metric

CHEYNEY THOMPSON

pedestal

MIT List Visual Arts Center,
Cambridge, Massachusetts

Koenig Books, London

cabengo

landlord

récit

Contents

The artist would like to thank Miguel Abreu, Jean-Michel Alberola, Monica Baer, Simon Baier, Tim Bailey, George Baker, Steven Baldi, Michelle Barré, Dan Berchenko, Yve-Alain Bois, Benjamin Bois, Sasha Braunig, Daniel Buchholz, Johanna Burton, Emanuela Campoli, Merlin Carpenter, Sylvia Chivaratanond, Pascale Consigny, Brendon Downey, Caroline Elder, Roe Ethridge, Katharina Forero de Mund, Nik Gambaroff, Tim Griffin, Nicolás Guagnini, Natalie Häusler, Paul Ha, Dustin Hodges, Hervé Ingrand, Yoshiko Ishhiki, Gareth James, David Joselit, Timo Kappeller, John Kelsey, Caitlin Keogh, Nobuhiko Kitamura, Kristina Kite, Jutta Koether, Michael Krebber, Andrew Kreps, Taylor Kretchmar, Ann Lauterbach, Daniel Lefcourt, Simon Leung, Sam Lewitt, Jason Loebs, Scott Lyall, Luca Marenzi, Charles Mayton, Sean McBride, Megan McClarney, Lucy McKenzie, Christopher Müller, Cora Muennich, Liz Mulholland, Leslie Norins, Rainey Norins, Lisa Overduin, Pat Palermo, Sean Paul, Gil Presti, Rebecca Quaytman, R.H. Quaytman, Eileen Quinlan, Umberto Raucci, Blake Rayne, João Ribas, Marina Rosenfeld, Carlo Santamaria, Elisa Santiago, Pieter Schoolwerth, Hendrik Schwartz, Amy Sillman, Billy Sothern, Taylor Thompson, Simon Thompson, Jim Thompson, T.J. Thompson, Ethan Wagner, Hilke Wagner, Osamu Wataya, Alexander Waterman, Liz Wendelbo, Stephen Westfall, Thea Westreich, Rachael Wicka, and Alun Williams.

Metric Pedestal Cabengo Landlord Récit

Cheyney Thompson has made the technology, production, and distribution of painting the subject of his work for over a decade.[1] Thompson employs rational structures, technological processes, and generative devices as part of "thinking through problems that organize themselves around the terms of painting."[2] With such a rigorous approach to the medium, he has produced visually engaging yet exacting work that addresses varieties of abstraction, including pictorial, economic, and technological.

The status of painting within competing technological modes of image production and the medium's historical and technical conditions have been central concerns in much of Thompson's recent work. As a technology, painting is both outmoded within the technics of the production and circulation of images, yet also able to continuously incorporate and internalize other technical modes of production. Thompson's paintings readily engage the image, as mediated by precisely such a series of technologies—from perspective and photography to the cinematic apparatus and the digital artifact.[3]

The luminous surfaces of his *Chronochromes* (2009–2011) are composed using the color system devised by Albert H. Munsell in the early 1900s. Thompson transposes Munsell's system—used to classify everything from archaeological artifacts to frozen french fries—onto a calendrical cycle: each day is assigned a complementary hue pair, and for each laboriously hand-rendered mark painted during that day, the value is determined by the hour when the painting occurs, the saturation determined by the month. This system produces paintings of subtle variations, "which register fatigue, distraction, and interruptions," as well as the flow of time itself.[4] Midday is represented by luminescent white and midnight by a saturated black. A continuous gradient could be achieved only if Thompson worked consistently, every single day, on each painting.[5]

The materiality of painting is the basis for his *Chromachromes* (2009), which depict a motif drawn from an enlarged scan of canvas.[6] Thompson's recursive process merges digital reproduction with the literal support: the woven pattern of the scanned linen is divided into values of highlight, midtone, and dark; it is then hand-painted using complementary colors drawn from Munsell's system.[7] Each painting is given a unique historical format, including those of an academic portrait painting, a diptych, and a Renaissance tondo.[8] The use of this typology continues Thompson's engagement with, and allusion to, the history of painting, from the conventions of still life[9] to what Meyer Schapiro called "the chromatic variations of a single motif."[10]

Thompson's long-standing interest in the circulation of painting, and in the artwork as commodity, is evident in eight paintings of his landlords, which are composed using the four-color CMYK process of commercial printing. These paintings comment on the historical relations of artistic production (artist and market, labor and value), as well as on the circulation and exchange of commodities and information. Through what he calls "a subtractive process, removing degrees of light from the image"—as the CMYK process "subtracts" luminance from white—Thompson's portraits combine the painterly with deskilled technology.[11]

Thompson's works often reframe or reiterate details and motifs from his previous work, approaching them as a kind of remainder.[12] These reflect his interest in the practice of painting—many are studies on the modernist trope of the grid—and the conceptual and material conditions of image production. Blurred photocopies of garbage are used to produce a digital artifact that serves as the source for Thompson's series of grisaille *Untitled* (2006) paintings. Various enlarged sections of these images are rendered in shades of gray; arranged in a grid, the tonal scheme used to produce them is itself presented in *Is-A* (2008), while another detail is reframed in a blue register for *Untitled* (2008). For his participation in the 2008 *Whitney Biennial*, Thompson reframed further details from the digital images to produce a series of black paintings whose titles refer directly to the digital coordinates of their source material.[13]

The artist's recent pedestal sculptures—many of which have the same surface area and yet are subject to radical formal iteration—reflect his interest in varying forms of display and what can be "folded" or contained within the "frame" of painting itself.[14] Rather than following the convention of presenting artworks, these sculptures self-reflexively address their function by offering research, supplemental, and informational materials related to the artist's work.[15] The data, references, documents, and codes that "*lie behind* Thompson's paintings, in terms of interpretation," are placed "*on top of the surface* of his liberated pedestals," as David Joselit has written.[16] These have included artifacts from Papua New Guinea, two lamps given to Thompson by his landlords (a kind of exchange exceeding the parameters of the lease),[17] numeric information used to develop five different motifs in his work, and a bound book collecting references to all of the materials employed in his work.[18]

In particular, these arrangements and collections function to address the putative autonomy of painting as a medium, which is so central to painting's discourse throughout the twentieth century. The notion of a limit between the interiority of content and what is supposedly exterior to it, between what is considered inside and outside of the work, in effect, is thus collapsed.[19] As such, a supplement that is seemingly external to the work, in fact, "does not stop disturbing the *internal* order of discourse on painting, its works, its commerce, its evaluations, its surplus values, its speculation, its law, and its hierarchies," in Derrida's words.[20]

In her contribution to this volume—which is being published on the occasion of Thompson's first solo museum exhibition, *Metric, Pedestal, Landlord, Cabengo, Récit* at the MIT List Visual Arts Center[21]—poet Ann Lauterbach addresses such complexities in Thompson's work by drawing on modernist poetics. Parsing the visual and verbal elements of the work, Lauterbach writes that Thompson's paintings "appear to emerge from a sequence of intensely negotiated, sometimes overlapping but disparate cognitive and material nodes, capable of engaging a range of contents." Art historian Simon Baier's close reading of the technological and procedural elements of several series of Thompson's works foregrounds questions of time, labor, and the body. As Baier explains, speaking of the relation between the laboring body and information, "The time of the hand, labor time itself, suddenly appears conversely as empty, useless time and comes across as an obsolete, rudimentary form of accumulation and of sacrifice." In his contribution, renowned art historian Yve-Alain Bois considers Thompson's economics of production and "quantification of labor time," linking the artist's practice, both formally and technically, to Seurat's attempts to "rationally decompose a continuous visual field." "It is perhaps with his *Chronochromes*," Bois writes, "that Thompson comes closest to and departs the most from Seurat." While Seurat mistakenly relied "on optical mixing to resynthesize in our eyes what he had patiently divided," Thompson, in contrast, "exposes the codes of division that he uses in his various series," according to Bois. His essay also subtly considers the materials presented through Thompson's pedestals in terms of their symbolic and metaphoric resonances—the economic and libidinal exchanges that these materials, like much of the artist's work, refer to and so richly evoke.

1 As Suzanne Hudson notes in her entry on Thompson for the 2008 *Whitney Biennial* catalog, "Questioning protocols of exhibition as much as techniques of production and their contingent modes of reception in the space of the gallery, Thompson assumes the history, practice, and circulation of painting as his subject." Suzanne Hudson, "Cheyney Thompson," in *Whitney Biennial 2008*, Henriette Huldisch and Shamim Momin, eds. (New Haven: Yale University Press, 2008), 241.

2 Cheyney Thompson, April 30, 2011, in conversation.

3 As David Joselit notes, "In an uncanny parallel to the photography's 19th century challenge to painting, Thompson and his generation are faced with a new question: why make painting in the digital age?" David Joselit, "Blanks and Noise: On Cheyney Thompson," *Texte Zur Kunst*, no. 77 (March 2010), 129–32.

4 As the artist writes, "I grafted the color system onto a calendar. Each day has a complementary hue pair, each hour changes the colors' value, and each month the saturation changes. Noon is absolute white and midnight is absolute black. This provides a system of producing paintings which would register fatigue, distraction, and interruptions as, in theory, it has the potential to produce a smooth gradient that would represent a continuous flow of time." Cheyney Thompson, artist's statement for the exhibition *Motifs, /Robert/, Paul de Casteljau, Socles, Menarches, Chronochromes*, Sutton Lane, Brussels, September 2010.

5 Ibid.

6 Cheyney Thompson, artist's statement for the exhibition *Robert Macaire Chromachromes*, Andrew Kreps Gallery, New York, 2009; Joselit, "Blanks and Noise"; and Caroline Busta, "Cheyney Thompson," *Artforum* (September 2010).

7 Thompson, artist's statement for *Robert Macaire Chromachromes*.

8 In comparison, each of the paintings comprising the *Chronochromes* are the same height but differ in width.

9 The influence of Chardin, for example, was central to his exhibition "of 134 paintings of building materials," *1998*, Andrew Kreps Gallery, New York, 2004. Meghan Dailey, "Cheyney Thompson: Andrew Kreps Gallery," *Artforum* (June 2004).

10 Meyer Shapiro, "The Nature of Abstract Art," *Marxist Quarterly* 1 (January–March 1937), 82.

11 Press release for the Cheyney Thompson exhibition *The End of Rent Control and the Emergence of the Creative Class*, Galerie Buchholz, Cologne, 2006.

12 This can be conceived either as what is left behind or is still contained in an image after it has been "consumed," or as an excess contained in an image or procedure that is then folded back in, as if through a kind of feedback loop.

13 For example, *Detail (0.147, 0.160)(5.558, 4.407)(15.779)* and *Detail (0.933, 1.425)(4.108, 5.181)(13.510)*, 2008.

14 Derrida, *The Truth in Painting*, (Chicago: University of Chicago Press, 1987), 9, 37.

15 Aude Launay, "Cheyney Thompson: Un Systeme contre le systeme," *ZéroDeux*, no. 56 (Winter 2010); press release for the Cheyney Thompson exhibition *Memphis, Pedestals, Chronochromes, Subincision, Papua New Guinea, /Macaire/, Motifs*, Overduin and Kite, Los Angeles, 2010; and press release for the Cheyney Thompson exhibition *Pedestals, Bias-cut, /Robert Macaire/, Chronochromes*, Galerie Buchholz, Cologne, 2009.

16 Joselit, "Blanks and Noise."

17 As Sam Lewitt has written, "The representation of contractual relations between things often produces the effect of an excess, a surplus, in the margins of the contract's legal conditions." Press release for *The End of Rent Control and the Emergence of the Creative Class*.

18 Joselit, "Blanks and Noise." Joselit writes, "Thompson's work begs the question of inclusion within a genre—of what belongs, for instance, to the category 'painting.'"

19 Perhaps one such important framing is the fact that the works included in the exhibition at the MIT List Visual Arts Center and in this monograph were produced for commercial galleries, beginning in the late 1990s; these works are now being brought into the "frame" of the institution and its discourse.

20 Jacques Derrida, *The Truth in Painting*, 9, 37-82.

21 Cheyney Thompson, *Metric, Pedestal, Landlord, Cabengo, Récit*, MIT List Visual Arts Center, February 10 - April 8, 2012, curated by João Ribas.

A Pedestal is a Pedestal is a Pedestal

"When asked the price of a picture . . . he wrote that he was very much embarrassed in fixing the price; that he reckoned it as one year's work at seven francs a day, but that he would be willing to reduce it if he liked the personality of the buyer." The painter in question is not Cheyney Thompson, but rather Georges Seurat. The writer, Meyer Schapiro, goes on: "Thus Seurat rationalized even his own labor as a sum of units of work, in contrast to his contemporaries, who identified every stroke with the experience of a lifetime or the priceless effect of inspired genius."[1] Schapiro's remark on Seurat's billing proposal is based on a letter the artist wrote on February 17, 1889, to the Belgian collector/critic Octave Mauss, one Seurat's most ardent defenders. After noting his lack of ease in determining a price and suggesting a method for doing so, Seurat adds, "In conclusion, I will say that the personality of the collector can compensate me for the difference between his price and mine."[2] I can't find the current value of a 1889 French franc, but a daily wage of seven of them sounds fairly paltry, even then.[3] The painting in question was *Les Poseuses*, which was sold a year after Seurat's death and is now at the Barnes Foundation. (It was purchased by Barnes for $75,000 in 1926.) In 1959, John Rewald calculated that Seurat's annual remuneration, following the artist's indications, would have been around 2,200 francs in 1889 (excluding Sundays, and thus leaving 313 working days per year).[4] But comparative data are more telling, as Rewald acknowledges. He notes that *L'Angelus* by Millet, a painter Seurat much admired, was bought by an American collector for 580,650 francs that same year—264 times the top price that the painter of *Les Poseuses* had arrived at for his work.[5]

It is obvious that there is a lot in common between Thompson's way of thinking and working and Seurat's. There is a vast literature on the relationship between Seurat's dots and the development of the printing industry—and it is doubtful that Thompson, whose forays into the field of art history seem wide and deep, would ignore at least the gist of this scholarship. In any event, from the series of portraits of his landlords that he painted in 2006 using the four-color CMYK distribution process borrowed from printing techniques, to his most recent *Chronochromes*, one can find in Thompson's work the same desire to rationally decompose a continuous visual field (a photographic image, in this case) into contiguous, discrete units. In fact, in his digitization frenzy, Thompson outdoes Seurat: while the pointillist artist (erroneously) counted on optical mixing to resynthesize in our eyes what he had patiently divided, Thompson exposes the codes of division that he uses in his various series. In his recent exhibition at MIT's List Center, for example, he showed a series of four large untitled "black" canvases dating from 2008, together with a small painting of a modular grid with sixteen shades of black and grey. This small grid painting is the visual caption of the series.[6] It identifies the sixteen shades through which the "abstract photographs" (failed scans) used for the production of these large canvases have been "separated," to use a technical term from the printing industry, and transferred into as many distinct "films," as if the artist had intended to make silkscreens. (Each of the sixteen films is projected, one at a time, onto the large canvas, upon which the tiny projected digits are manually painted with the requisite shade of color.) Other examples include the CMYK portraits and other images created using the same technique. Here the code need not be specified because it is well known to anyone who has ever looked closely at an offset reproduction of a color photograph (any illustrated magazine, any poster will do). The mere intimation of it suffices, which Thompson provides by hanging four "identical" versions of each portrait side by side. Each is slightly different because it is done by hand, even though they have all been realized through exactly the same process. This time there are more than sixteen films per painting: eight values for each of the four colors of the CMYK system—cyan, magenta, yellow, and black, or "key." (In his use of silkscreen on canvas, Andy Warhol had been a champion of what is called "high tolerance" in engineering lingo, perhaps as a way of signaling that the silkscreens were still handmade—his dream of being like a machine notwithstanding. In any case, the high tolerance of Thompson's process is far less staged, far less avoidable: Warhol used four or five films per image, at most, and each film was inked in one go; Thompson separates his colors into many more films, and each is made of a myriad of units, each painted separately.)

1 Meyer Schapiro, "Seurat and *La Grande Jatte*," *The Columbia Review*, vol. XVII, no. 1 (November 1935), 16.

2 Quoted in Norma Broude, ed., *Seurat in Perspective* (Englewood Cliffs, NJ: Prentice Hall, 1978), 16. The last sentence in the original French reads as: "Pour me résumer, je vous dirais que la personnalité de l'amateur peut me payer de la différence de son prix au mien." Quoted in Henri Dorra and John Rewald, *Seurat* (Paris: Les Beaux-Arts, 1959), 218.

3 According to the latest chart provided by the French Institut National de la Statistique et des Études Économiques (INSEE), one franc in 1911, the earliest date for which data is given, had the same buying power as €3.24 today, thus about $4.27. It was probably not much different in 1889, given the extremely low rate of inflation around 1900. This amounts to roughly $30 per day — far below the nearly $60 that a worker would receive for an eight-hour day under the current US federal minimum wage of $7.25 per hour.

4 Dorra and Rewald, *Seurat*, p. lxviii, note 49. In the chronology that she established for the catalog of the massive 1991 Seurat retrospective at the Met, Anne Distel confirms Rewald's estimate (the figure she gives is "between 2,000 and 2,500 francs"). See Robert L. Herbert, ed., *Georges Seurat 1859–1891* (New York: The Metropolitan Museum of Art, 1991), 409.

5 Rewald comes up with other comparative figures, but all of them are staggering. (The lowest is the 5,000 francs that Vincent Van Gogh had been urging his brother Theo to pay, the previous year, for *Les Poseuses*.) Distel's comparative figures confirm the amazing discrepancy between Seurat's modest computation of his fee (for one of his largest paintings) and the art market of the time. Noting that Raffaëlli "budgeted himself at 1,500 francs per month," she adds, "As for the Impressionists, Renoir was selling his small canvases for between 500 and 1,500 francs; Monet and Degas for twice that and more. Manet's *Olympia* brought his widow almost 20,000 francs. Finally, in 1888 the State paid 4,000 francs for Puvis de Chavannes's *Le pauvre pêcheur*, even though his dealer was asking 6,000 francs." Herbert, *Georges Seurat 1859–1891*, Ibid.

6 The series had already been exhibited in this manner at the artist's solo show at the Sutton Lane gallery in Paris in 2008. At his exhibition *Quelques Aspects de l'Art Bourgeois* (Andrew Kreps Gallery, New York, 2009), a series of large untitled gray canvases were similarly "captioned" by a row of eight folding tables, whose surfaces were made from a sequence of sixteen black-and-white photos that "showed" the sixteen-value progression.

It is perhaps with his *Chronochromes* that Thompson comes closest to and departs the most from Seurat. Once again, the insistence on the man-made is patent. As has been described many times by the artist and by his most eloquent critics, the base photograph projected onto these canvases (as well as those of the previous series, called *Chromachromes*) is that of an enlarged piece of similar canvas that has been digitized into three values corresponding to the weave of the fabric under light (highlights, shadows, midtone). The midtone, or "neutral" value, which is that of the ground, is left unpainted on the gessoed canvas, so only the projections of the highlights and shadows are registered with paint. In order to assign, differently for each canvas, the colors of the binary pair corresponding to the highlight/shadow division, Thompson turned to the Munsell color system, still in use in many branches of industry. Unlike other theories, it has the advantage of classifying color according to coordinates on three axes (hue, value, and saturation, or chroma): each binary pair is represented by a complementary contrast arbitrarily chosen in Albert H. Munsell's taxonomic cornucopia. In the *Chromachromes*, the arbitrariness of that choice is plain—intently laid bare, so to speak, and in tandem with the arbitrariness of the various formats of the paintings. (The fact that these generic, typical formats—tondo, landscape, portrait, etc.—have been naturalized by their use throughout centuries of Western painting does not make them any less arbitrary.) With the *Chronochromes*, this arbitrariness is dramatized by its structural opposite (motivation), as both the format and the binary pairs become indexes of labor time. Each canvas has the same height (seventy-five inches), each is of a different width, but two motivating rules clash with these arbitrary requirements. The first concerns the width of the series as a whole, which varies according to site. (The paintings, hung sequentially side by side, with a two-inch interval between them, take the longest running axis of the gallery as their total width for any given exhibition.)[7] The other motivating mechanism concerns the binary pairs: the choice of their color is time sensitive. The projected image (of a canvas) is divided into vertical rows of binary pairs, painted sequentially from top to bottom, but the value of the color of each pair is determined by the time of day when it was painted, with pure white "representing" noon and pure black corresponding to midnight. Similarly, the hue of each pair is determined by the day when it was painted; the saturation is determined by the month. Of course, the indexical status of the mark is perturbed by the happenstances of daily life, for the artist is never able—even with the help of assistants—to paint continuously, 24/7. In some canvases, the zone of light value marks (with high-noon white at its center) occupies a band that is far thinner than in others (which could mean that the work on a canvas was interrupted during day X at noon and taken up again the next day at 3 p.m., for example); sometimes the midnight pure black is totally absent; and the intervals between the opposite poles on the scale of values vary immensely in width, even within a single canvas. In short, it is impossible to infer from the canvases themselves when they were actually painted, and we can't determine, just by looking at them, if or when ellipses (moments when no one was at work) took place. But we can ascertain the amount of time required to complete each canvas: this is something no one would have been able to say in front of a Seurat, except for the artist himself.

Why this insistence on the quantification of labor time? For Seurat, whose circle was known for its leftist political views, it partakes of a genuine democratic identification with (manual) workers: he refused the idea of a difference between the production of art and that of any other object, considering his artwork to be like any other commodity, whose exchange value is determined, according to Marx (in his revision of Ricardo and Smith), by the quantity of "social" labor that has been expended in its production and is "crystallized" in it. In other words, Seurat chose to ignore the perturbations of the exchange value system engendered by the fluctuations of supply and demand, which are notoriously extreme in the market of luxury goods—and particularly in the art market. Since such perturbations (and the speculations that come along with them) cannot have escaped Thompson, one can only assume that his indexing on his canvases of the quantity of time necessary to produce them, as well as his unremitting recourse to the age-old technique of applying paint with a brush, often deemed obsolete, is parodic. One could say that Thompson's mode partakes of what Hal Foster, in his recent analysis of the pictorial strategies of pop art, has termed "mimetic troping," but in reverse direction.[8] What is mimicked is no longer the "hardened" characteristics of life and culture under the conditions of consumer capitalism but the "real" economy that had long been its soil (think manufacturing) and is now being gradually replaced by the virtual economy of financial markets. Parodying Seurat imagining himself as a day laborer, Thompson underscores how much has changed in our lives, not only since Seurat's time but, say, since 1968, when a certain kind of utopian fantasy was still credible (classless society, unalienated labor, no difference between artist and nonartist, etc.). This is not to say that Thompson's art is nostalgic, though, but rather that it is critical—that it points, with very concrete means, to the sweeping transformations that the capitalist system has undergone in the last few decades.

Since 2010, Thompson has exhibited five pedestals together several times. These pedestals posit their exchangeability (their commodity status) not in regard to the quantity of labor necessary to their production but rather on the basis that, despite their obviously (even ostentatiously) different shapes, they "all have the exact same surface area," Thompson notes. "In theory," he adds, "the most distinguishing feature of a pedestal (its verticality) could topologically become its opposite (horizontality). The pedestals then retain their nominal function as supports for artifacts, while proliferating the mutability of their capacity to signify /pedestal/."[9] The issue is obviously one of identity, and it is not by chance that the figure of Robert Macaire—about whom Thompson had already devoted a series

7 Shown in Brussels from September to October 2010, the series was forty-two feet wide; shown in Los Angeles from November to December of the same year, it was thirty-nine feet wide, etc.

8 As Foster writes, "In his early interviews, Lichtenstein is explicit about the 'hard' and 'deadening' aspects of the [contemporary] culture; at the same time he insists, these 'brazen and threatening characteristics . . . are also powerful in their impingement on us'; more, they 'give a kind of brutality and maybe hostility that is useful to me in an aesthetic way.' This point is key to his practice, for implicit here is a strategy that goes beyond a provocative troubling of artistic oppositions (such as manual and mechanical) toward a critical redoubling of lived conditions in consumer capitalism. That is to say, what Lichtenstein intimates is a mimetic troping of the 'brazen and threatening characteristics of our culture'—a mimesis of the industrial (he underscores the 'hard steely quality' of his work), the informational ('I want my painting to look as if it had been programmed'), and, of course, the commercial. ('I got some of these colors from supermarket packaging,' he remarked in 1971; 'I would look at package labels to see what colors had the most impact on one another.')" Hal Foster, *The First Pop Age* (Princeton: Princeton University Press, 2012), 79–80. See also note 39, 279, where the roots of this strategy of mimetic troping are traced back to Baudelaire via Adorno and Benjamin.

of works on paper exhibited in 2009, at the same time as his *Chromachromes*—should have reappeared next to the pedestals, and even, literally, on one of them. (The bound volume of photocopies placed there to be perused by gallery visitors includes James Rousseau's *Physiologie du Robert-Macaire*, published in 1842, with illustrations by Daumier.[10]) Robert Macaire was a real or perhaps imaginary fourteenth-century criminal (convicted for a murder on testimony given by a dog, and hanged), but his name has since come to signify villainy and fraudulence as such. (His proper name evolved into a common noun: the English translation of the book's title is *Physiology of the Robert-Macaire*—as in, *Physiology of the Married Man* or *Physiology of the Spinster*, which were volumes offered in the same series.)[11]
Each chapter of Rousseau's book, except the first, which is dedicated to "the Robert-Macaire in general," concerns a Robert-Macaire in a different trade (lawyer, playwright, philanthropist, notary, journalist, doctor, stock broker, etc.): they are all as interchangeable as the pedestals. (It should be noted that the pedestals are coated with Formica of different colors and patterns—Formica, the Robert-Macaire of materials, the ur-ersatz renowned for its infinite plasticity.) Yet, as we have just noticed, the pedestals do have a function, a use value. Thompson uses them to present objects and documents that accompanied and nurtured the production of his work in painting and sculpture. The objects are sometimes contingent and incidental (two lamps given to him by his landlords; a flute from Papua New Guinea), but they are not interchangeable. (This is made clear by the volume of Xeroxes I just mentioned, which contains information pertinent to most of them.)

One of the strangest documents made available by Thompson in this compendium is an essay by Alan Dundes entitled "A Psychoanalytic Study of the Bullroarer" and published in *Man*, the journal of the Royal Anthropological Institute of Great Britain and Ireland, in 1976.[12] Immediately following this essay in Thompson's handbook is a compilation of about fifty grainy black-and-white full-page photographs that are hard to stomach. Almost all of them are close-up shots of a penis that has been mutilated or is in the course of being mutilated—knife, blood, and all—through subincision (an unimaginably excruciating operation during which the urethra is slit open lengthwise). At first, these unsettling images seem to be illustrations of Dundes's essay, but it does not take long to realize that no images are mentioned in the text. (Moreover, the obsessive nature of their redundancy would seem very out of place in an academic paper.) The case is soon put to rest: they must be the results of a frantic Web search by Thompson. It takes a while, however, to grasp the link between Dundes's long-winded essay on the bullroarer, a musical instrument dating back to the Paleolithic period, and the gory photographs.

Dundes is short on the shape and material of the bullroarer (a rhomboid slat of wood that is pierced at one end so that it can be attached to a rope) and on how one produces sound with it (it is swung rapidly with a circular motion); he is more interested in the sound itself. The latter, a vibrato, seems to be universally associated with wind (which Dundes's psychoanalytically bent mind immediately translates into "fart" and thus puts in the "anal" column of his ledger). Allusions to the role of the bullroarer in male initiation rites and to Papua New Guinea as one of several current sites of such rites come early in the text (so at least we realize that the essay is correlated to the flute placed on another one of Thompson's pedestals, and are thus encouraged to keep reading), but mention of the subincision affair appears only quite late and fairly casually, with a reference to Bruno Bettelheim's highly praised interpretation of its recurring inclusion in male initiation rites. (For Bettelheim, the subincision stems from men's jealousy of female procreativity: through this process, as it were, the young male is transformed into a woman—he'll need to squat in order to pee, for example, and the bleeding produced in the operation is aligned with menstruation.) Dundes does not wholly contest this view but wishes to amend/supplement it. Here is the abstract of the text proposed by the author:

> The bullroarer's widespread distribution (in Australia, New Guinea, North and South America, Africa, and Europe) plus its common occurrence in male initiation rites has made it one of the classic subjects of cross-cultural enquiry among anthropologists since 1880. Features of the so-called bullroarer complex include its being kept secret from women and its association with thunder and wind. Previous scholarship has suggested the bullroarer is phallic, but this theory does not satisfactorily explain why women may not see it nor why it is associated with making wind. The present psychoanalytic essay draws attention to the possible anal components of male initiation arguing that the bullroarer is a flatulent phallus. The anal component of the bullroarer complex is amply demonstrated by unequivocal ethnographic and linguistic data from myth. Myths also state that the bullroarer was originally possessed by women. Men claimed the bullroarer for themselves just as in male initiation, the initiates are reborn from men through anal symbolic ritual. In addition, through ritual masturbation and ritual homosexuality, men seek to carry out other sexual behavior without women. Men acting like women do not wish women to observe this behavior. This may explain why women are not permitted to see the bullroarer—with its associations of male anal creation and its whirling masturbatory motion.[13]

One imagines that Thompson was intrigued by this essay because it deals with exchanges of identity recorded in myths affiliated with the bullroarer or performed through rituals in which the ancient instrument plays an essential part. Multiple types of exchanges having to do with sexual roles and gender positions are proposed in a vast array of anthropological studies and a few psychoanalytical ones—they are all discussed by Dundes, some of them disregarded. Needless to say, he devotes most of his criticism to essays by his psychoanalyst peers. No need here to enter into this debate. Suffice it to say that in their discussion of bullroarer myths and rituals, psychoanalysts—Dundes included—seem to obsess over the phallus, the One and only One, posited as the gold standard of all drives, desires, and libidinal exchanges.

I have next to zero understanding of the economy, and thus of the history of the gold standard. Consequently, I am unable

9 Press release for the Cheyney Thompson exhibition *Motifs, /Robert/, Paul de Casteljau, Socles, Menarches, Chronochromes*, Sutton Lane, Brussels, 2010.

10 James Rousseau, *Physiologie du Robert-Macaire*, illustrated by Honoré Daumier (Paris: Jules Laisné, 1842).

11 Along with the totality of Rousseau's book, Thompson reproduces the cover of thirteen of these volumes, as well as an advertisement for the series, making sure we understand the Robert-Macaire of the title as a common noun (the Robert-Macaire, the Married Man, the Spinster) and not as a particular individual called Robert Macaire.

12 Alan Dundes, "A Psychoanalytic Study of the Bullroarer," *Man*, Vol. 11, No. 2 (June 1976), 220–38.

13 Ibid., 220.

to pursue the metaphor Phallus/Gold, splendidly explored fifty years ago by Jean-Joseph Goux, or to gauge its pertinence today.[14] (Should we explore instead the pair Phallus/Dollar?) My bet, however, is that Thompson would rather see his artistic practice associated with a libidinal/economic system in which the standard is no longer the Phallus/Gold (or Phallus/Dollar)—or rather, in which there is no longer a standard. A passage in Gilles Deleuze and Felix Guattari's *A Thousand Plateaus: Capitalism and Schizophrenia* might help us and Thompson to envision just such a system.[15] In the second chapter of the book, entitled "One or Several Wolves?," Deleuze and Guattari lambaste Freud for convincing himself that the six or seven wolves in the famous dream of the Wolf Man, and the five included in his no-less-famous drawing, were in fact the result of a displacement. Their multiplicity, as imagined by Freud, is a disguise for the One, concocted in the clever brewery of the Wolf Man's unconscious. But in order to introduce their critique, Deleuze and Guattari refer to another extraordinary text by Freud, dating from 1915 and entitled "The Unconscious," no less, "which deals with the difference between neurosis and psychosis":

> Freud says that hysterics or obsessives are people capable of making a global comparison between a sock and a vagina, a scar and castration, etc. Doubtless, it is at one and the same time that they apprehend the object globally and perceive it as lost. Yet it would never occur to a neurotic to grasp the skin erotically as a multiplicity of pores, little spots, little scars, or black holes, or to grasp the sock erotically as a multiplicity of stitches. The psychotic can: "we should expect the multiplicity of these little cavities to prevent him from using them as substitutes for the female genital." Comparing a sock to a vagina is OK, it's done all the time, but you'd have to be insane to compare a pure aggregate of stitches to a field of vaginas: that's what Freud says. This represents an important clinical discovery: a whole difference in style between neurosis and psychosis.[16]

But alas, Deleuze and Guattari observe, "No sooner does Freud discover the greatest art of the unconscious, this art of molecular multiplicities, than we find him tirelessly at work bringing back molar unities, reverting to his familiar themes of the father, the penis, the vagina, Castration with a capital C . . . (On the verge of discovering a rhizome, Freud always returns to mere roots.)"[17] Thus follows a rigorous dismantling of Freud's reduction of the "multiplicity of stitches" of his psychotic patient to just one, by way of the unicity of the word (e.g., the word "hole": a hole is a hole is a hole, just as a pedestal is a pedestal is a pedestal), and a rebuttal of his conclusion that psychotic processes of displacement and condensation traffic in representations of words (as opposed to neurotic processes, which traffic in representations of things).

This is no more the place to elaborate on the concepts of Deleuze and Guattari's schizo-analysis than it is to keep score between the various participants in the bullroarer debate. It is important to note, however, that certain types of fetishism are precisely what Deleuze and Guattari wish to dissipate, in their optimistic ode to multiplicity. (These include the fetishism of the commodity, described by Marx as the core illusion upon which the capitalist consumer system rests, and the fetishism of the neurotic, who, for example, zeroes in on a sock. Both types presuppose a central "general equivalent," to use the concept forged by Marx and elaborated by Goux, a standard functioning as the anchor and the gauge of everything.) Perhaps in the multiplicity of digits that Thompson patiently paints onto his canvases—digits of the image of a canvas that is itself made of many "stitches"—and in the multifarious documents he brings into the fray, all of them sprouting in multiple, interconnected directions, perhaps in these infinitely expansive ramifications, Thompson is also celebrating, in his own way, the band of wolves that Deleuze and Guattari wanted to rescue from Freud's synthesizing unification. Modernism was a fetishist affair on many scores, and particularly with regard to its fantasy of medium specificity. As Foster notes, Lichtenstein's paintings suggest "that 'media' had trumped 'medium.'"[18] According to David Joselit, Thompson's works acknowledge that the virtuality of networks has trumped both media and medium.[19] It might not be Seurat's divisionism and identification that the artist is "mimetically troping" (in reverse) in his *Chronochromes*, after all. Rather, fully engaged in the present, he could be troping the virtual economy of financial markets that caused the current economic nightmare. (That would tally well with Thompson's investment in the Occupy Wall Street movement.) Or rather, he could be mimicking both moments in the history of capitalism, with the kind of slim hope that can only come from despair.

14 Jean-Joseph Goux, *Symbolic Economies: After Marx and Freud* (Ithaca, NY: Cornell University Press, 1990). The book appeared in French in 1973.

15 Gilles Deleuze and Felix Guattari, *A Thousand Plateaus: Capitalism and Schizophrenia* (Minneapolis: University of Minnesota Press, 1987).

16 Ibid., 27.

17 Ibid.

18 Foster, *The First Pop Age*, 79.

19 David Joselit, "Blanks and Noise: On Cheyney Thompson," *Texte Zur Kunst*, no. 77 (March 2010), 129–32, and "Painting Beside Itself," *October*, no. 130 (Fall 2009), 125–34.

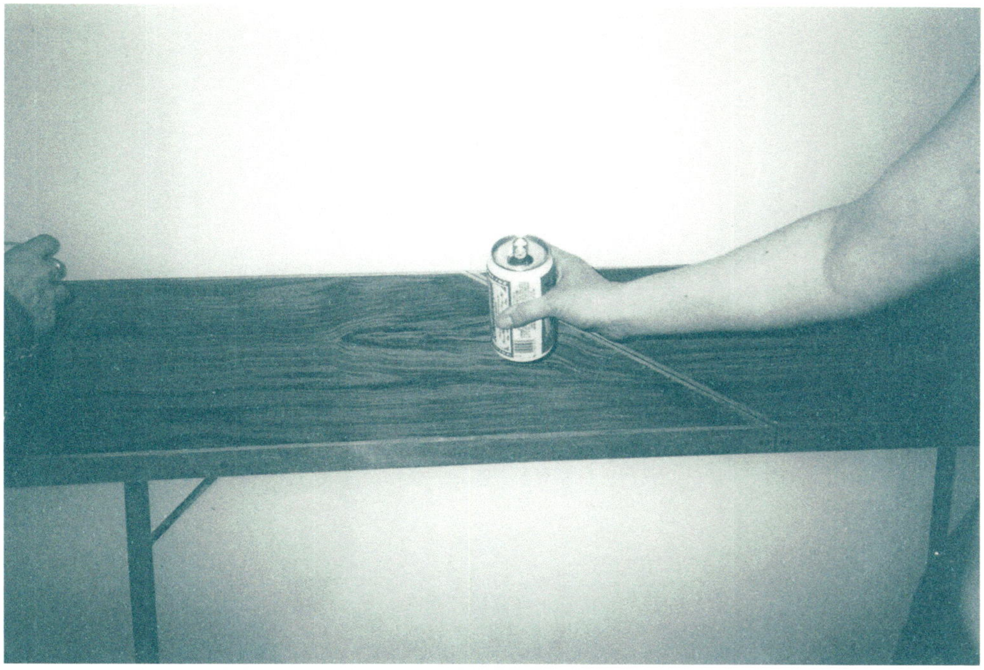

1924, 2000, acrylic on organza, 60 × 192 in.

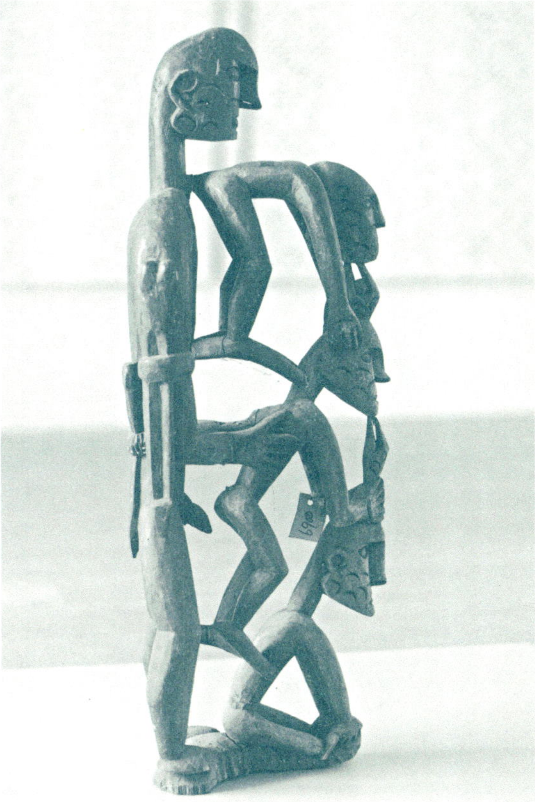

Installation view, *Chronochromes, Menarches, Socles, Paul de Casteljau, /Robert/, Motifs* (Sutton Lane, Brussels, courtesy of Campoli Presti, London/Paris), 2010, 19 mm MDF, Formica K1994, 3,200 sq. in., artifact from Papua New Guinea, 3 × 40 × 36 in.

Installation view, *Sean Paul / Cheyney Thompson, Caisse Blanche* (Sutton Lane, Paris, courtesy of Campoli Presti, London/Paris), 2007.

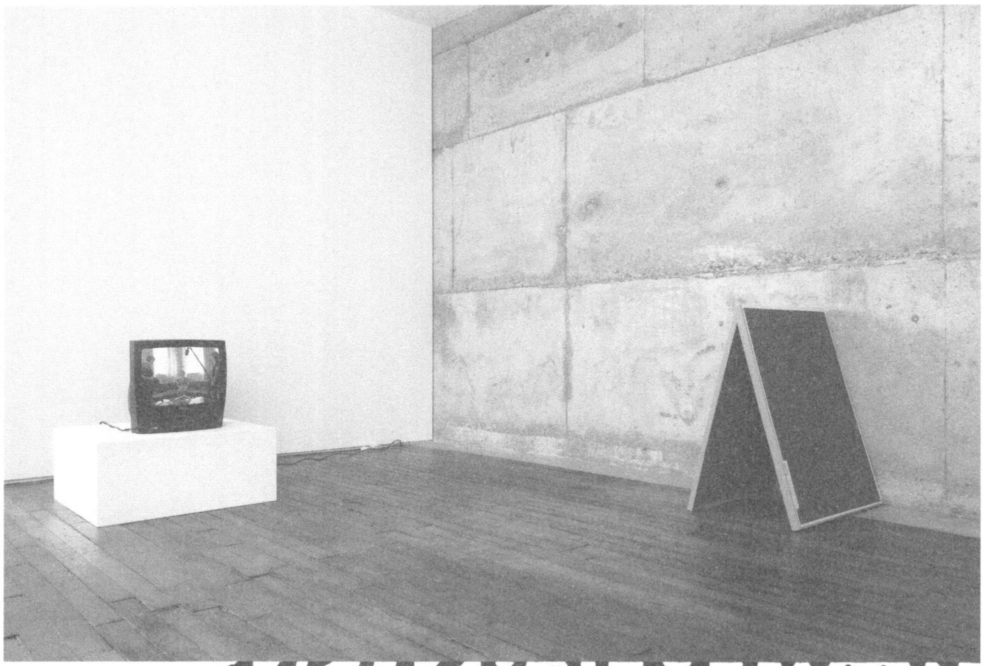

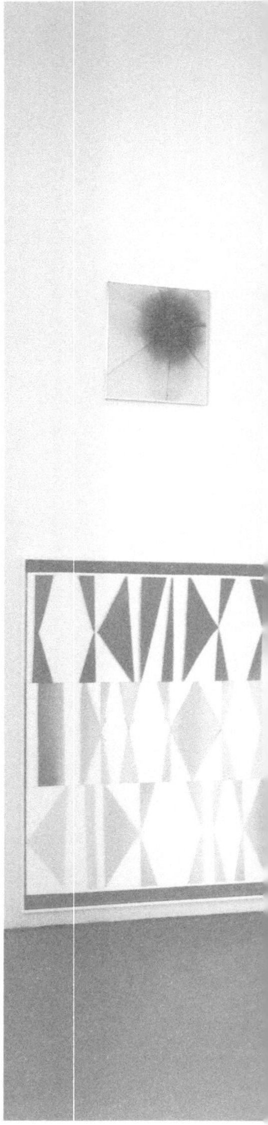

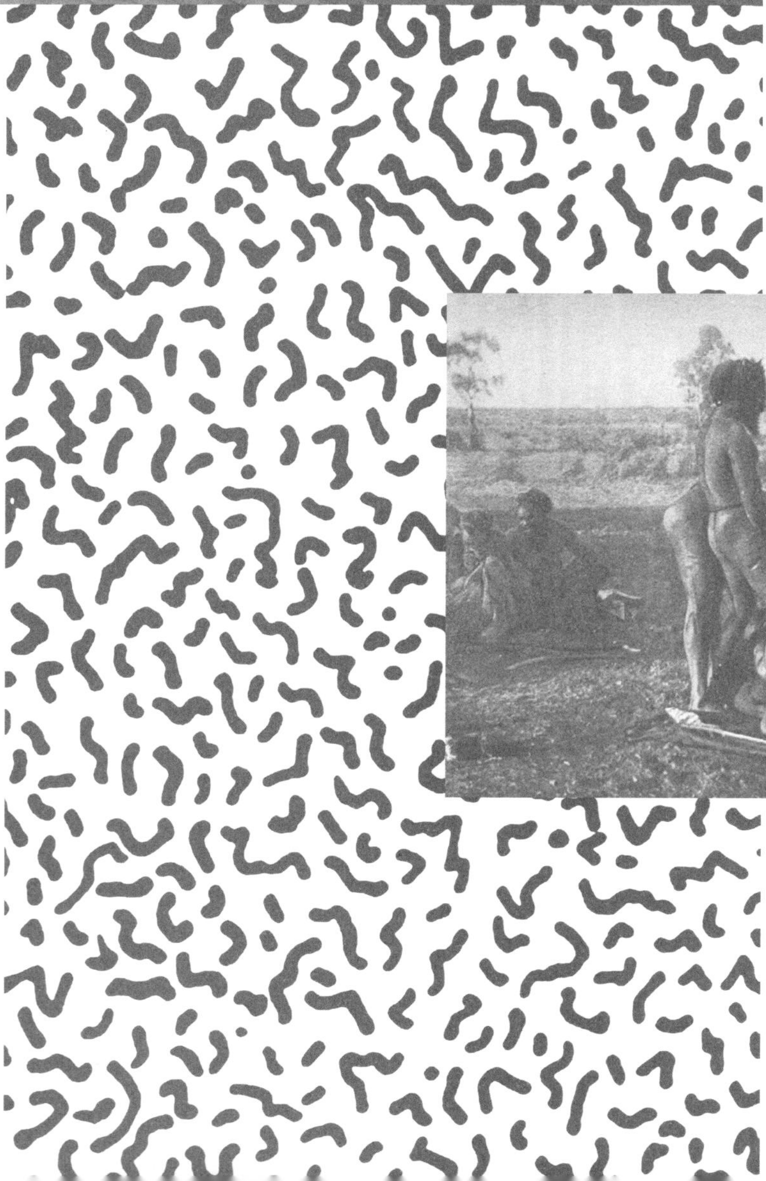

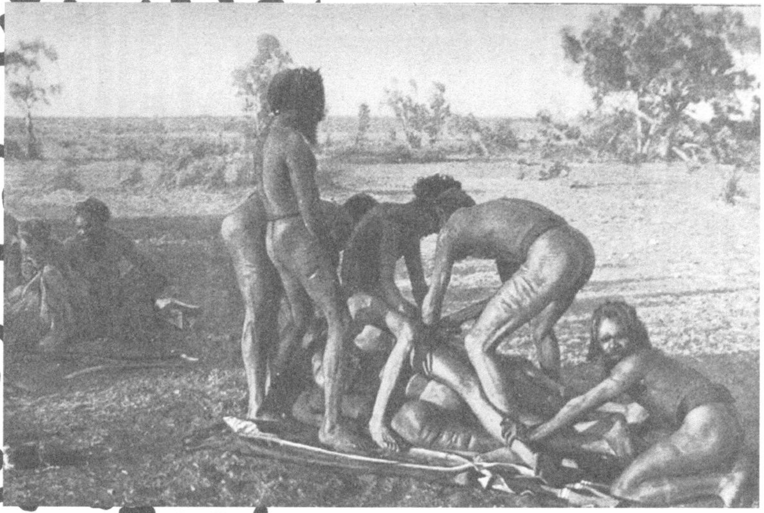

From *Subincisions,* 2010, artist book.

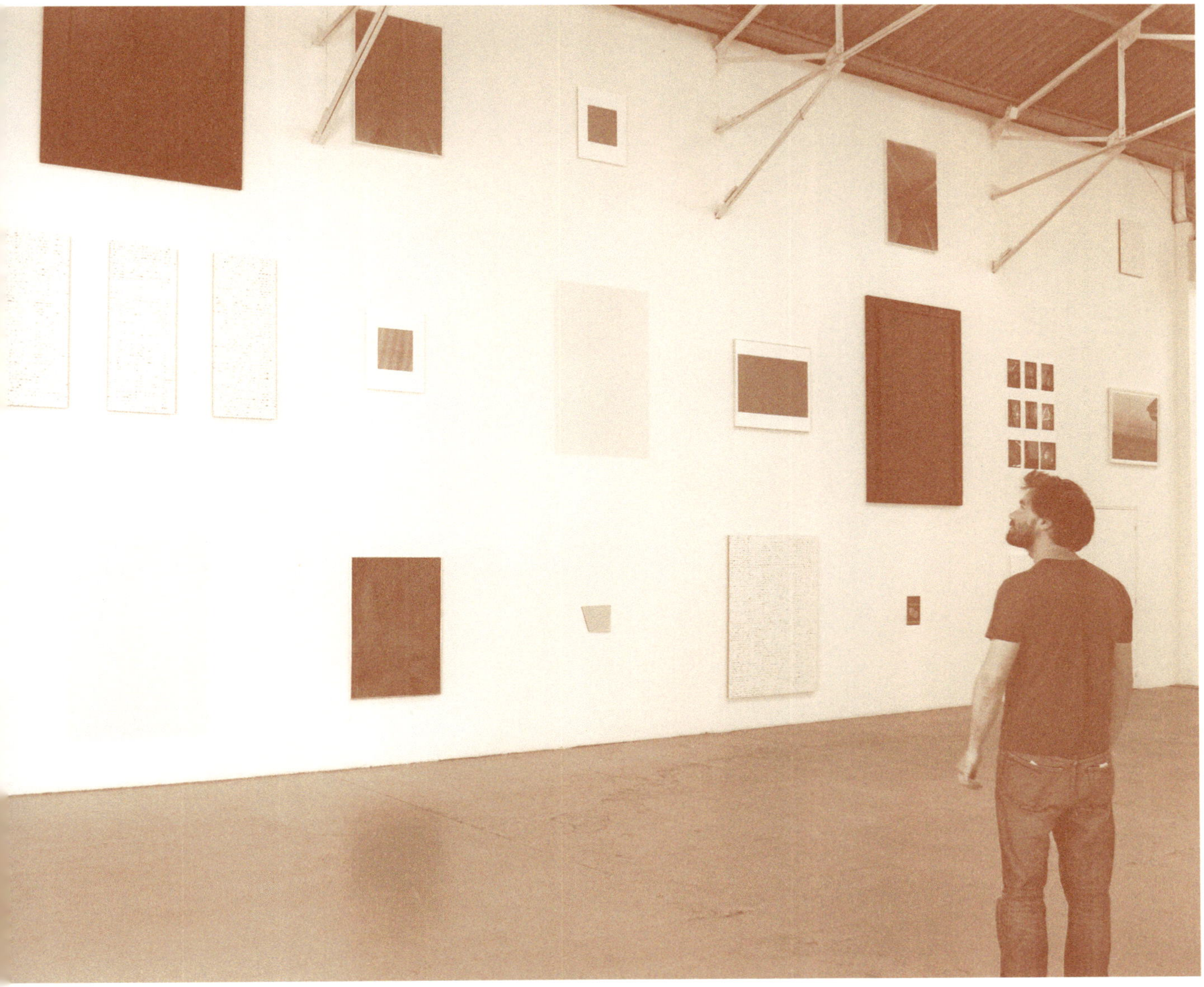

Installation view, *Collatéral* (Le Confort Moderne, Poitiers, courtesy of Campoli Presti, London/Paris), 2009.

Study for 1817, 2003, ink on paper, 16 × 20 in.

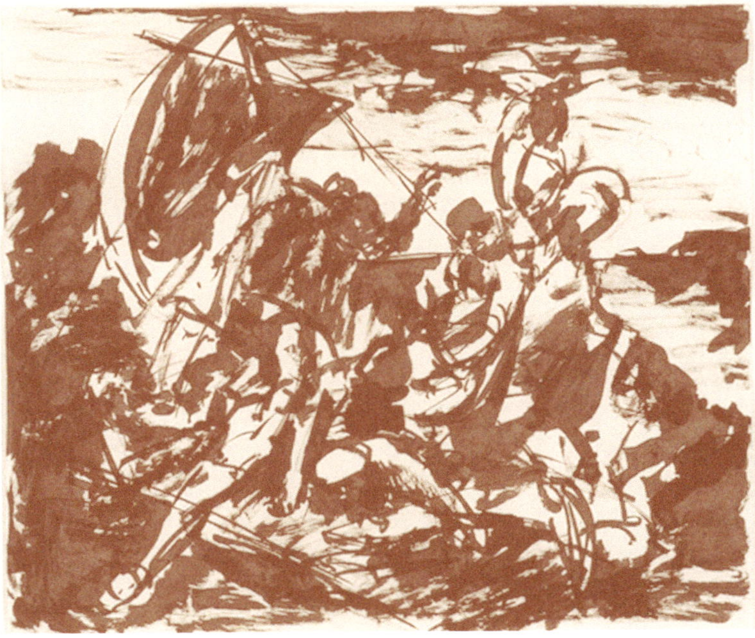

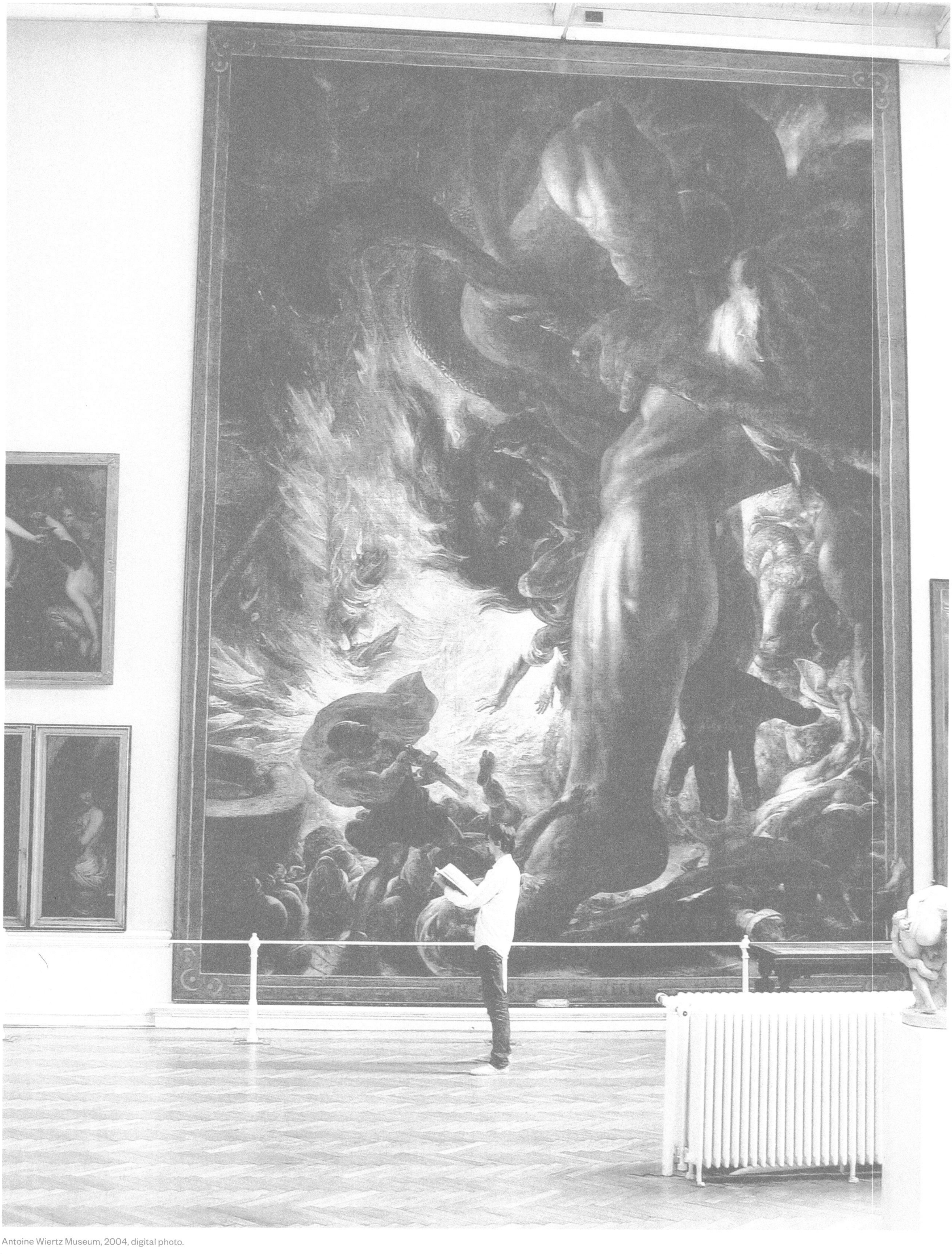

Antoine Wiertz Museum, 2004, digital photo.

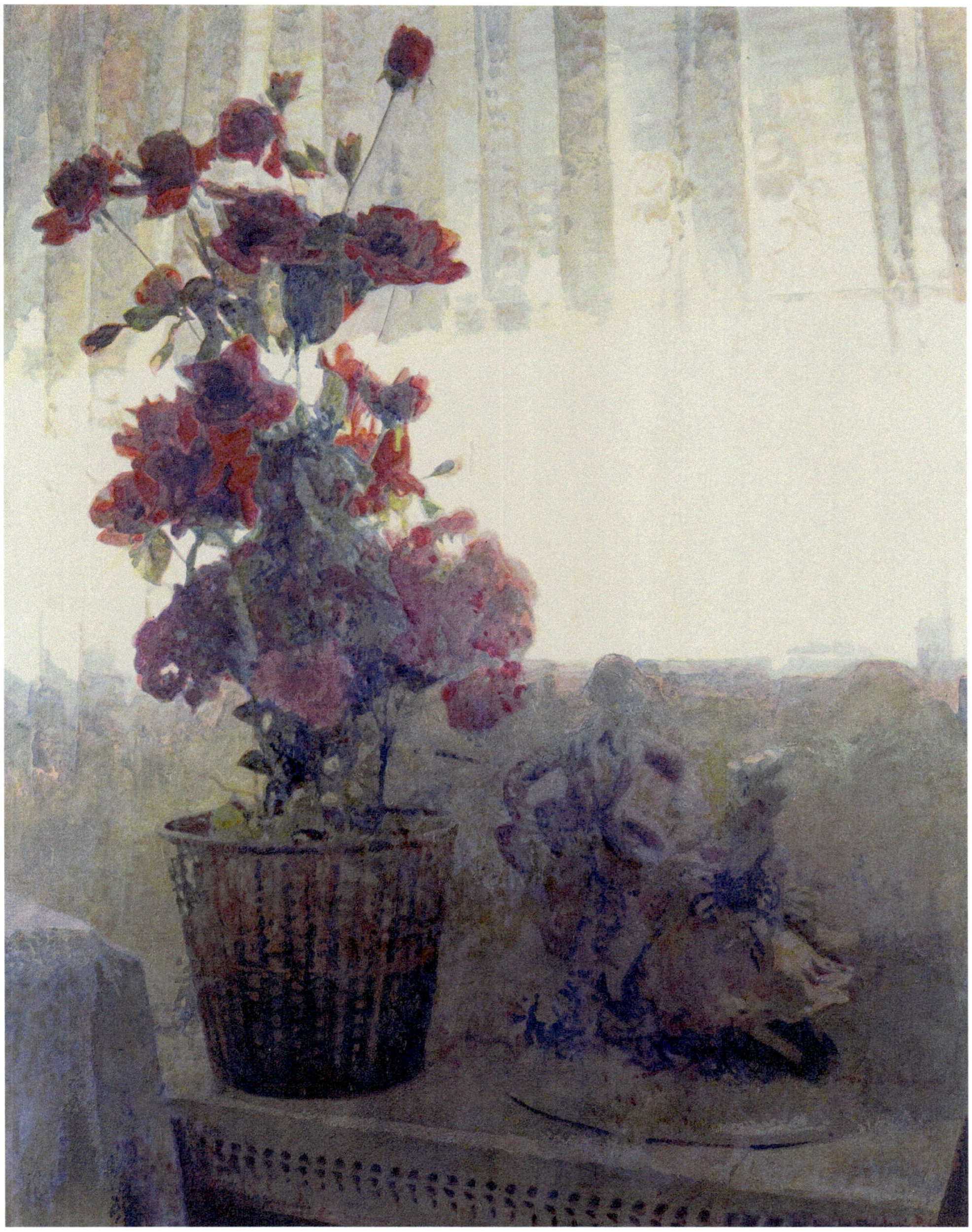

The Subtraction of Light from the Room Produces the Illusion of a Bourgeois Interior
2006, oil on canvas, 36 ¼ × 28 ¾ in.

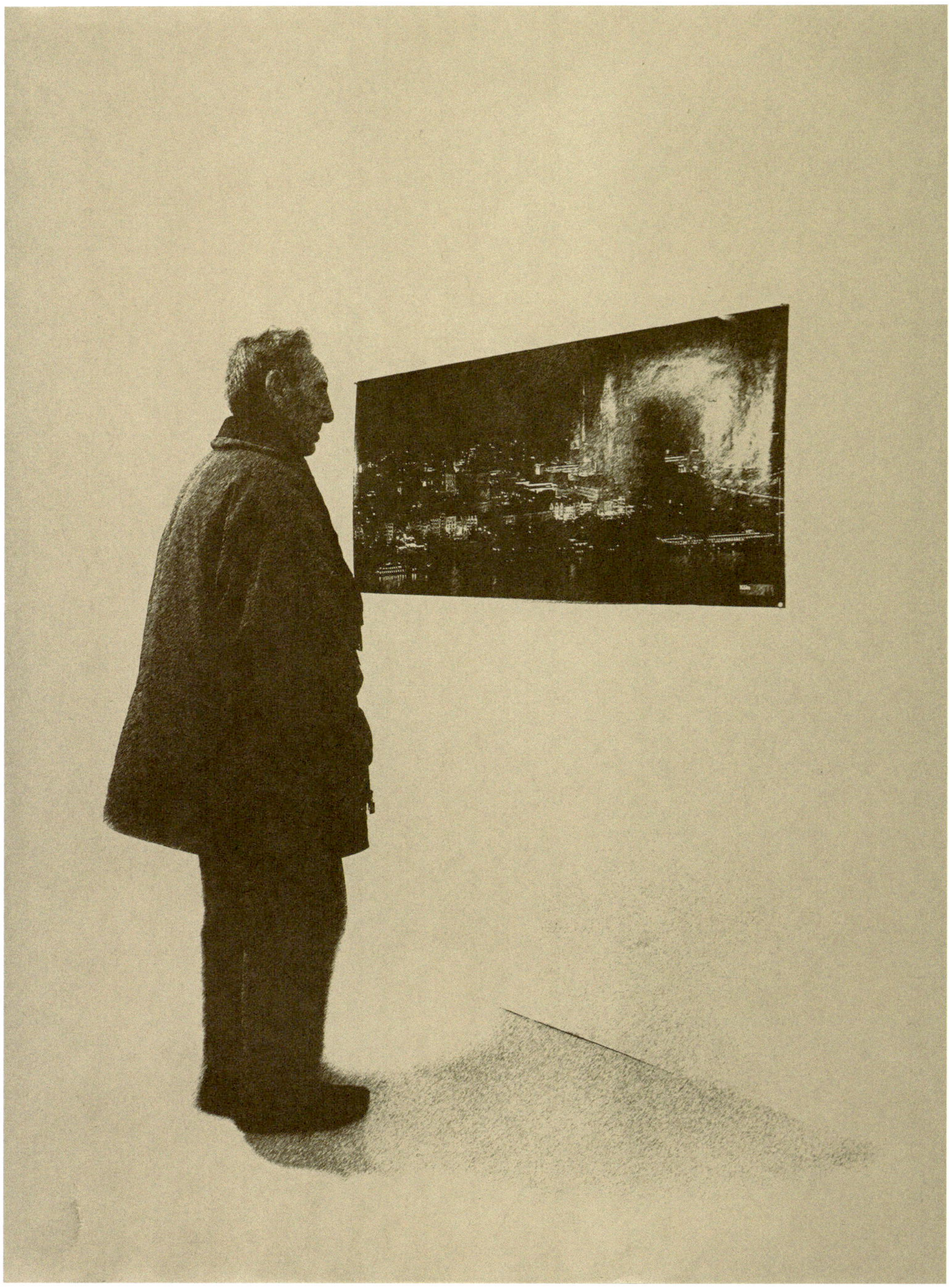

Property Owner Looking at a Poster of Cologne. No Response.
2006, inkjet print on newspaper, 24 × 17 ⅞ in.

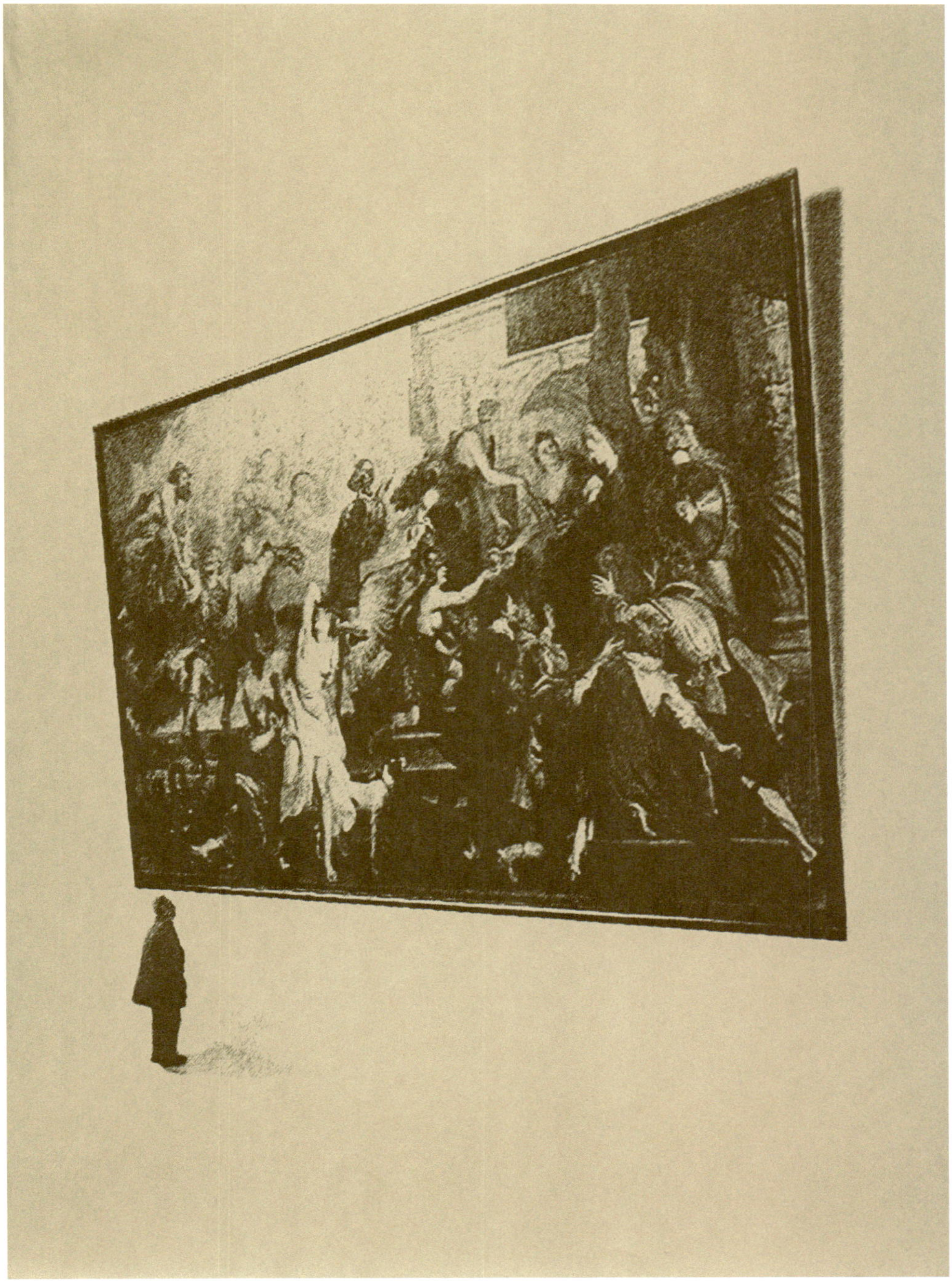

Property Owner in the Louvre Looking at Bellona. No Response.
2006, inkjet print on newspaper, 24 × 17 ⅞ in.

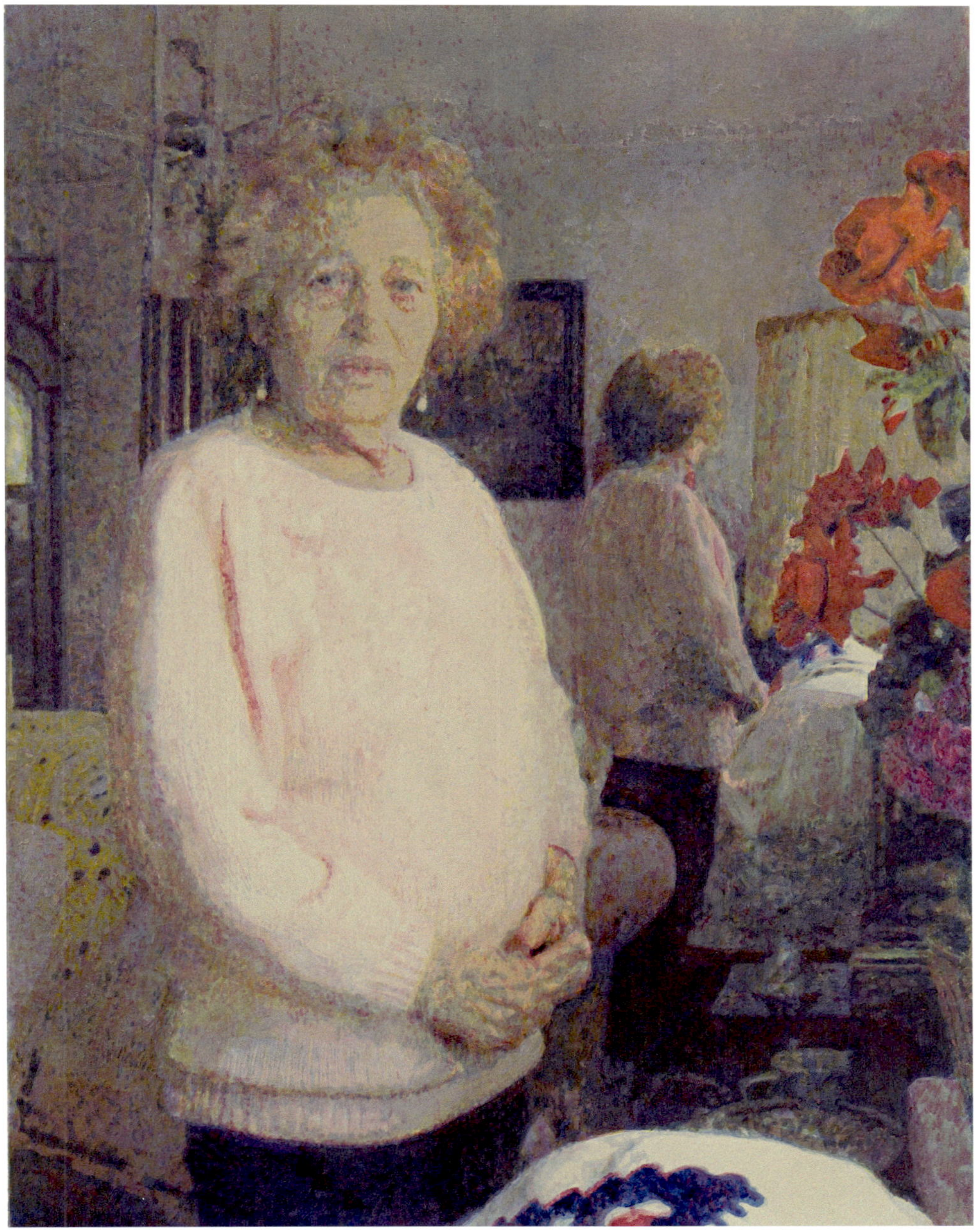

4 Colors Subtracting Light from the Room in 6 Degrees of Intensity Repeated 4 Times, II
2006, oil on canvas, 36 ¼ × 28 ¾ in.

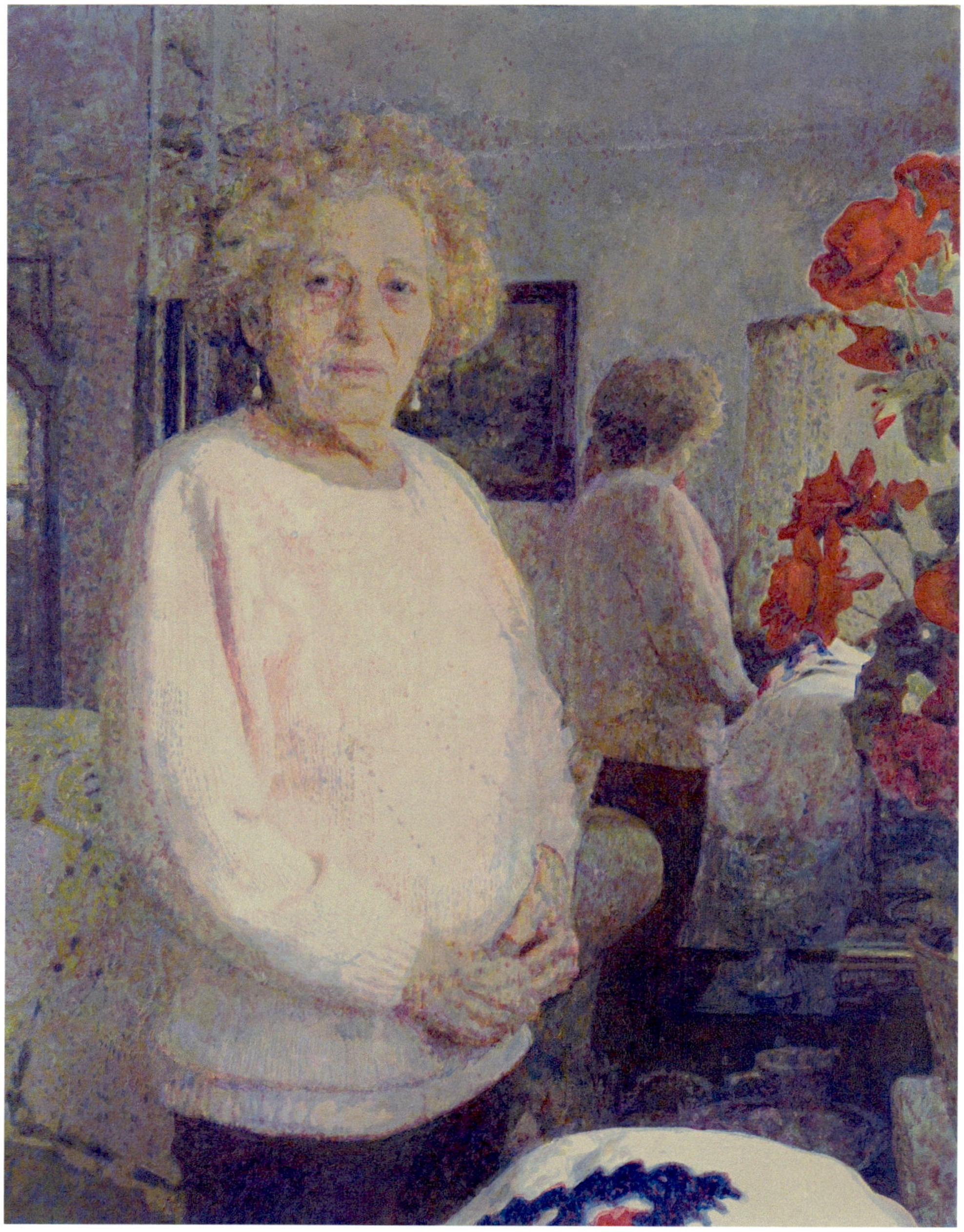

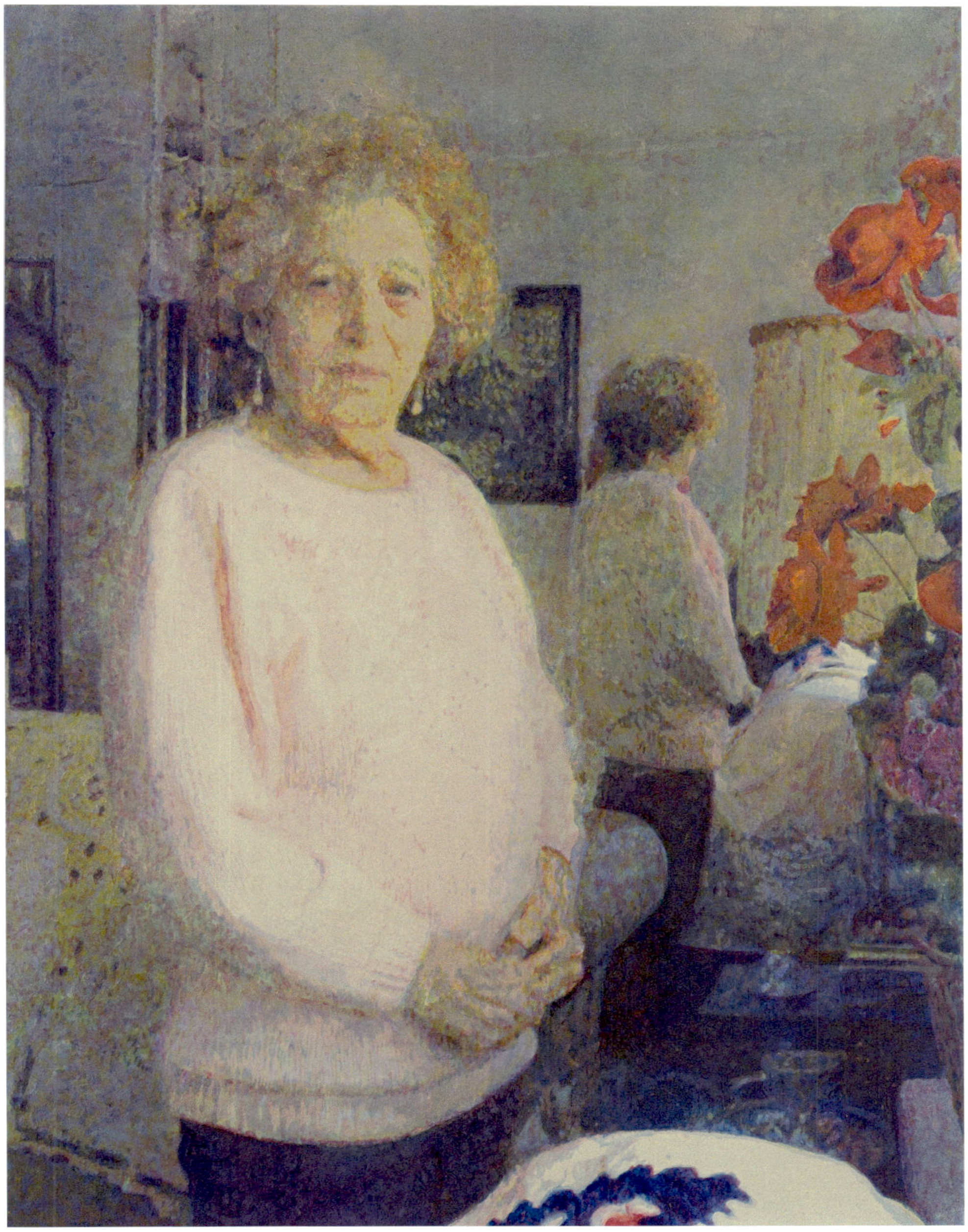

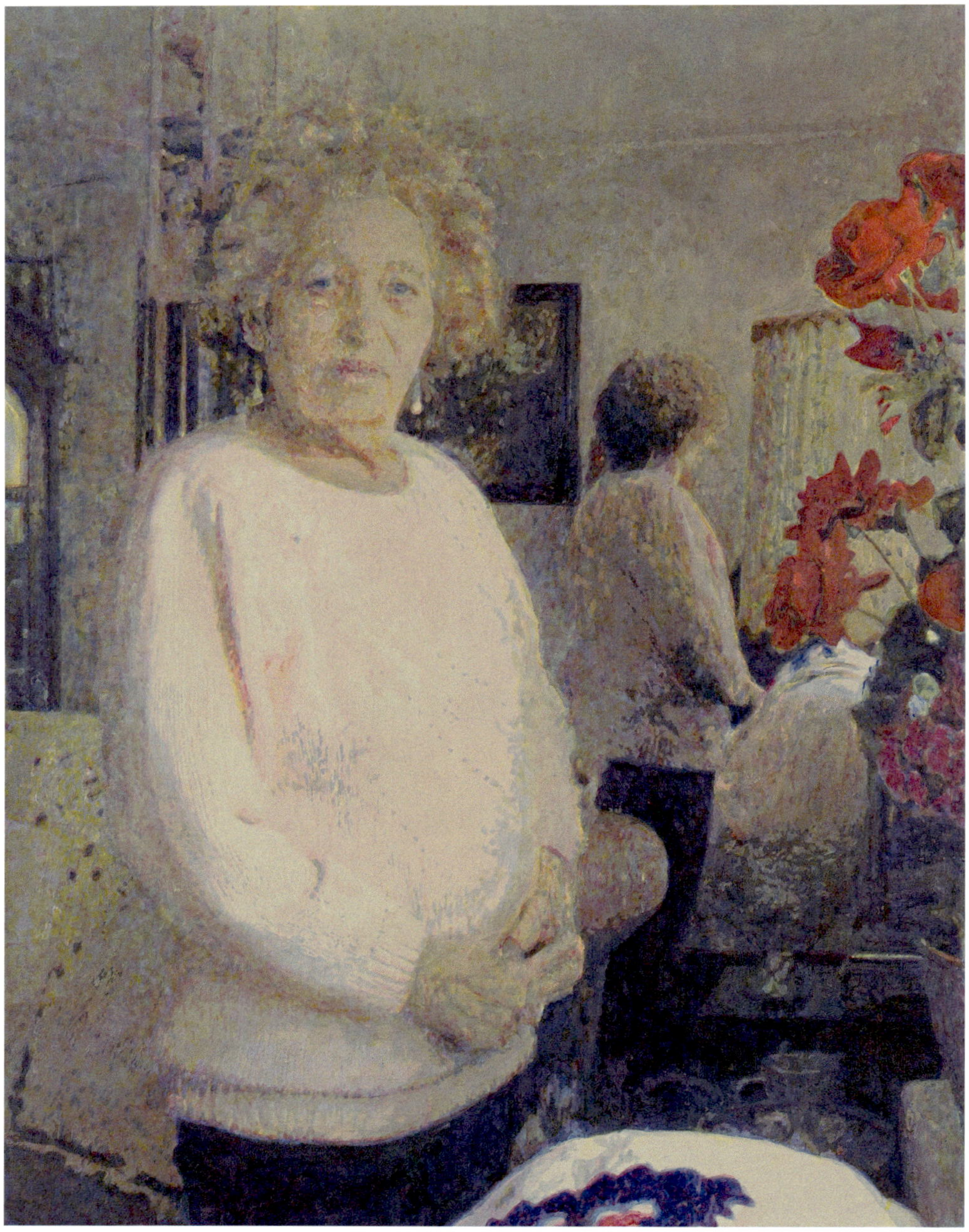

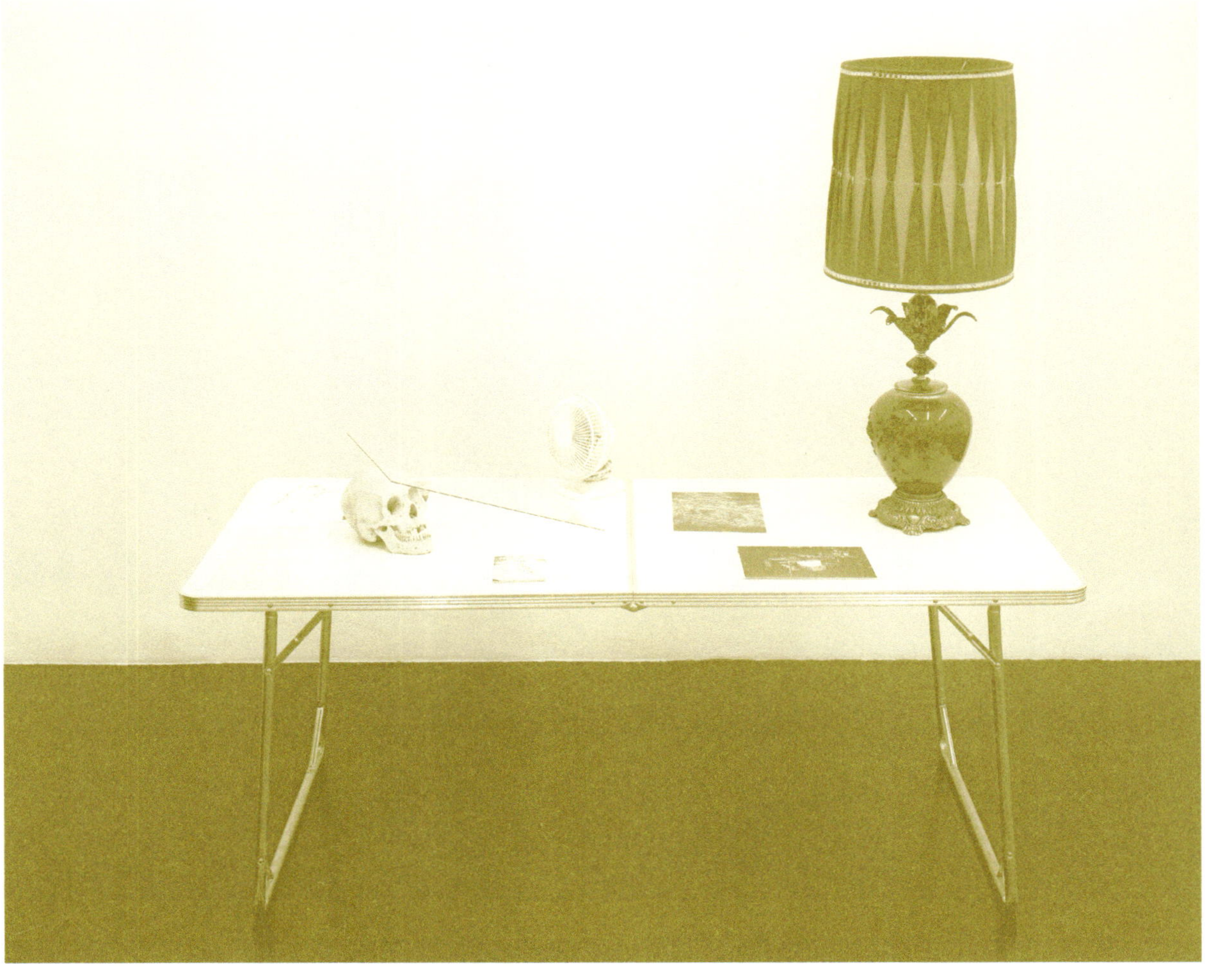

Table Displaying Gifts from the Landlord and Working Papers, 2006, table, lamp, four computer printouts, Xeroxed text with handwritten insertions, skull, glass, postcards, ventilator, 68 ½ × 72 ½ × 30 ⅛ in.

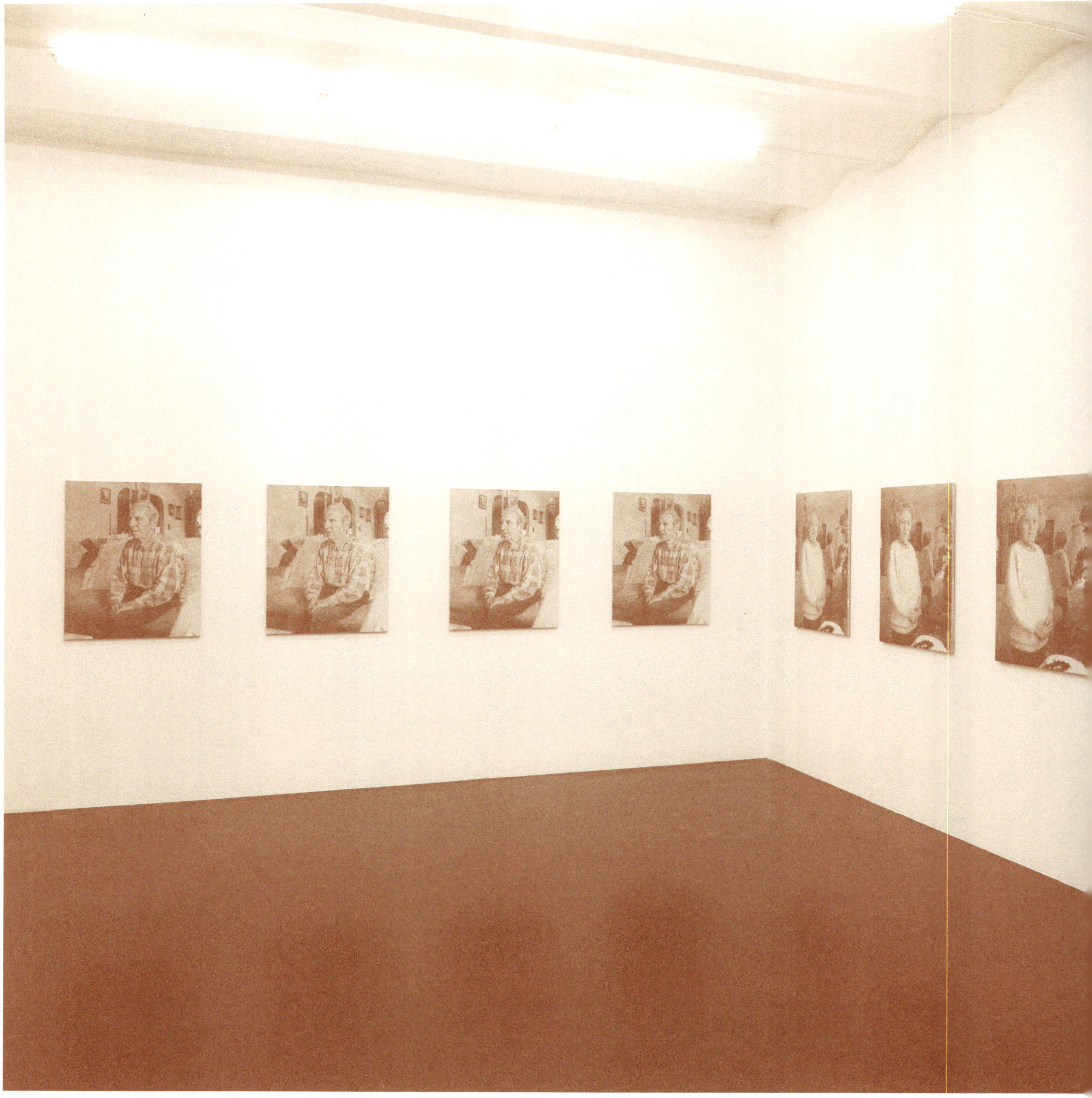

Installation view, *The End of Rent Control and the Emergence of the Creative Class* (Galerie Buchholz, Cologne), 2006.

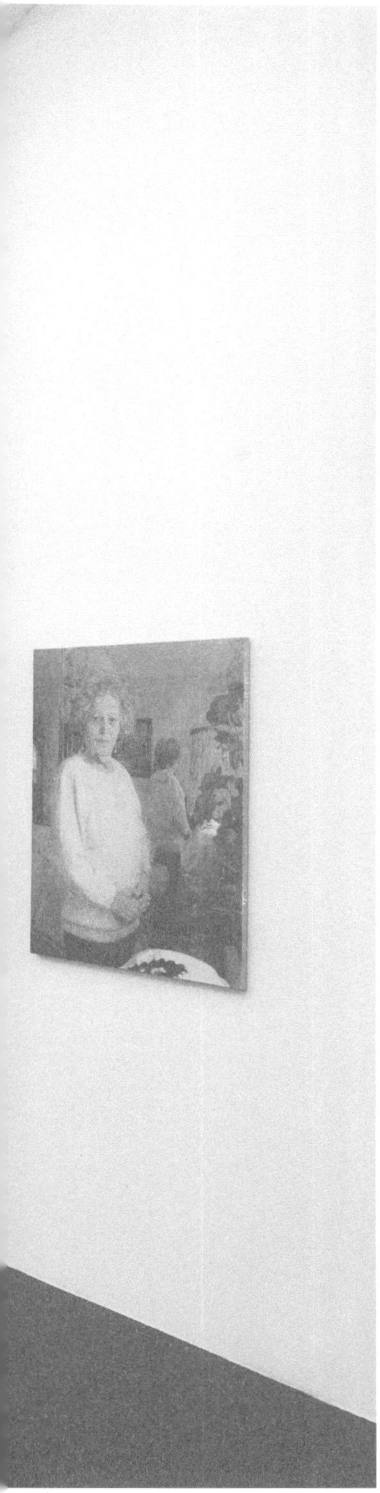

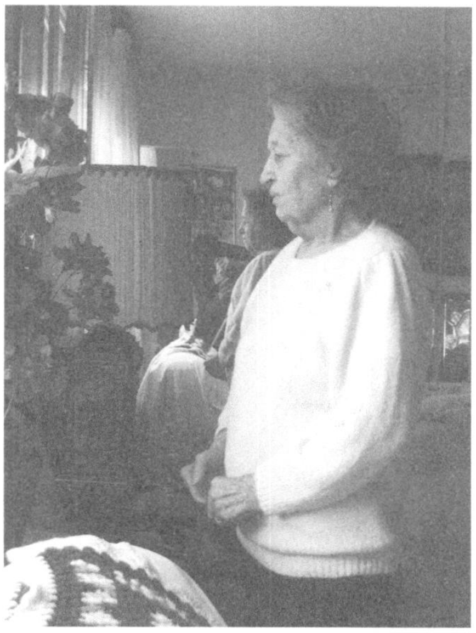

Carmella, 2006, digital photo.

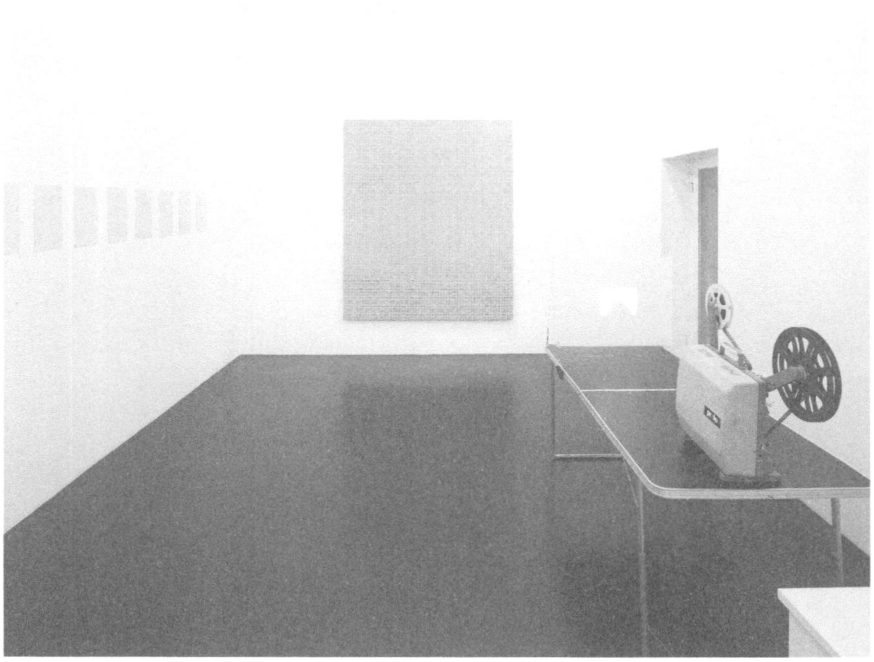

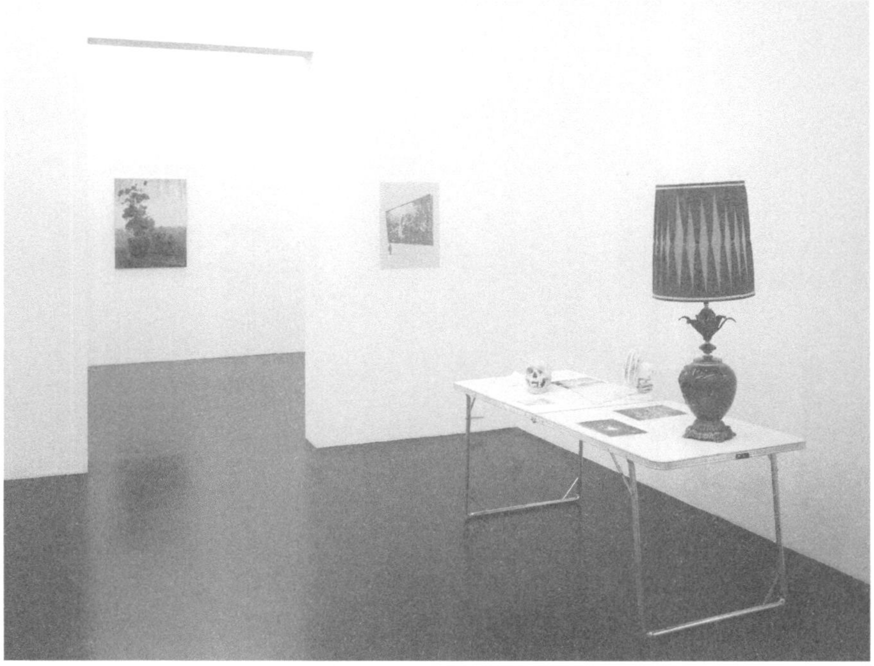

Installation view, *The End of Rent Control and the Emergence of the Creative Class* (Galerie Buchholz, Cologne), 2006.

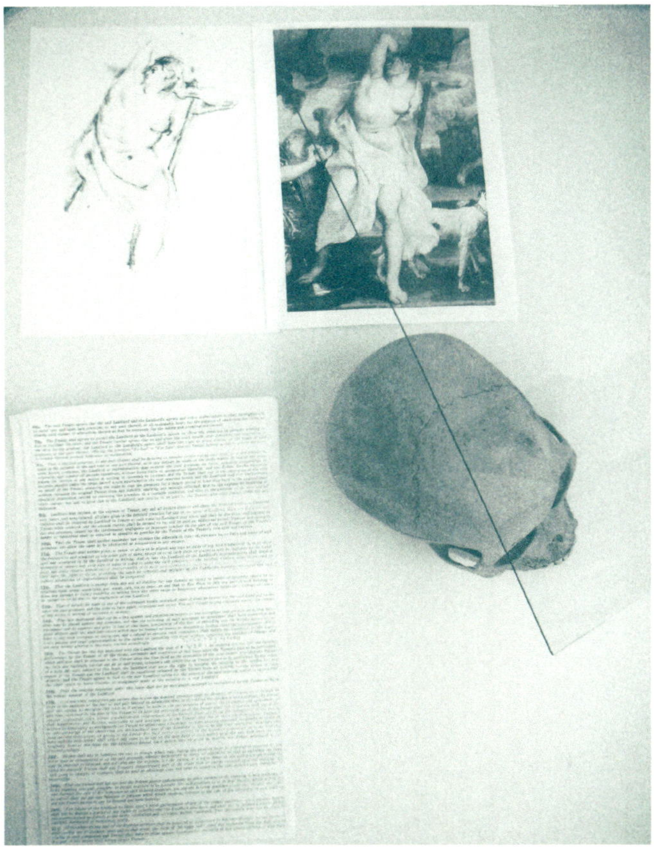

Table Displaying Gifts from the Landlord and Working Papers (detail), 2006, table, lamp, four computer printouts, Xeroxed text with handwritten insertions, skull, glass, postcards, ventilator, 68 ½ × 72 ½ × 30 ⅛ in.

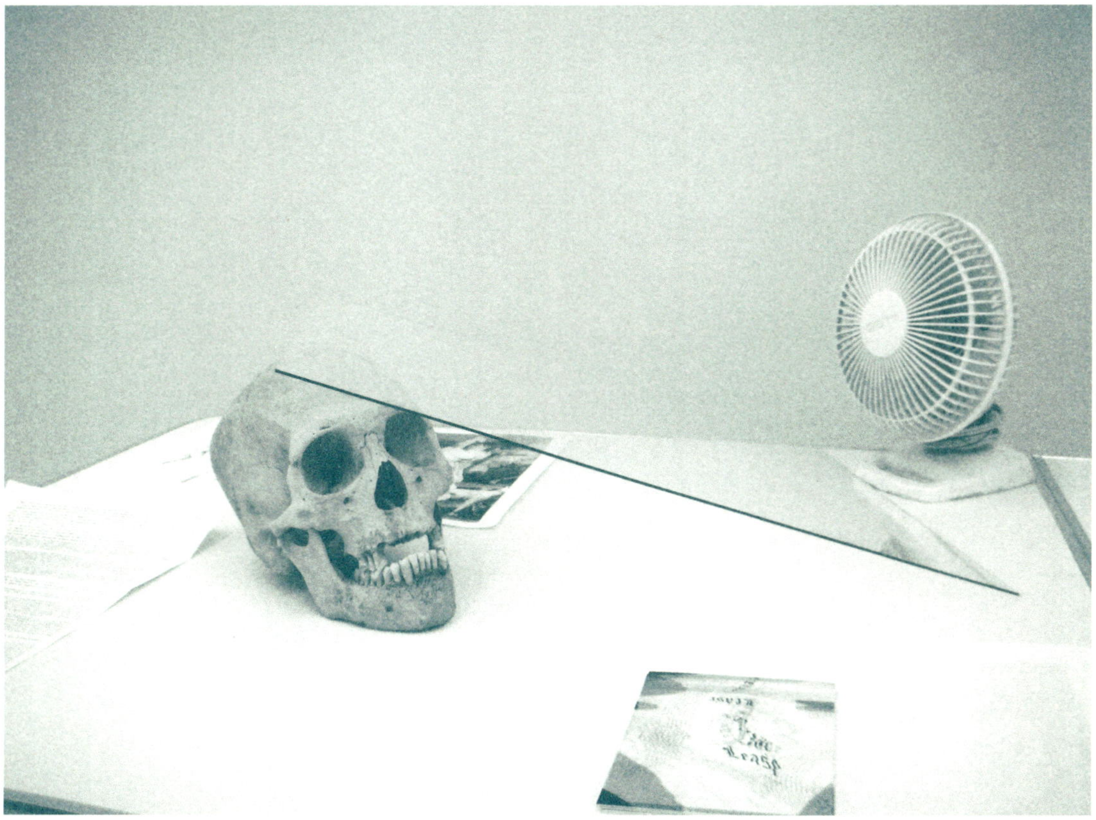

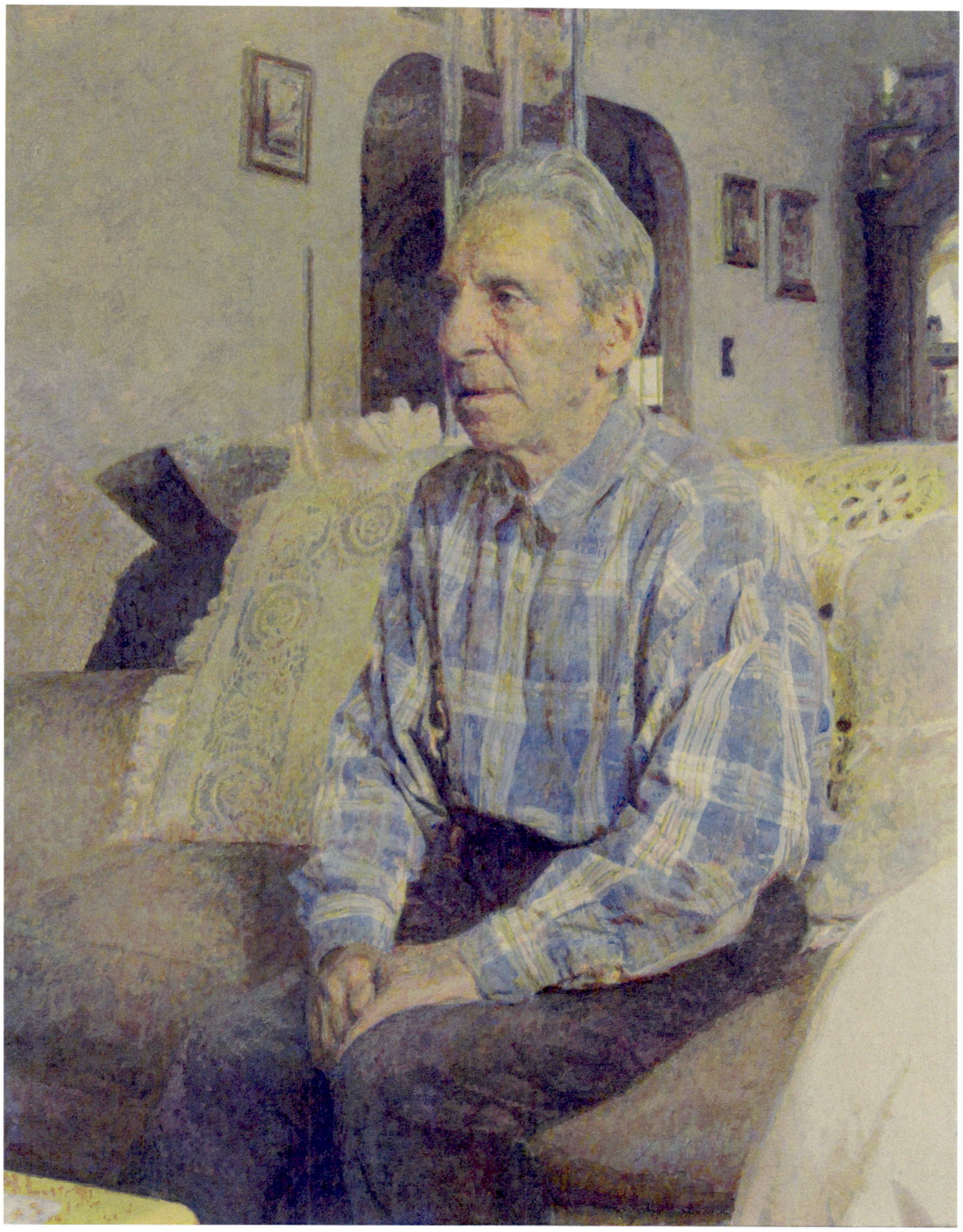

4 Colors Subtracting Light from the Room in 6 Degrees of Intensity Repeated 4 Times, I
2006, oil on canvas, 36 ¼ × 28 ¾ in.

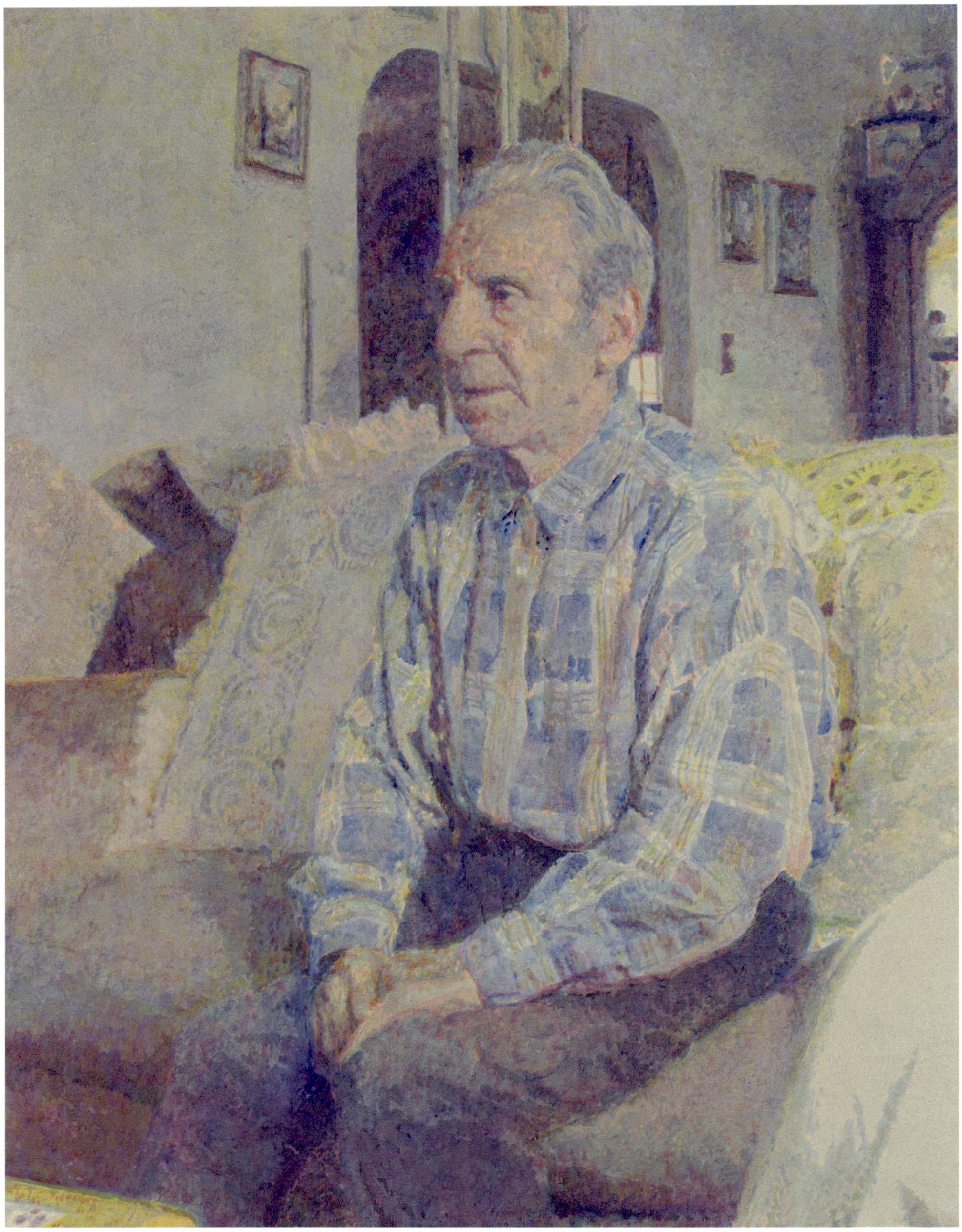

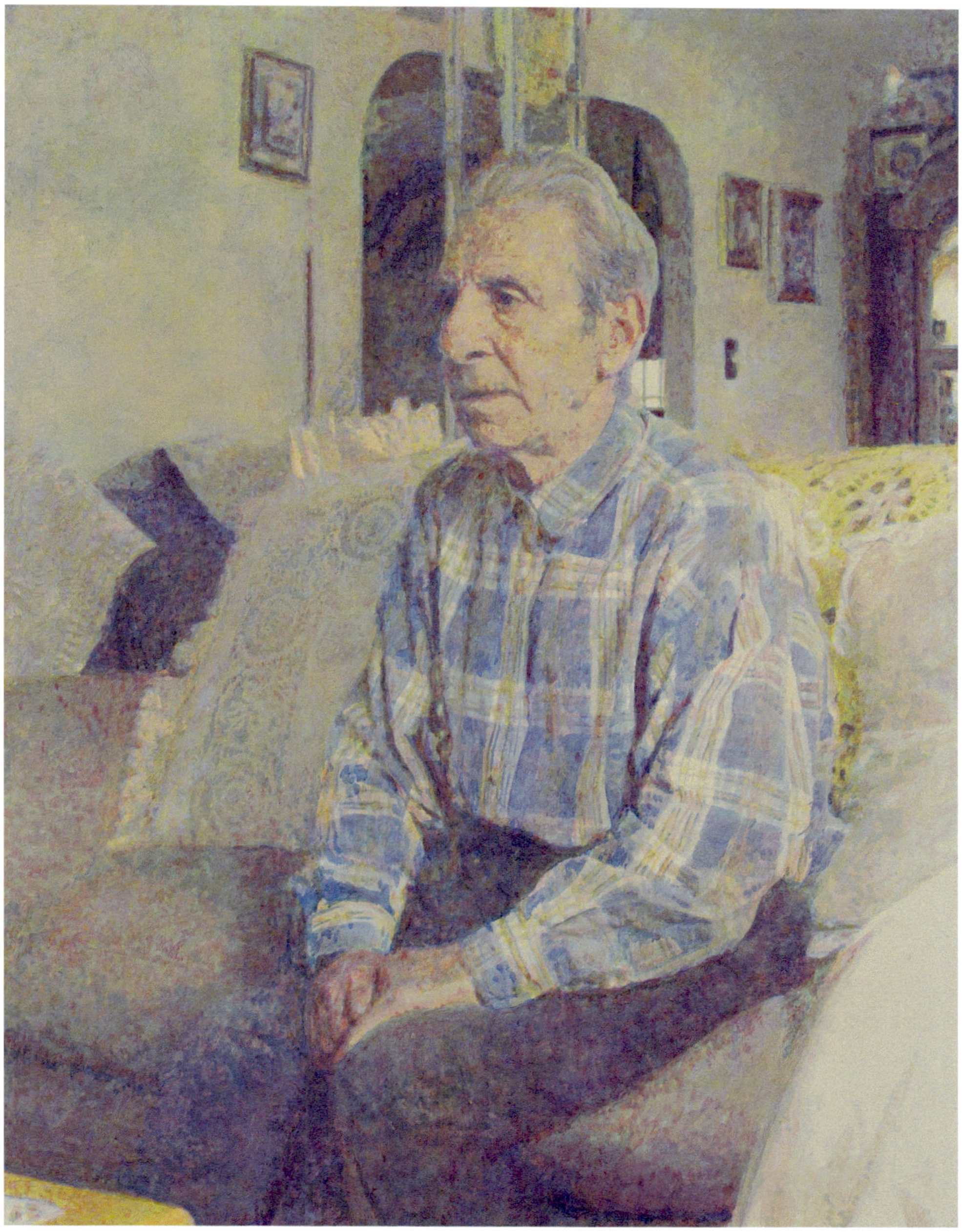

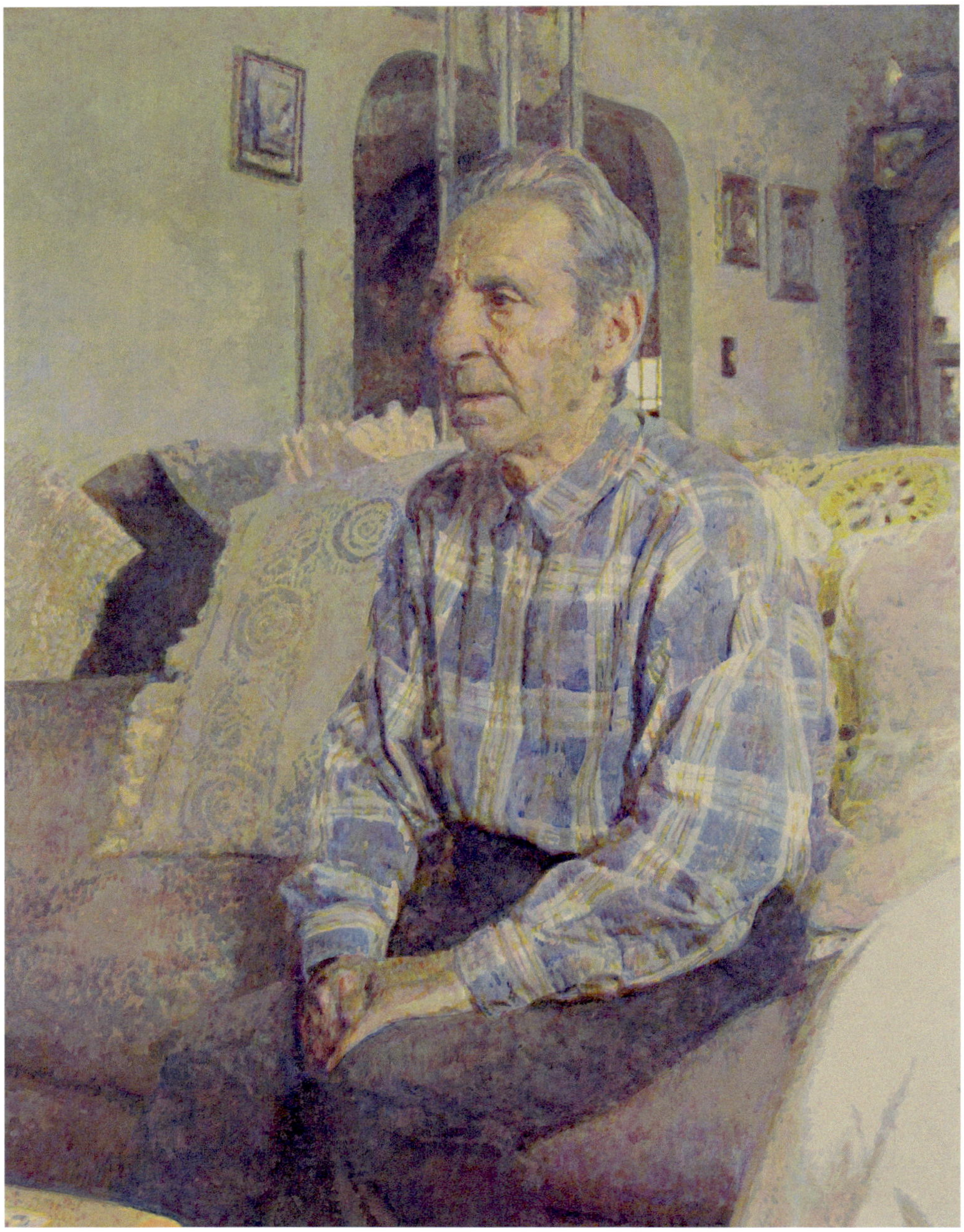

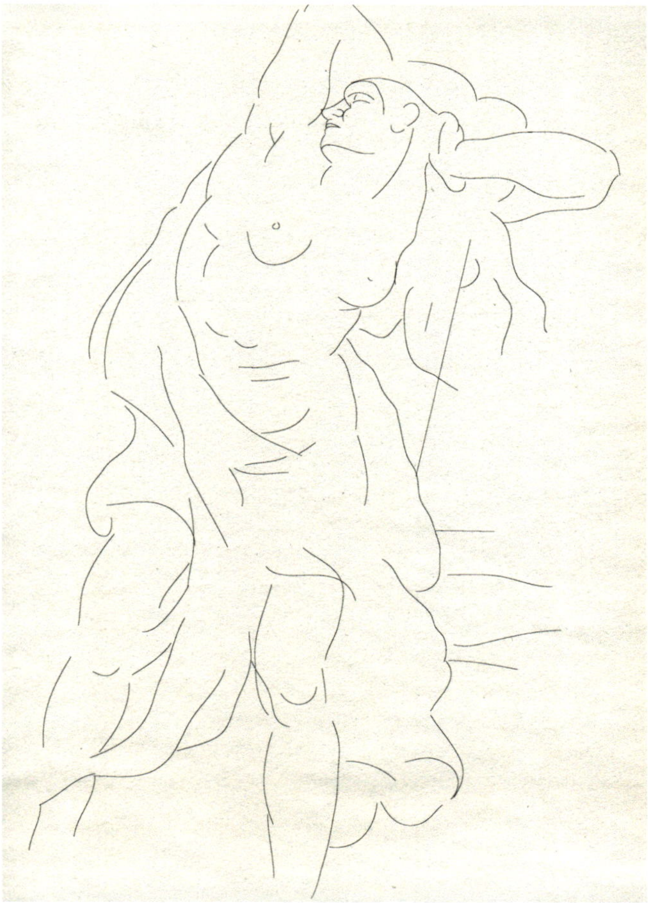

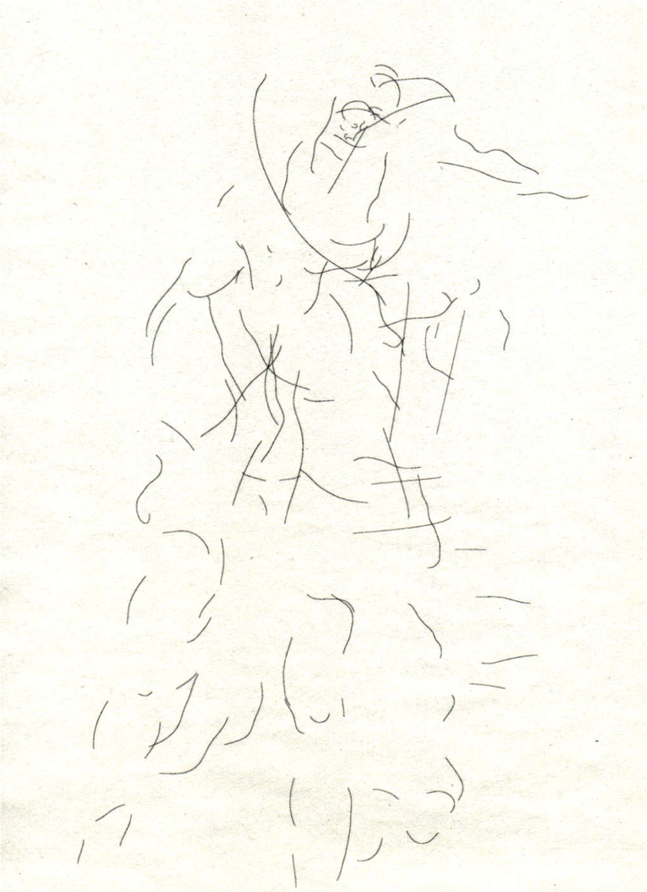

Sets of Curves from Bellona to Rubens to Cézanne to Bezier
2006, 17 inkjet prints on newspaper in cardboard box, 14 × 8 ⅝ in. each.

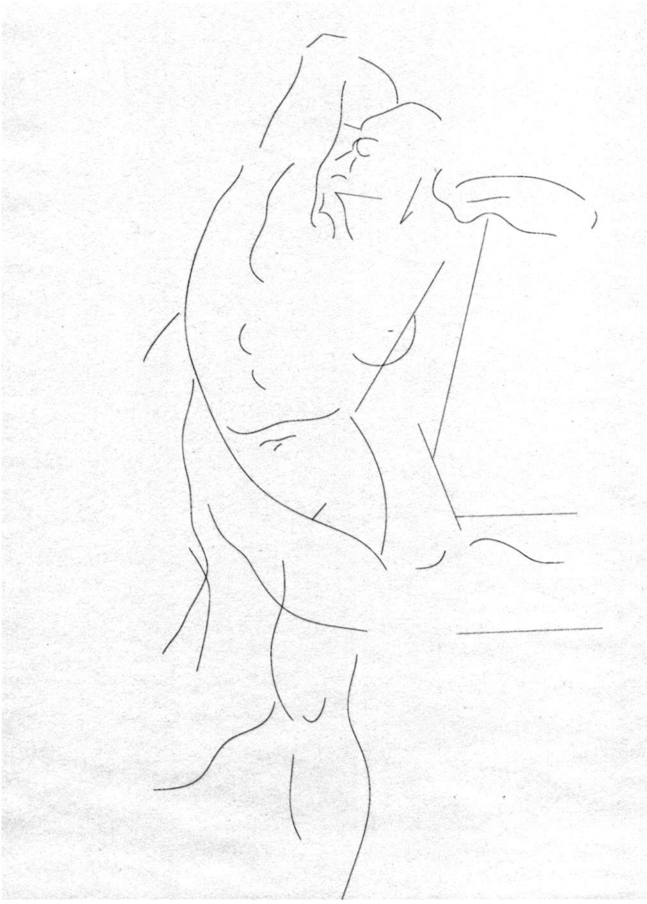
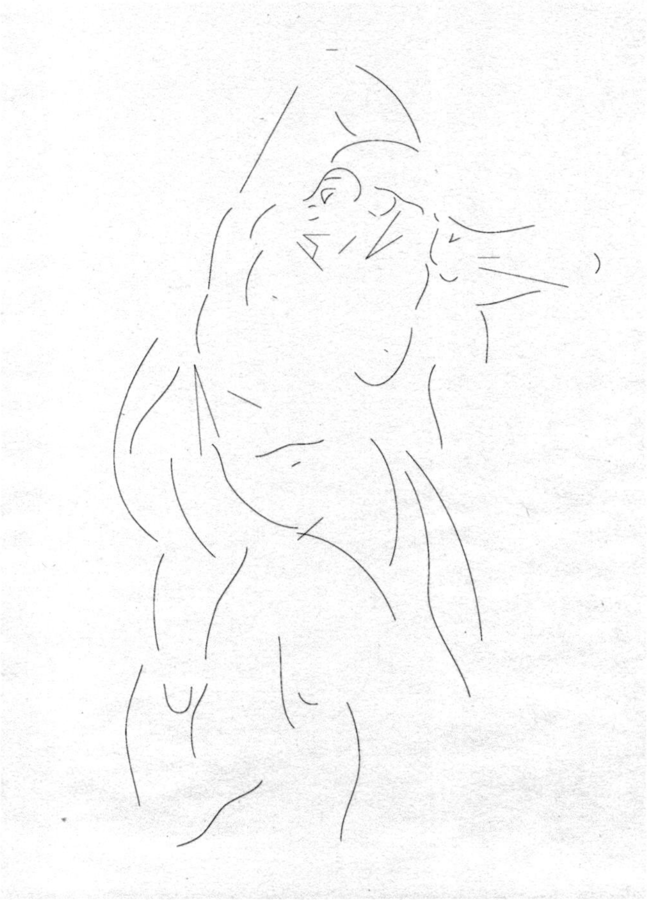
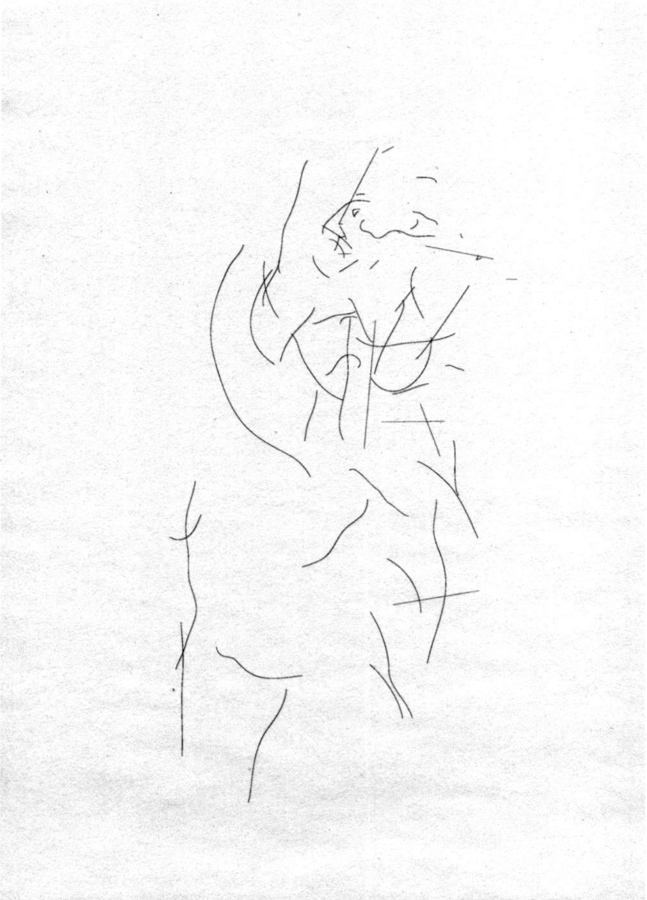
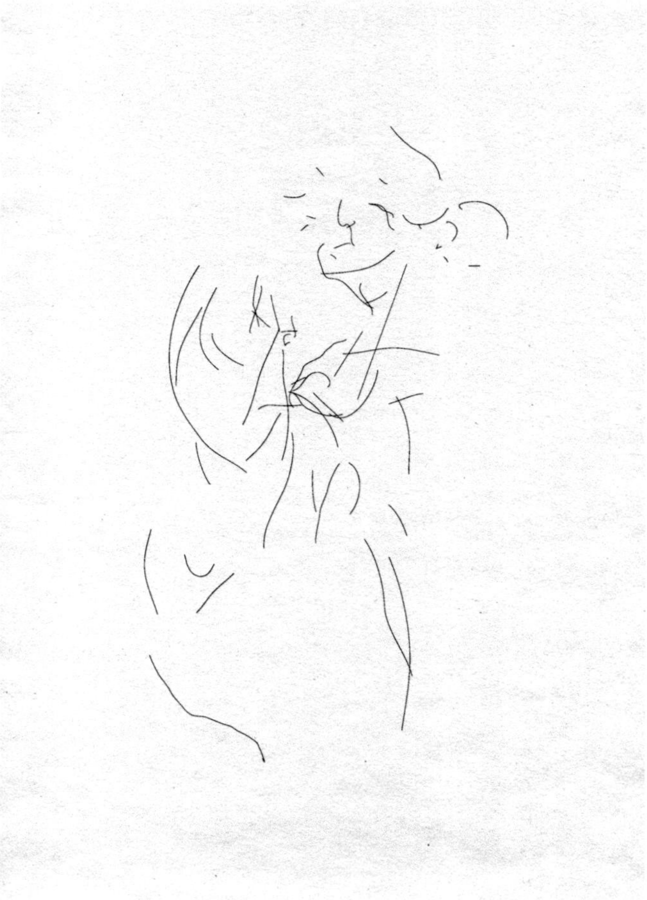

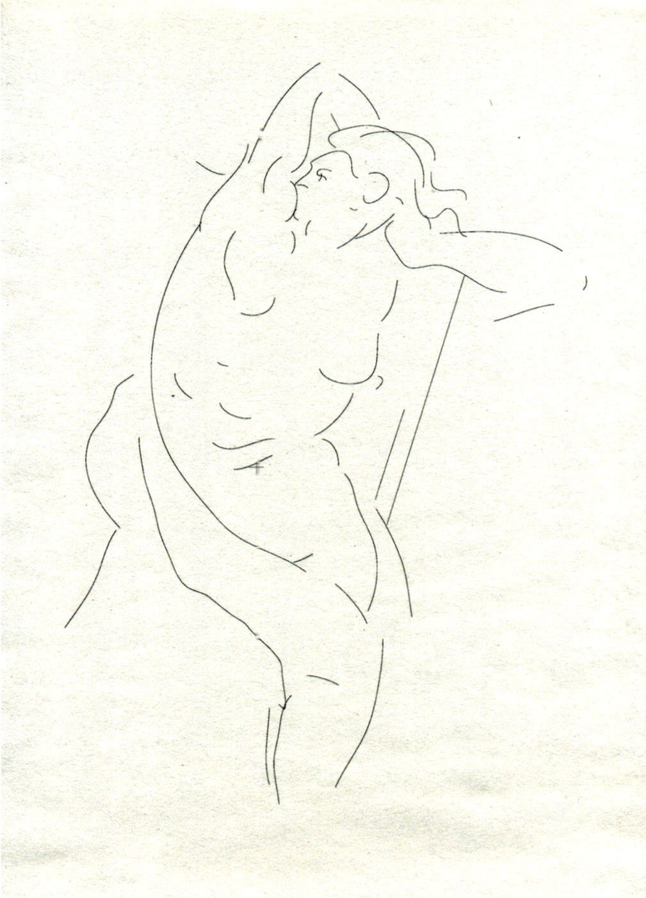

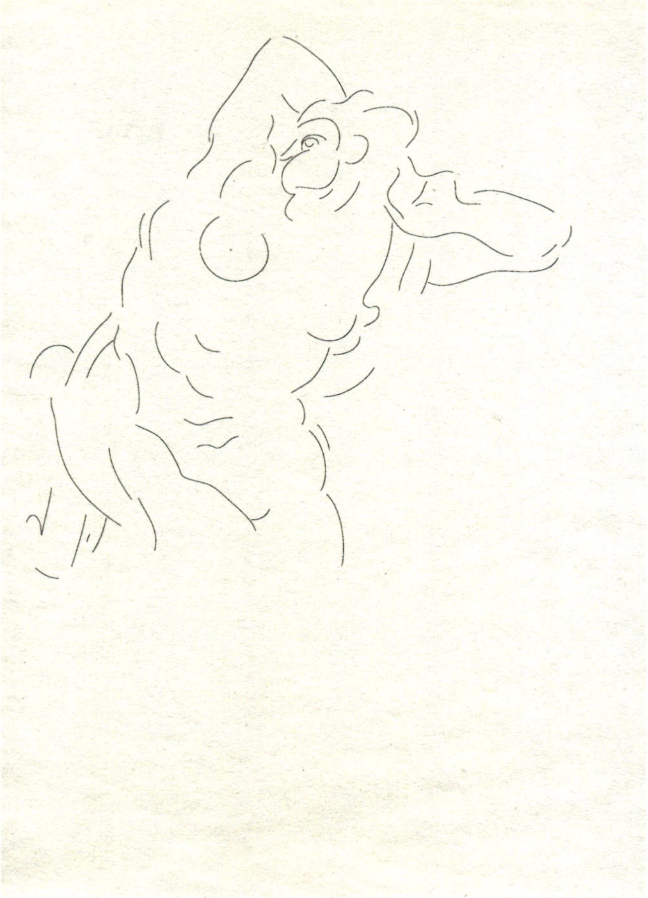

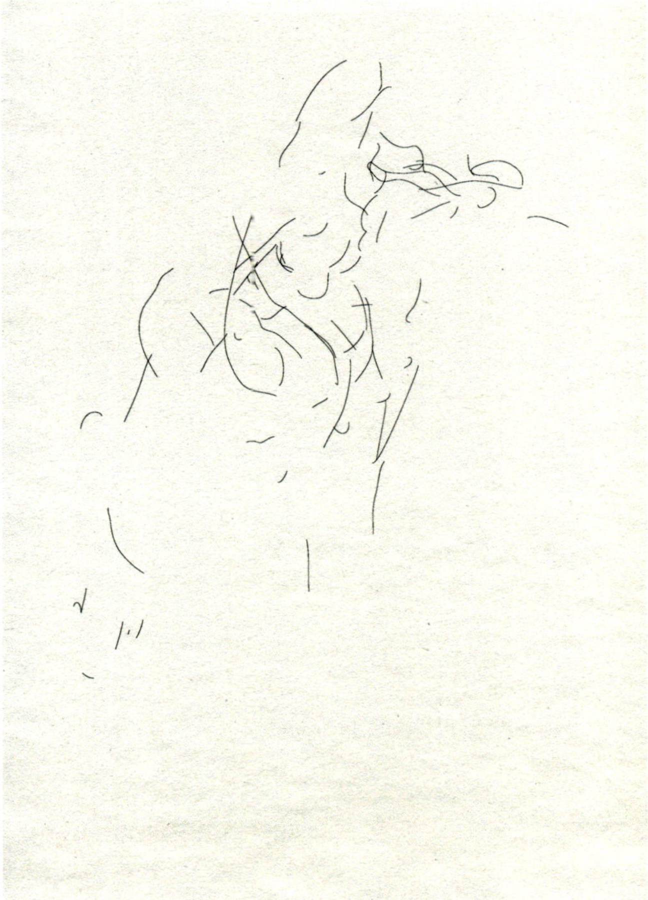

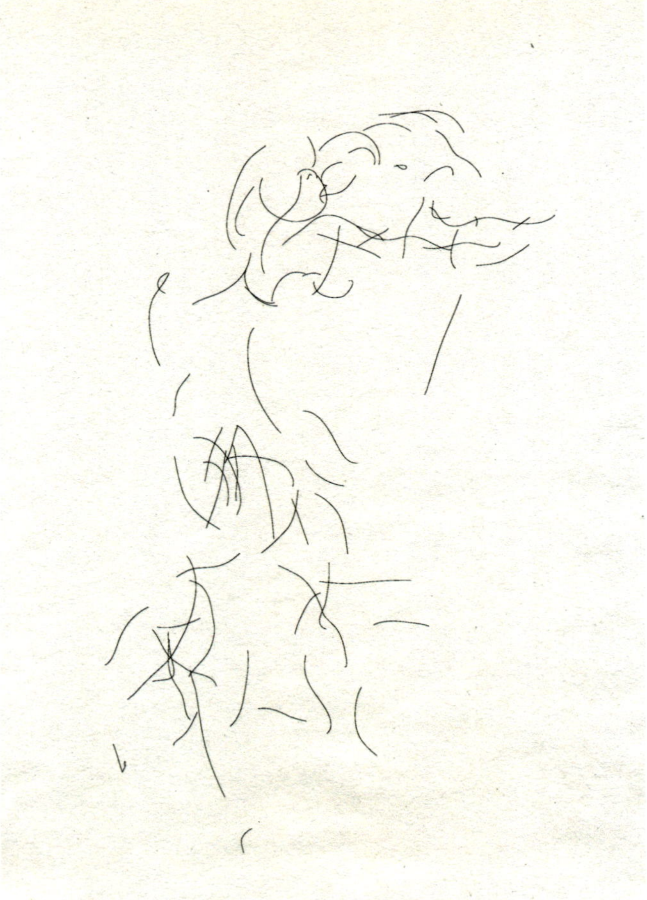

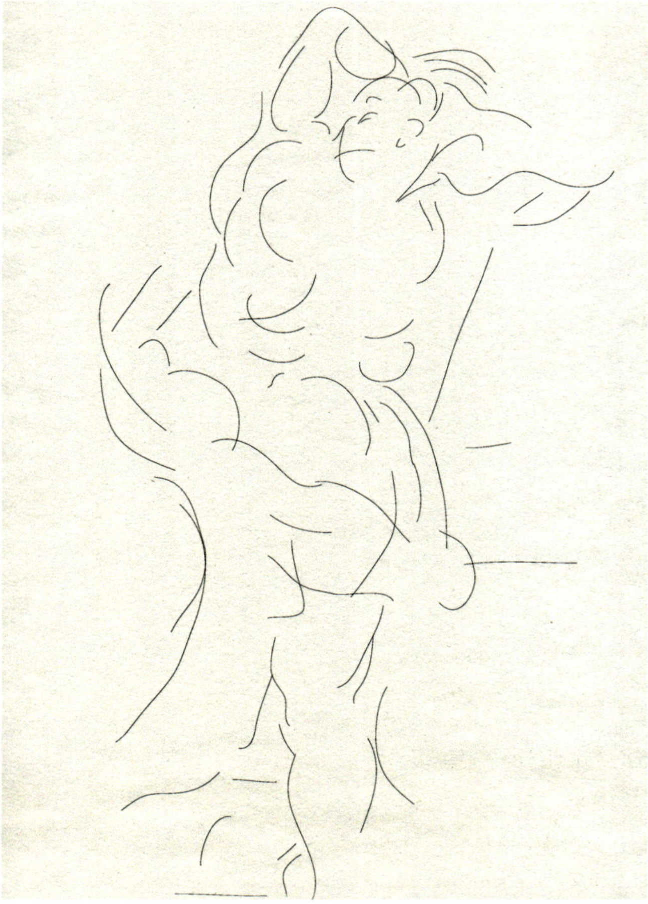
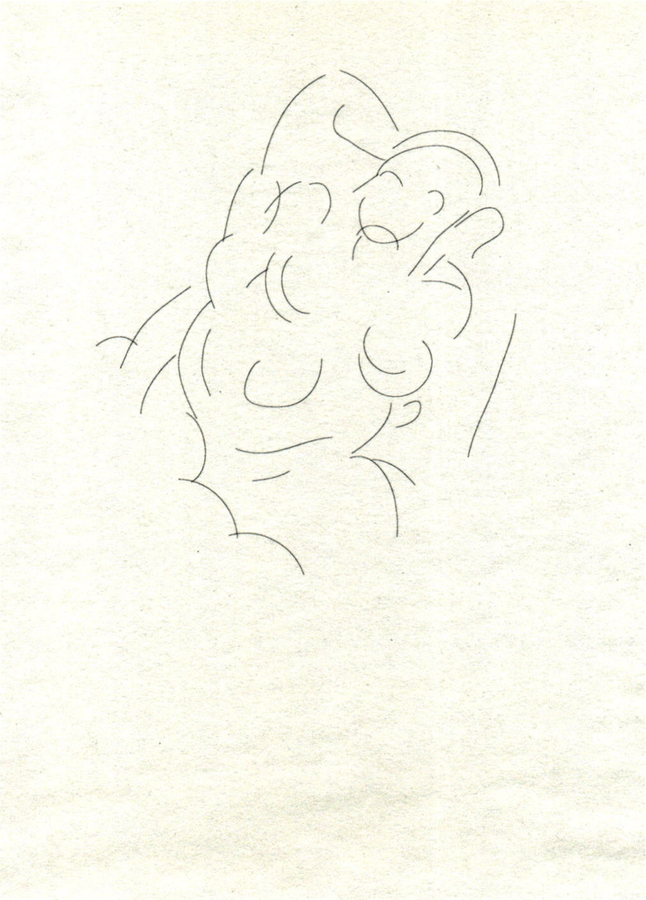
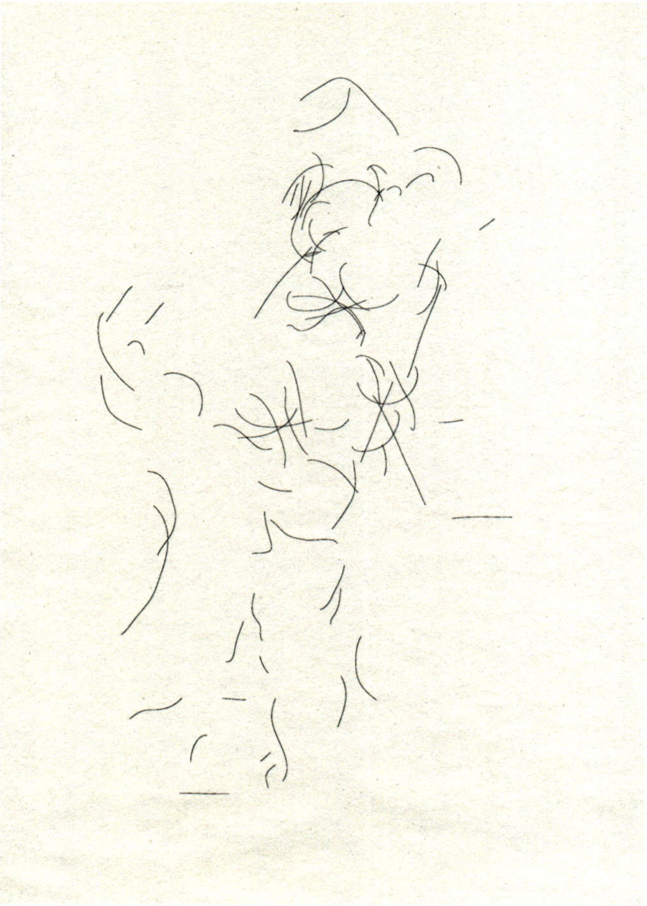
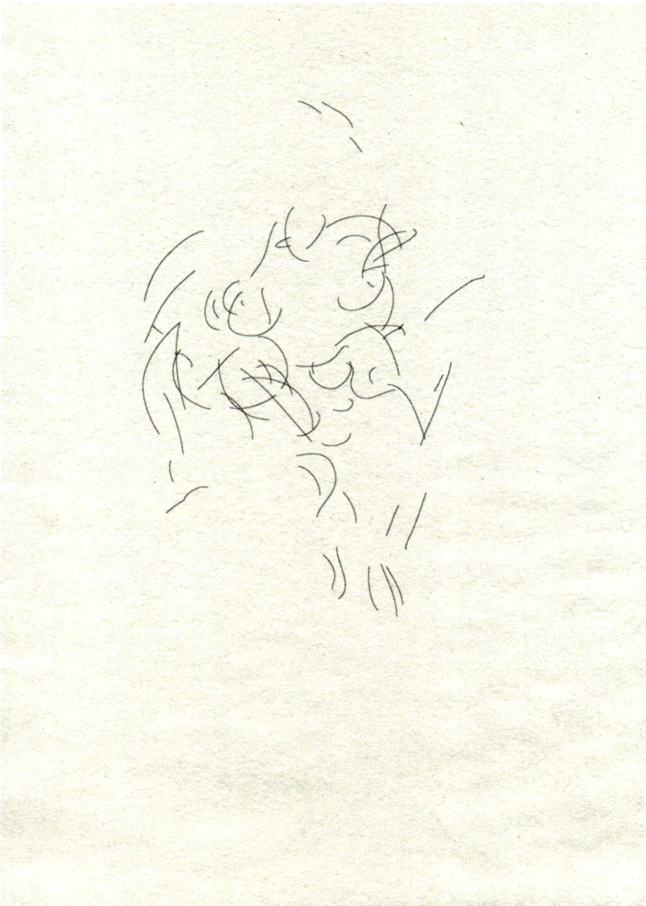

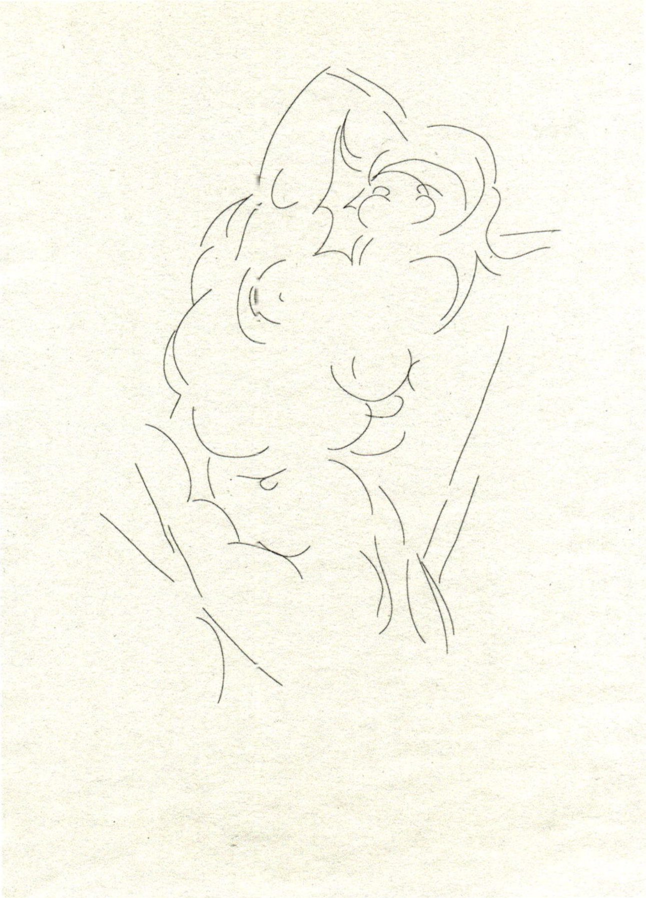
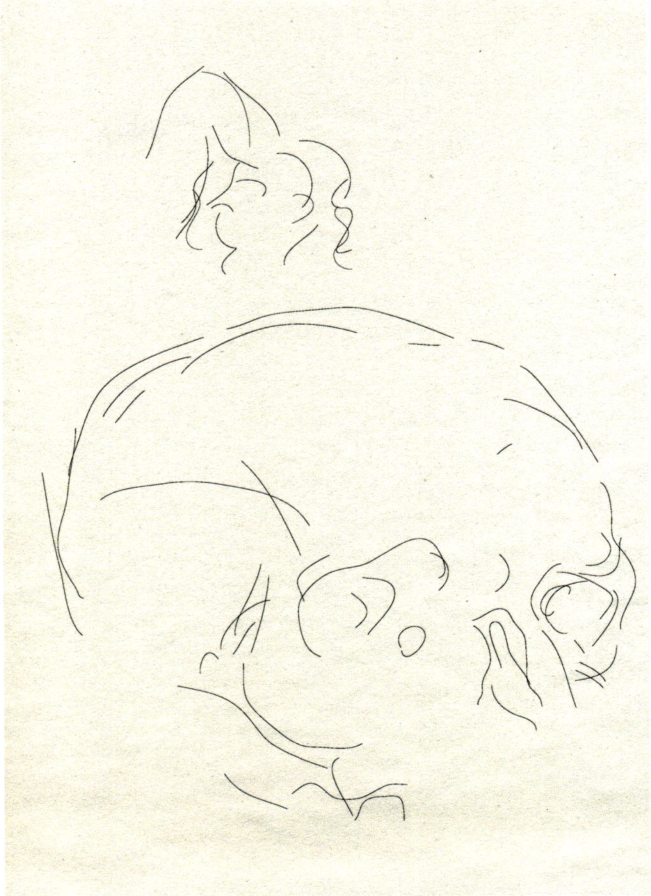

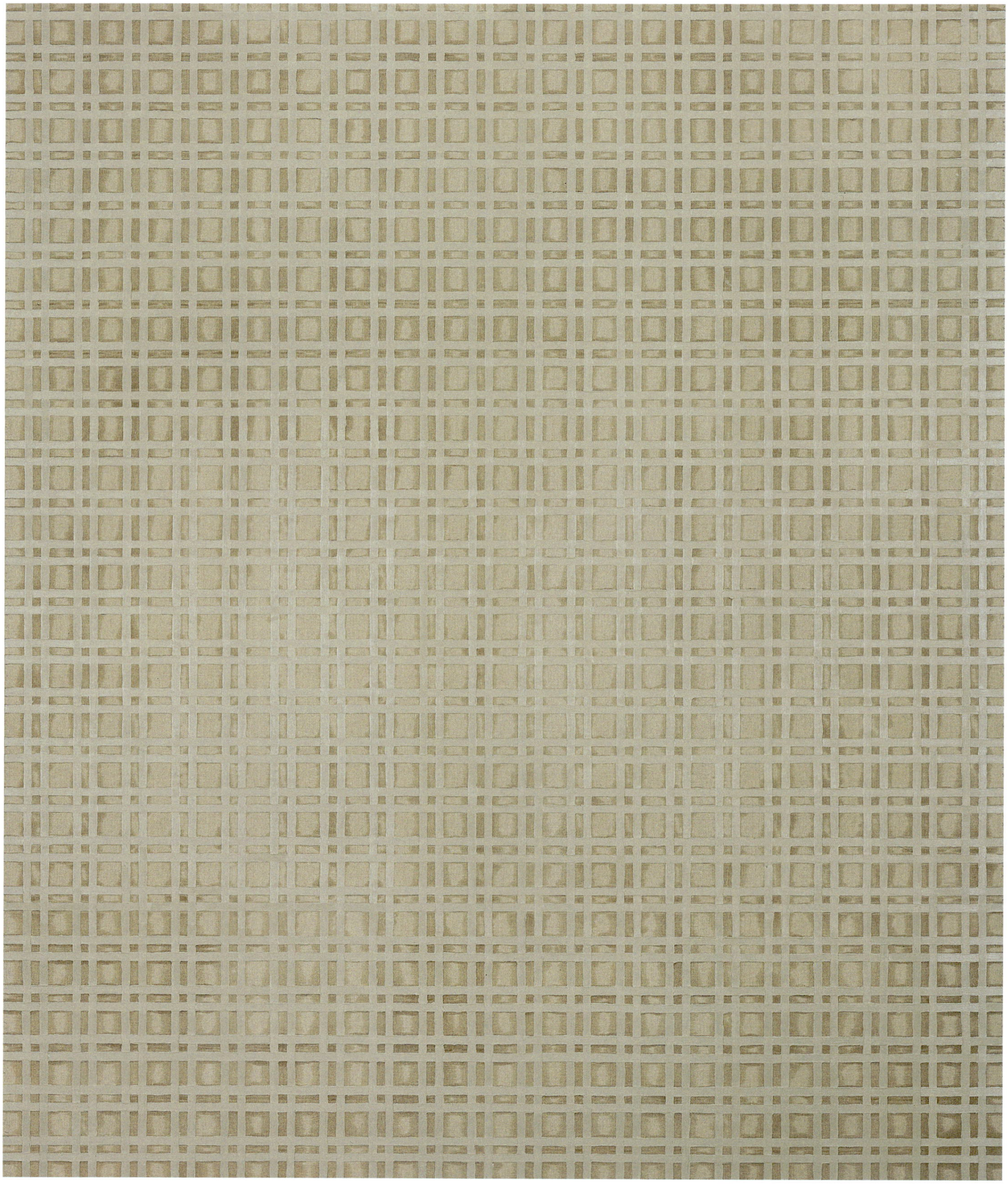

The Production of an Unevenly Distributed Surplus Results from the Facticity of Format and Ground
2006, oil on canvas, 84 ⅝ × 72 ¼ in.

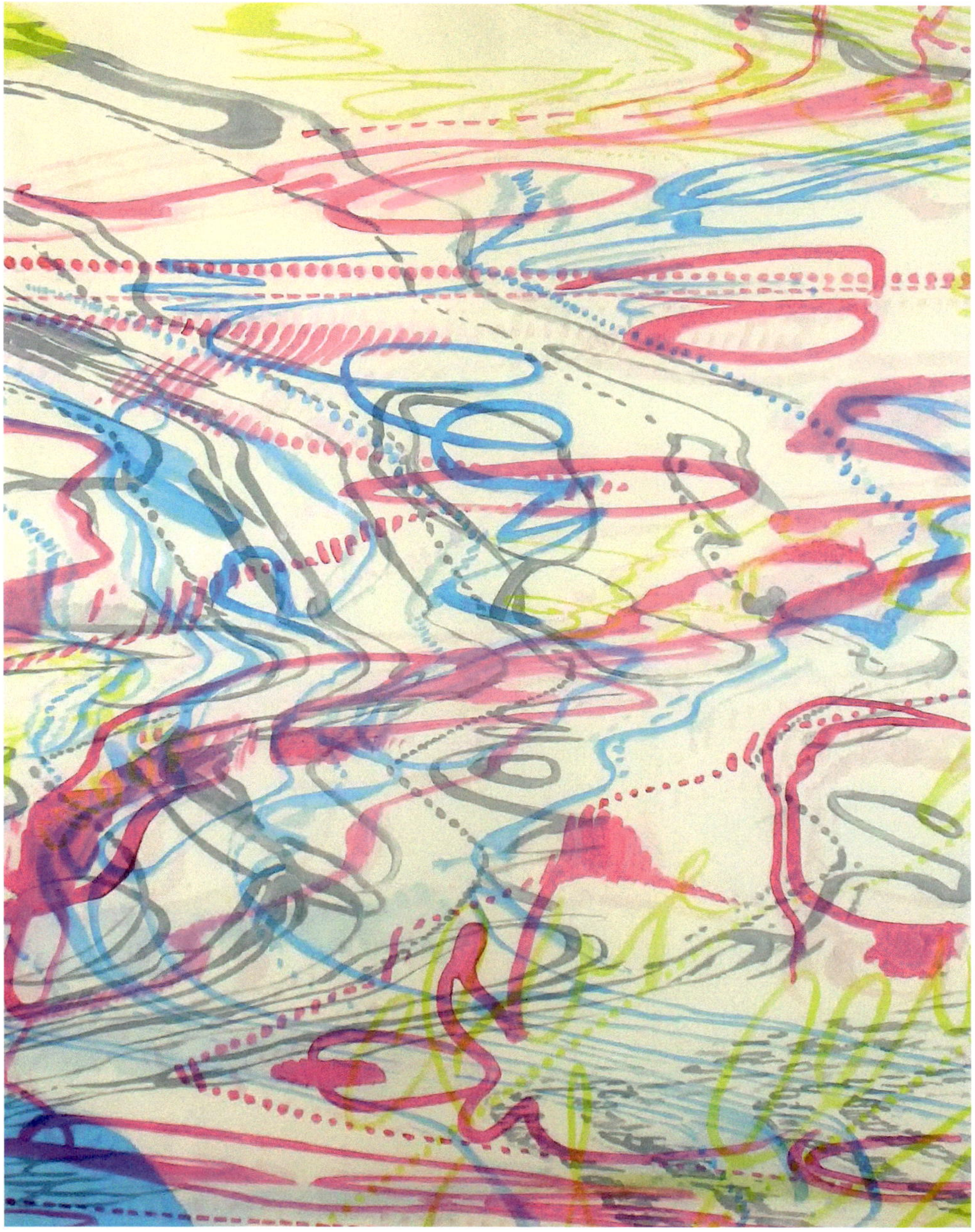

Untitled (Lease)
2006, oil on canvas, 37 × 28 ¾ in.

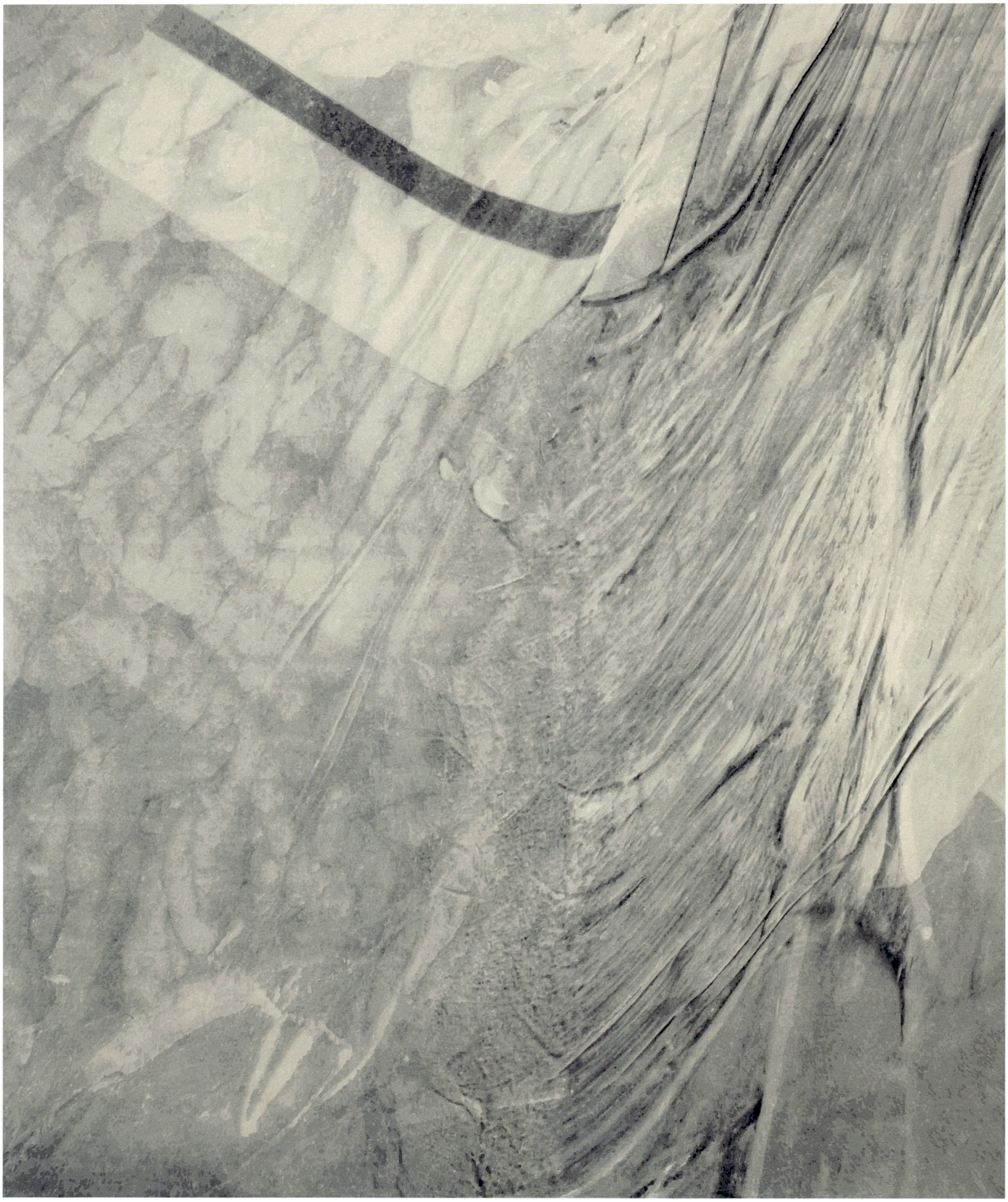

Untitled
2006, oil on canvas, 84 × 72 in.

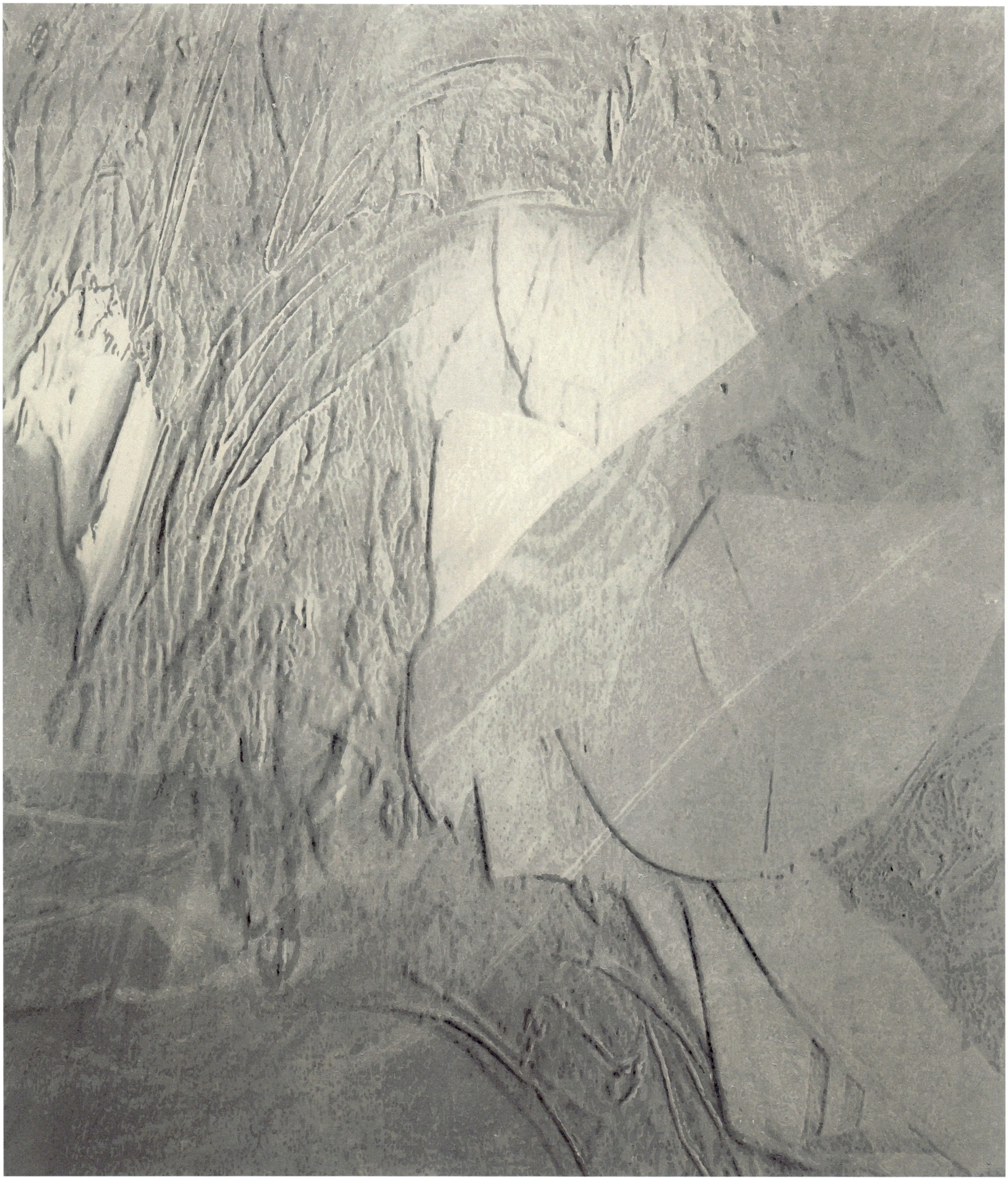

Untitled
2006, oil on canvas, 84 × 72 in.

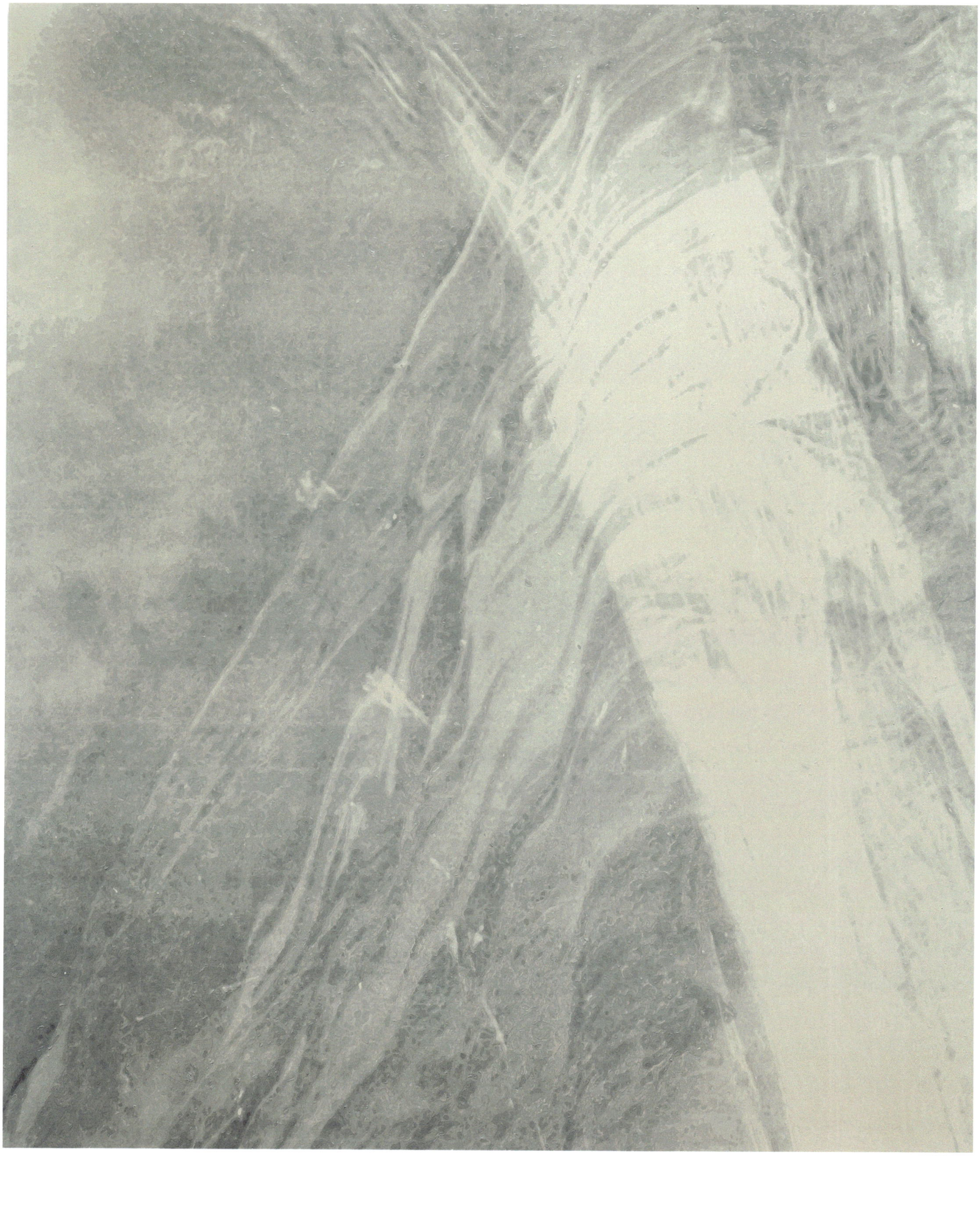

Untitled
2006, oil on canvas, 84 × 72 in.

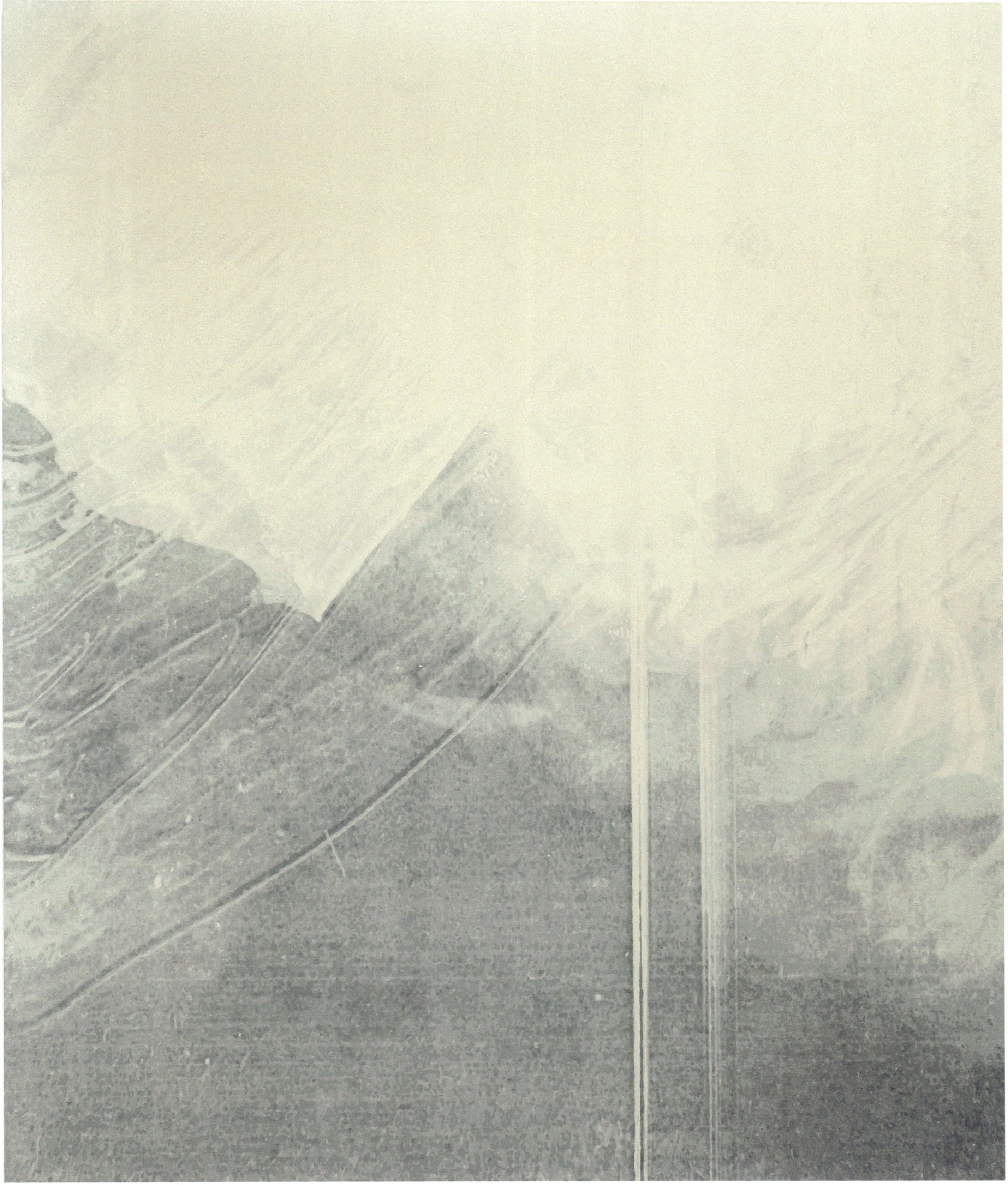

Untitled
2006, oil on canvas, 84 × 72 in.

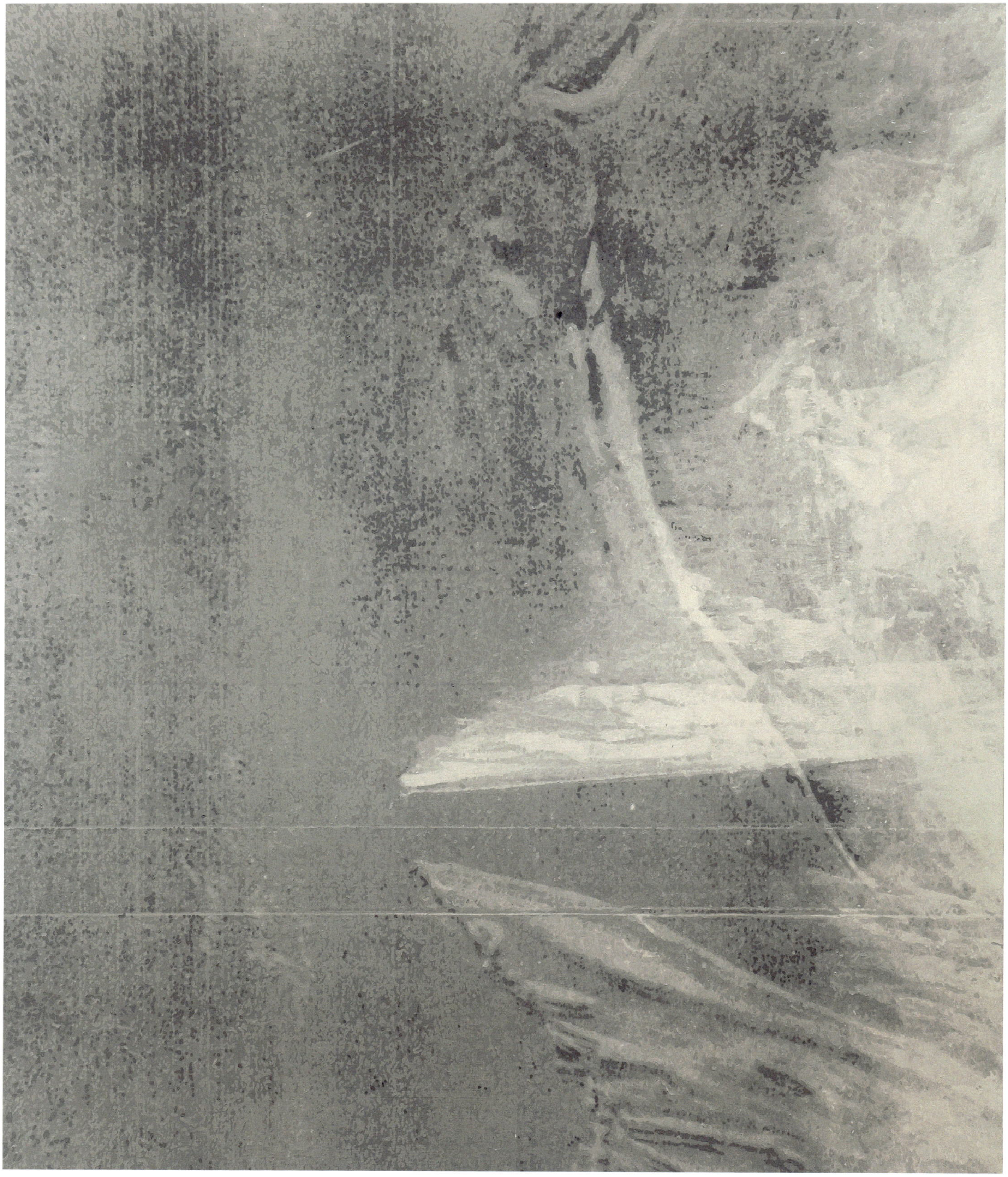

Untitled
2006, oil on canvas, 84 × 72 in.

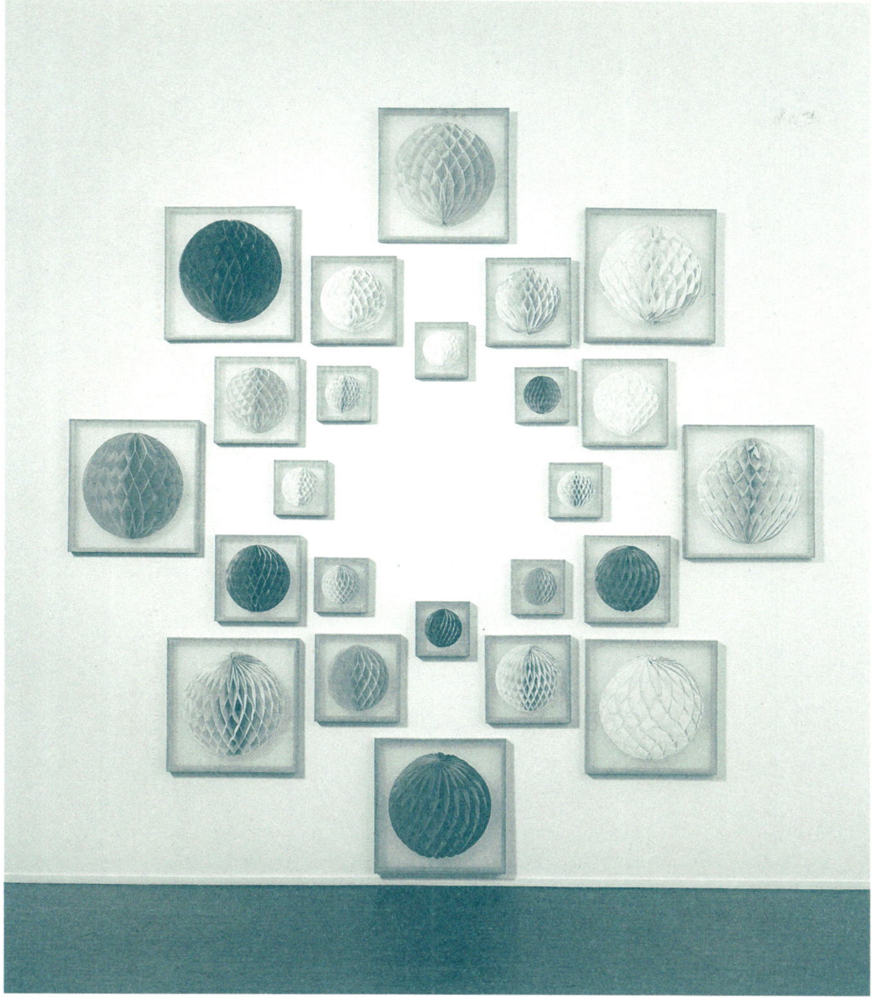

Sweet Authority, 2003, 24 oil on organza paintings, 132 × 132 in.

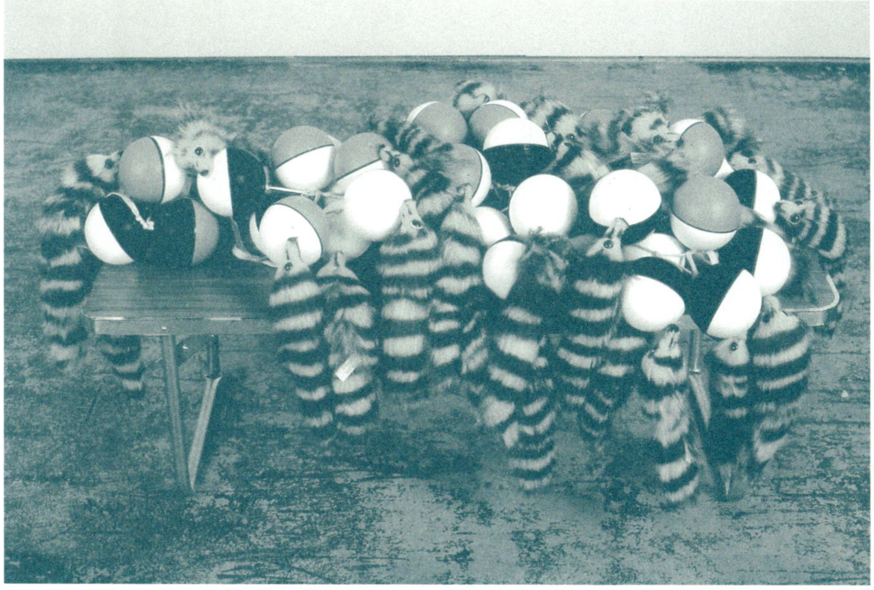

Table of Hubris, 2002, weasel balls, shoelaces, aluminum, metal tape, wood panel, 15 × 36 × 15 in.

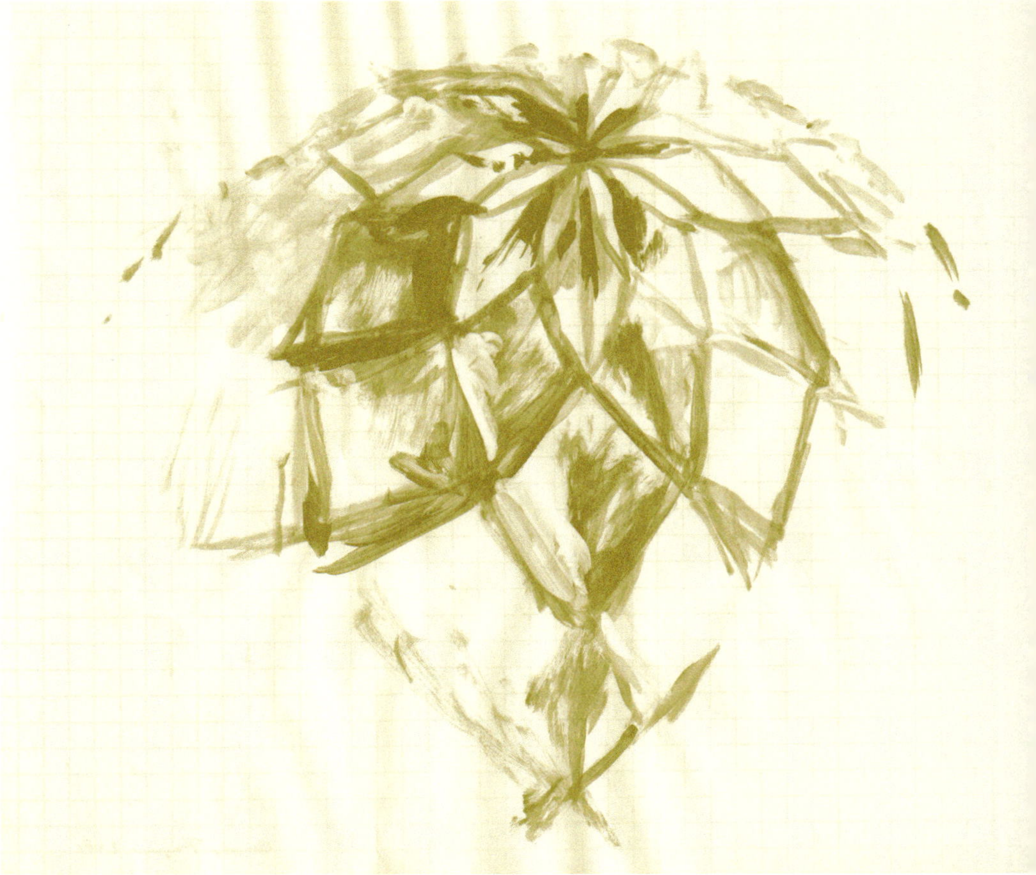

Untitled, 2002, watercolor on graph paper, 8 ½ × 11 in.

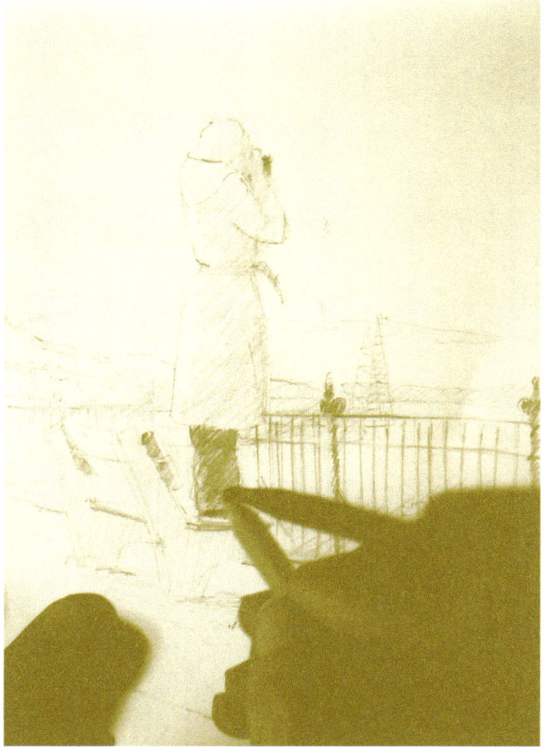

Eileen in Hudson, 1999, C-print, cardboard, cellophane bag, bulldog clips, metal grid, 9 ½ × 13 in.

Chair study, 1997, oil on canvas, 30 × 48 in.

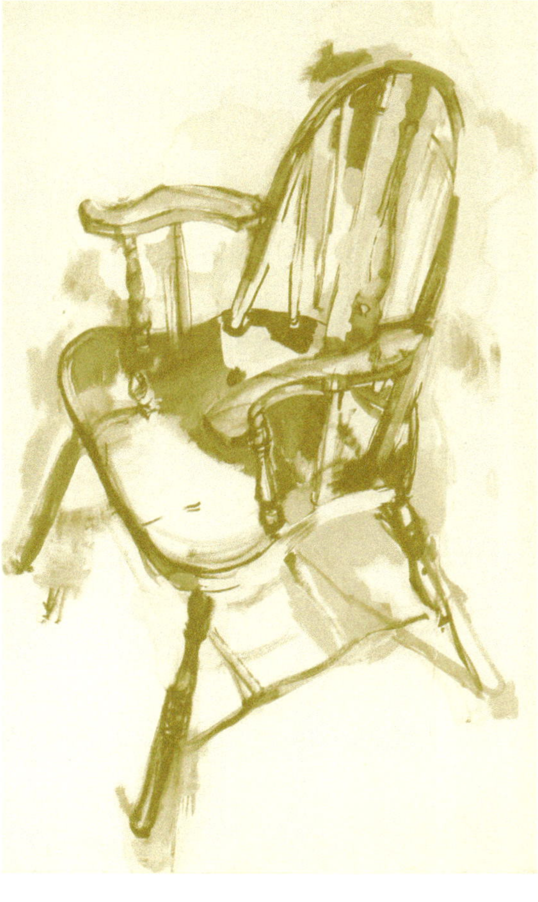

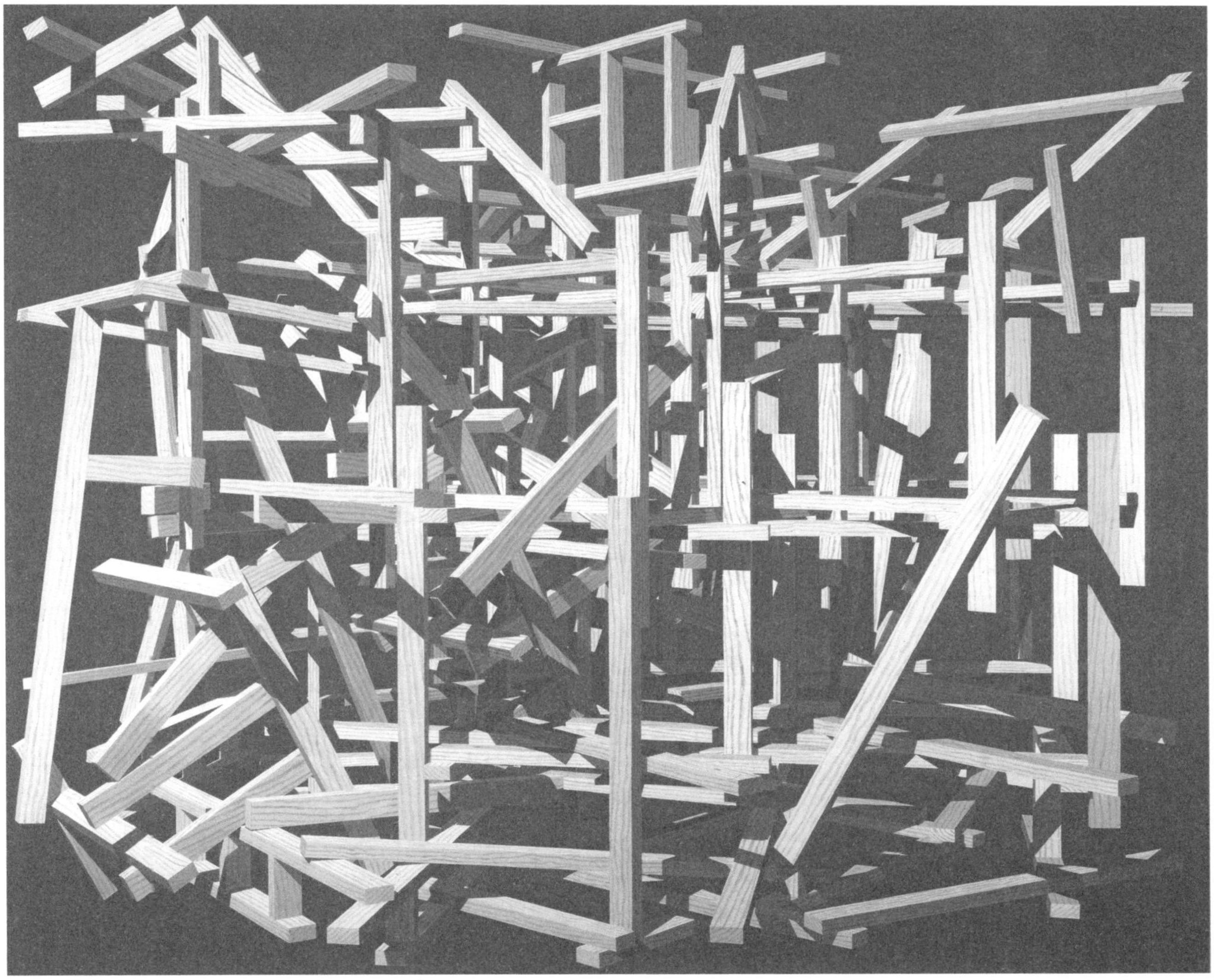

January 14, 1743, Paris (Deaf, Dumb and Blind), 2005, acrylic on canvas, 96 × 120 in.

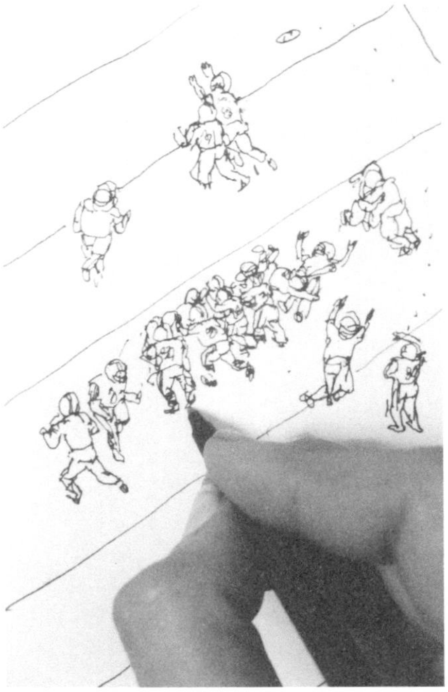

Drawing for Roe, 1998, C-print, cardboard, cellophane bag, bulldog clips, metal grid, 9 ½ × 13 in.

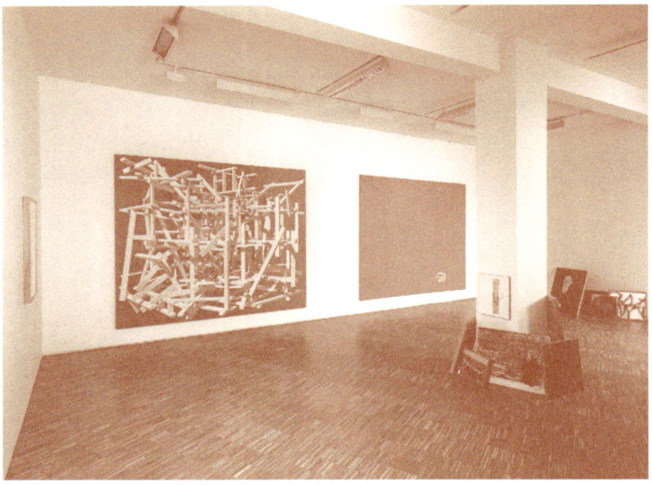

Installation view, *Cheyney Thompson* (Galleria Raucci/Santamaria, Naples), 2005.

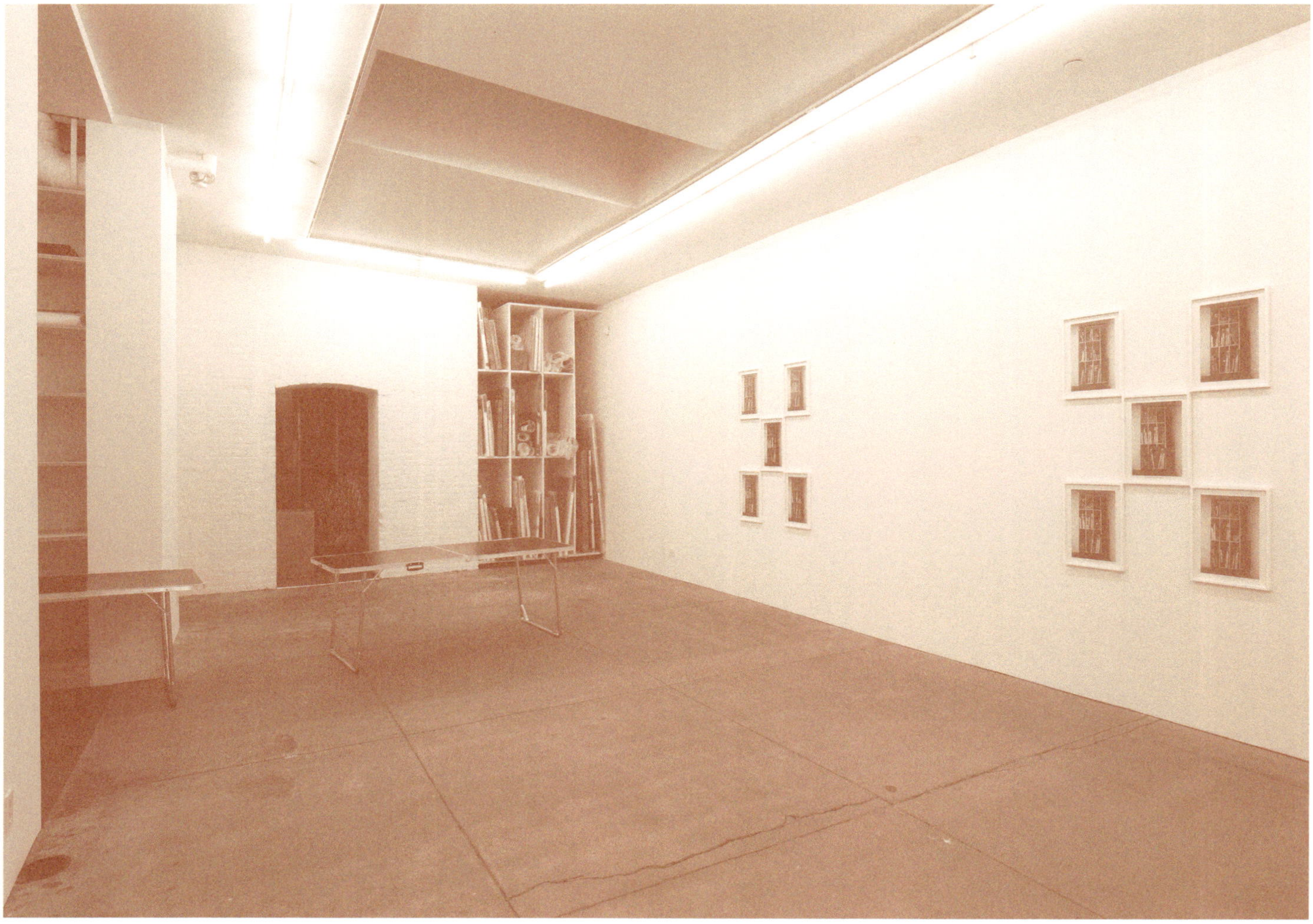

Installation view, *Quelques Aspects de l'Art Bourgeois: La Non-Intervention* (Andrew Kreps Gallery, New York), 2006.

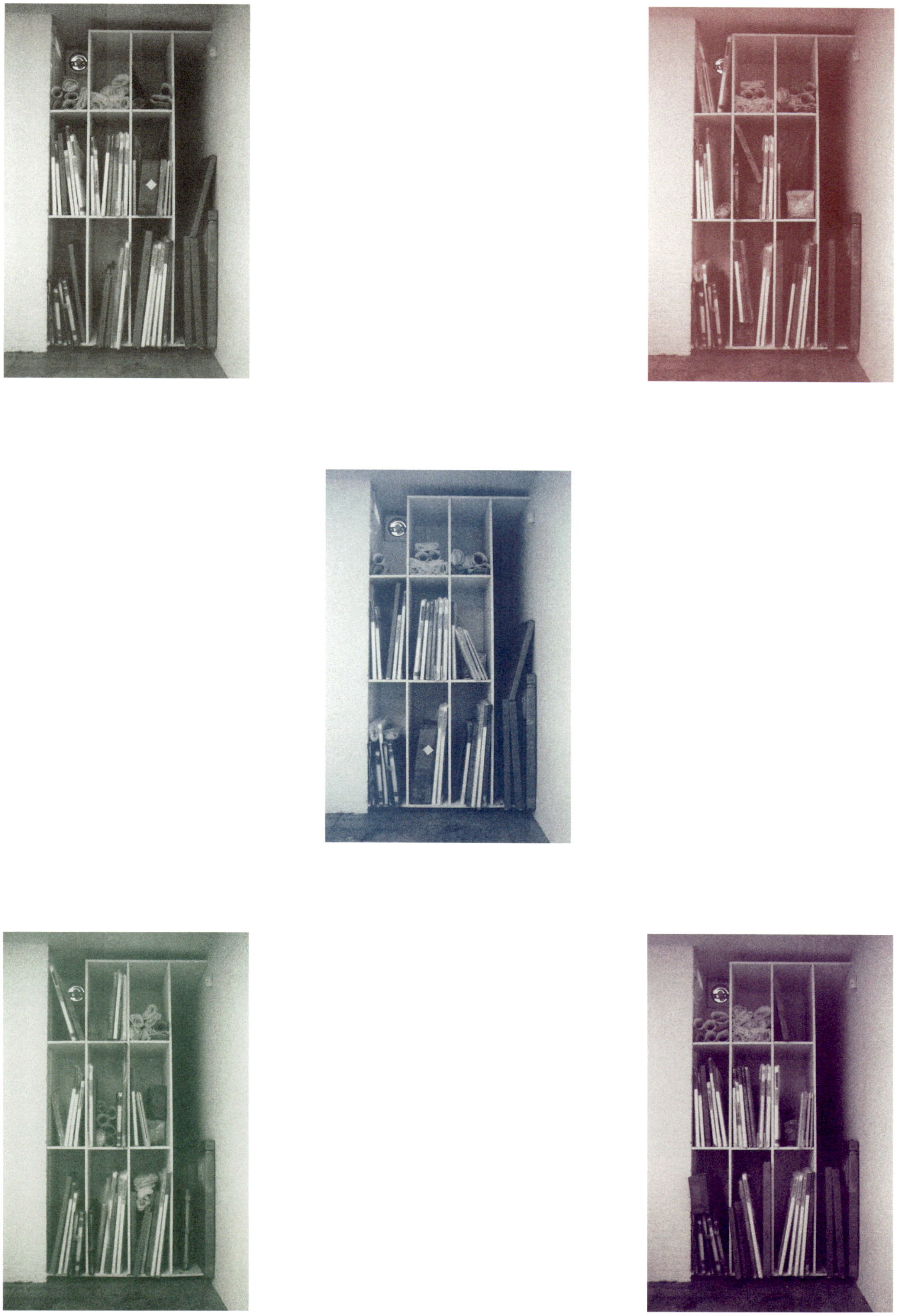

Sets of Color from Robho to Storage
2006, offset lithographs, 58 × 42 in.

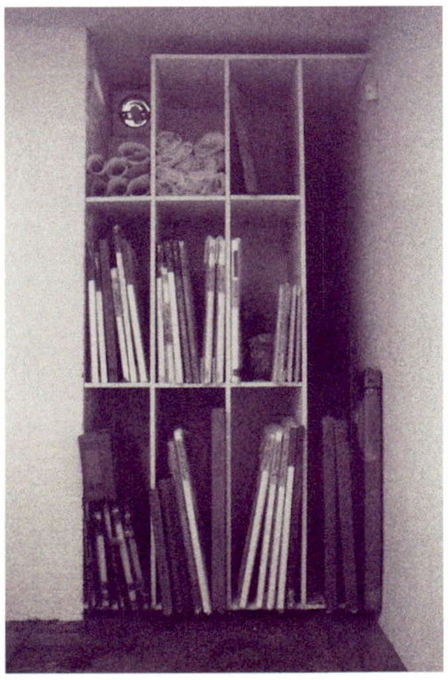
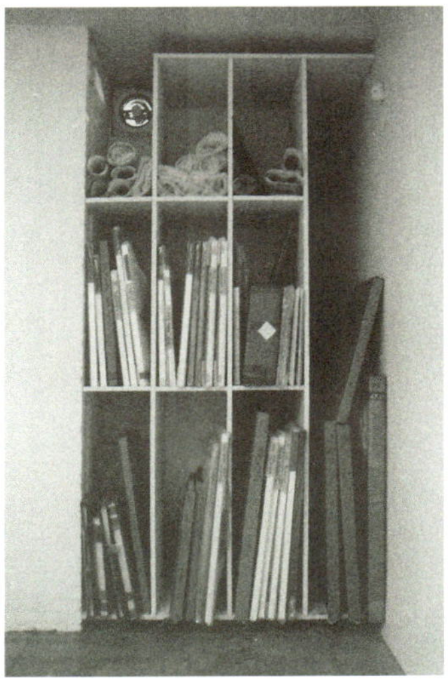
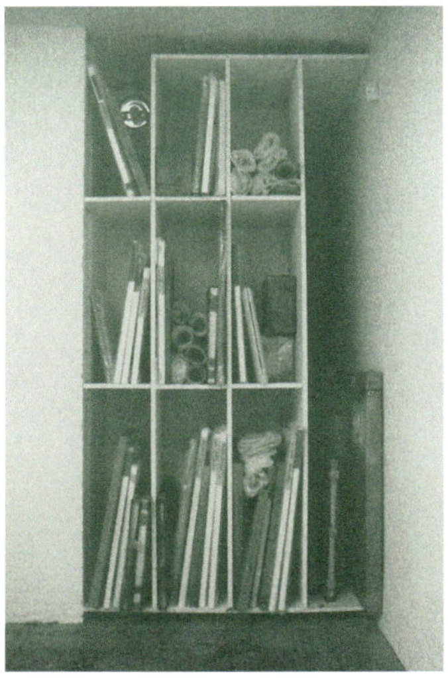
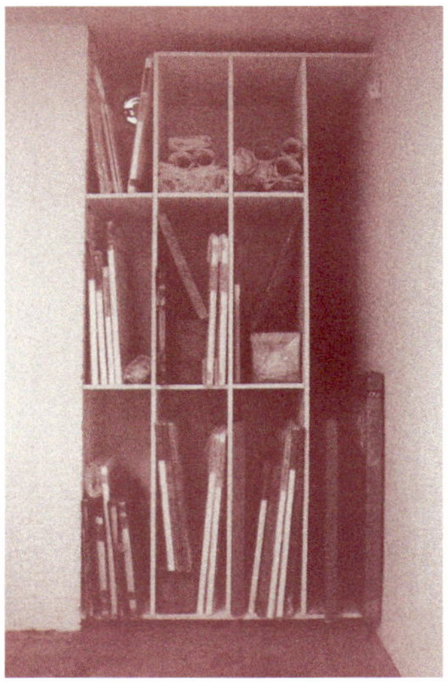
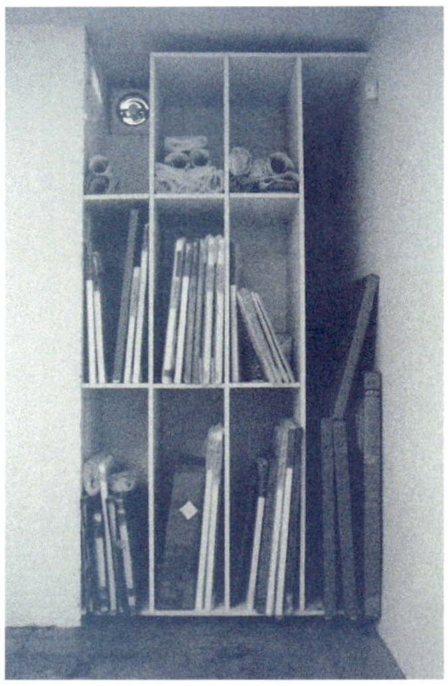

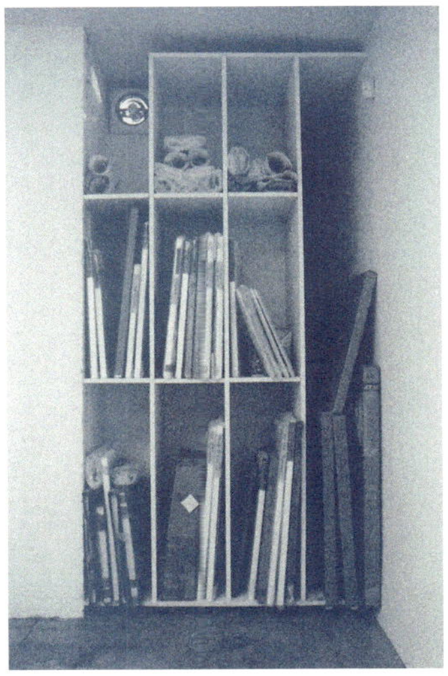

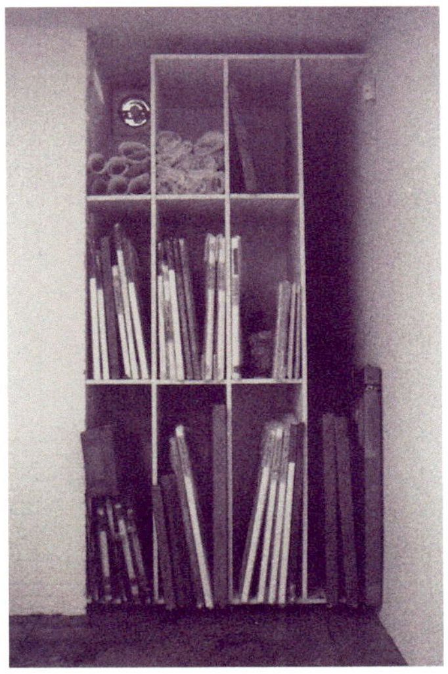

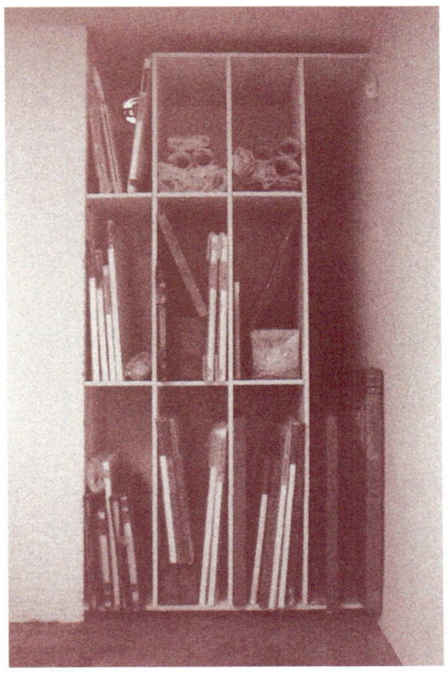

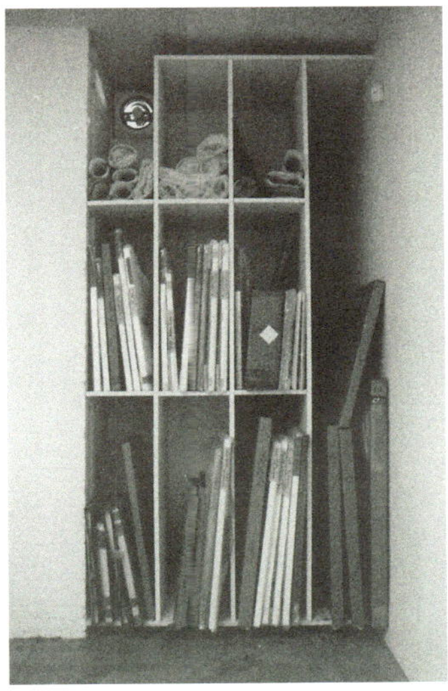

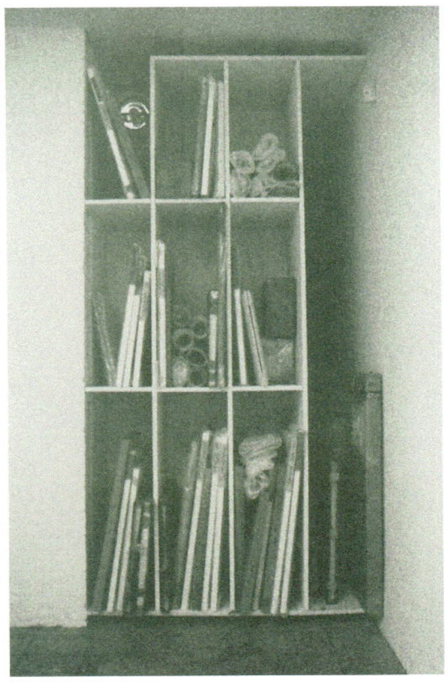

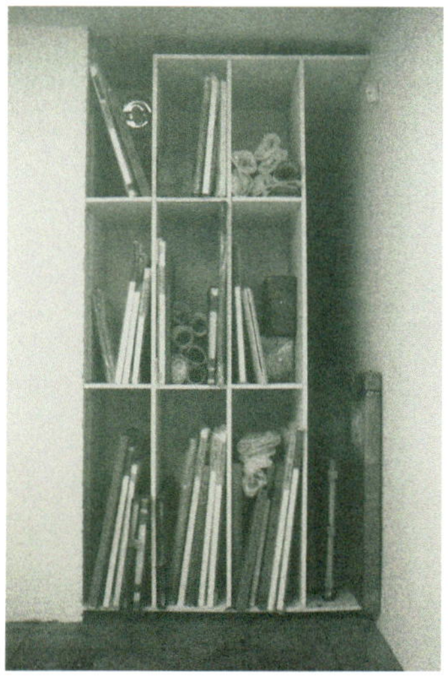
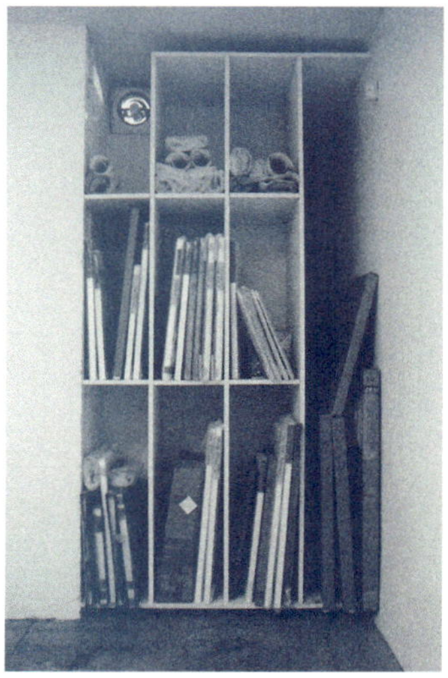
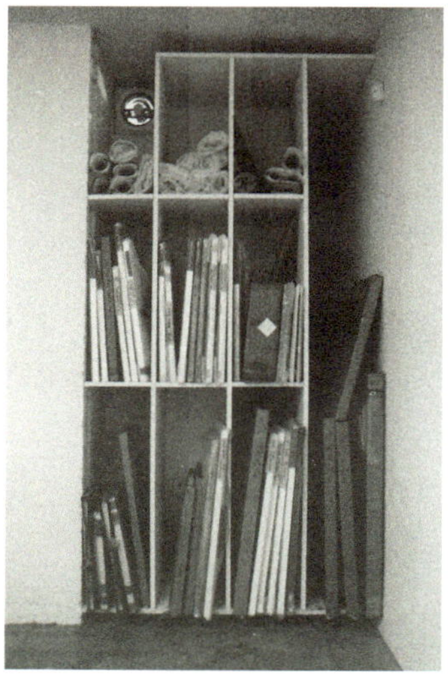
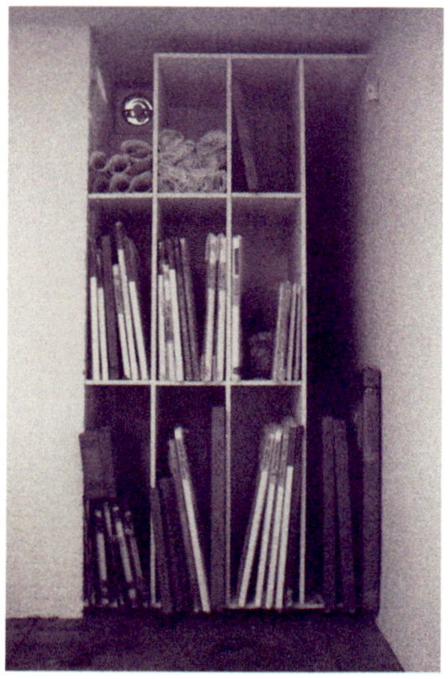
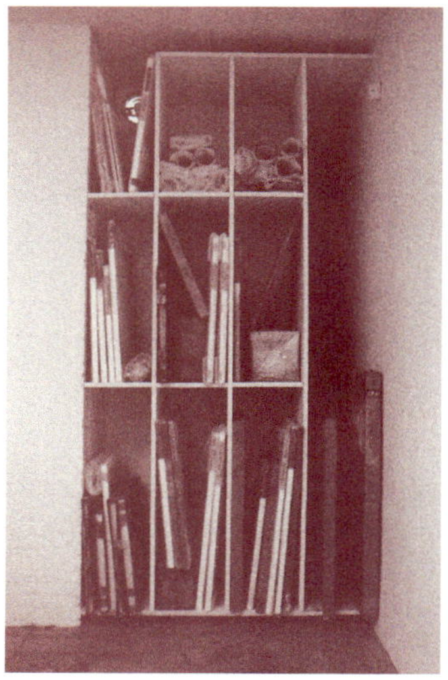

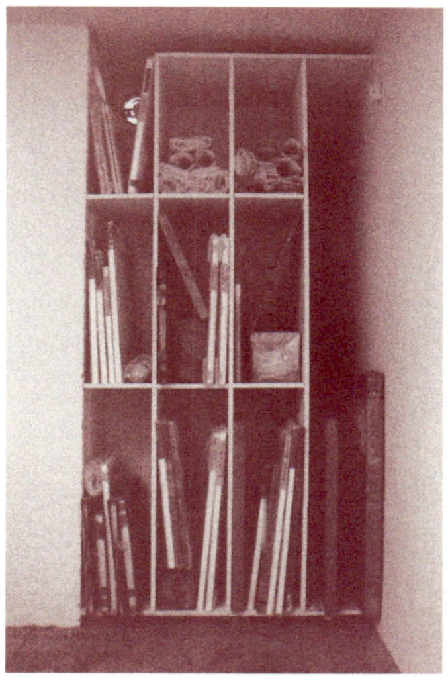

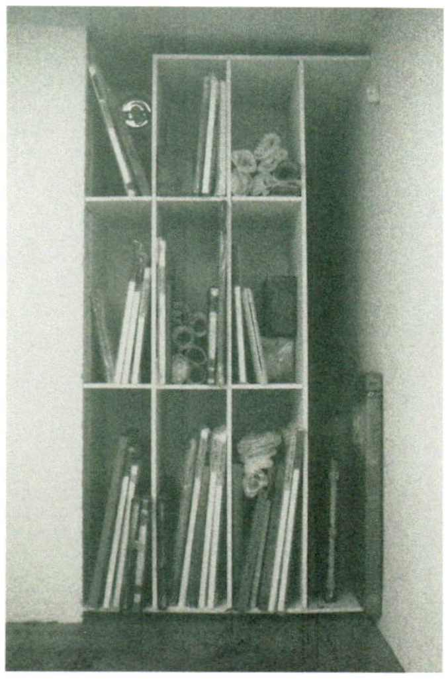

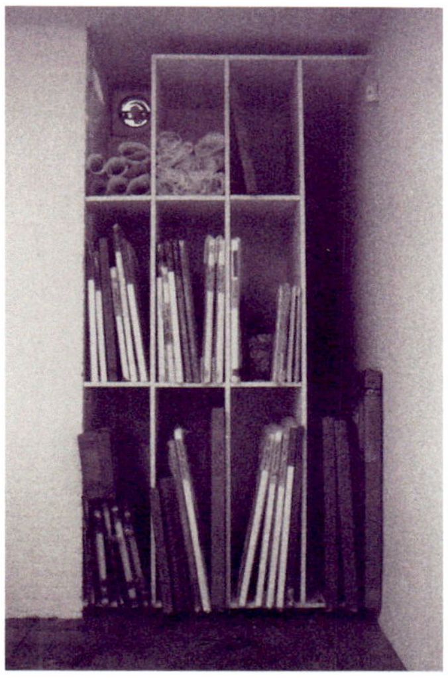

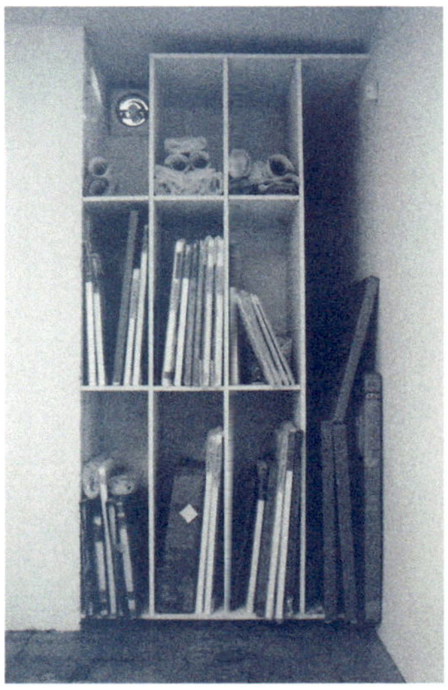

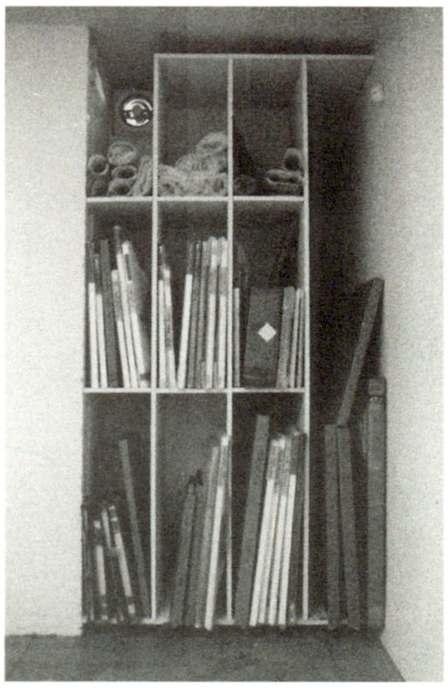

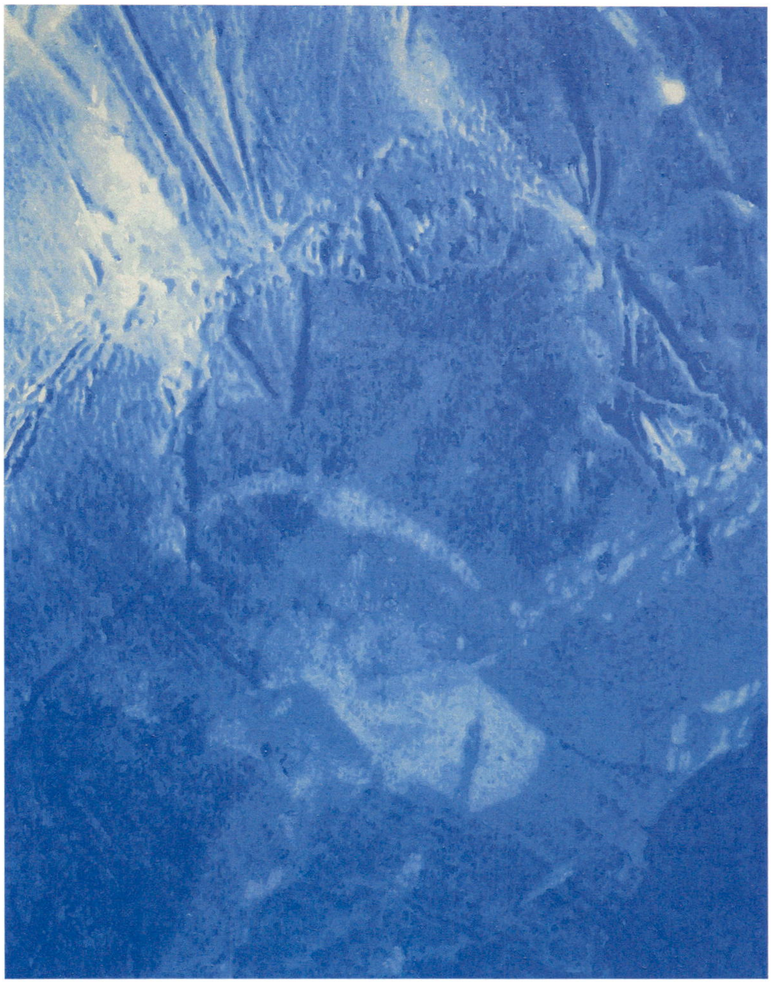

Untitled
2008, oil on canvas, 36 × 30 in.

Untitled
2008, oil on canvas, 24 × 20 in.

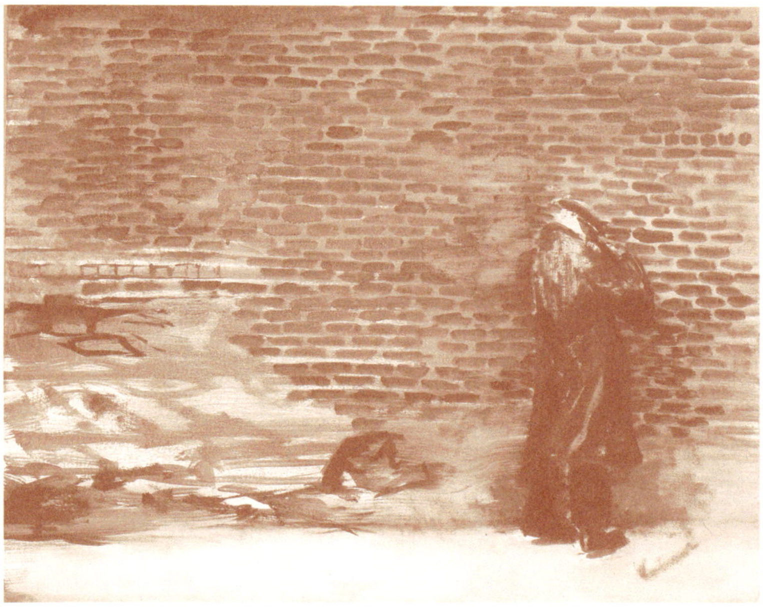

Untitled film still, 2005, oil on canvas, 22 × 28 in.

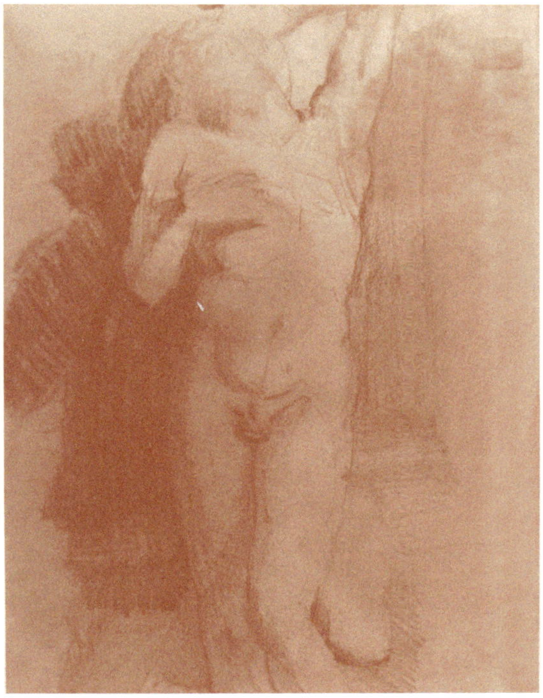

Art|36| Basel |15-20|6|2005, 2005, black and white photograph, wood frame, and velvet curtain with silkscreen, 22 × 18 in.

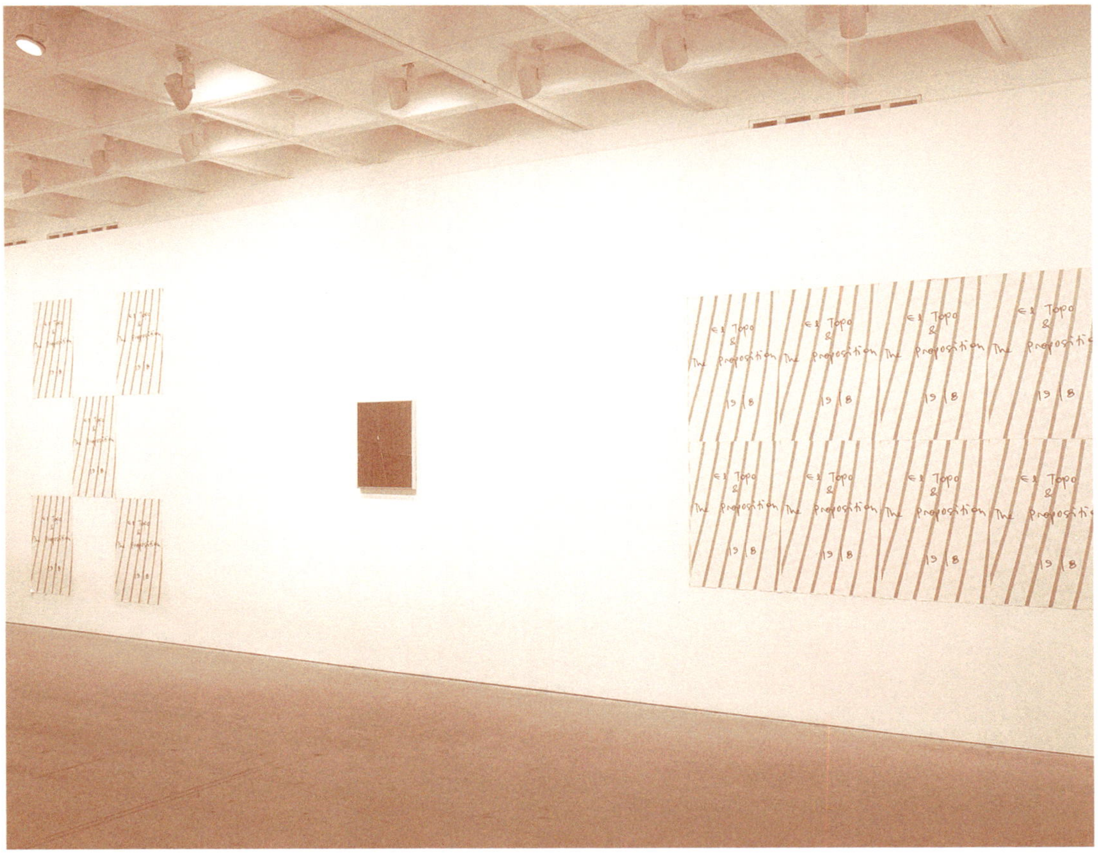

Installation view, *TBA: Cheyney Thompson and Eileen Quinlan* (Arnolfini, Bristol, courtesy of Campoli Presti, London/Paris), 2007.

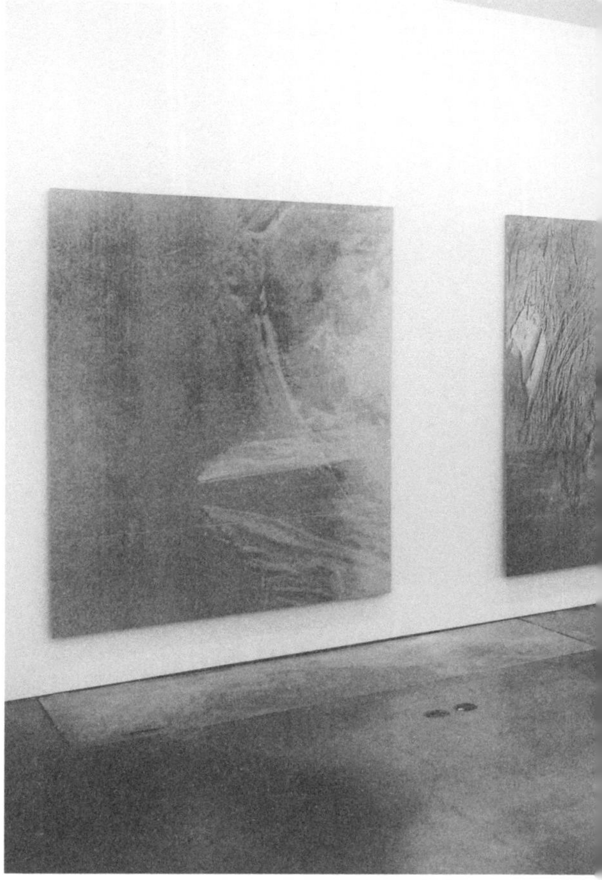

Installation view, *Quelques Aspects de l'Art Bourgeois: La Non-Intervention* (Andrew Kreps Gallery, New York), 2006.

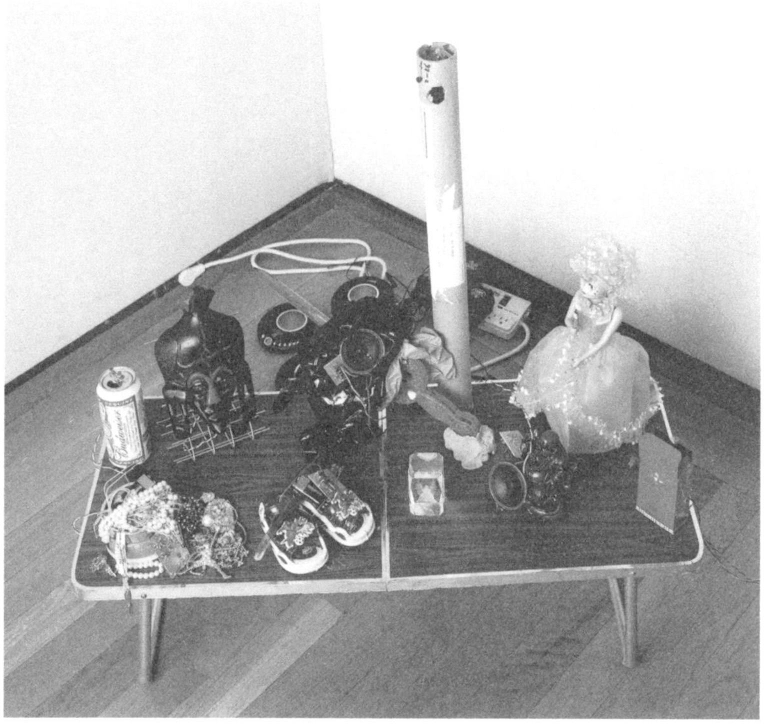

Table of Tragedy, 2005, table, CDs, CD players, toys, shoes, beer, 15 × 36 × 15 in.

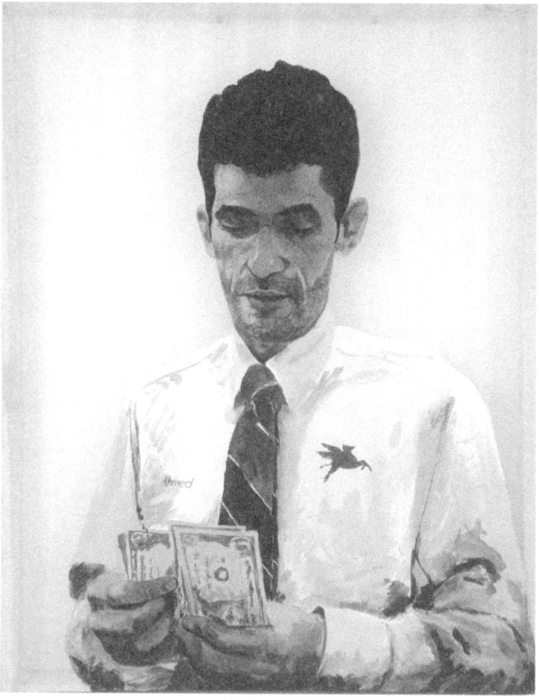

Ahmed, 1998, acrylic on organza, 28 × 32 in.

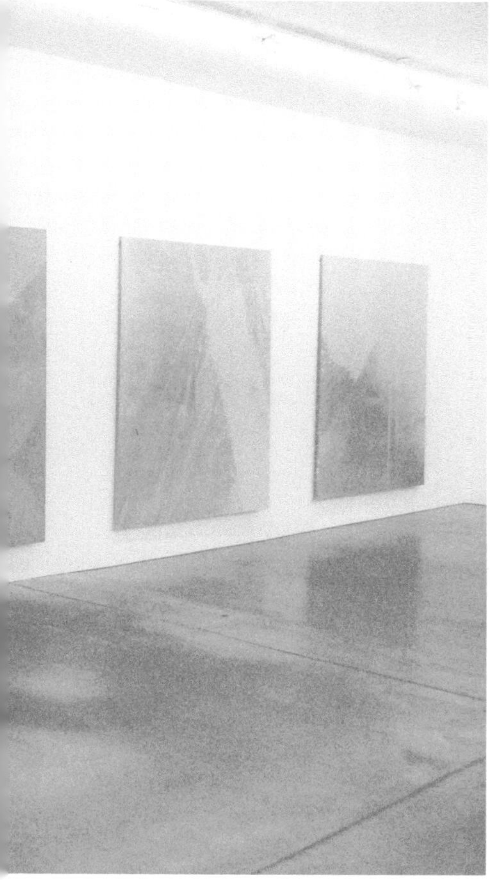

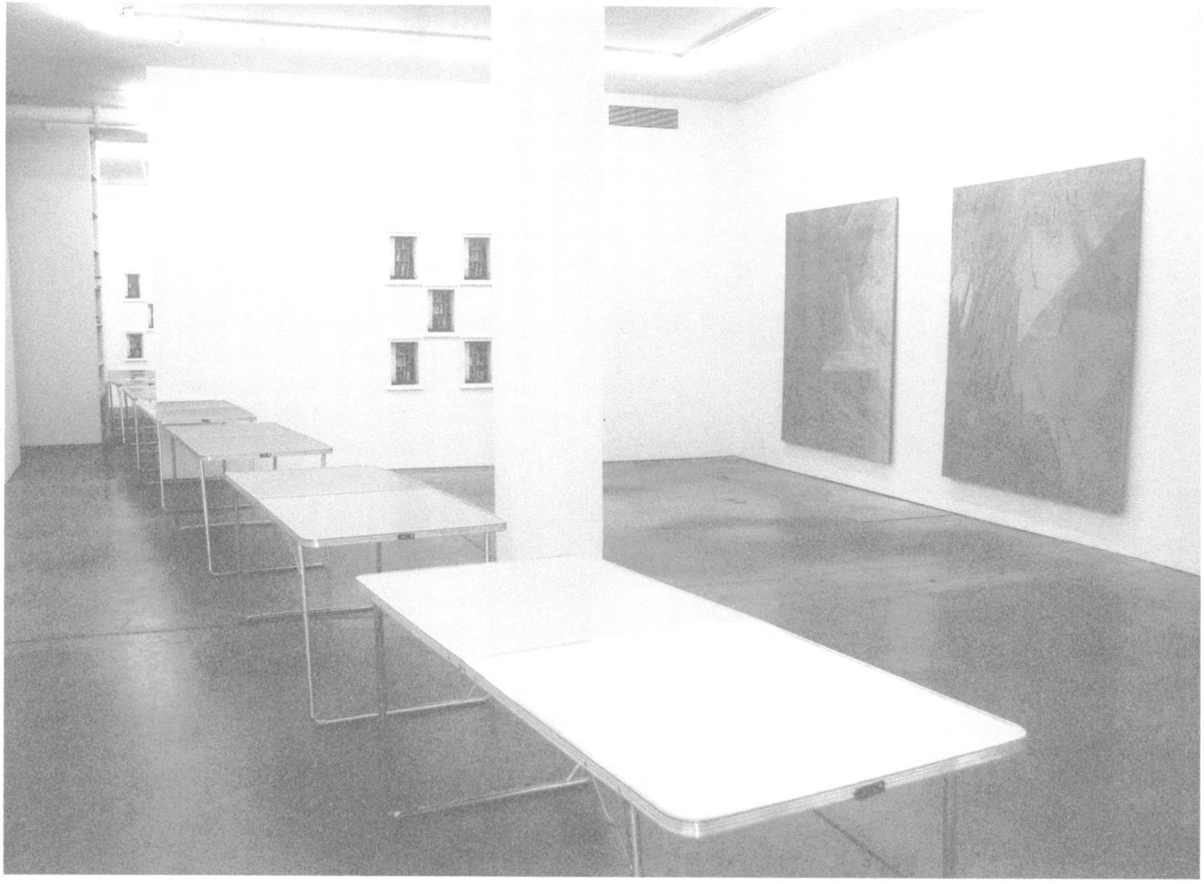

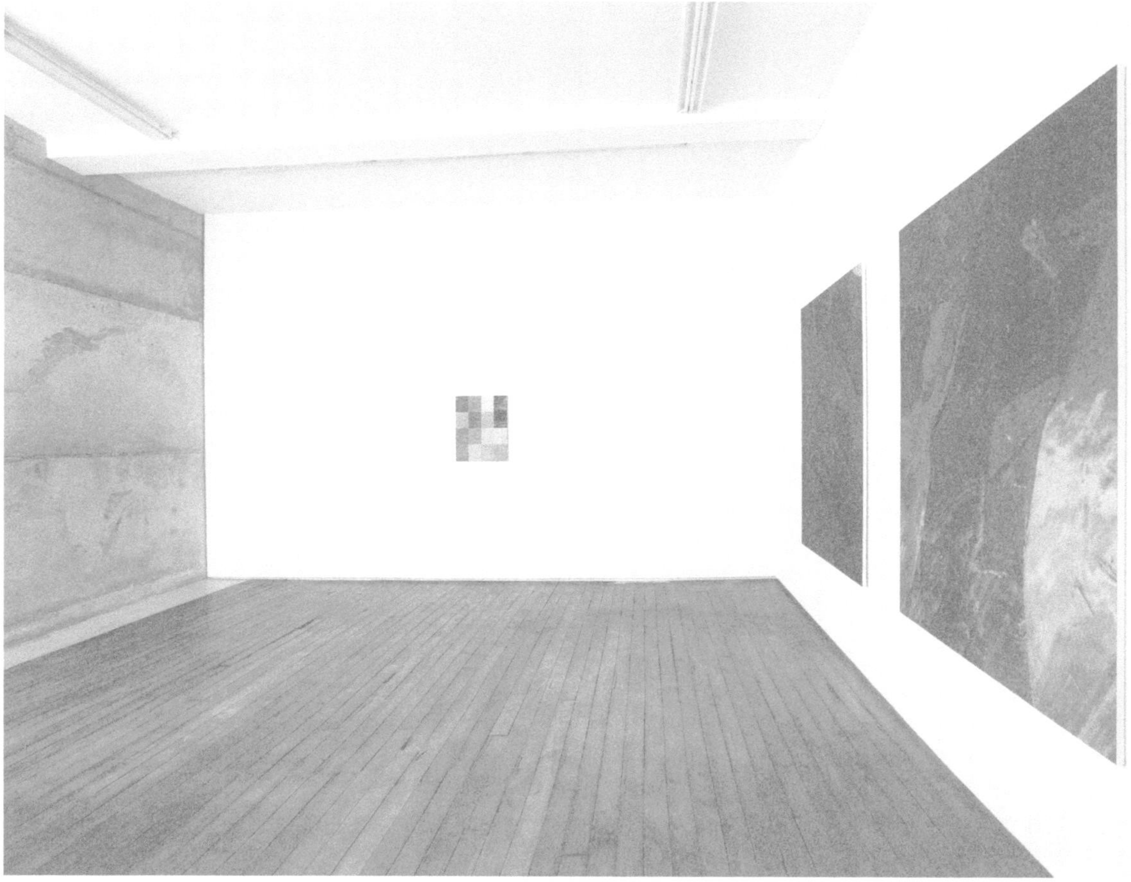

Installation view, *New Works* (Sutton Lane, Paris, courtesy of Campoli Presti, London/Paris), 2008.

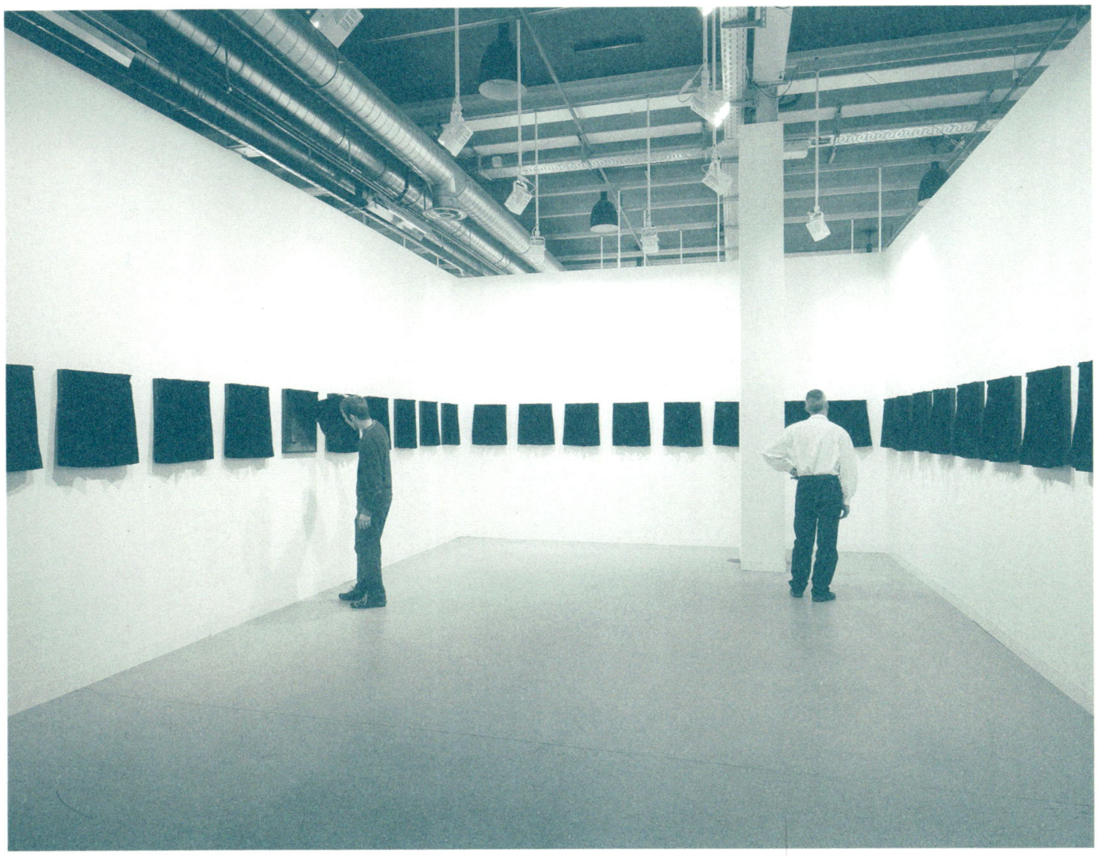

Installation view, *Art Statements (Art|36|Basel|15–20|6|2005)*, 2005.

Detail (0.93,1.518)(4.058,5.118)(13.676): Untitled
2008, oil on canvas, 70 × 55 ½ in.

Detail (0.147,0.160)(5.558,4.407)(15.779): Untitled
2008, oil on canvas, 70 × 88 ½ in.

Detail (0.933,1.425)(4.108,5.181)(13.510): Untitled
2008, oil on canvas, 70 × 55 ½ in.

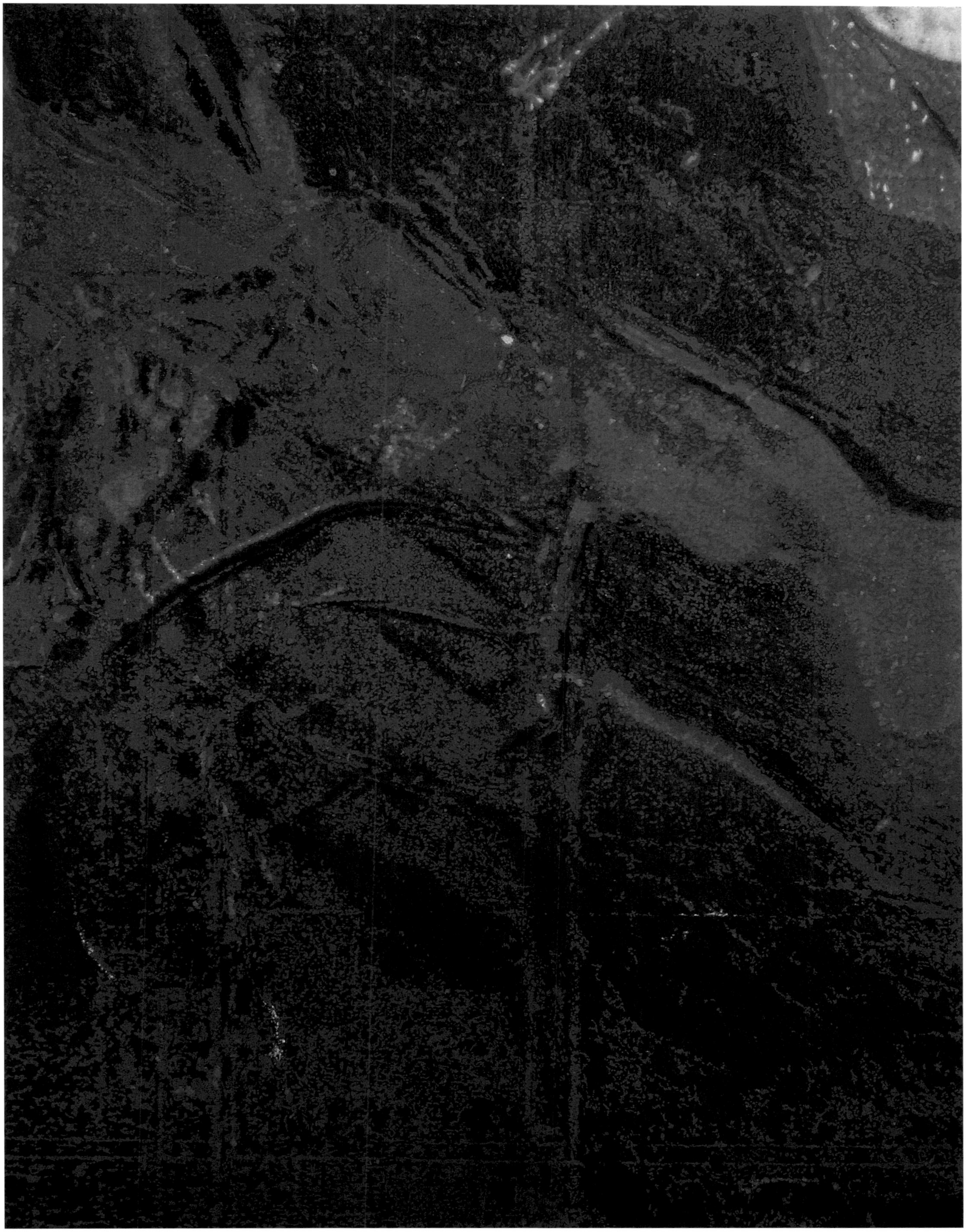

Detail (x.xxx,x.xxx)(x,x)(x): Untitled
2008, oil on canvas, 70 × 55 ½ in.

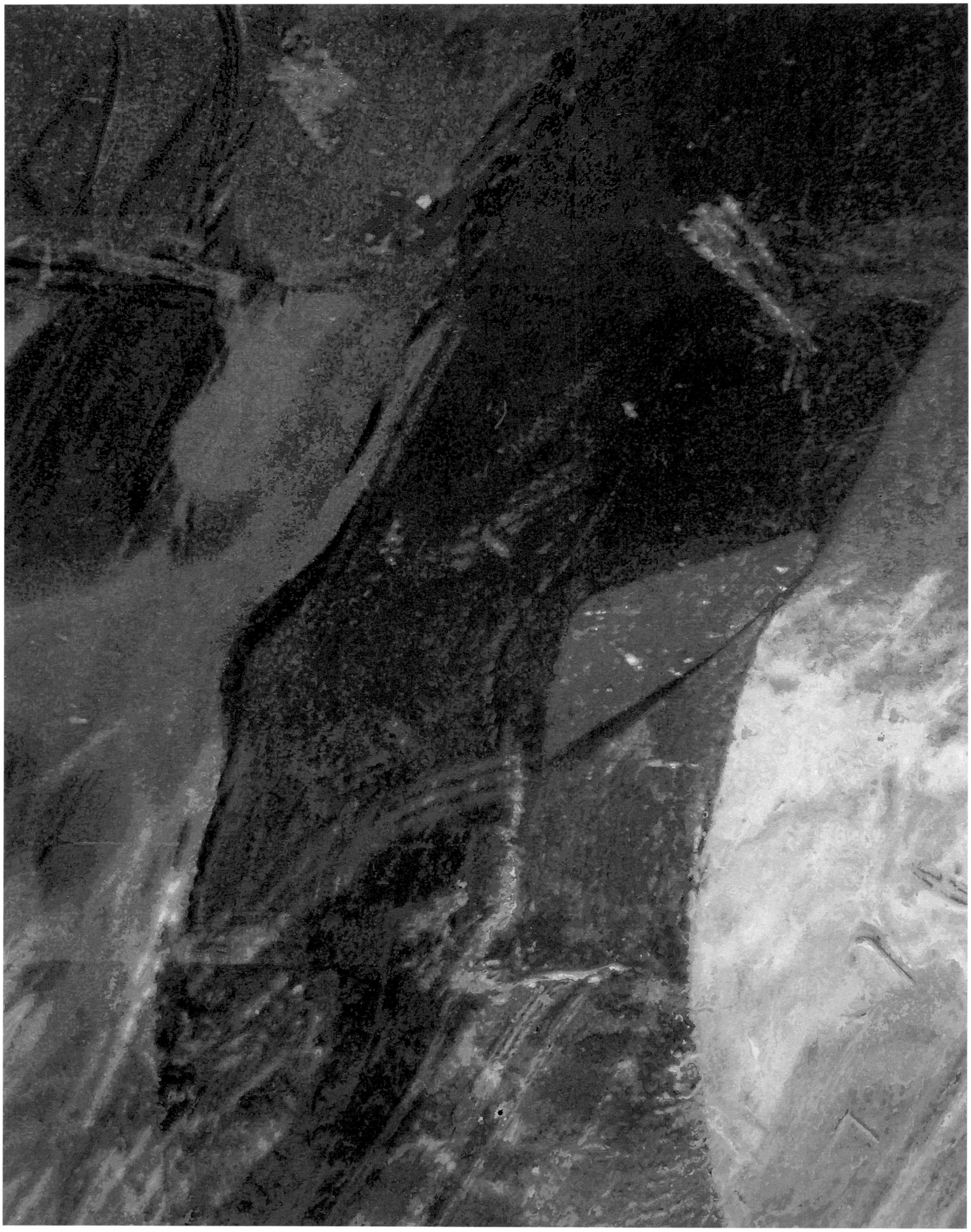

Detail (x.xxx,x.xxx)(x,x)(x)(2): Untitled
2008, oil on canvas, 70 × 55 ½ in.

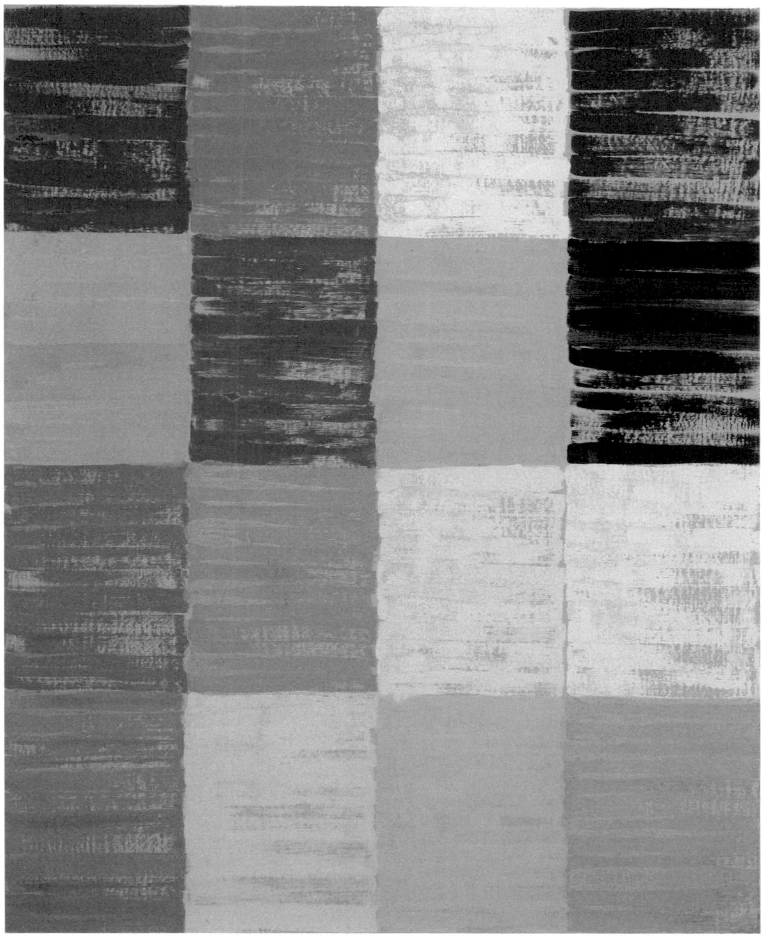

Is-A
2008, oil on canvas, 24 × 20 in.

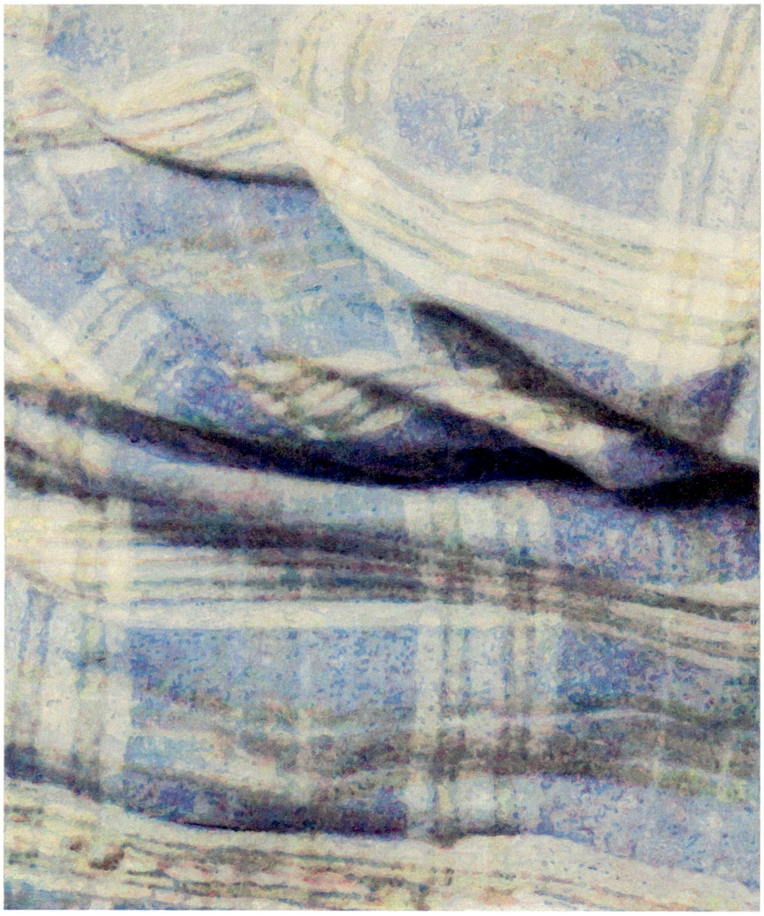

Detail (1.958,2.063)(1.111,0.931)(21.602): 4 Colors Subtracting Light from the Room in 6 Degrees of Intensity Repeated 4 Times
2008, oil on canvas, 24 × 20 in.

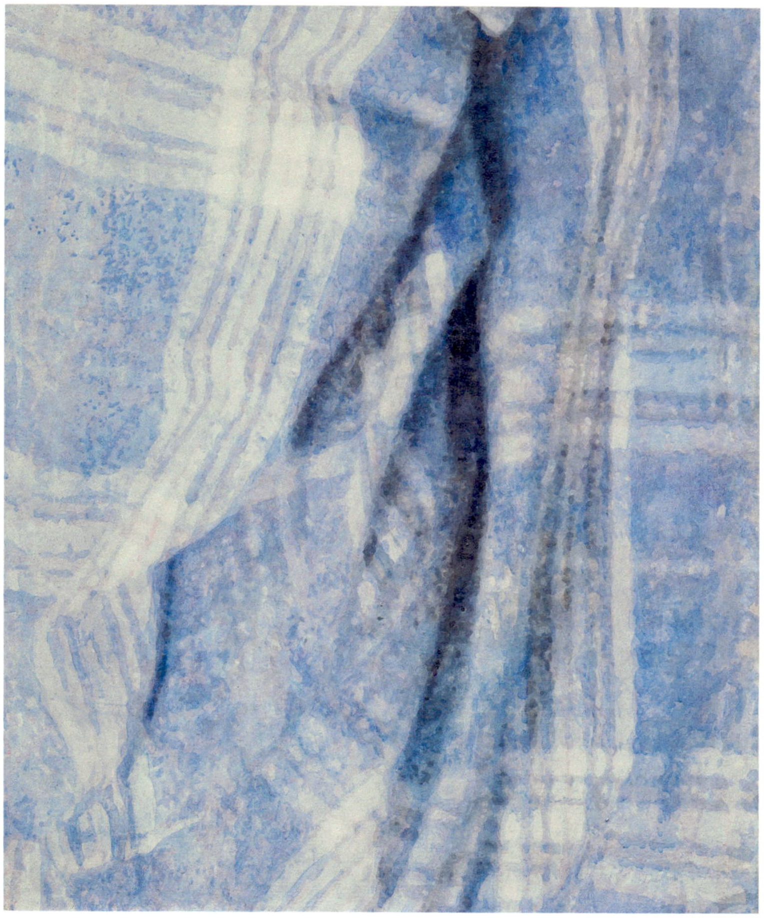

Detail (1.958,2.063)(0.931,1.111)(21.602): 4 Colors Subtracting Light from the Room in 6 Degrees of Intensity Repeated 4 Times
2008, oil on canvas, 24 × 20 in.

Untitled
2008, oil on canvas, 24 × 20 in.

Untitled
2008, oil on canvas, 24 × 20 in.

Untitled
2008, silkscreen on canvas, 36 × 30 in.

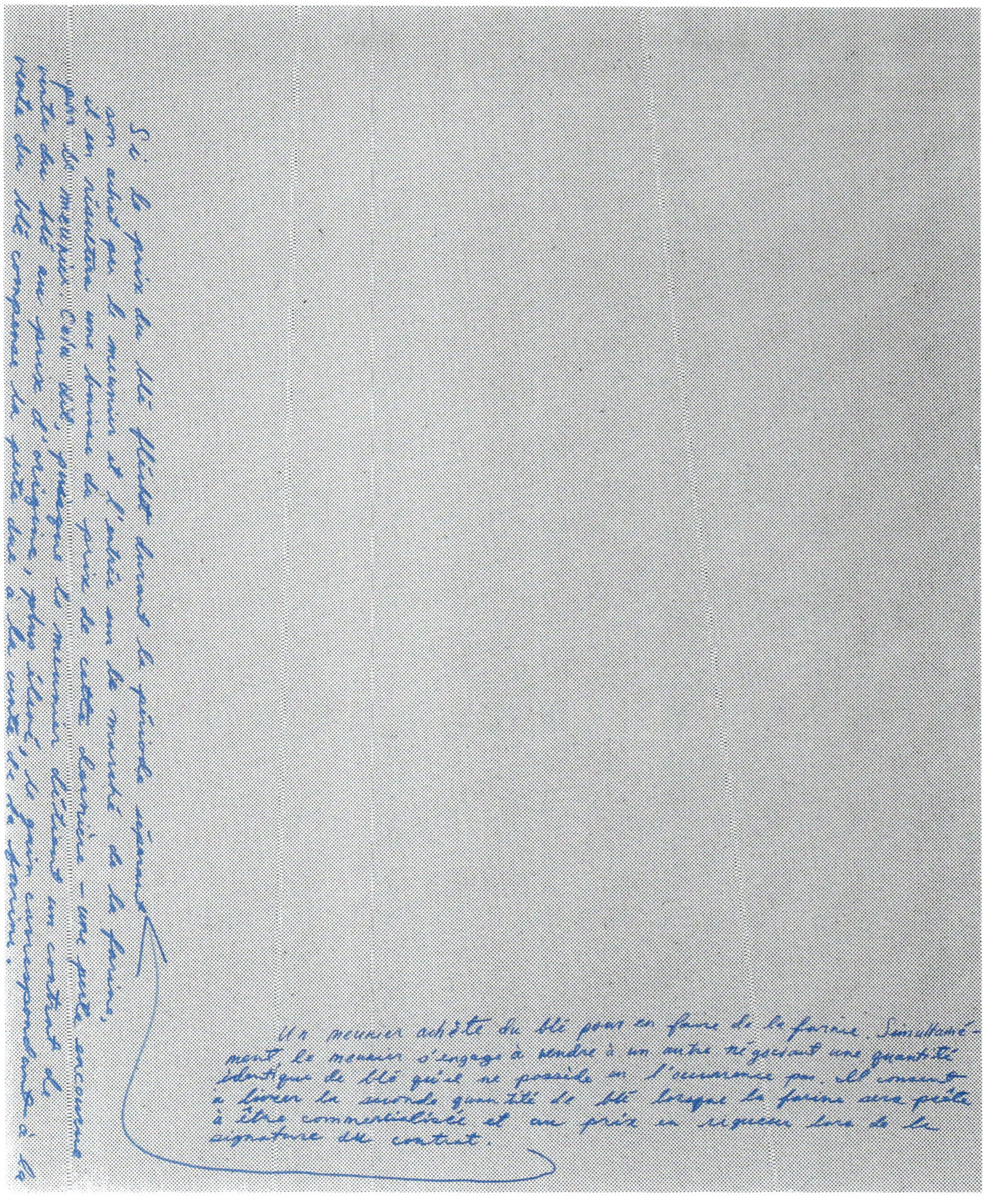

Untitled, with Sean Paul
2007, silkscreen on canvas, 40 × 36 in.

Untitled
2008, silkscreen on canvas, 36 × 30 in.

Untitled, with Sam Lewitt
2008, silkscreen on canvas, 36 × 30 in.

Untitled
2008, silkscreen on canvas, 36 × 30 in.

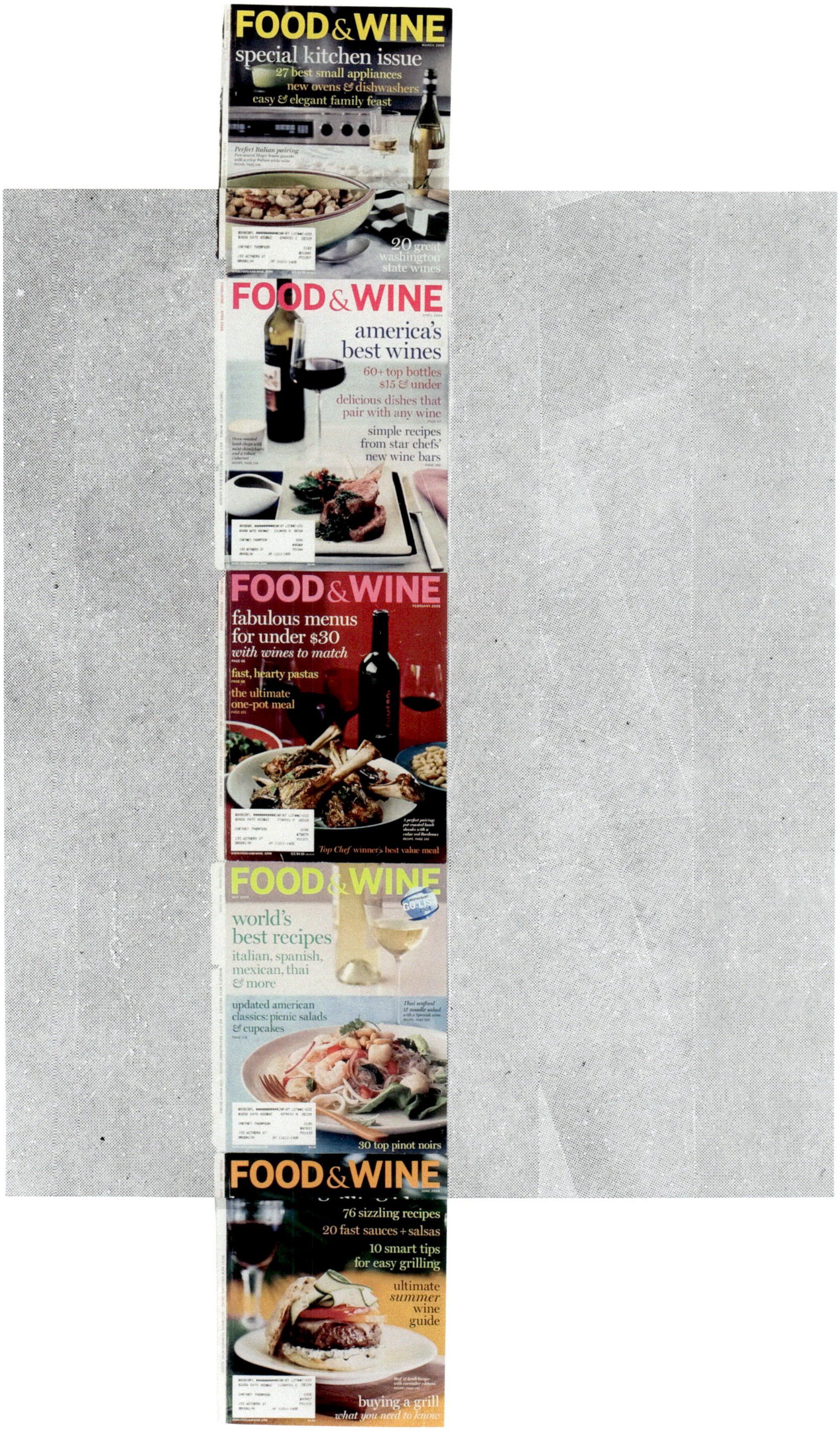

Untitled
2008, silkscreen on canvas, 36 × 30 in.

Abstract Picture (Y/YM)
2008, oil on canvas, 55 ¼ × 43 ⅞ in.

Property Owner (YM/M)
2008, oil on canvas, 55 ¼ × 43 ⅞ in.

Property Owner (M/CM)
2008, oil on canvas, 55 ¼ × 43 ⅞ in.

Blue (CM/C)
2008, oil on canvas, 55 ¼ × 43 ⅞ in.

Grid (C/CY)
2008, oil on canvas, 55 ¼ × 43 ⅞ in.

Linen (CY/Y)
2008, oil on canvas, 55 ¼ × 43 ⅞ in.

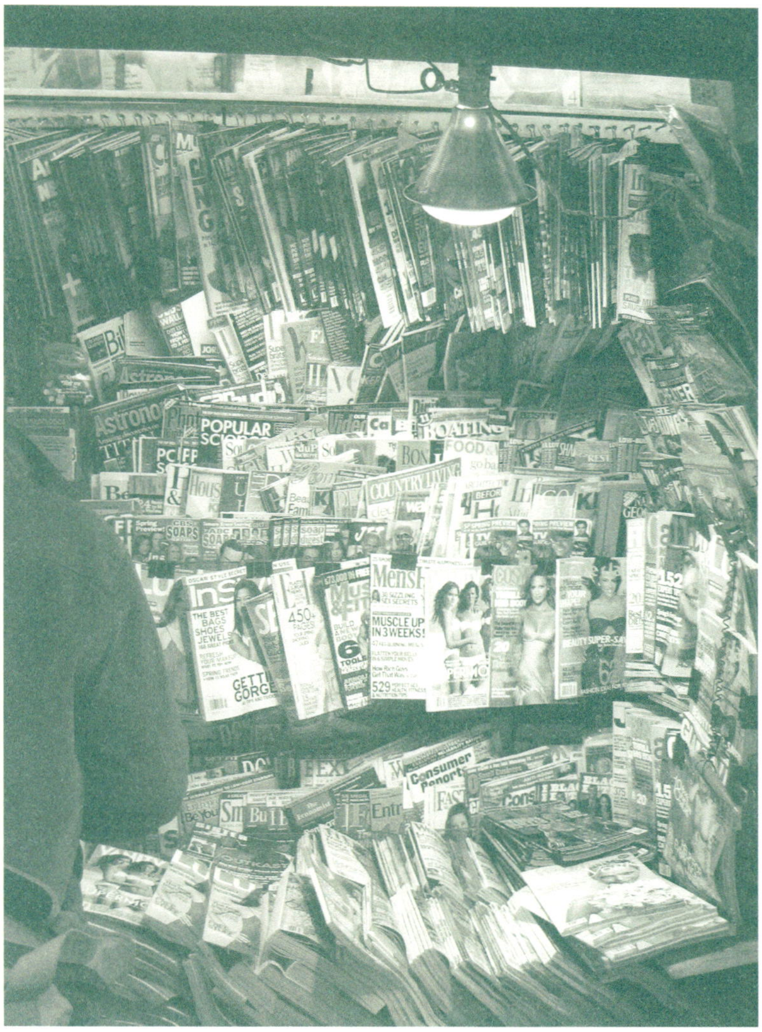

Newsstand, 2001, digital photo.

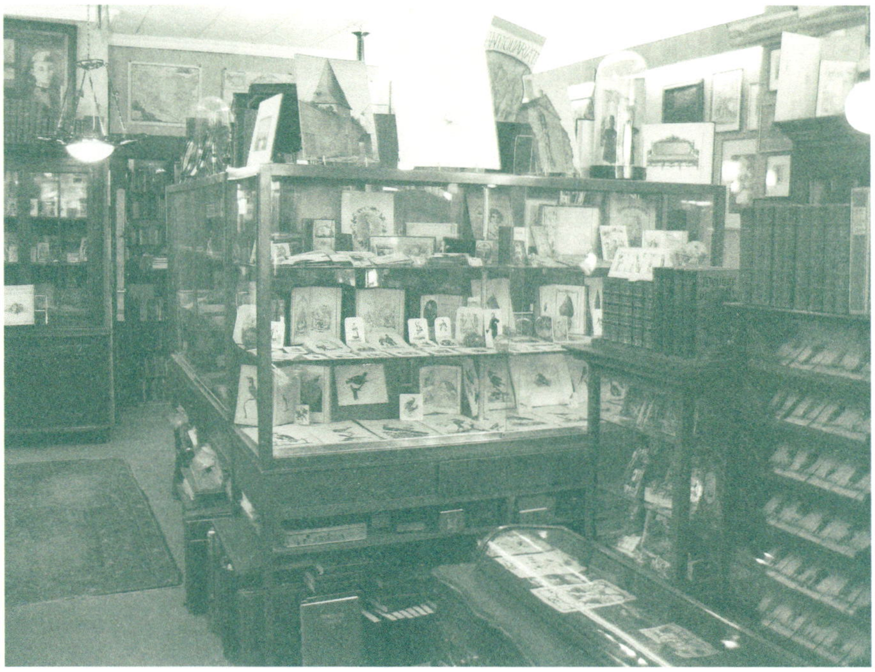

Interior (Antiquariat Buchholz, Cologne), 2004, digital photo.

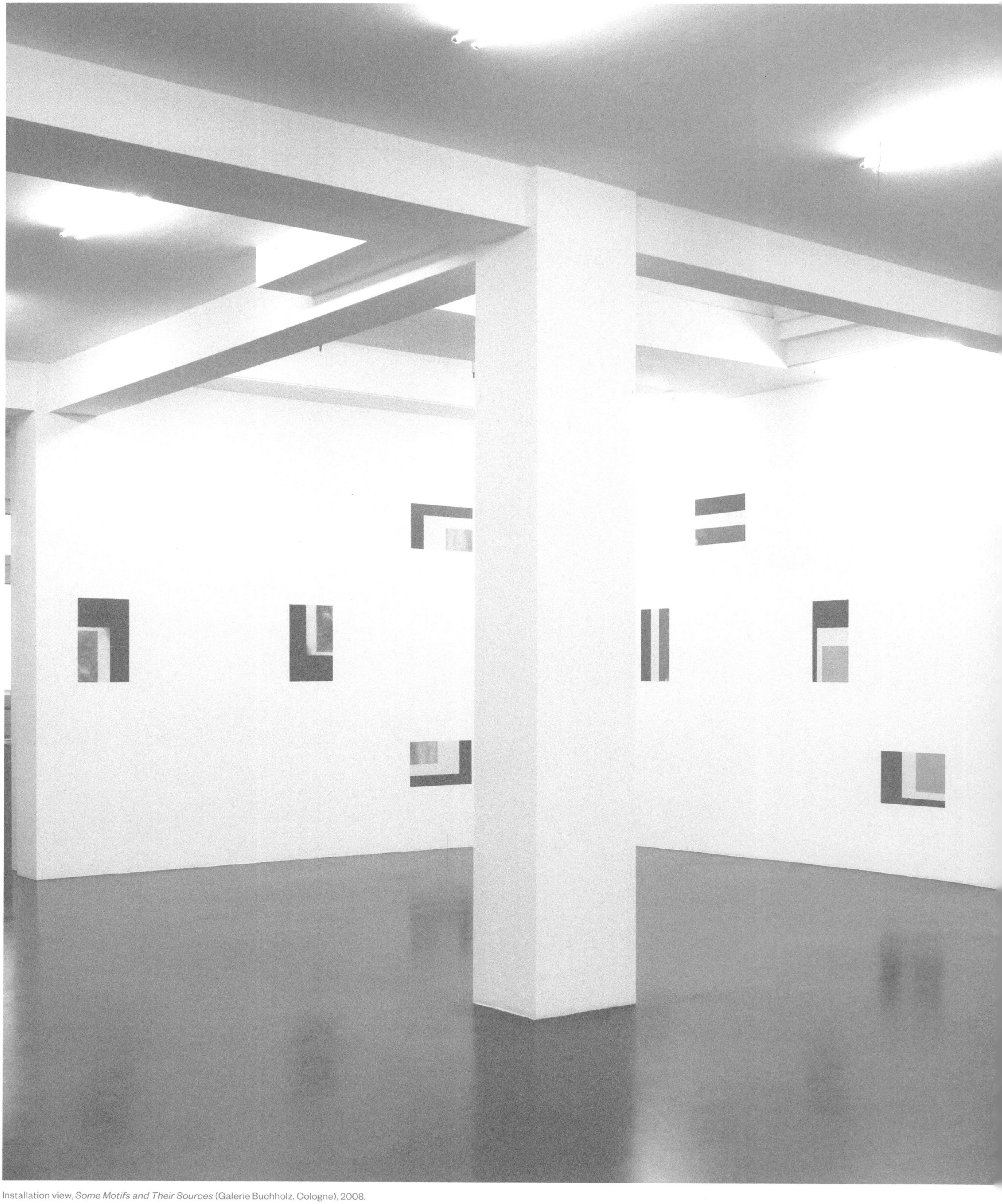

Installation view, *Some Motifs and Their Sources* (Galerie Buchholz, Cologne), 2008.

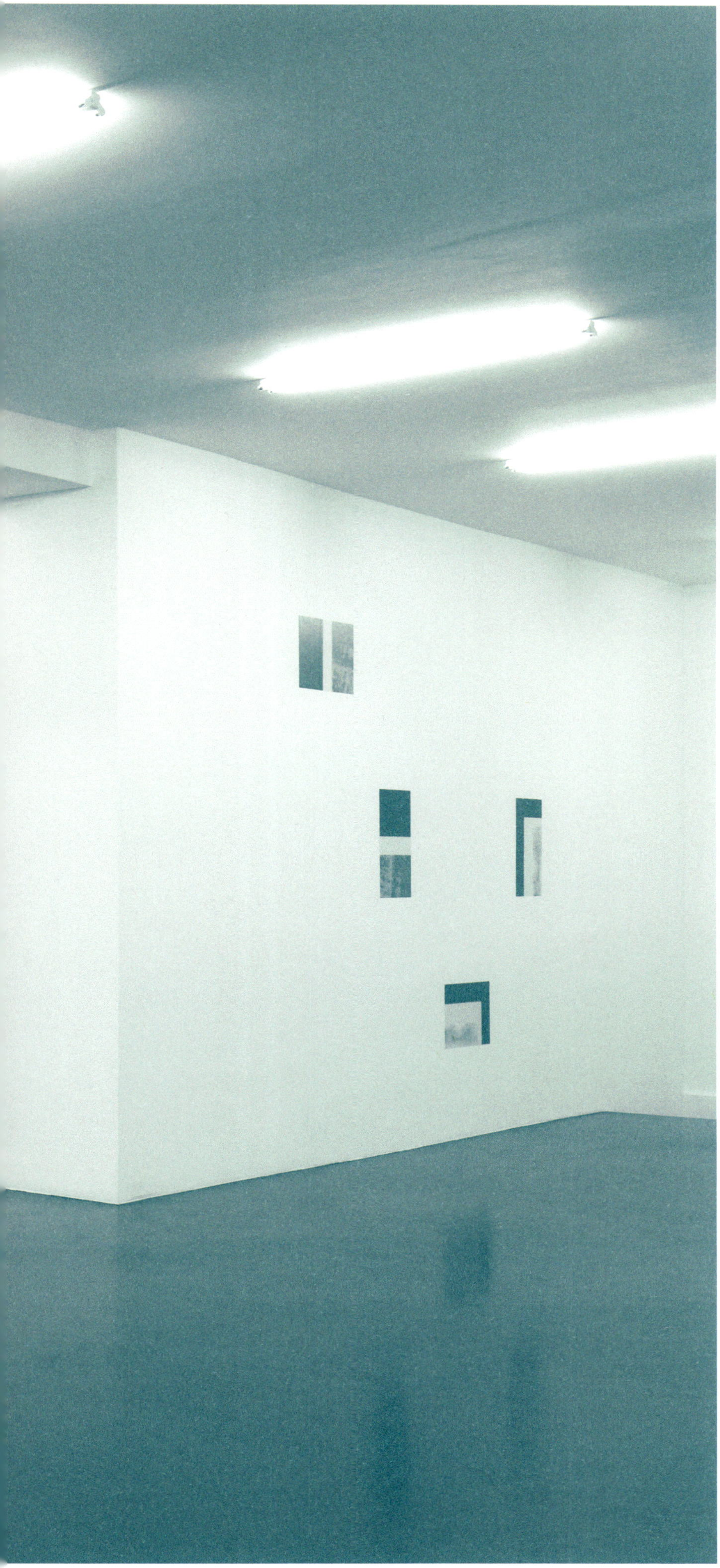

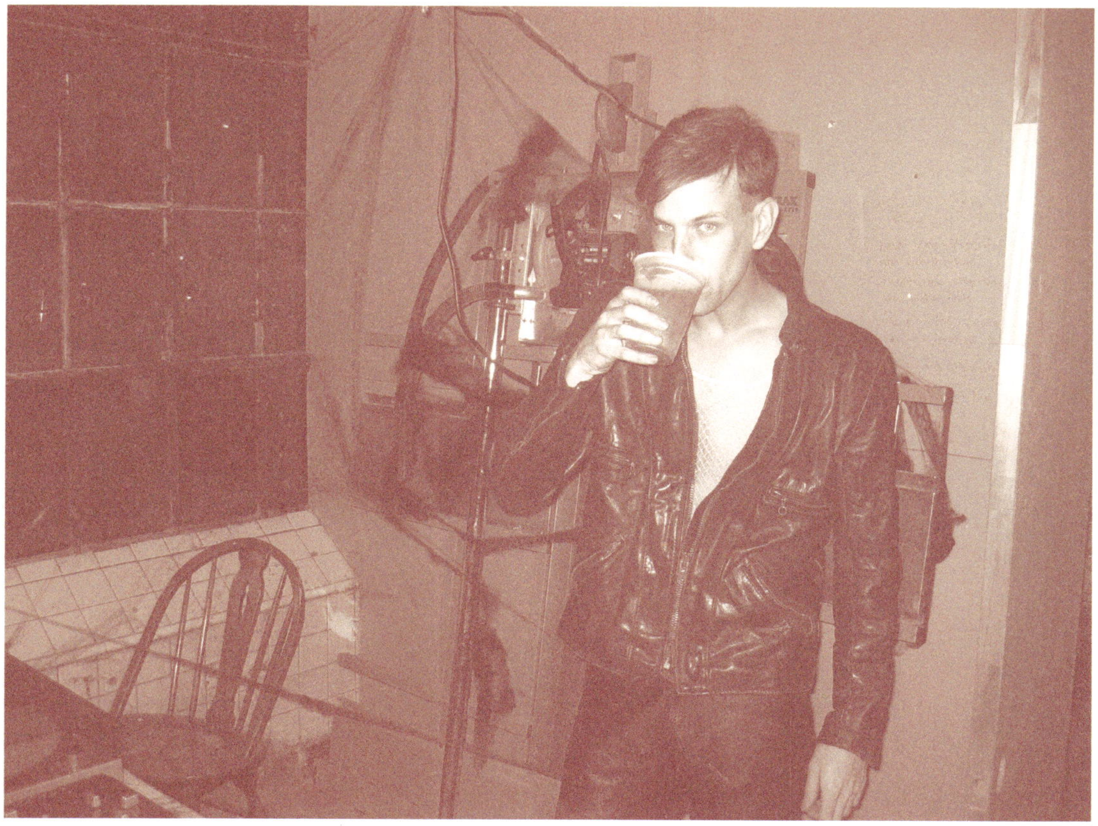

Martial Canterel, 2005, digital photo.

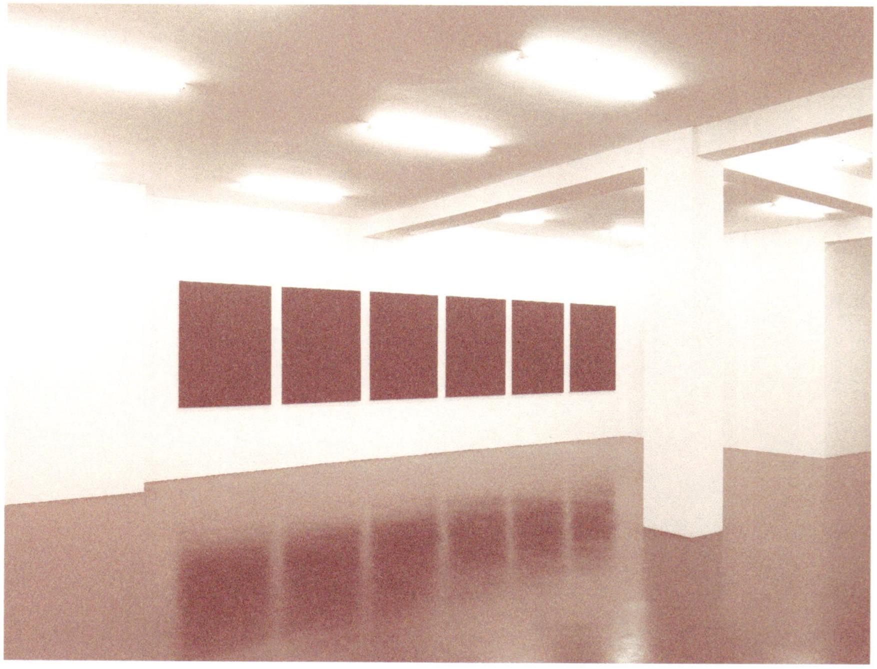

Installation view, *Some Motifs and Their Sources* (Galerie Buchholz, Cologne), 2008.

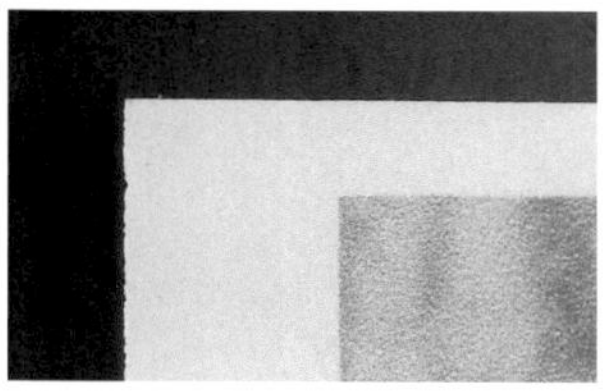

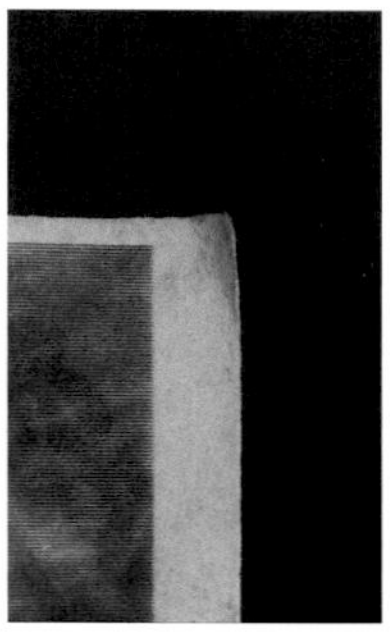

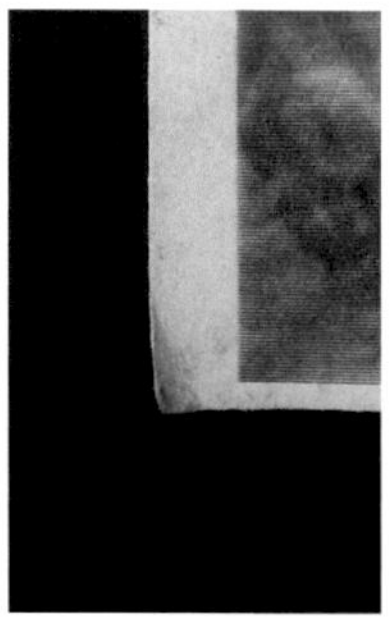

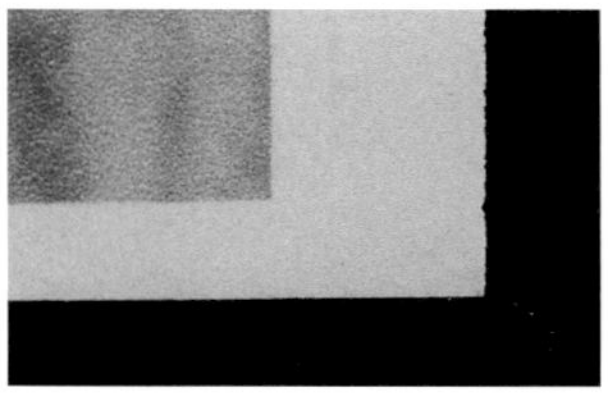

Working Papers (detail)
2008, 12 duotone offset prints, 20 ⅞ × 13 in. each.

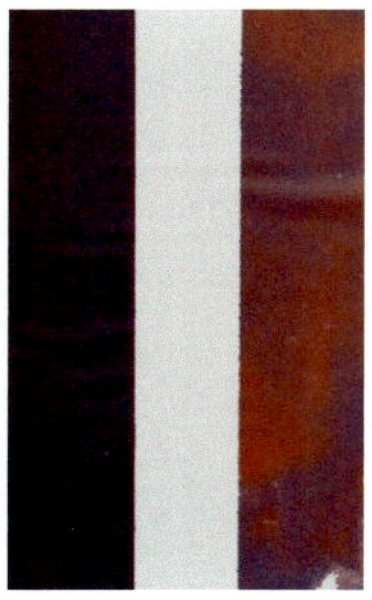

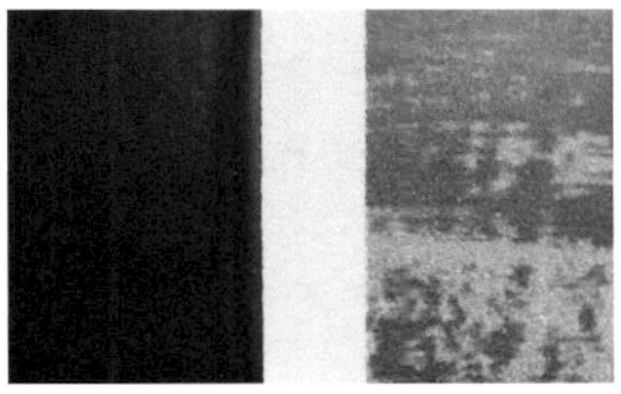

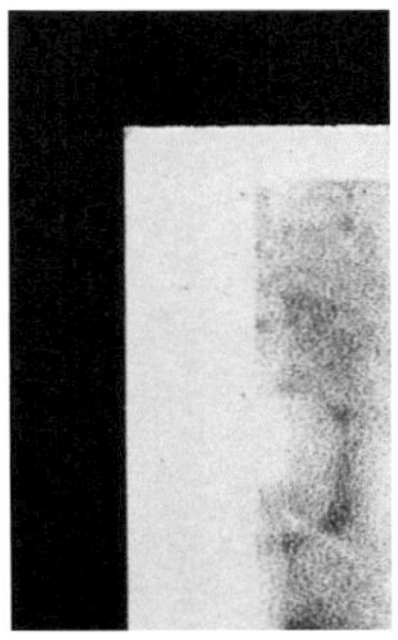

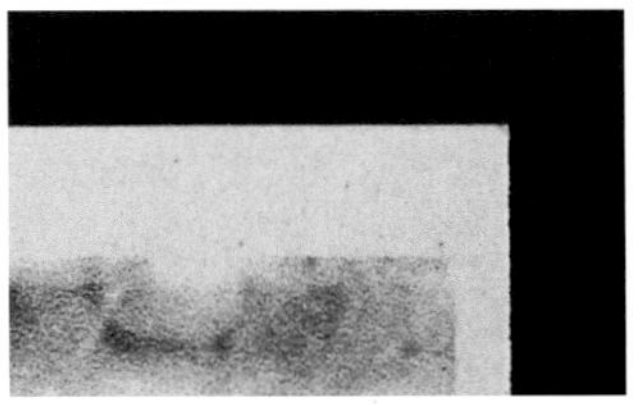

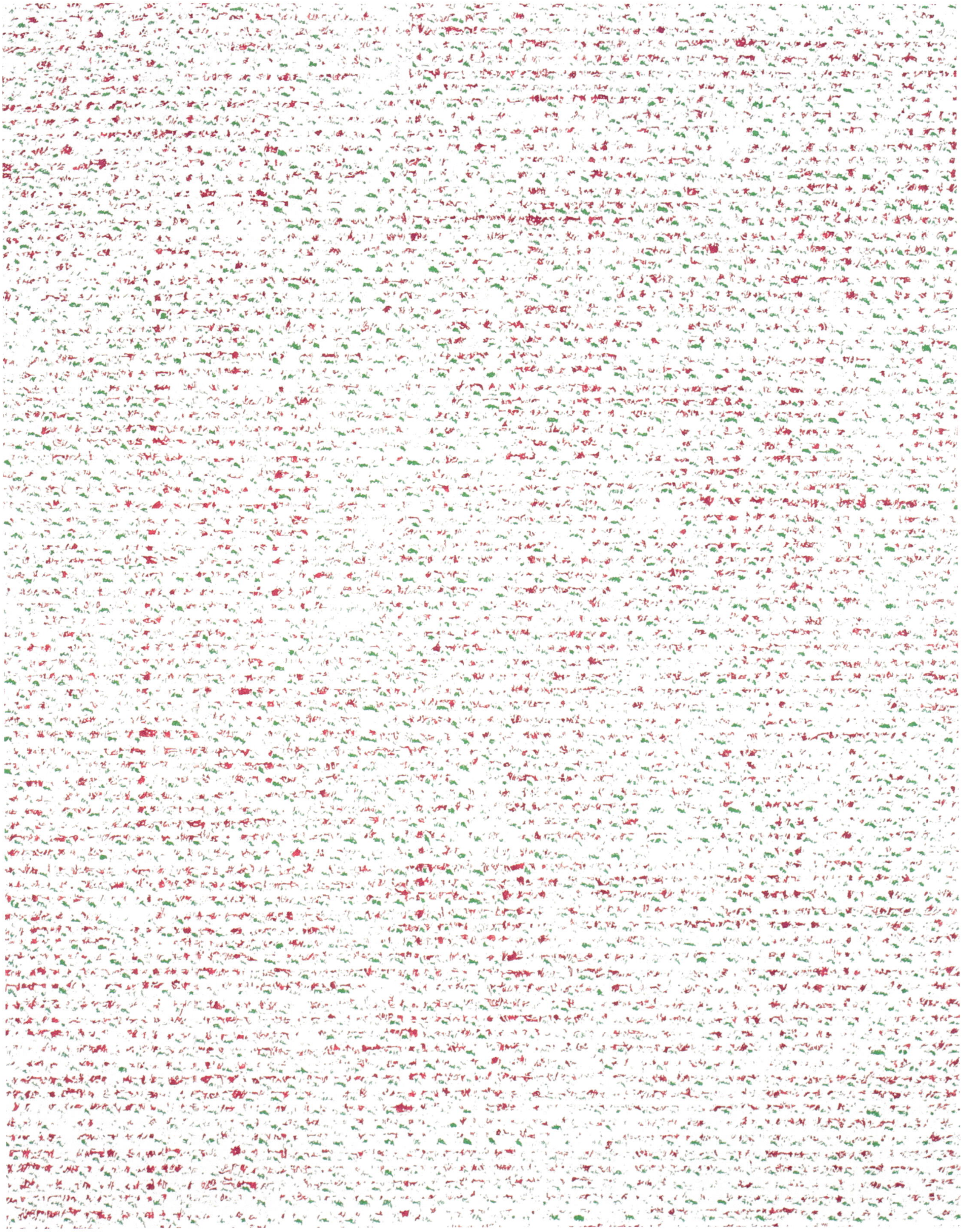

Untitled (Magenta-Yellow Green)
2009, oil on canvas, 55 ½ × 44 in.

Untitled (Cyan-Red Orange)
2009, oil on canvas, 55 ½ × 44 in.

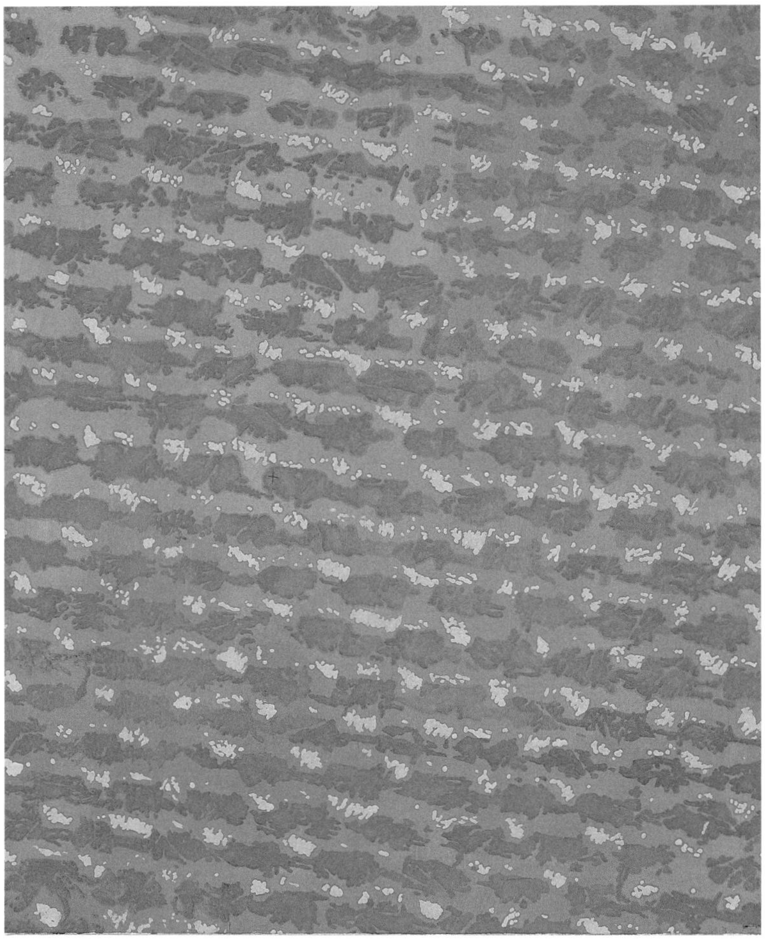

Untitled (Grey)
2009, oil on canvas, 24 × 20 in.

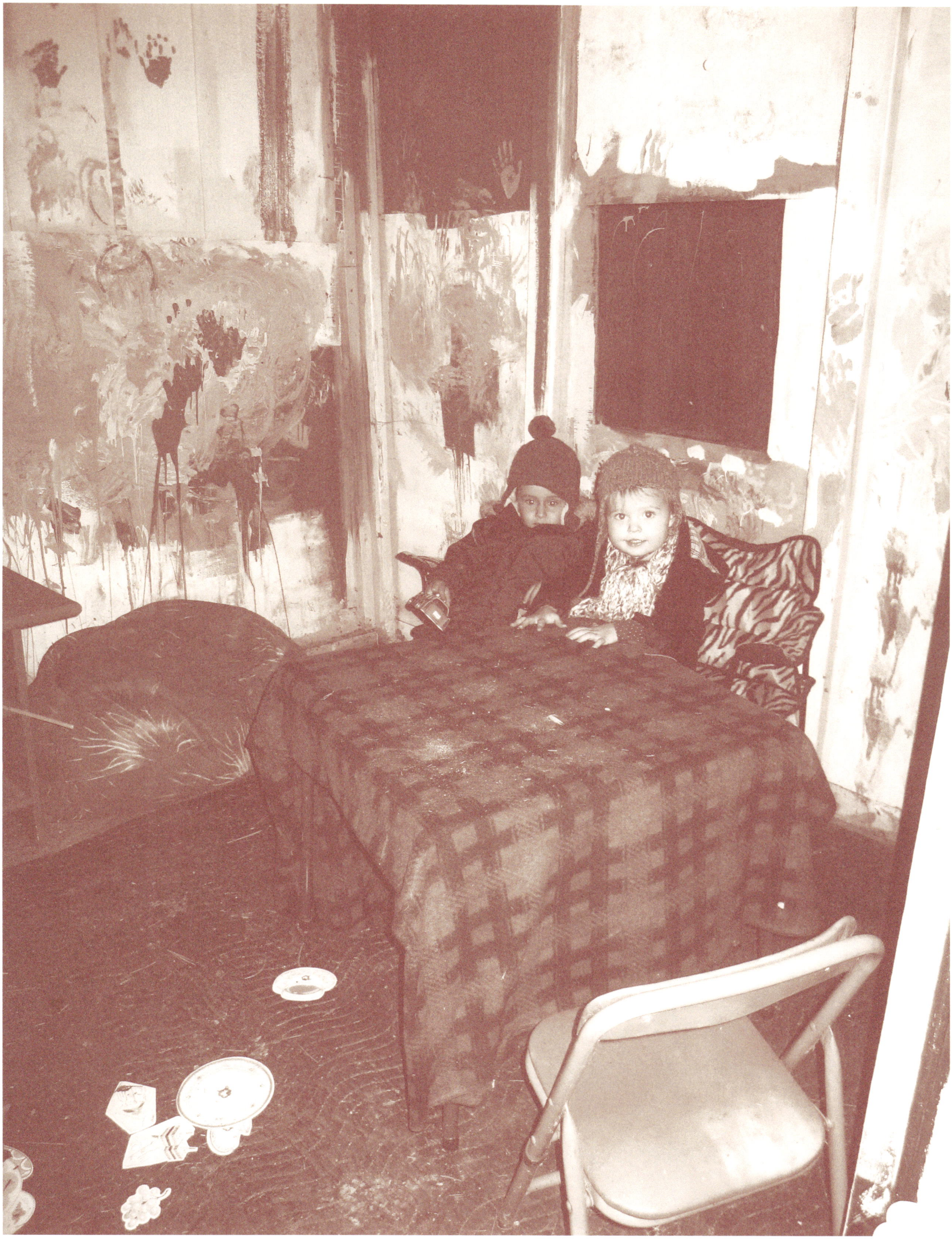

L and P, 2009, digital photo.

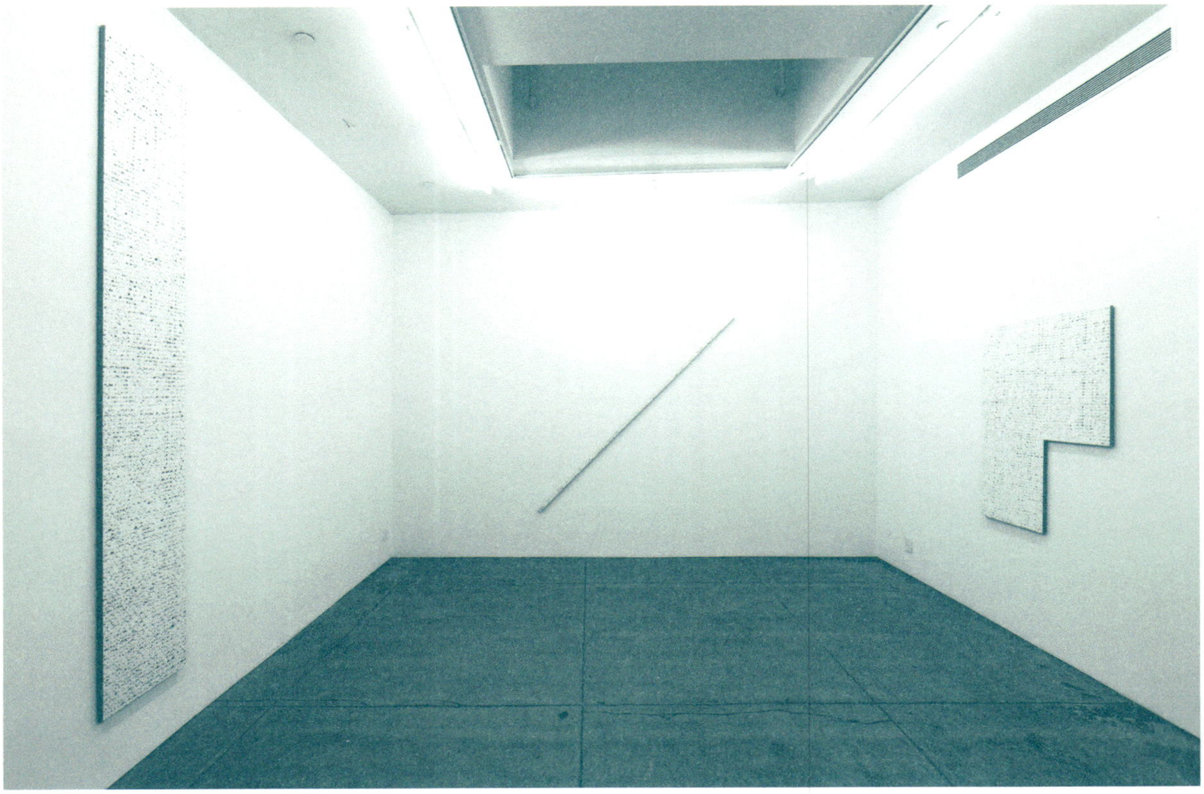

Installation view, *Robert Macaire Chromachromes* (Andrew Kreps Gallery, New York), 2009.

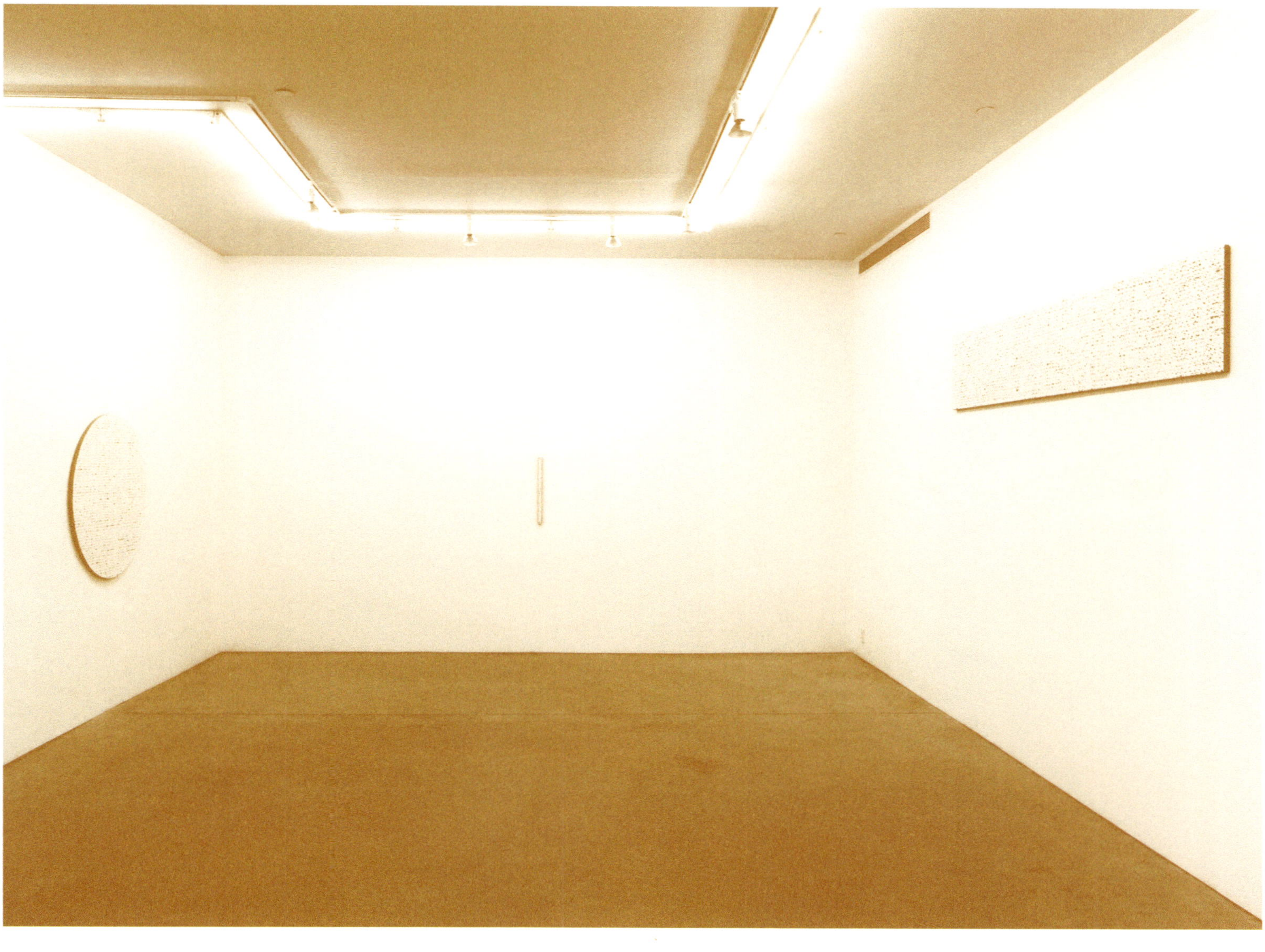

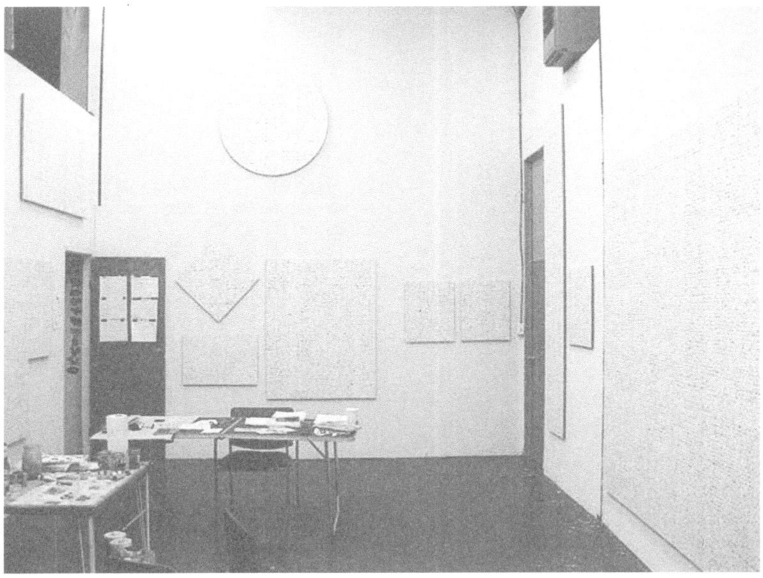

Studio, 2008, digital photo.

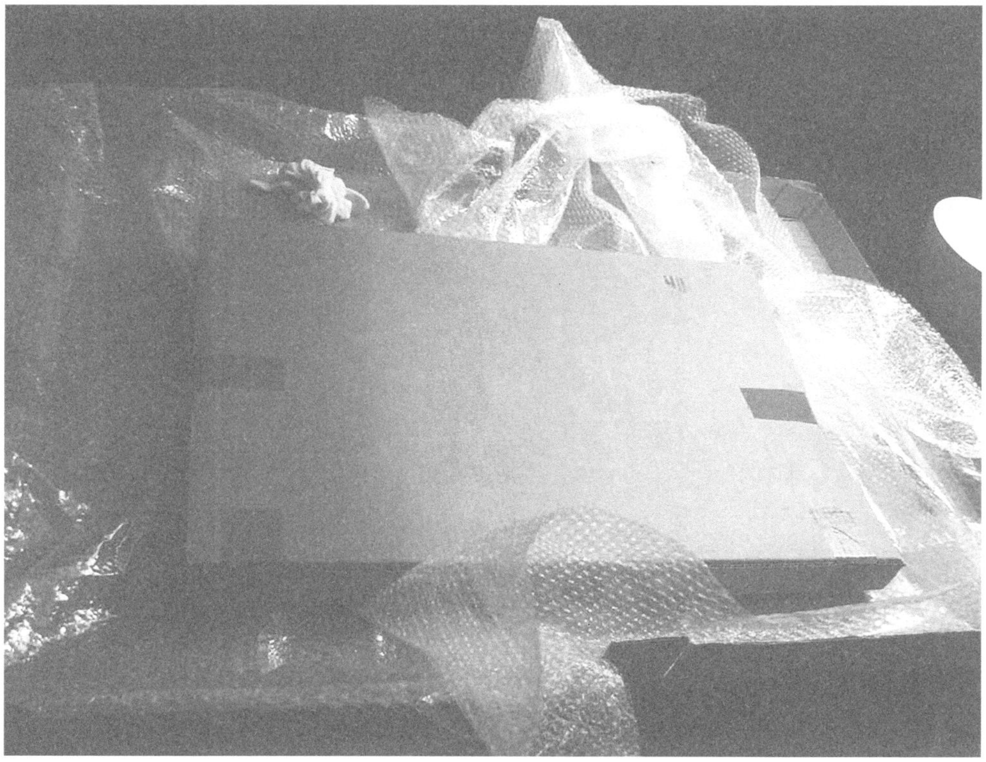

Collatéral (Le Confort Moderne, Poitiers), 2009, digital photo.

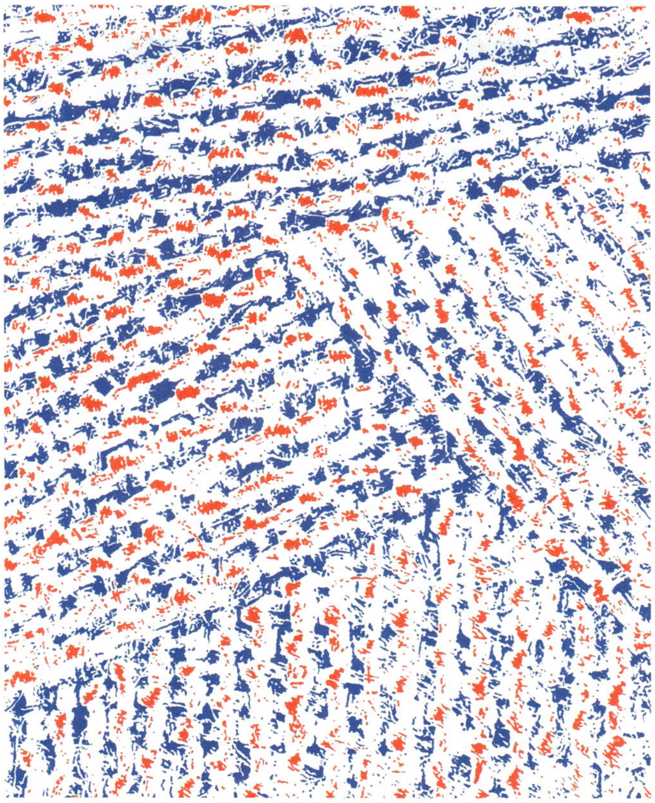

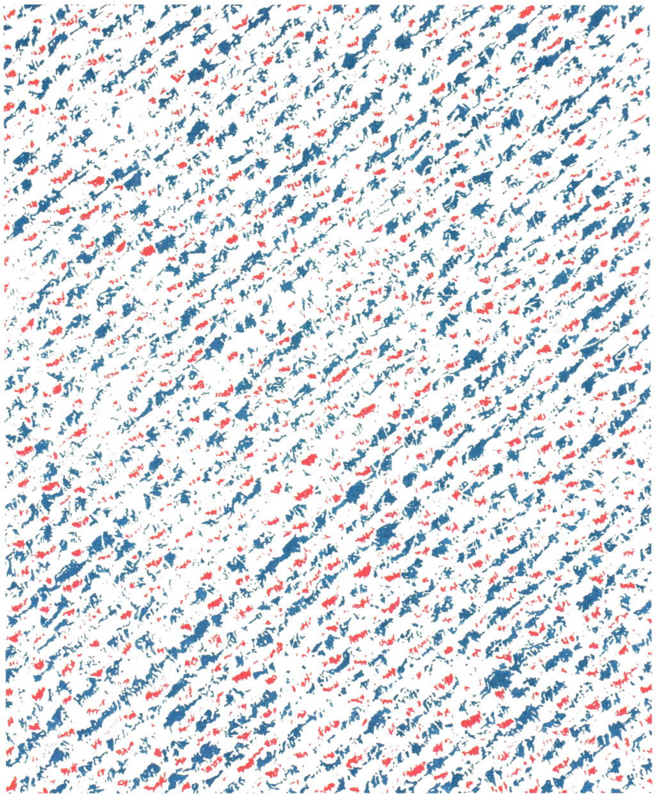

Untitled (Blue-Red)
2009, oil on canvas, 24 × 20 in.

Untitled (Magenta-Blue Green)
2009, oil on canvas, 24 × 20 in.

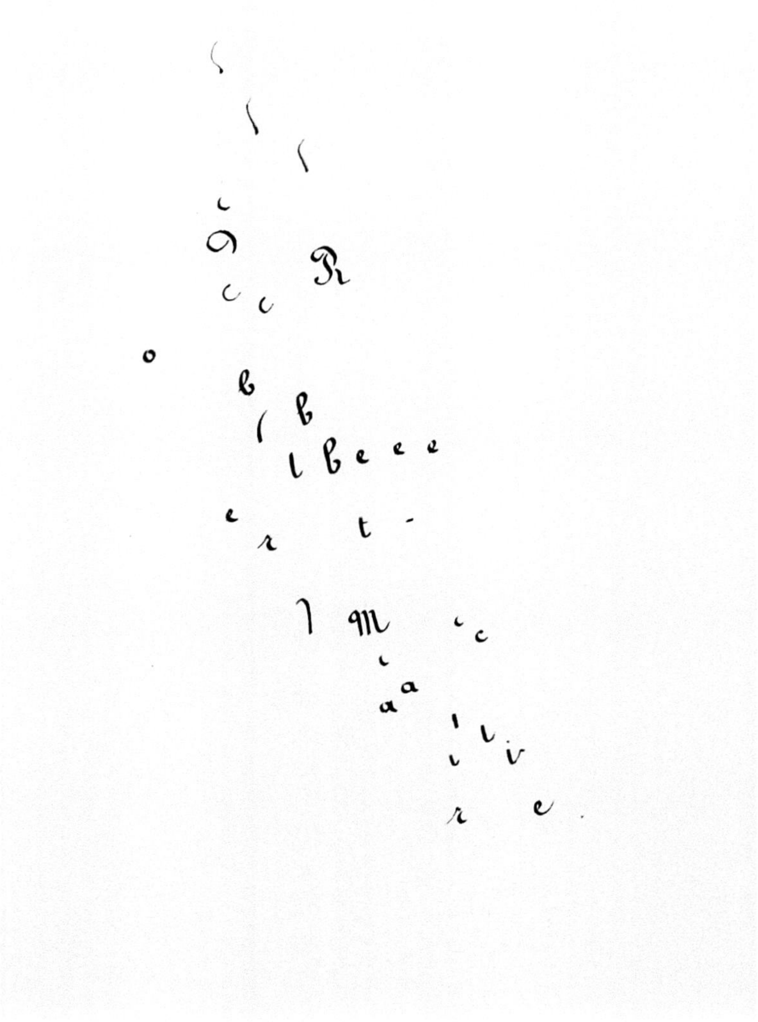

Untitled
2009, ink on paper, 14 × 8 ⅝ in.

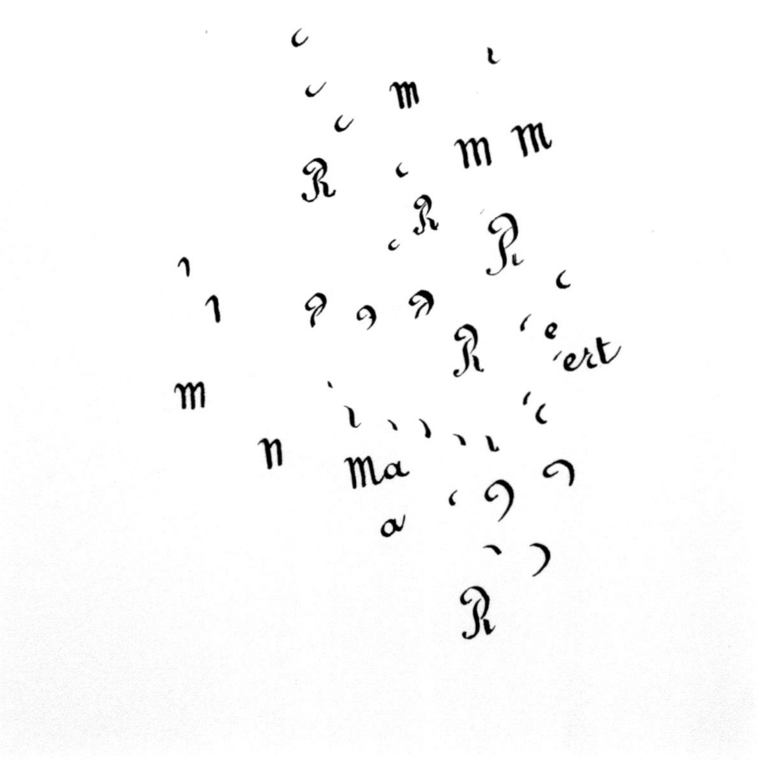

Untitled
2009, ink on paper, 14 × 8 ⅝ in.

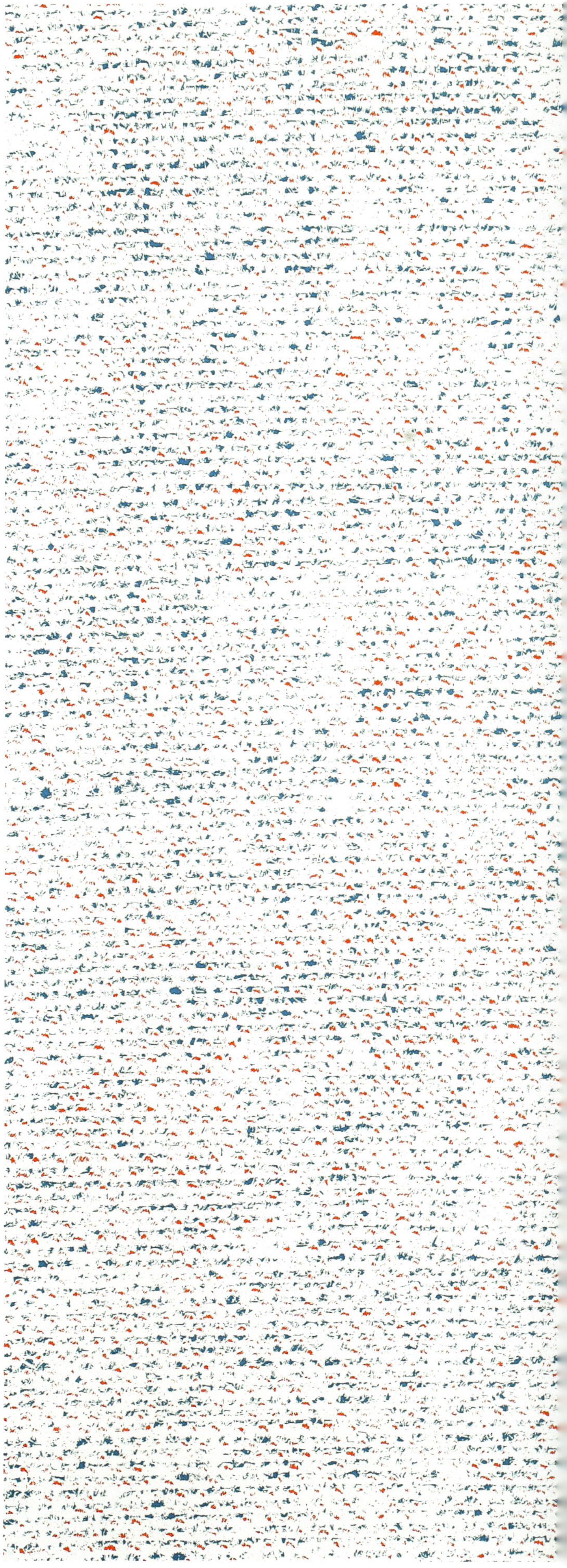

Chromachrome 19 (5BG/5R) macaire
2009, oil on canvas, 88 × 111 in.

Chromachrome 15 (5PB/5Y) shape
2009, oil on canvas, 56 × 44 in.

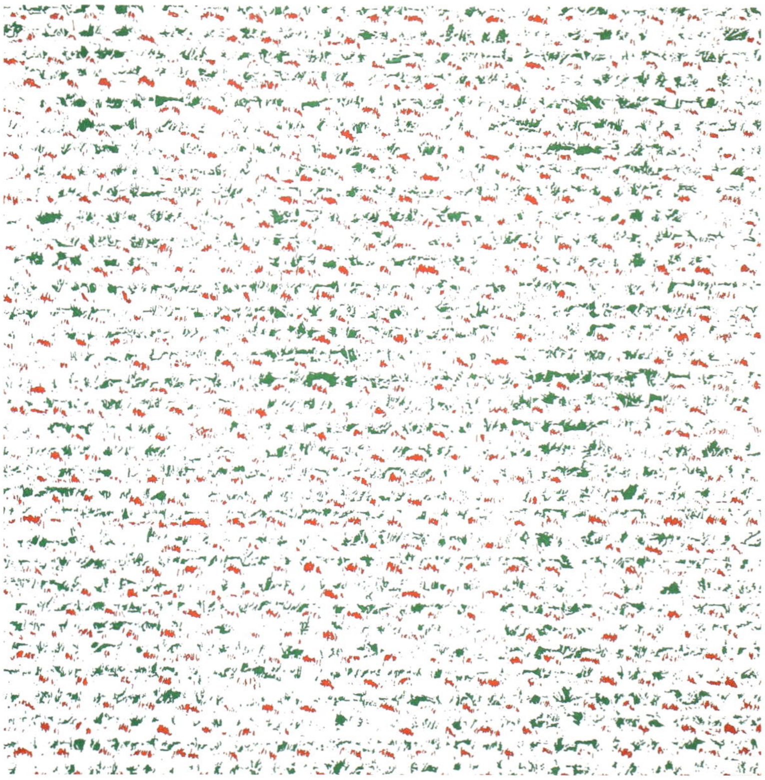

Chromachrome 18 (5G/5RP) square
2009, oil on canvas, 24 × 24 in.

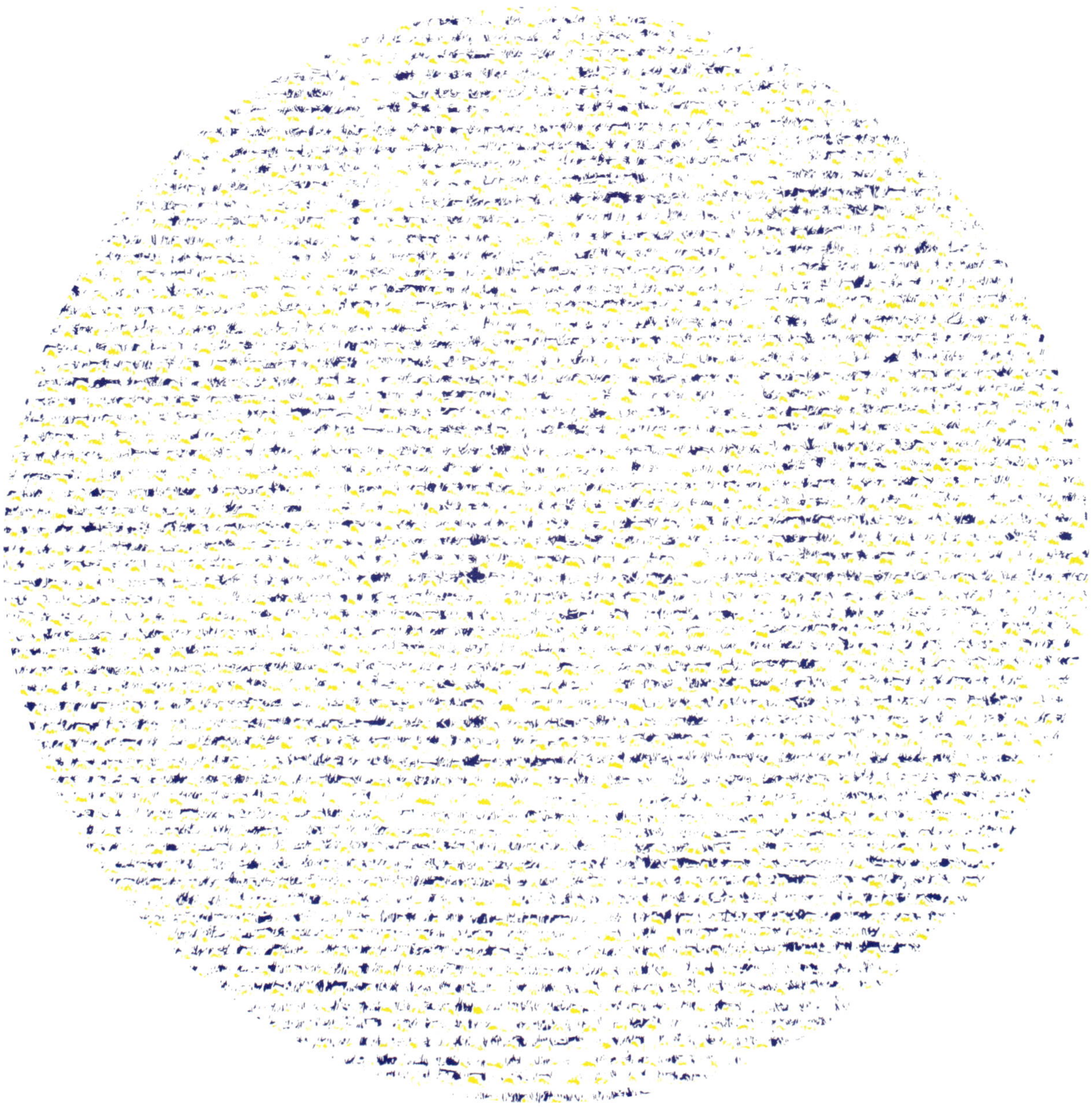

Chromachrome 9 (5PB/5Y) tondo
2009, oil on canvas, 44 in.

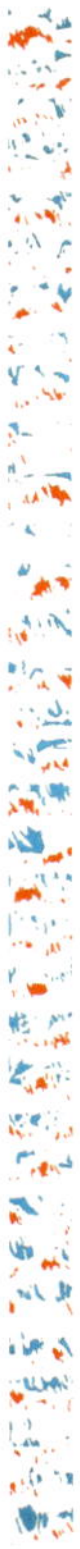

Chromachrome 11 (5BG/5R) edge
2009, oil on canvas, 24 × 1 in.

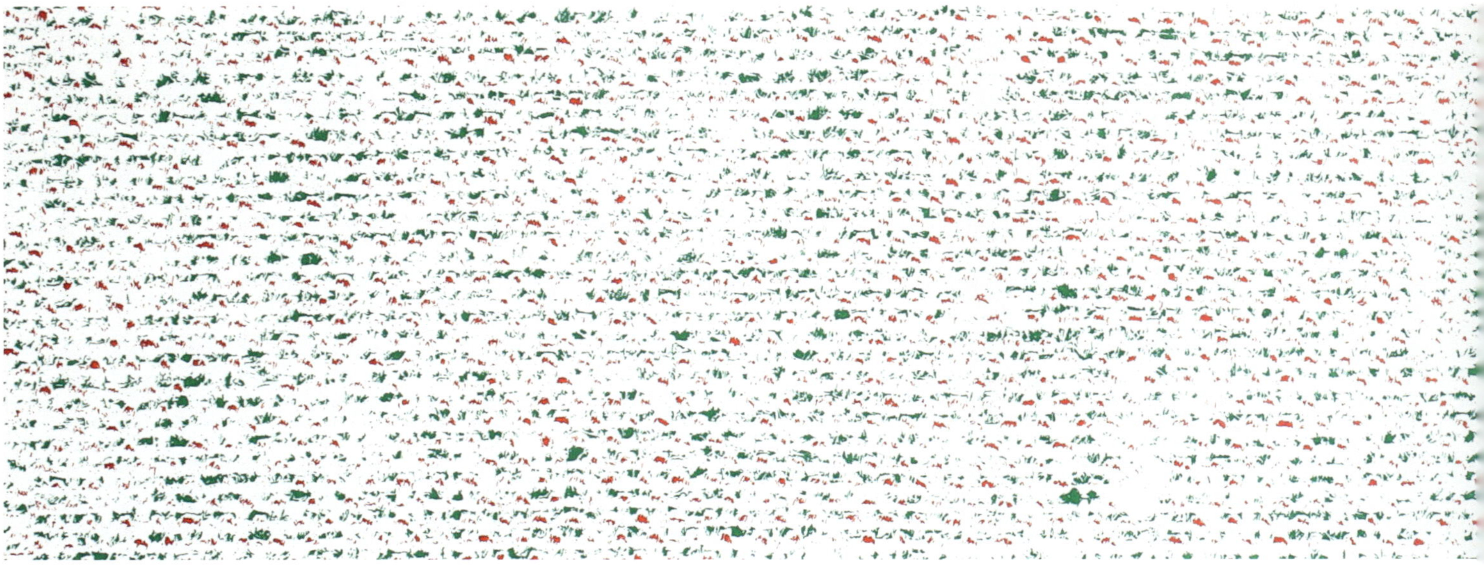

Chromachrome 10 (5G/5RP) frieze
2009, oil on canvas, 20 × 111 in.

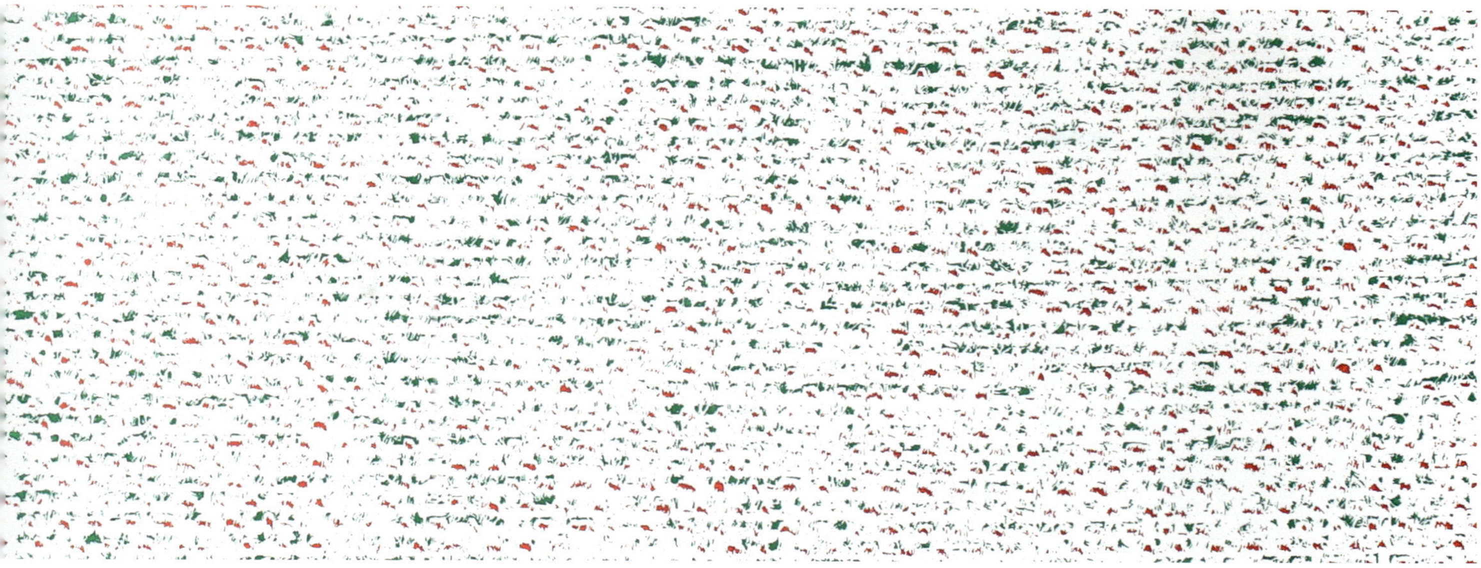

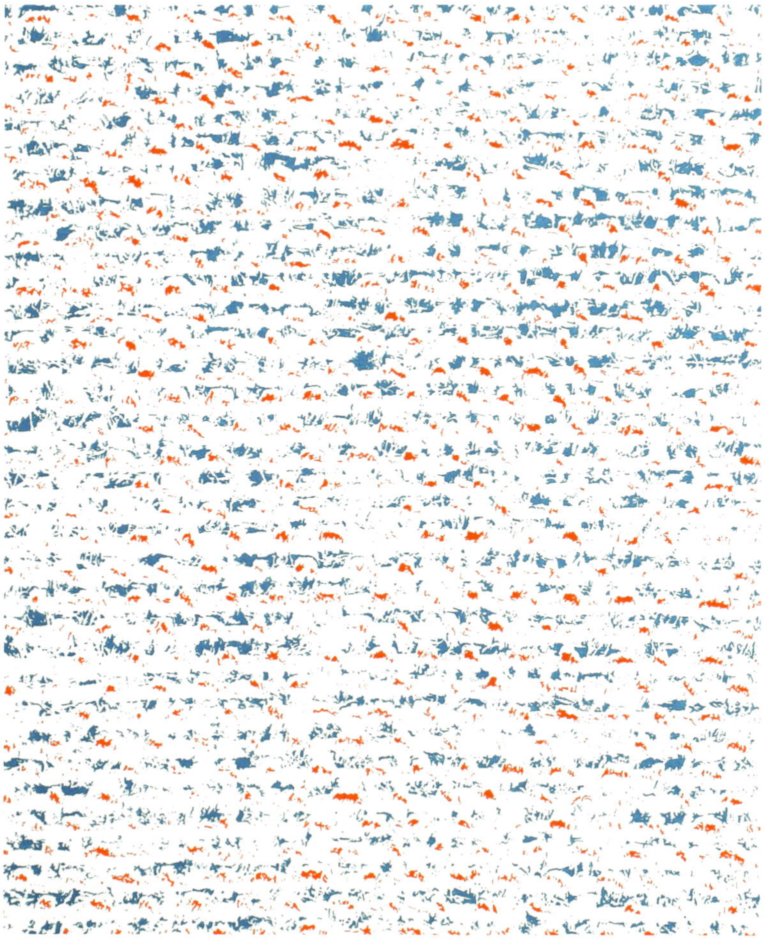

Chromachrome 8 (5BG/5R) diptych
2009, oil on canvas, 24 × 20 in.

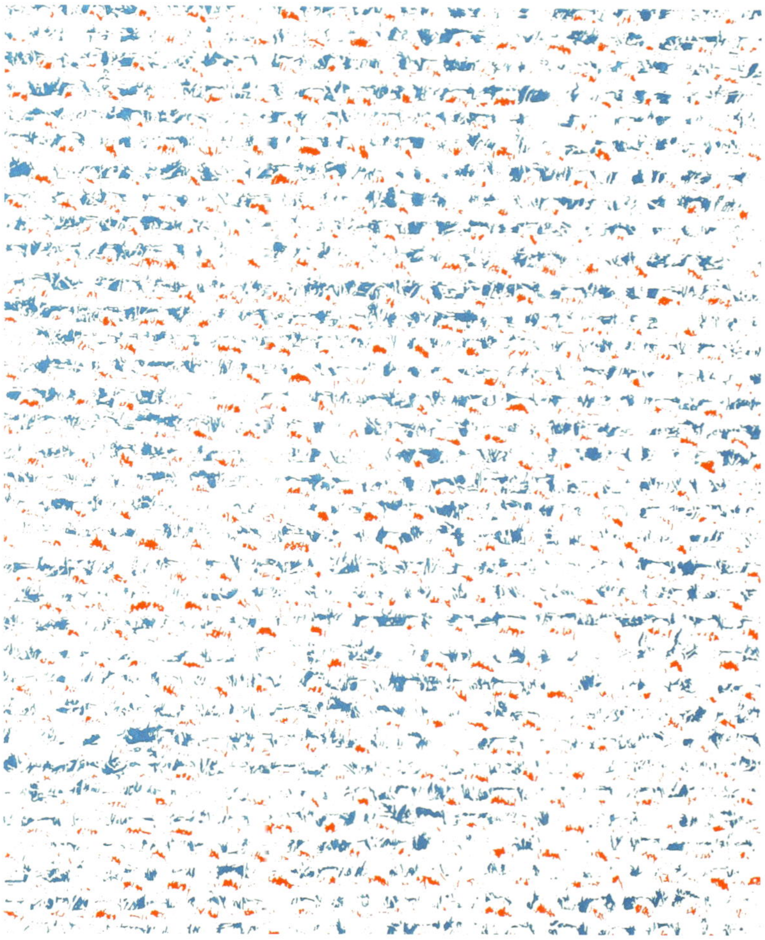

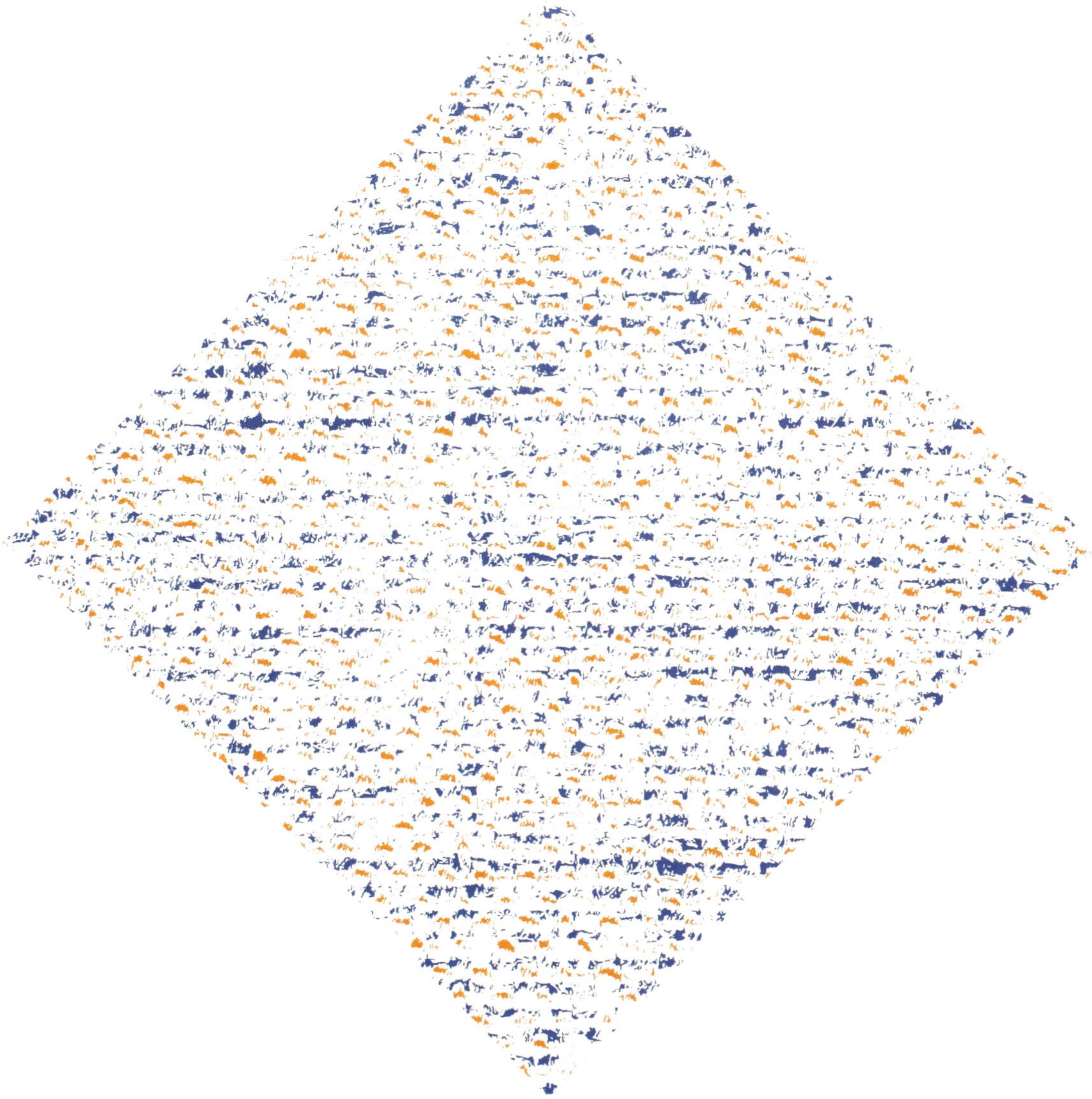

Chromachrome 12 (5P/5YR) lozenge
2009, oil on canvas, 34 × 34 in.

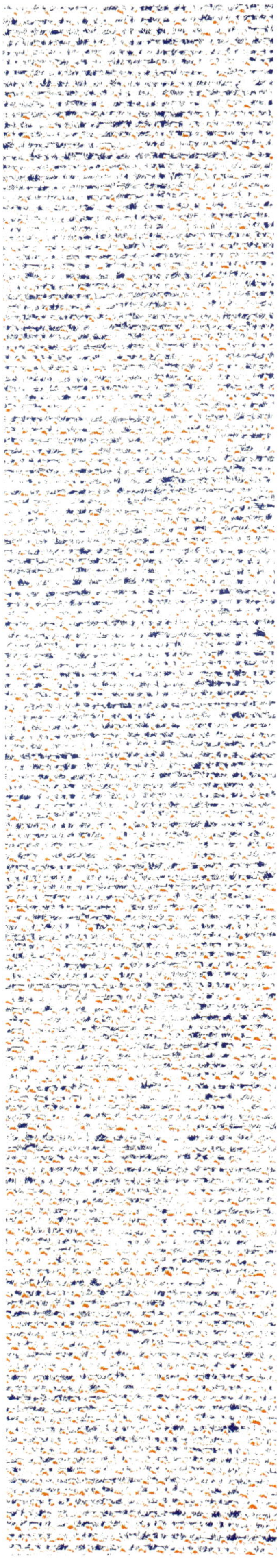

Chromachrome 14 (5B/5YR) column
2009, oil on canvas, 111 × 20 in.

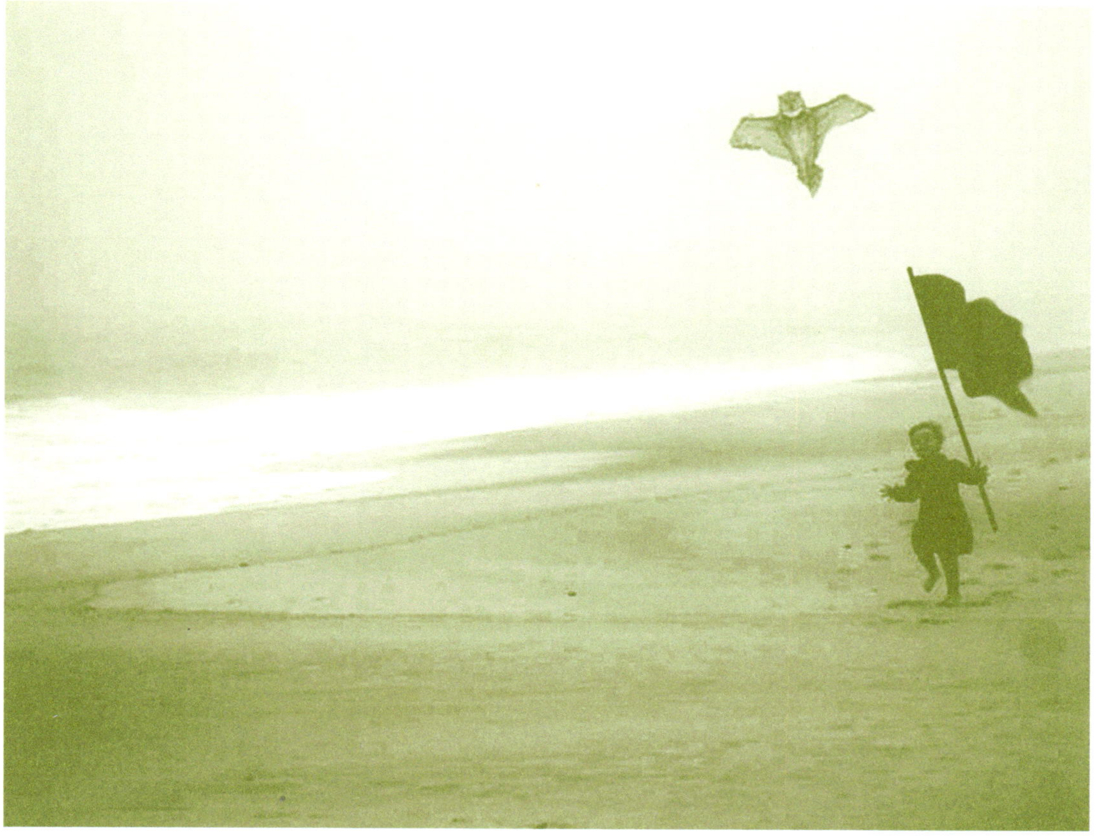

P leaving New York, 2010, digital photo.

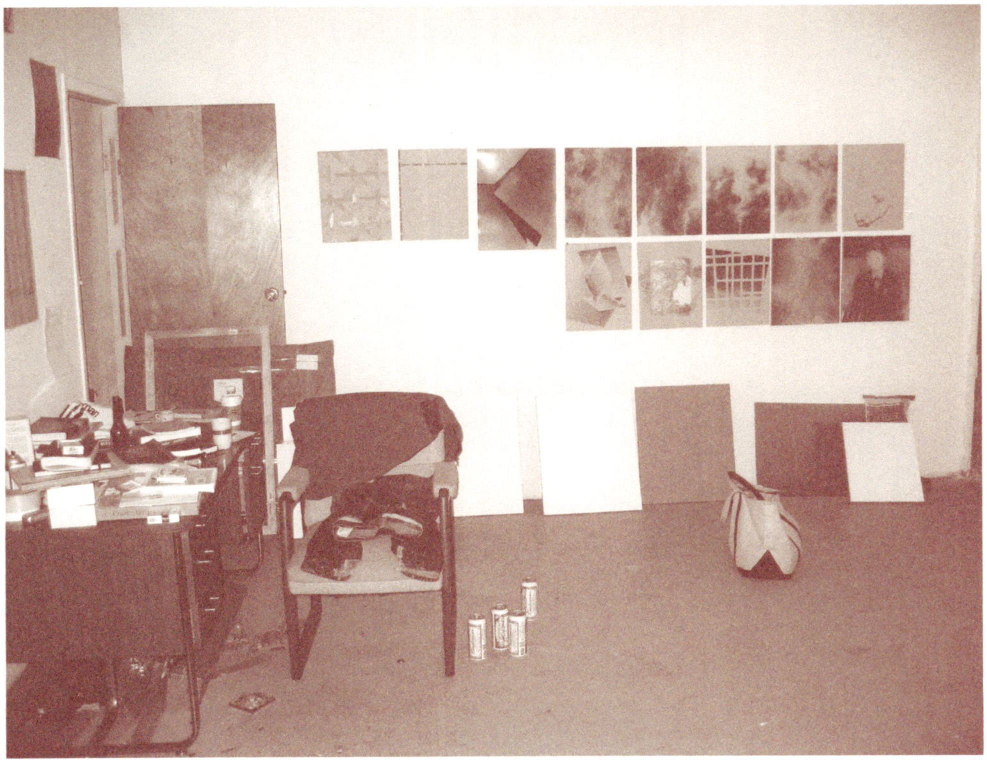

Studio, 2005, digital photo.

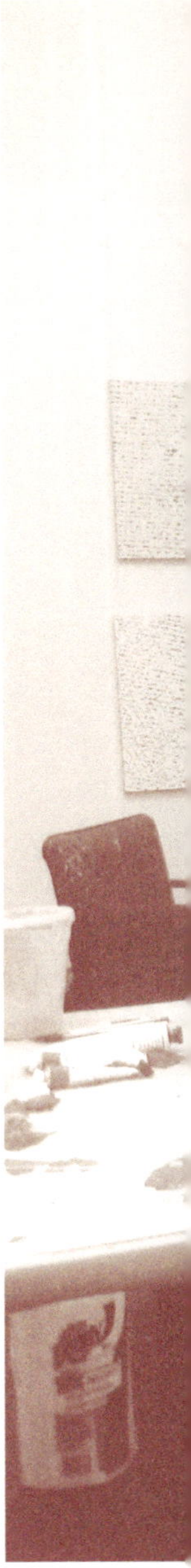

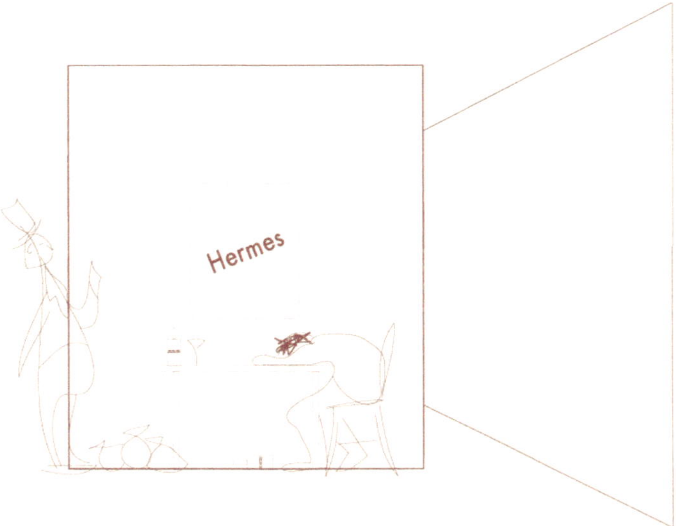

Study for *Art Basel*, Miami Beach, with Roe Ethridge, 2009, computer drawing.

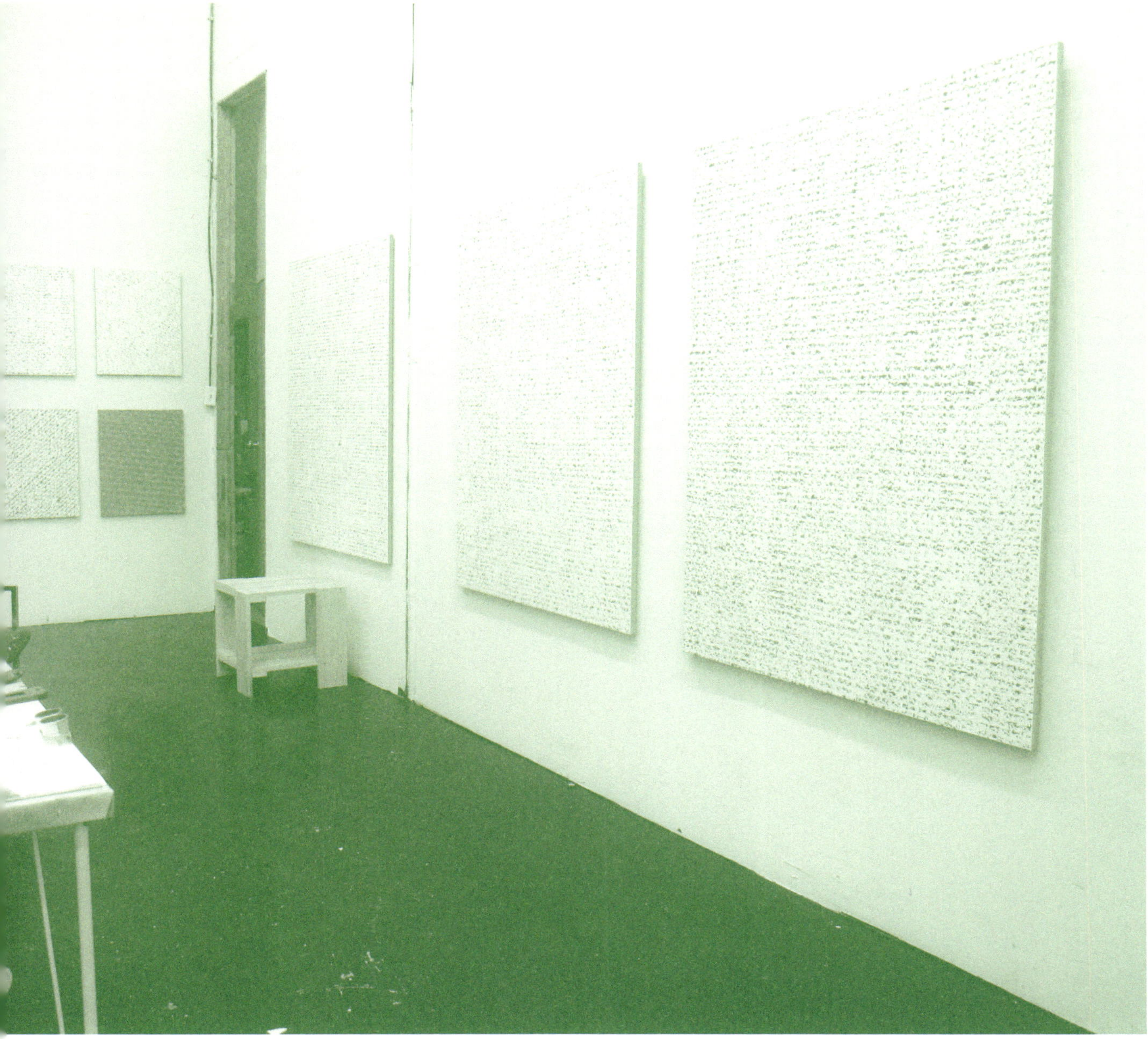

Studio, 2009, digital photo.

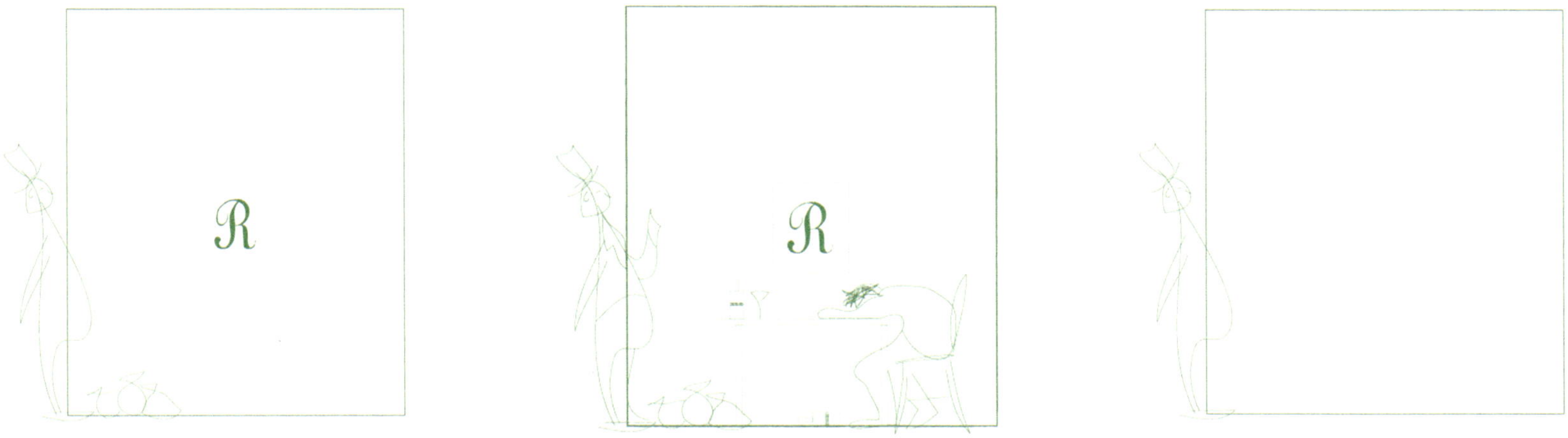

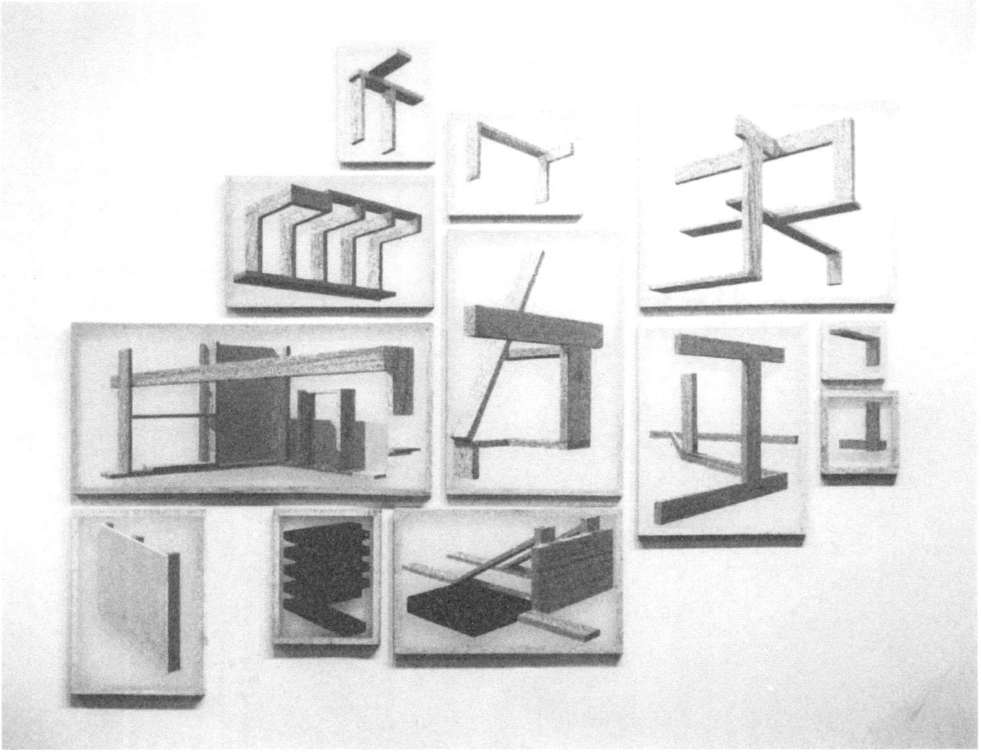

1731, 1998, acrylic on organza, 96 × 120 in.

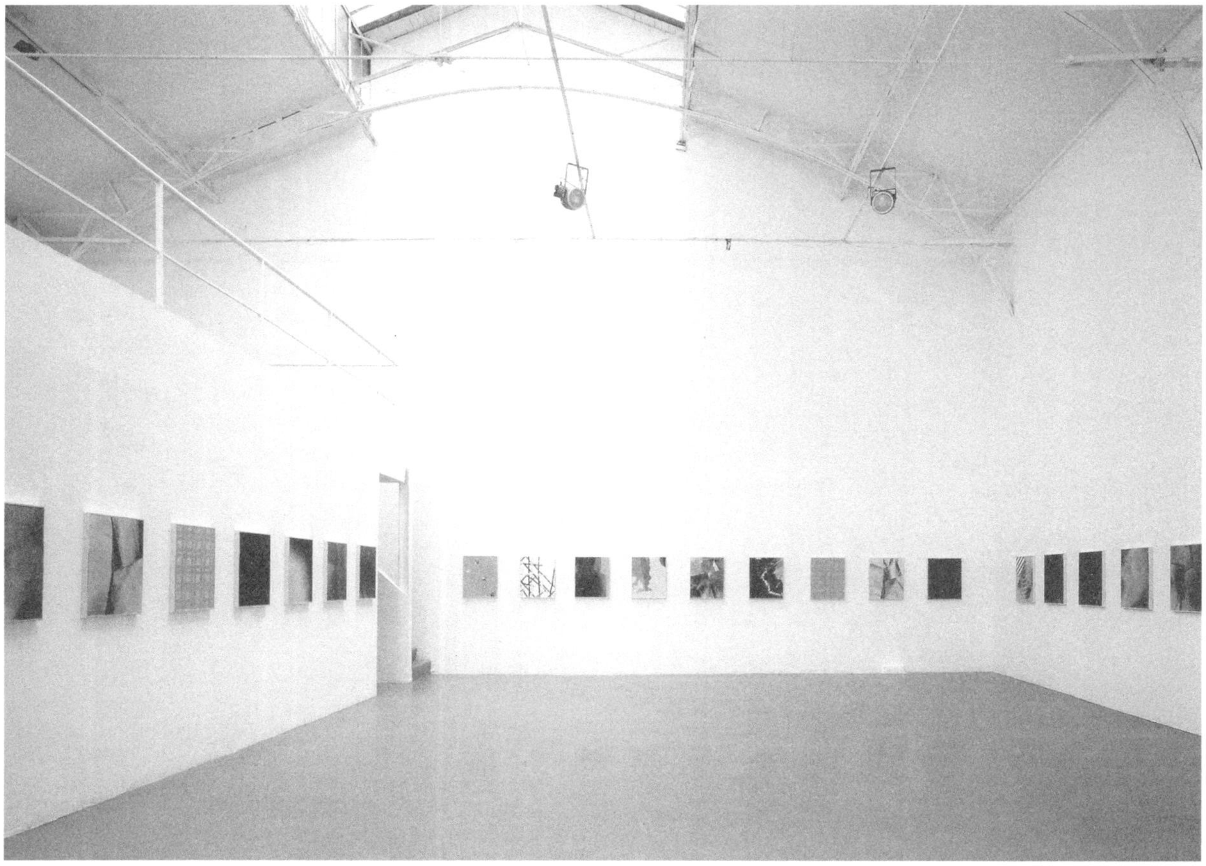

Installation view, *S&M* (Sutton Lane, Paris, courtesy of Campoli Presti, London/Paris), Eileen Quinlan & Cheyney Thompson, 2005.

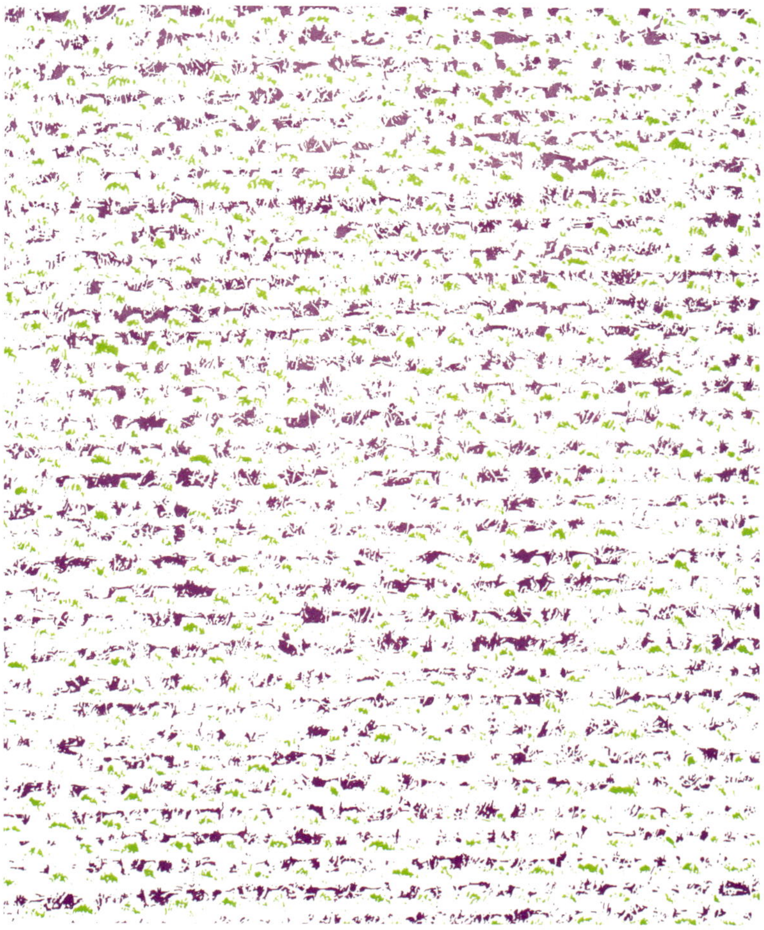

Chromachrome 7 (5GY/5P) portrait
2009, oil on canvas, 24 × 20 in.

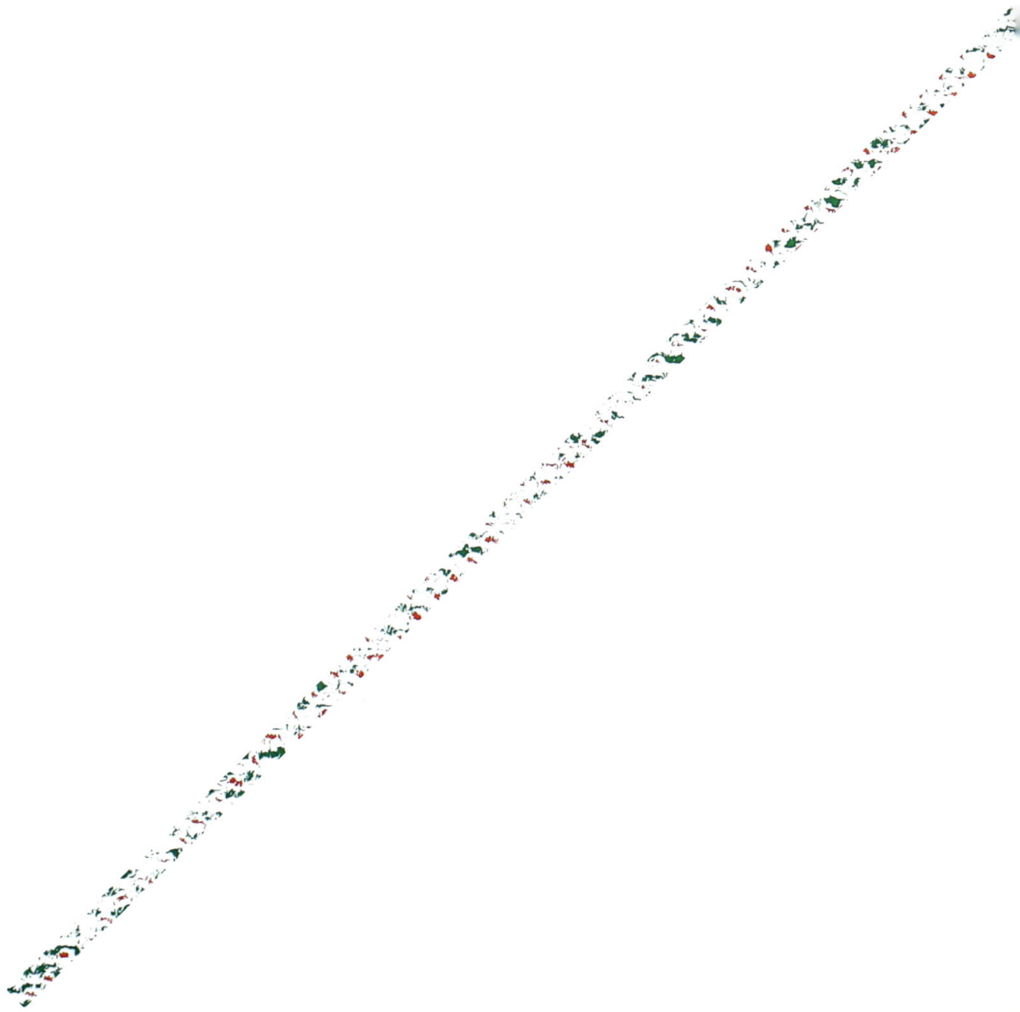

Chromachrome 13 (5G/5RP) angle
2009, oil on canvas, 111 × 1 in.

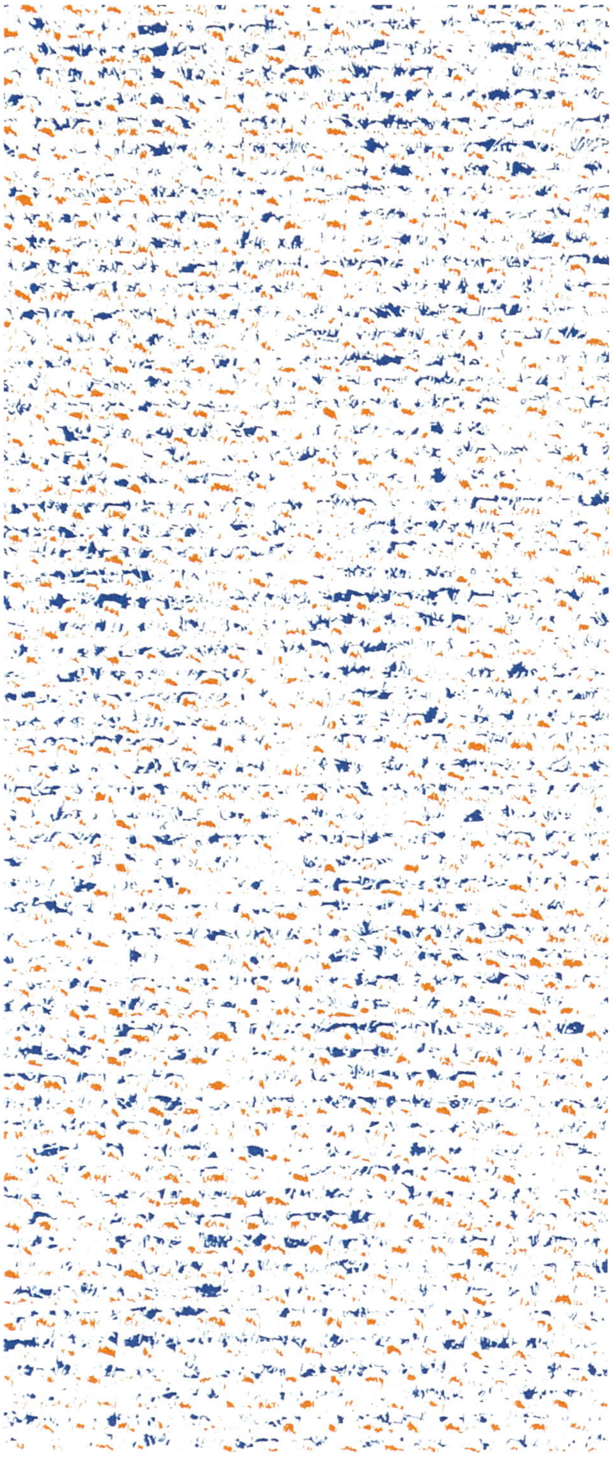

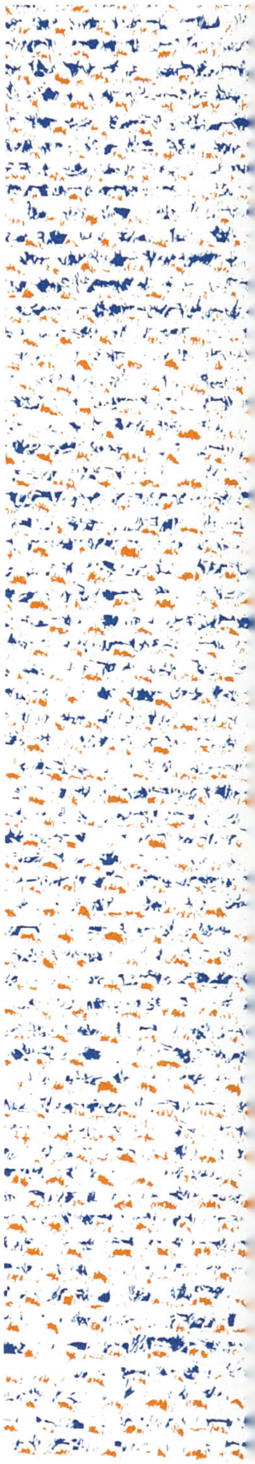

Chromachrome (58/5YR) triptych
2009, oil on canvas, 80 × 44 in.

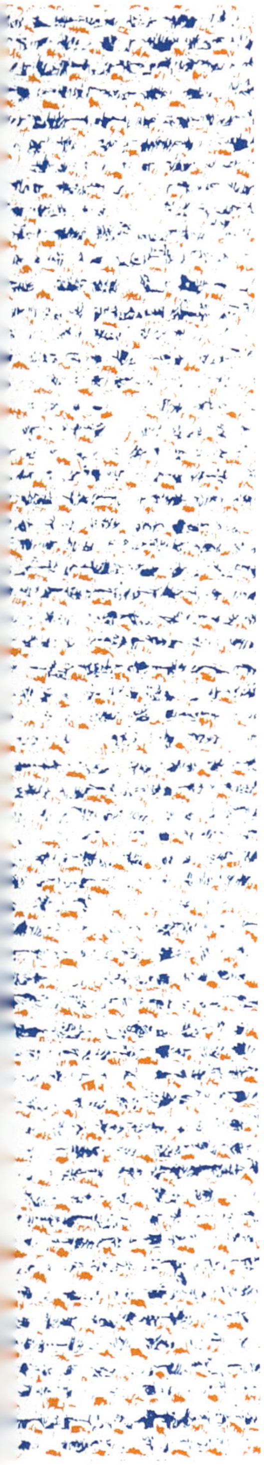

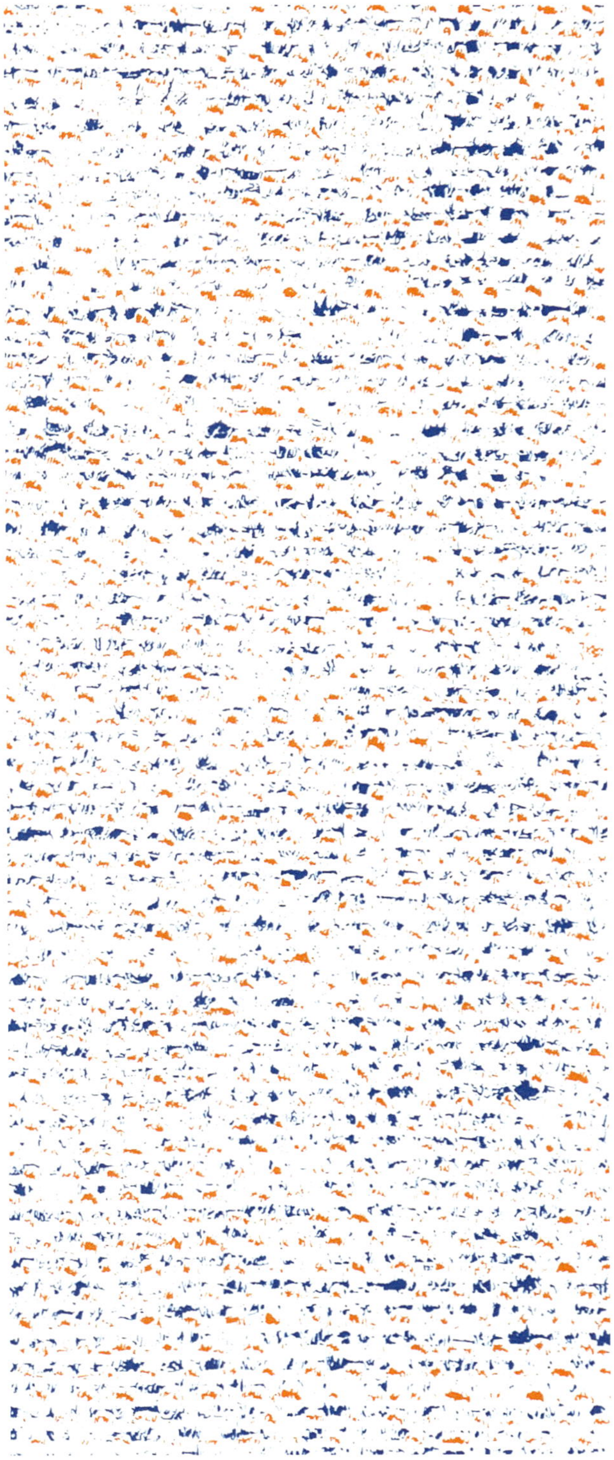

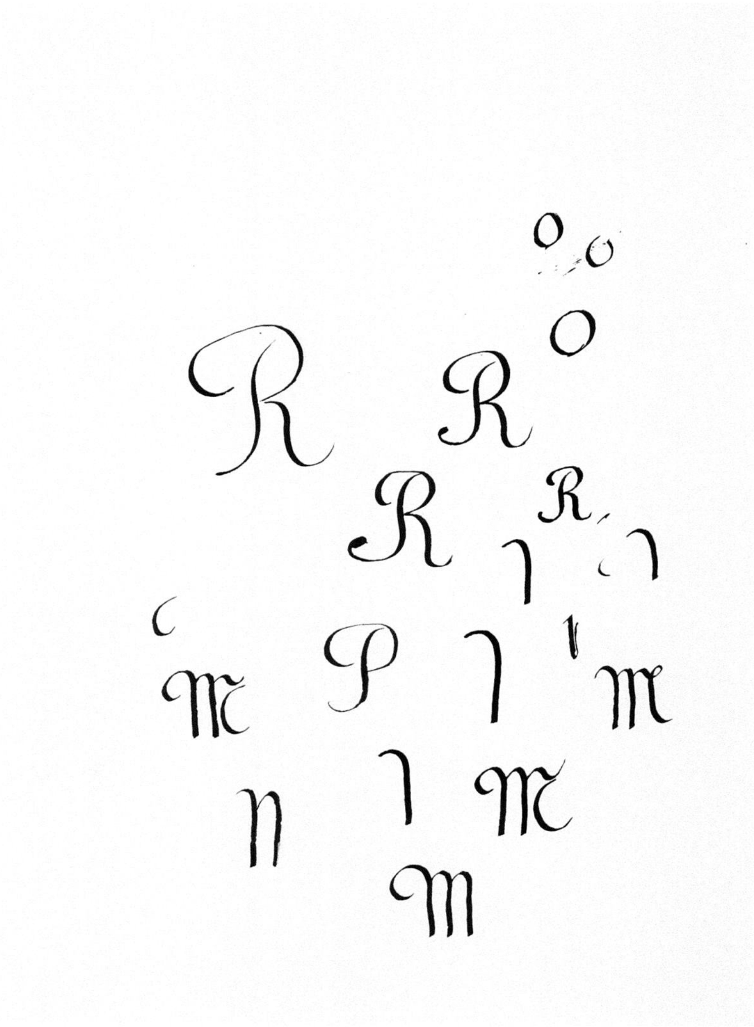

Untitled
2009, ink on paper, 17 ¾ × 14 ⅝ in.

Chronochrome 1
2009, oil on canvas, 55.1 × 42 in.

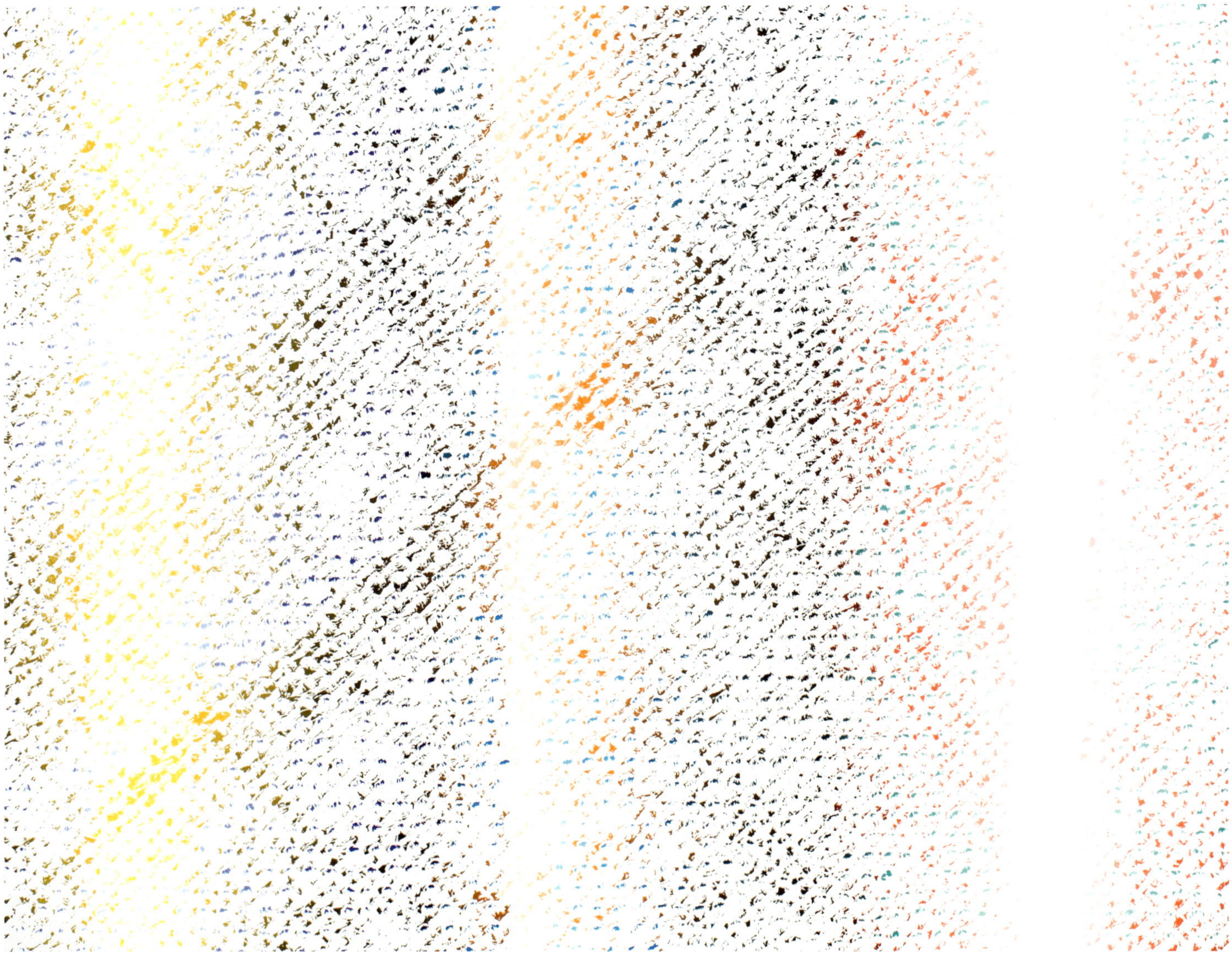

Chronochrome 8
2009, oil on canvas, 55.1 × 72 in.

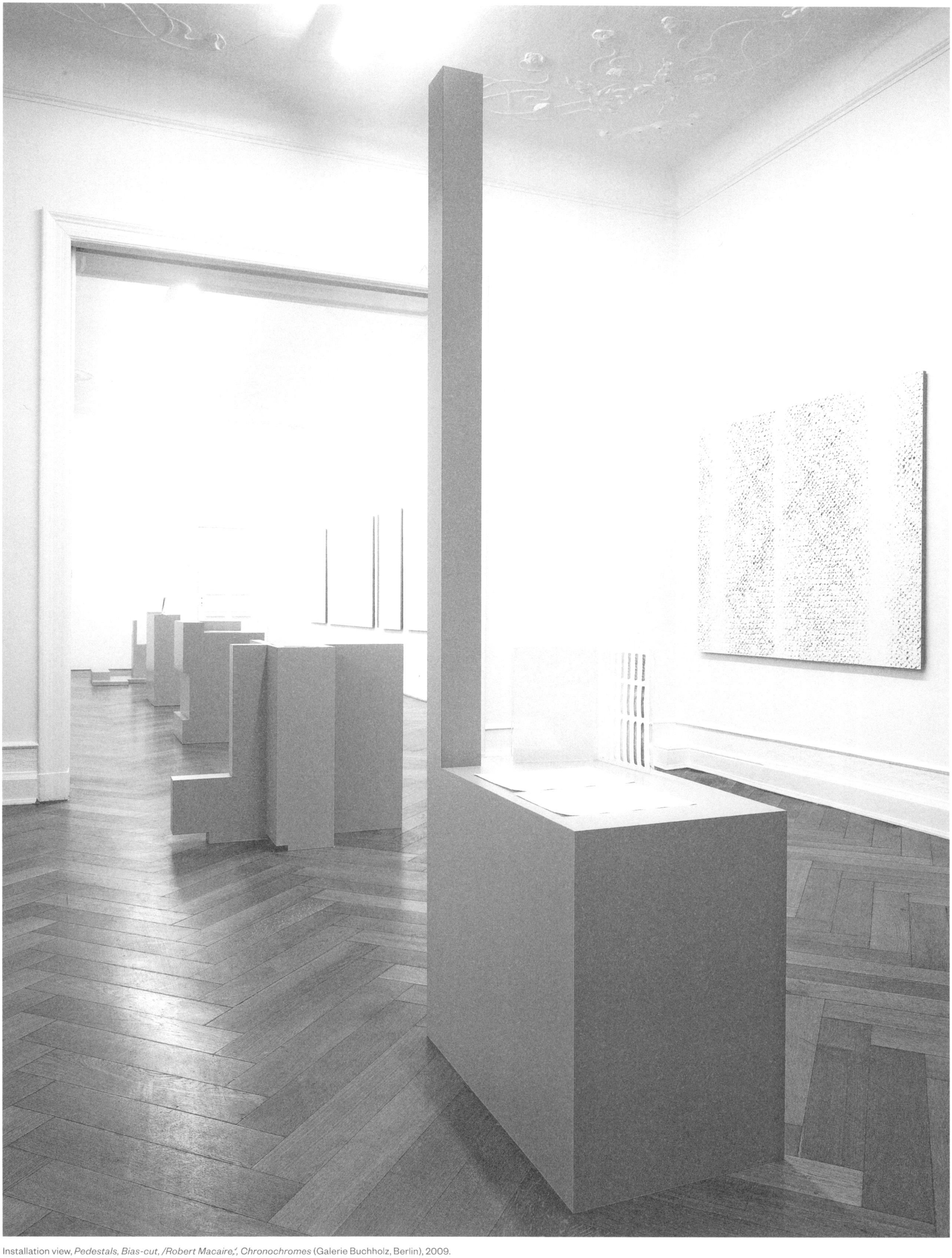

Installation view, *Pedestals, Bias-cut, /Robert Macaire,', Chronochromes* (Galerie Buchholz, Berlin), 2009.

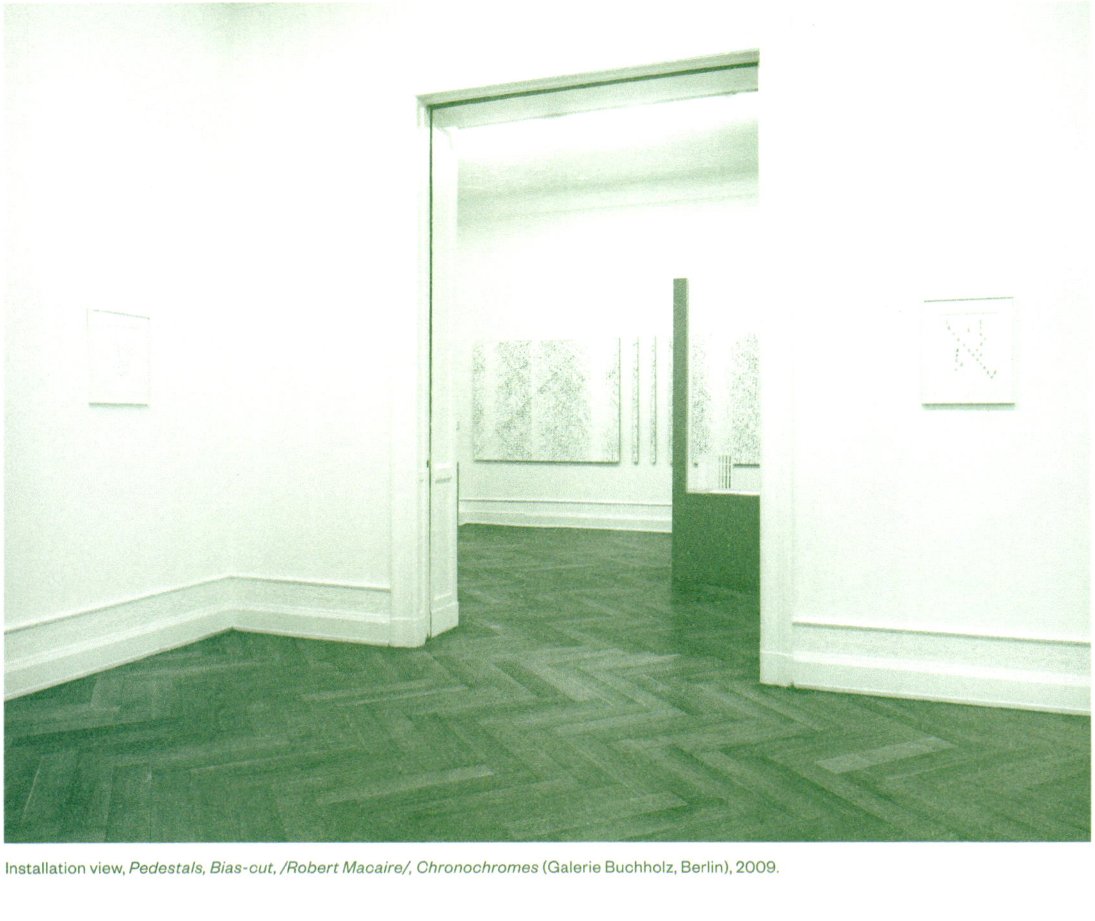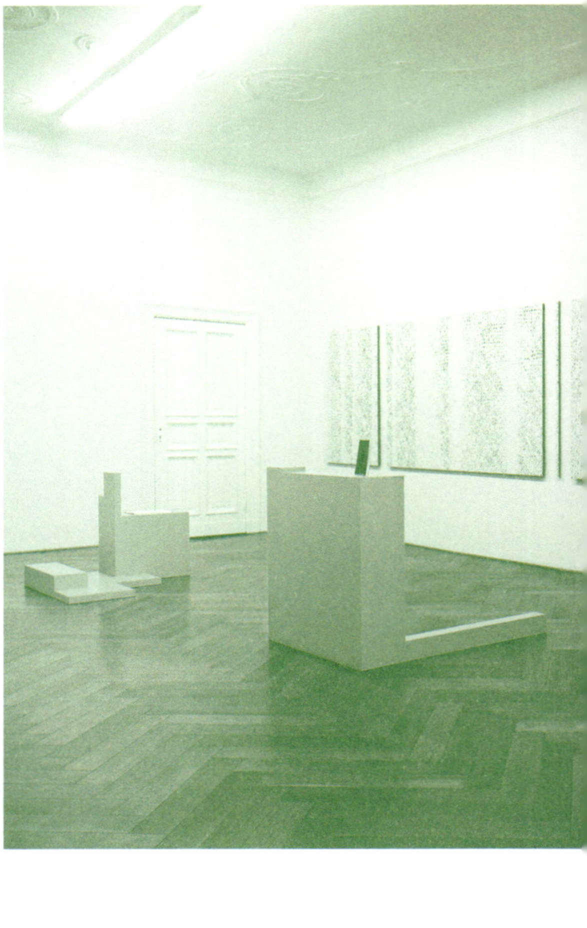

Installation view, *Pedestals, Bias-cut, /Robert Macaire/, Chronochromes* (Galerie Buchholz, Berlin), 2009.

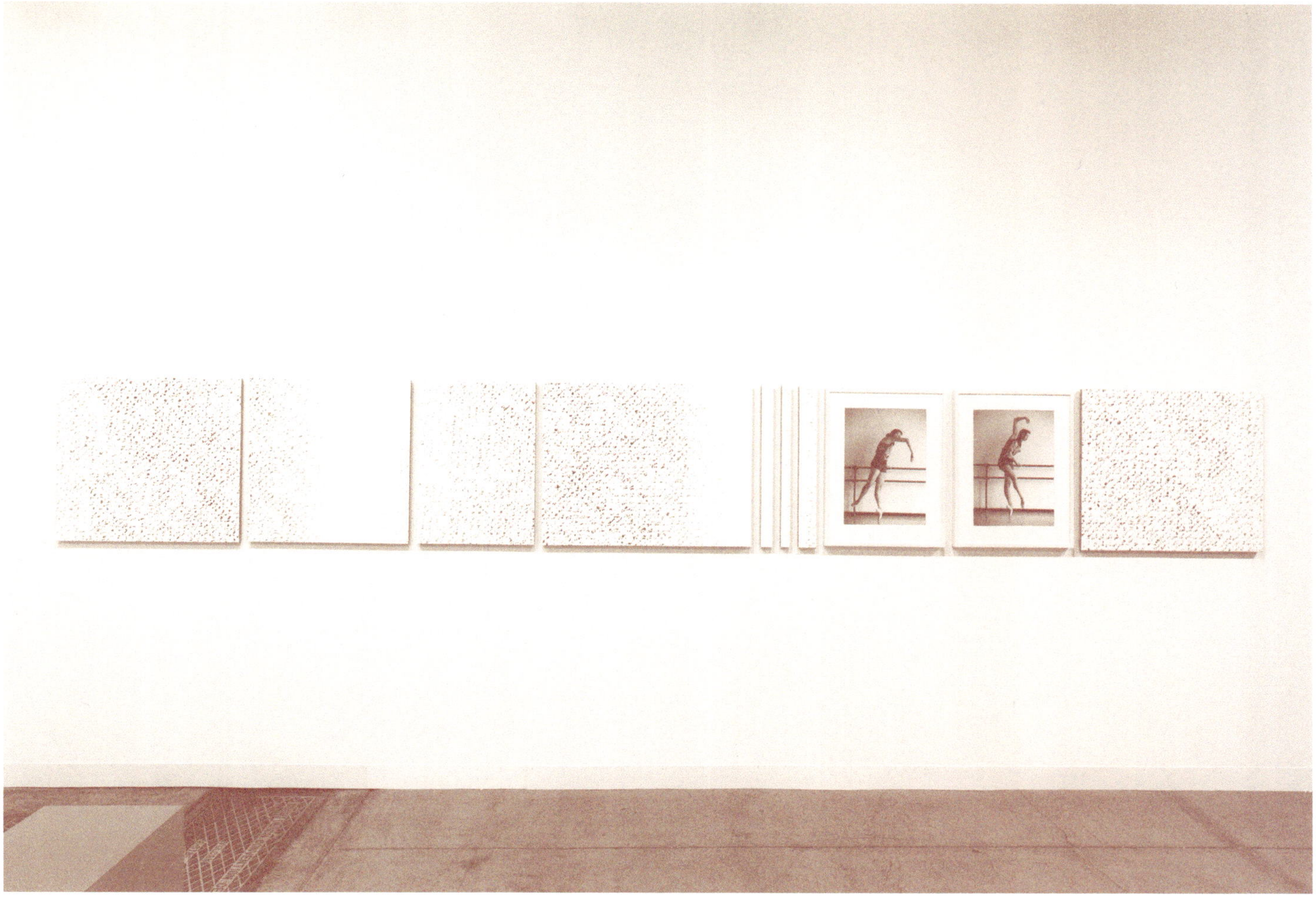

Installation view, with Roe Ethridge (*Art Basel*, Miami Beach) , 2009.

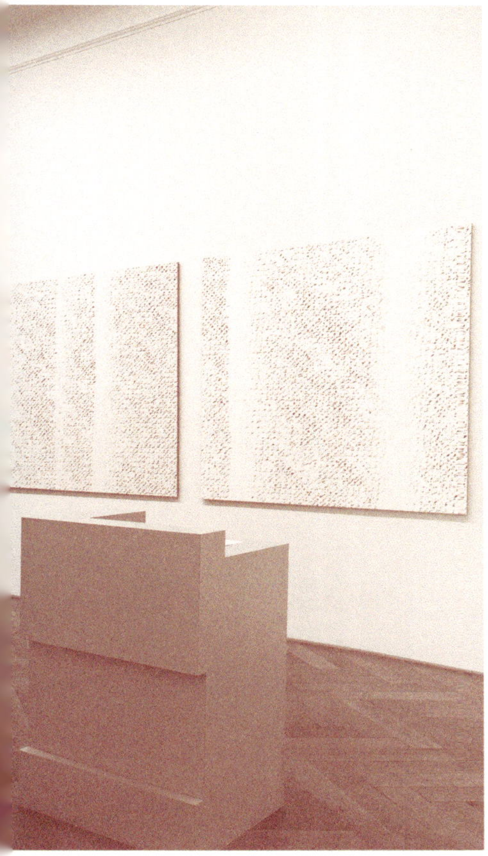

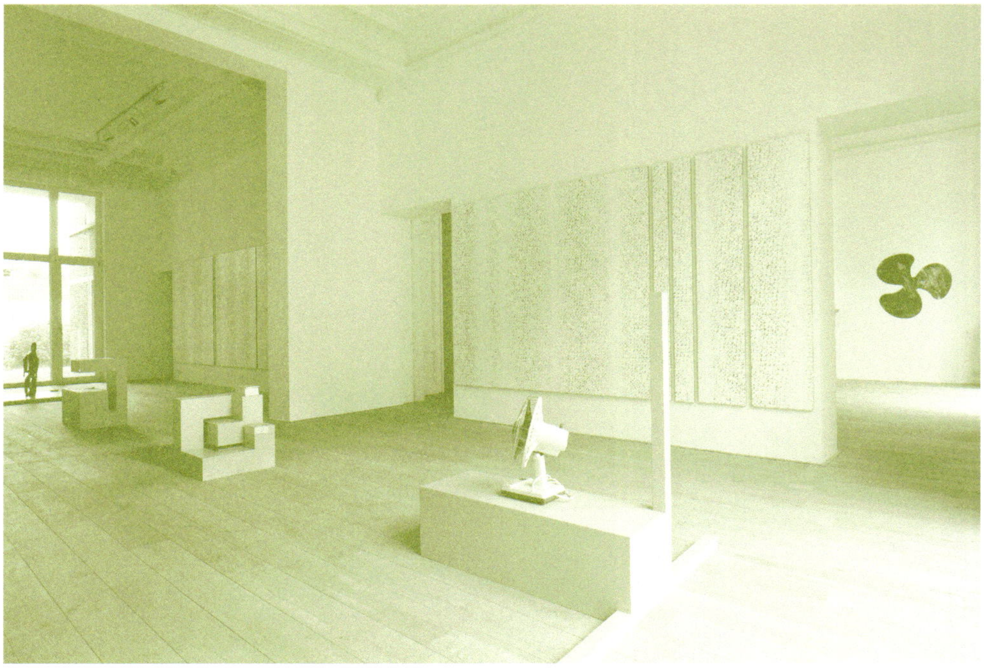

Installation view, *Chronochromes, Menarches, Socles, Paul de Casteljau, /Robert/, Motifs* (Sutton Lane, Brussels, courtesy of Campoli Presti, London/Paris), 2010.

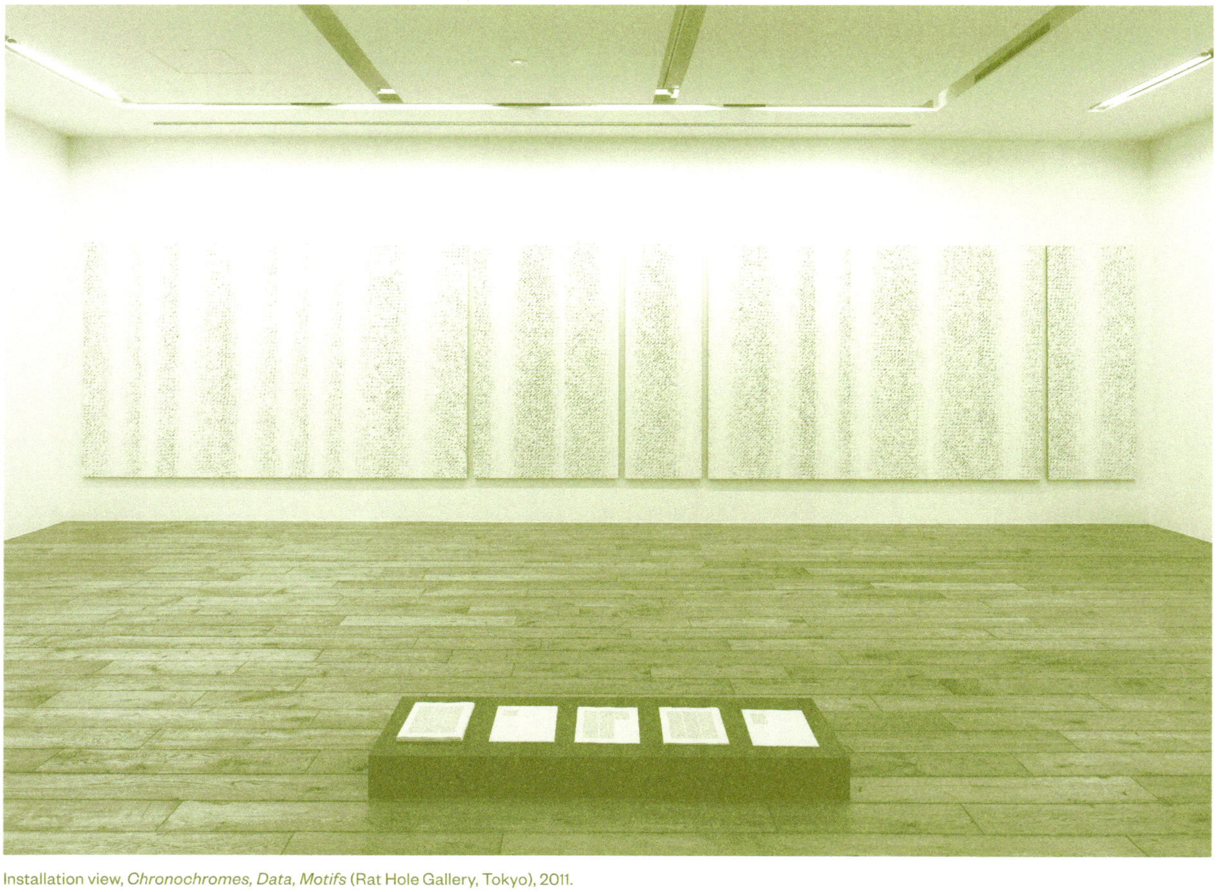

Installation view, *Chronochromes, Data, Motifs* (Rat Hole Gallery, Tokyo), 2011.

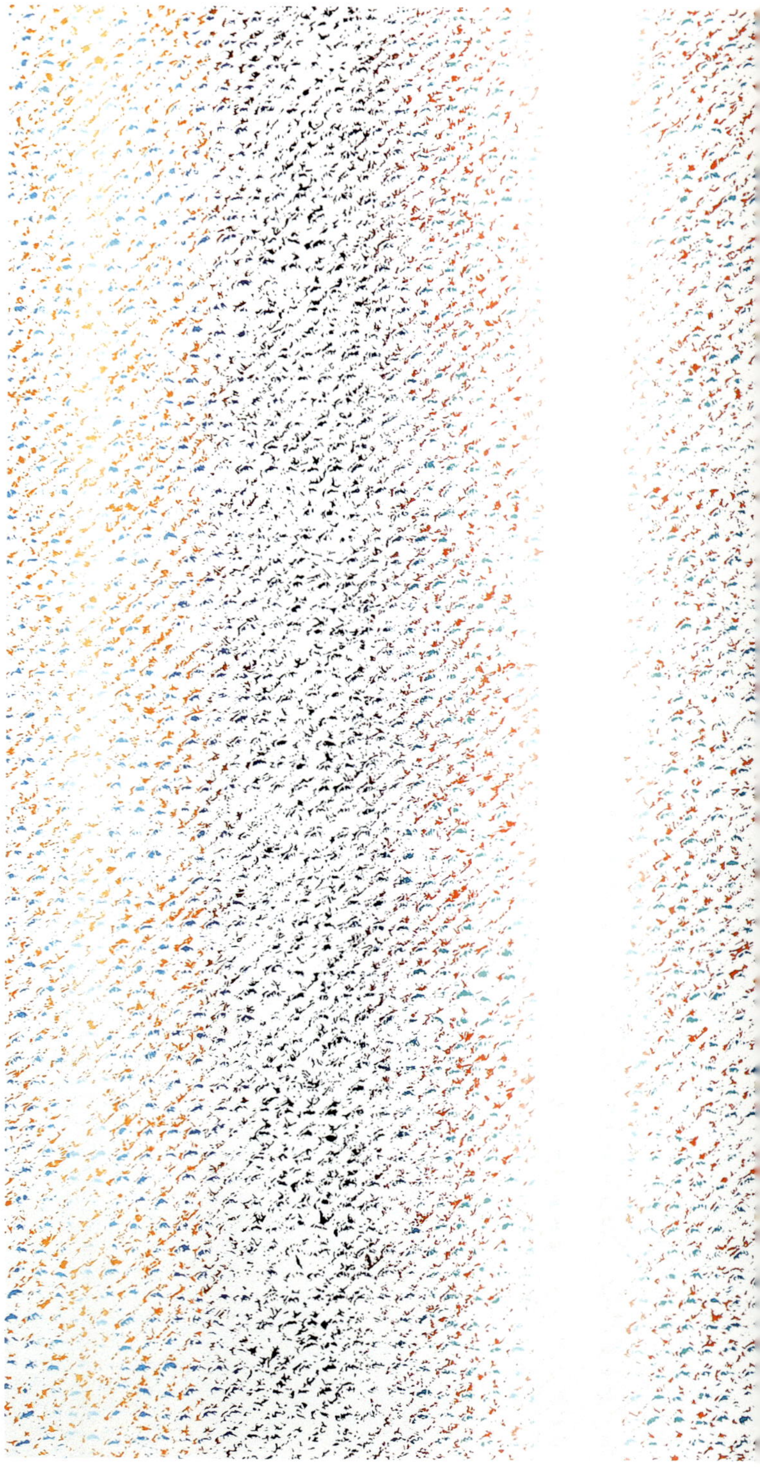

Chronochrome sets 1–4
2010, 75 × 384 in.

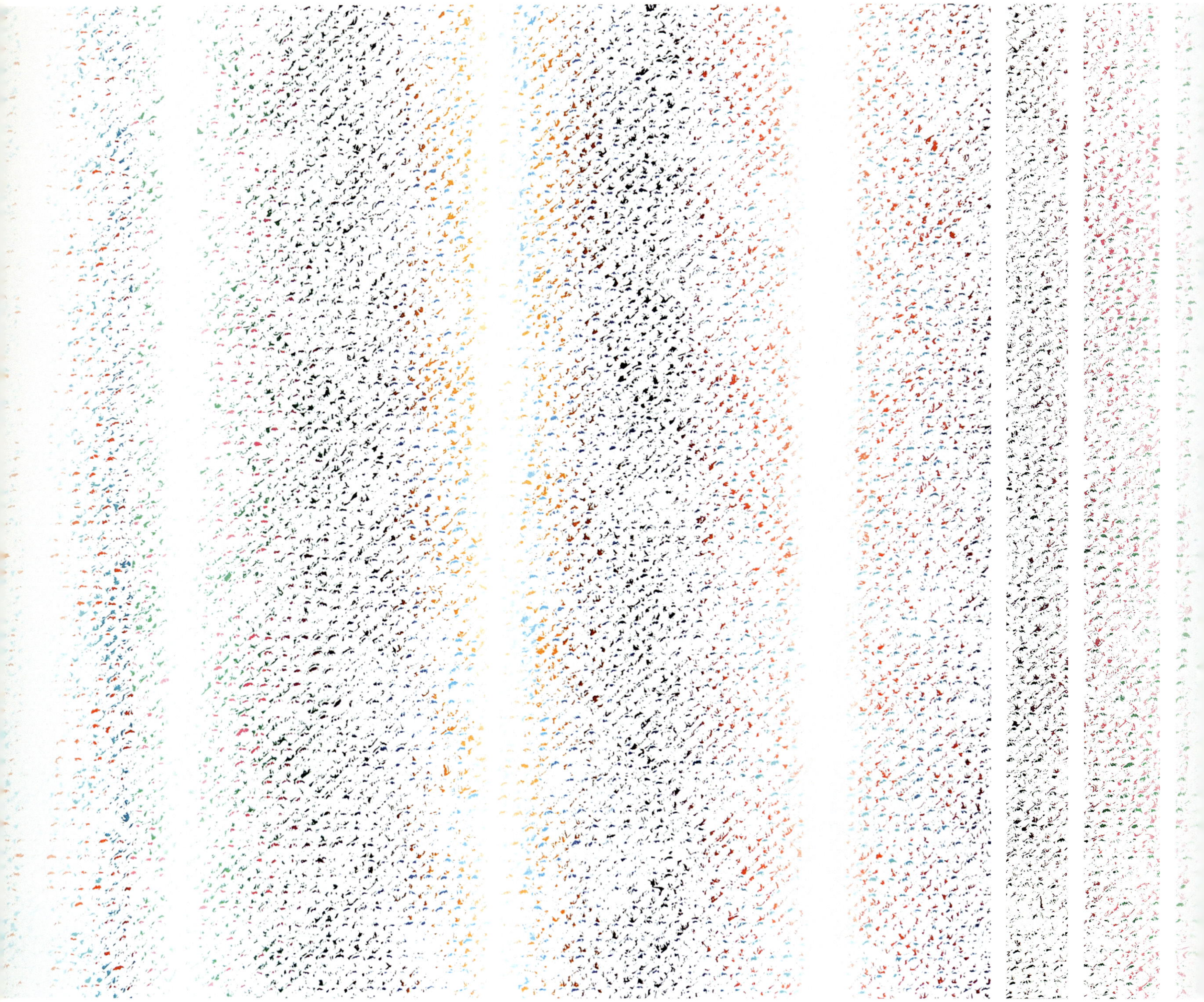

Chronochrome sets 5–8
2010, 75 × 418 in.

Chronochrome sets 9–11
2011, 75 × 384 in.

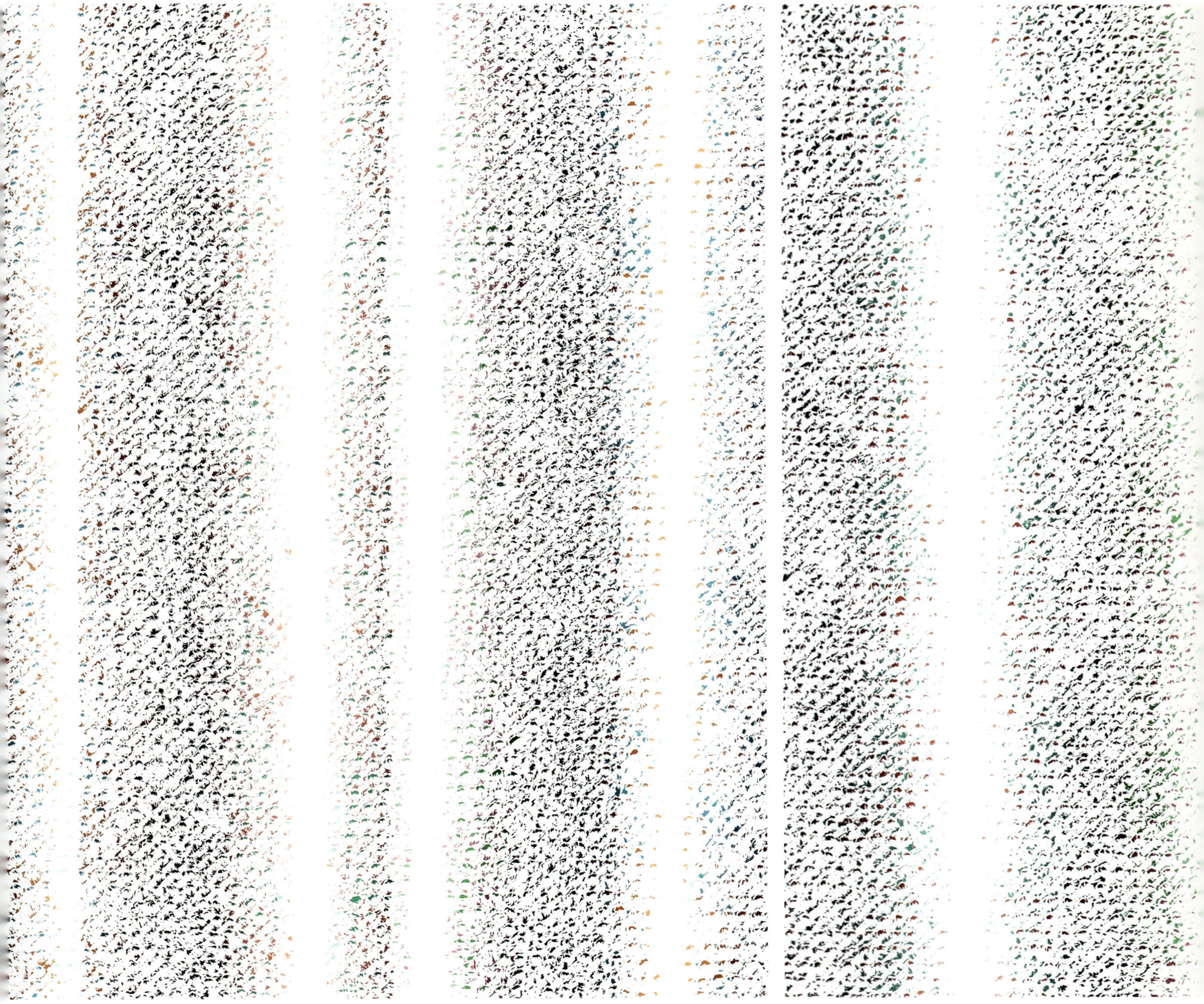

Chronochrome sets 12–14
2011, 75 × 352 in.

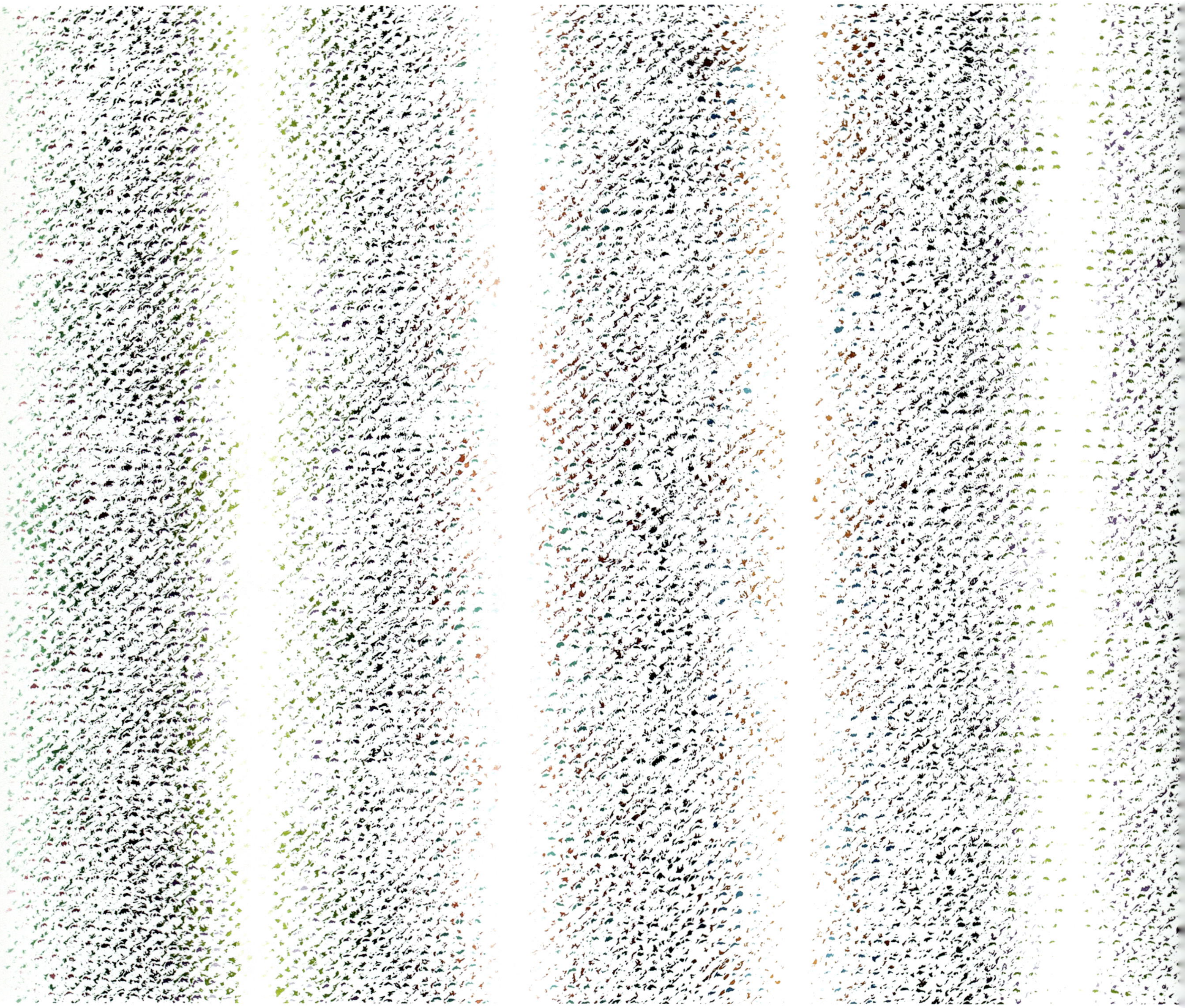

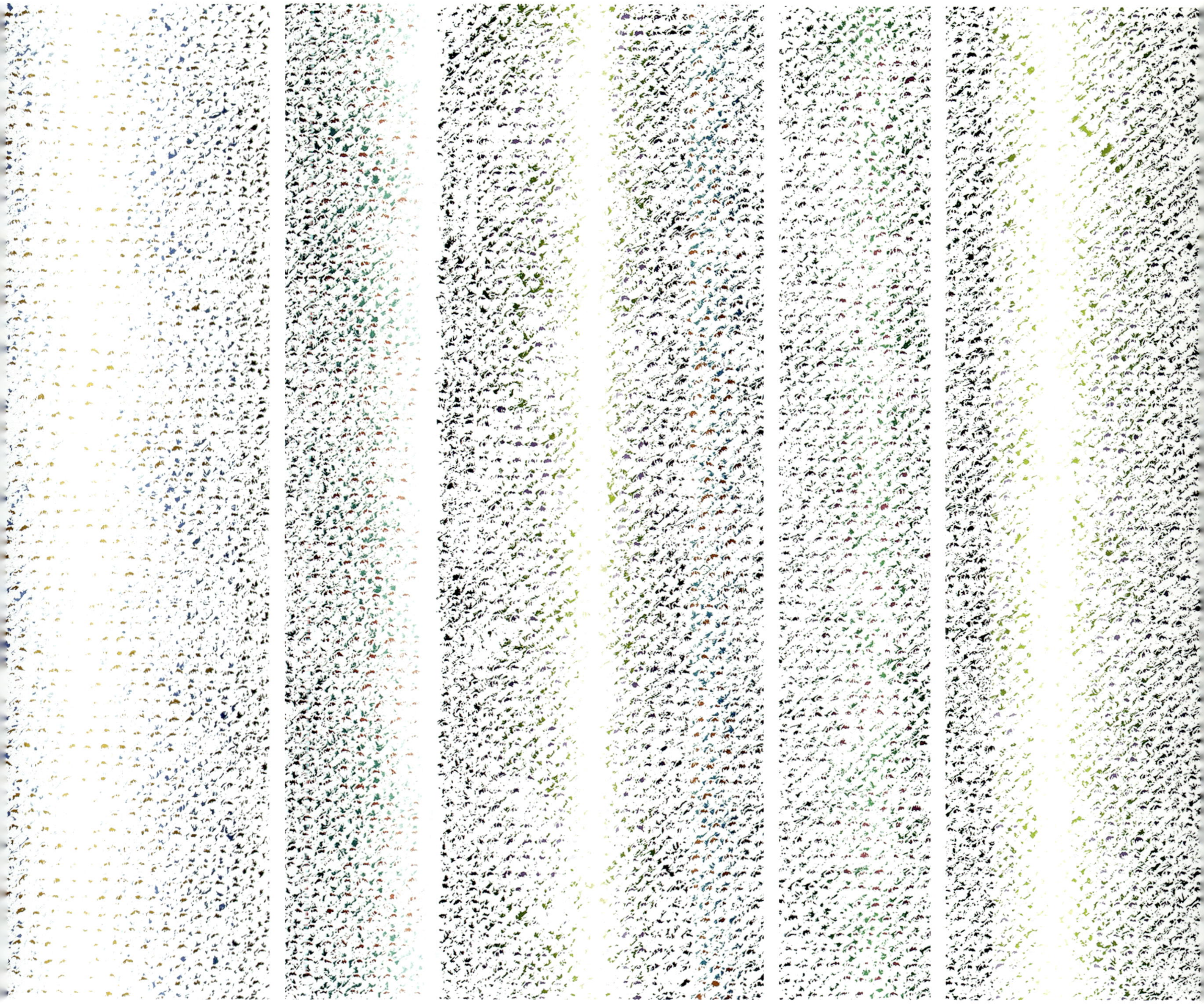

XNXVXRSXTX' DXGLX STXDX DX NXPXLX

FXDXRXCX II

FXCXLTX' DX LXTTXRX X FXLXSXFXA

CXRSX DX LRRRXX XN LXTTXRX MRDMRNR

TXSX DX LRRRXX

XN

STXRXX DMLL'XRTX CRNTXMPXRMNXX

"GXGLXXLMX RRRHRSSMM

X XL FXTXRXSMX NXPRLXTXNX"

Rrlrtrrr

Ch.mx Prxf.ssx

Mmrmmntmnxxtx Pxcxnx

Cxndxdxtx

Gxxrgxx Sxlzxnx

Mrtr. 01/1111

X.X. 2010-2011

From Wikipedia, the free encyclopedia

In colorimetry, the **Munsell color system** is a color space that specifies colors based on three color dimensions: hue, value (lightness), and chroma (color purity or colorfulness). It was created by Professor Albert H. Munsell in the first decade of the 20th century and adopted by the USDA as the official color system for soil research in the 1930's.

Several earlier color order systems had placed colors into a three dimensional color solid of one form or another, but Munsell was the first to separate hue, value, and chroma into perceptually uniform and independent dimensions, and was the first to systematically illustrate the colors in three dimensional space.[1] Munsell's system, and particularly the later renotations, is based on rigorous measurements of human subjects' visual responses to color, putting it on a firm experimental scientific basis. Because of this basis in human visual perception, Munsell's system has outlasted its contemporary color models, and though it has been superseded for some uses by models ... today.[2]

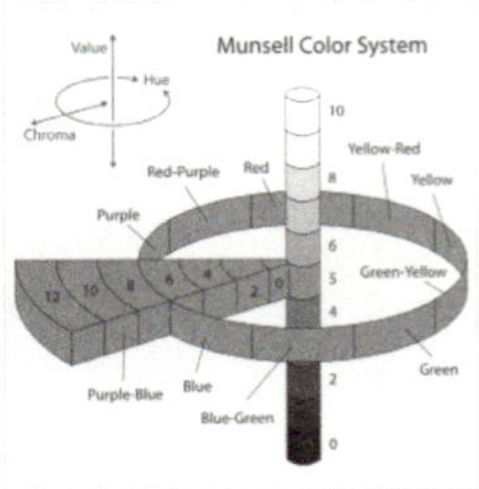

The Munsell color system, showing: a circle of hues at value 5 chroma 6; the neutral values from 0 to 10; and the chromas of purple-blue (5PB) at value 5.

The system consists of three independent dimensions which can be represented cylindrically in three dimensions as an irregular color solid: *hue*, measured by degrees around horizontal circles; *chroma*, measured radially outward from the neutral (gray) vertical axis; and *value*, measured vertically from 0 (black) to 10 (white). Munsell determined the spacing of colors along these dimensions by taking measurements of human visual responses. In each dimension, Munsell colors are as close to perceptually uniform as he could make them, which makes the resulting shape quite irregular. As Munsell explains:

> Desire to fit a chosen contour, such as the pyramid, cone, cylinder or cube, coupled with a lack of proper tests, has led to many distorted statements of color relations, and it becomes evident, when physical measurement of pigment values and chromas is ... contour will serve.
>
> —Al...

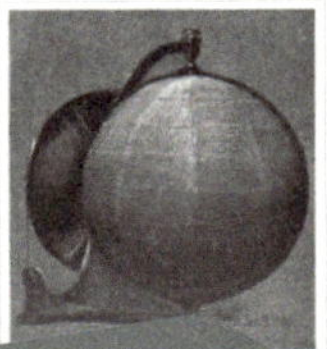

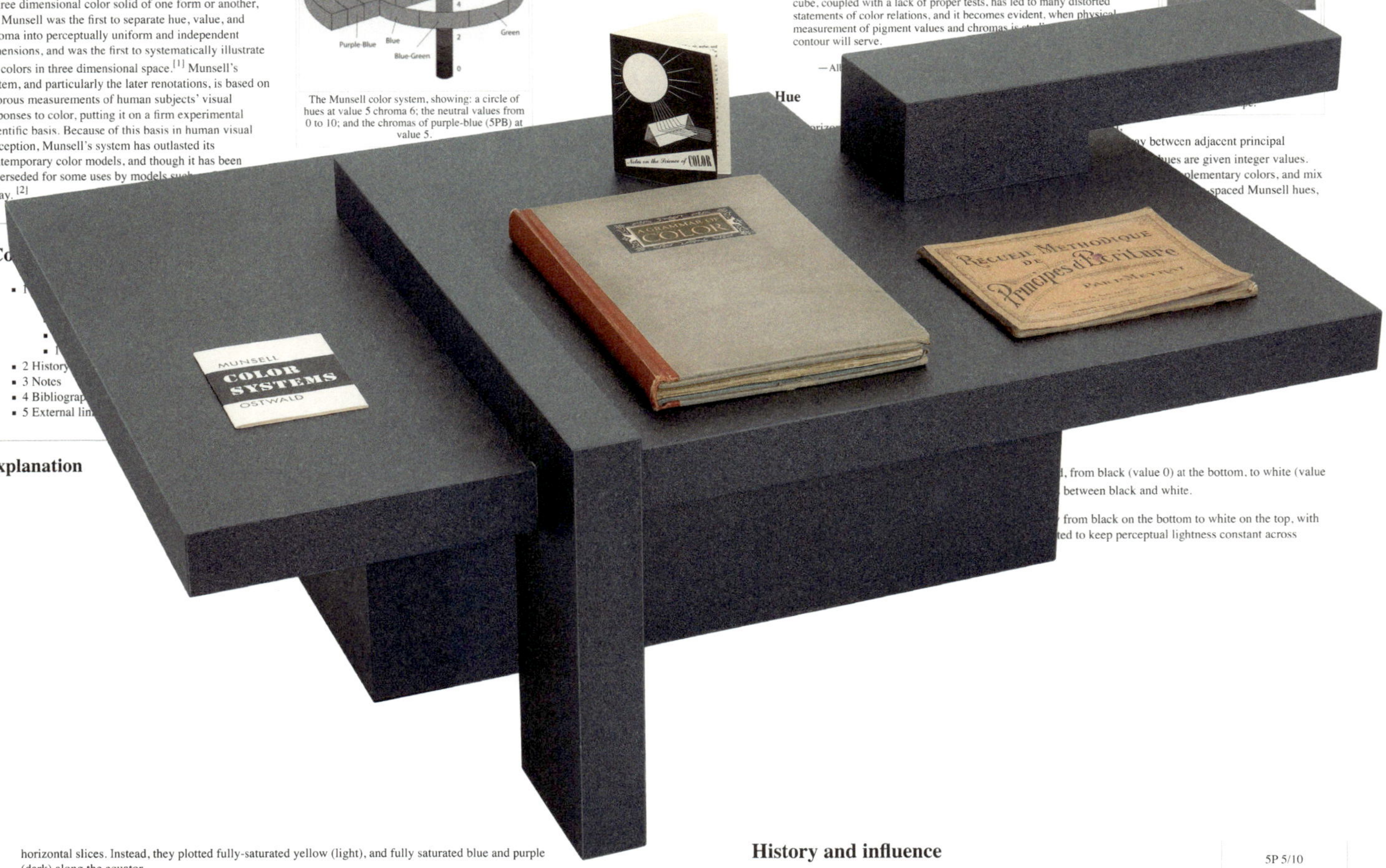

Co...

- 2 History...
- 3 Notes
- 4 Bibliograp...
- 5 External lin...

Explanation

Hue

...ay between adjacent principal ... ues are given integer values. ... plementary colors, and mix ... spaced Munsell hues,

..., from black (value 0) at the bottom, to white (value ... between black and white.

... from black on the bottom to white on the top, with ... ted to keep perceptual lightness constant across

horizontal slices. Instead, they plotted fully-saturated yellow (light), and fully saturated blue and purple (dark) along the equator.

Chroma

Chroma, measured radially from the center of each slice, represents the "purity" of a color, with lower chroma being less pure (more washed out, as in pastels).[6] Note that there is no intrinsic upper limit to chroma. Different areas of the color space have different maximal chroma coordinates. For instance light yellow colors have considerably more potential chroma than light purples, due to the nature of the eye and the physics of color stimuli. This led to a wide range of possible chroma levels—up to the high 30s for some hue–value combinations (though it is difficult or impossible to make physical objects in colors of such high chromas, and they cannot be reproduced on current computer displays). Vivid soil colors are in the range of approximately 8.

Munsell *value* (vertical) and *chroma* (horizontal); hue 5Y and 5PB

... 4 2 0 2 4 6 8 10 12

Note that the *Munsell Book of Color* contains more color samples than this chart for both 5PB and 5Y (particularly ... yellows, up to 5Y ... they are not

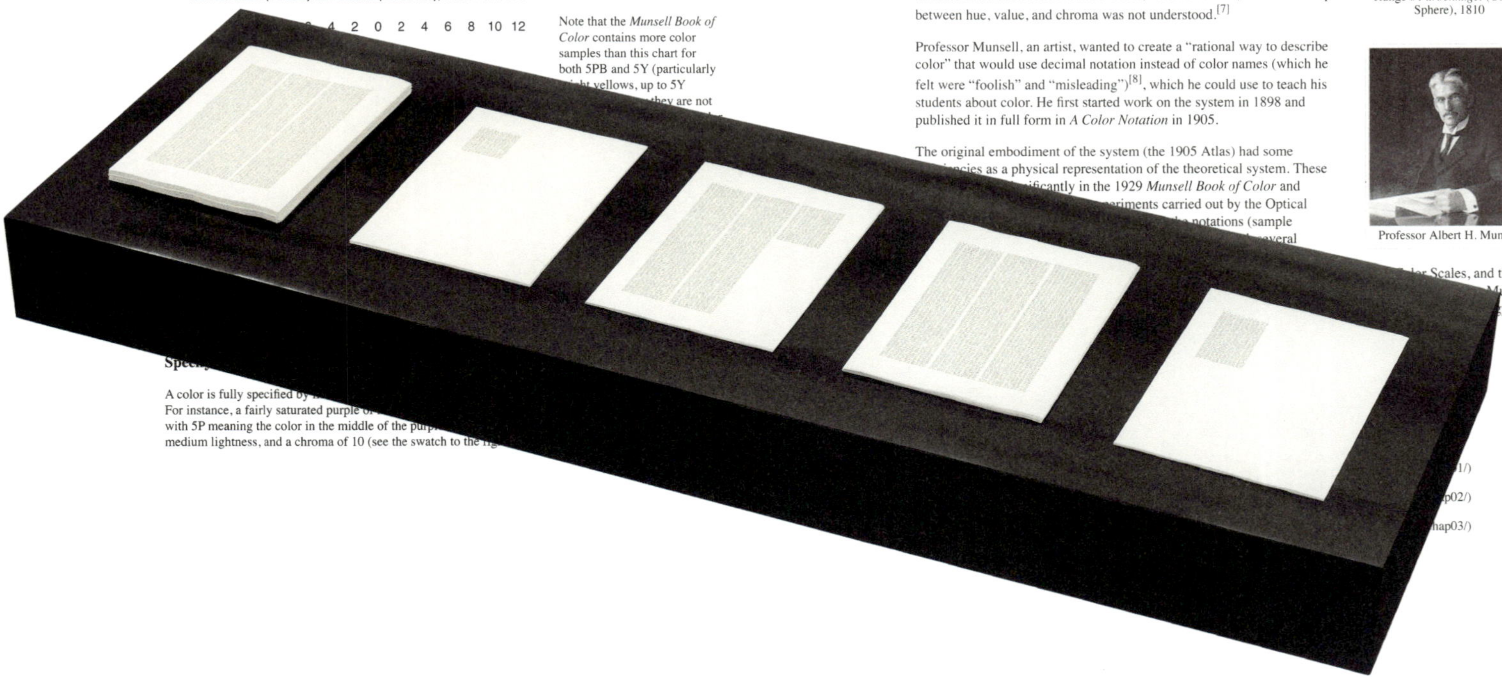

Spec...

A color is fully specified by ... For instance, a fairly saturated purple ... with 5P meaning the color in the middle of the purp... medium lightness, and a chroma of 10 (see the swatch to the rig...

History and influence

The idea of using a three-dimensional color solid to represent all colors was developed during the 18th and 19th centuries. Several different shapes for such a solid were proposed, including: a double triangular pyramid by Tobias Mayer in 1758, a single triangular pyramid by Johann Heinrich Lambert in 1772, a sphere by Philipp Otto Runge in 1810, a hemisphere by Michel Eugène Chevreul in 1839, a cone by Hermann von Helmholtz in 1860, a tilted cube by William Benson in 1868, and a slanted double cone by August Kirschmann in 1895.[7] These systems became progressively more sophisticated, with Kirschmann's even recognizing the difference in value between bright colors of different hues. But all of them remained either purely theoretical or encountered practical problems in accommodating all colors. Furthermore, none was based on any rigorous scientific measurement of human vision; before Munsell, the relationship between hue, value, and chroma was not understood.[7]

Professor Munsell, an artist, wanted to create a "rational way to describe color" that would use decimal notation instead of color names (which he felt were "foolish" and "misleading")[8], which he could use to teach his students about color. He first started work on the system in 1898 and published it in full form in *A Color Notation* in 1905.

The original embodiment of the system (the 1905 Atlas) had some ...ncies as a physical representation of the theoretical system. These ...ificantly in the 1929 *Munsell Book of Color* and ...periments carried out by the Optical ... notations (sample ... several

...lor Scales, and the ...unsell ...y, the

5P 5/10

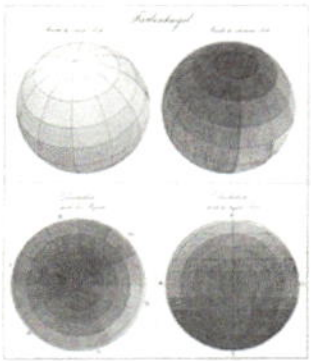

Runge's *Farbenkugel* (Colour Sphere), 1810

Professor Albert H. Munsell

...1/)

...ap02/)

...hap03/)

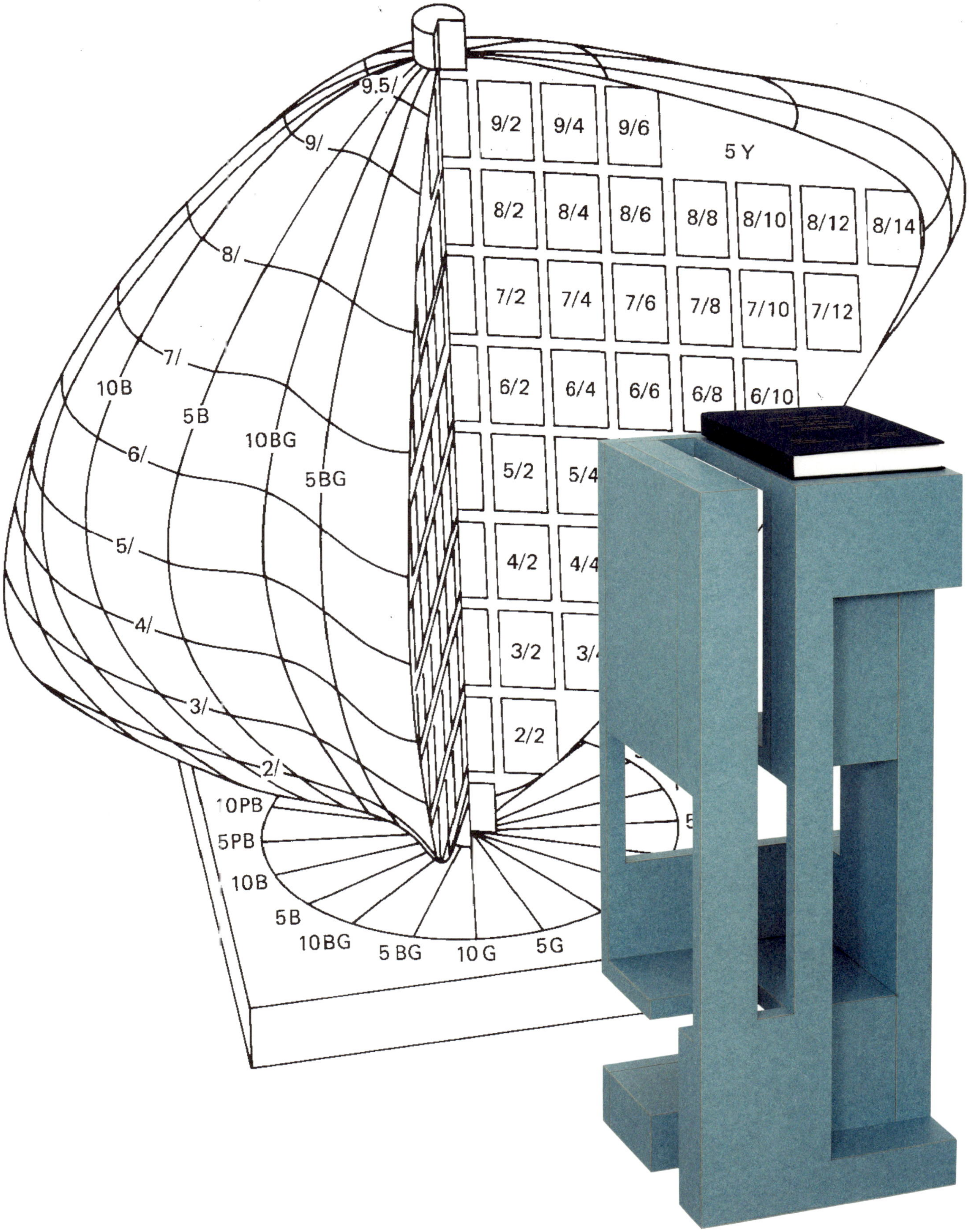
9.5/
9/
8/
7/
6/
5/
4/
3/
2/
10B
5B
10BG
5BG
9/2
9/4
9/6
5 Y
8/2
8/4
8/6
8/8
8/10
8/12
8/14
7/2
7/4
7/6
7/8
7/10
7/12
6/2
6/4
6/6
6/8
6/10
5/2
4/2
3/2
2/2
10PB
5PB
10B
5B
10BG
5 BG
10 G
5G

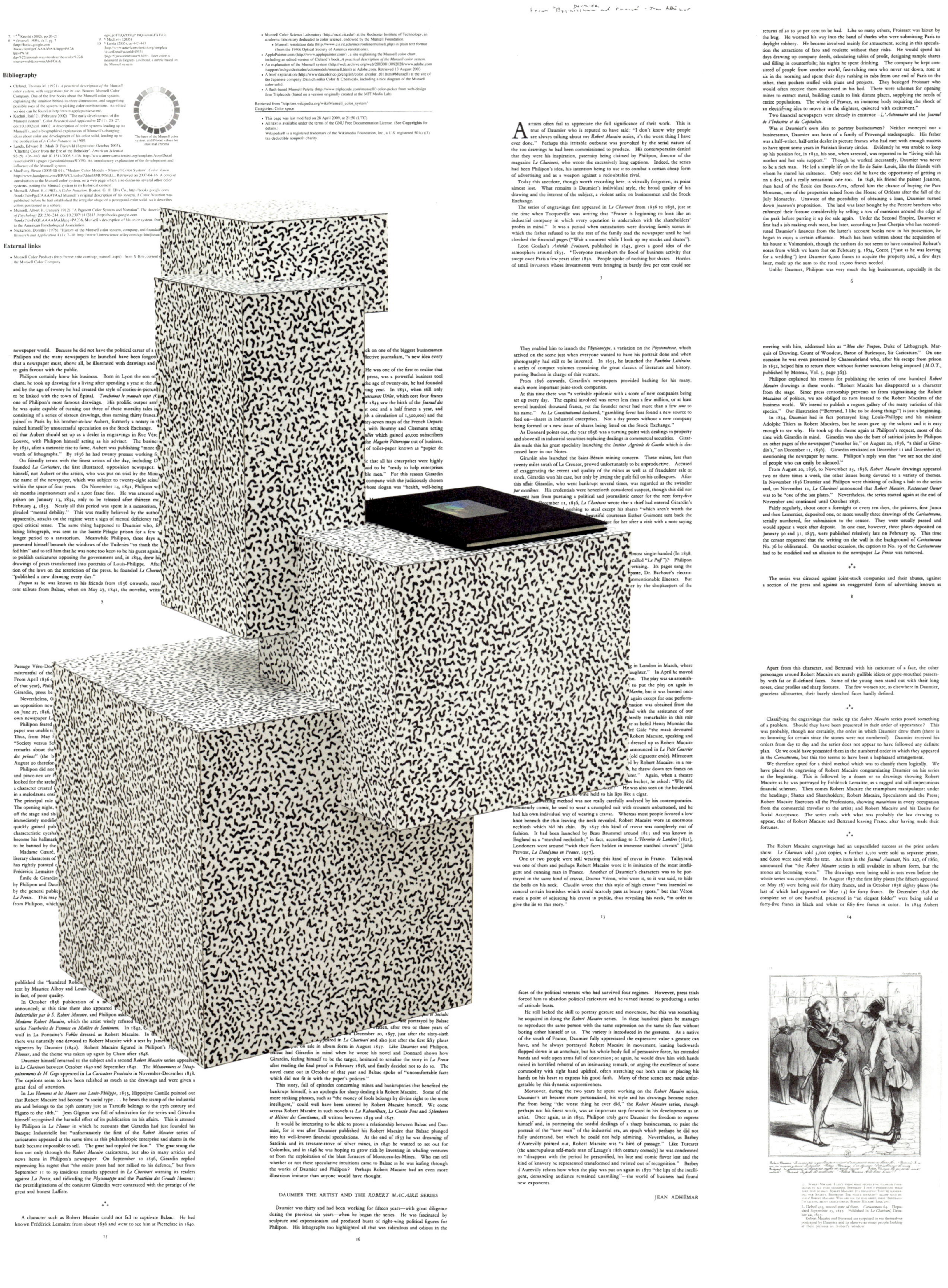
Bibliography
External links
DAUMIER THE ARTIST AND THE ROBERT MACAIRE SERIES
JEAN ADHÉMAR

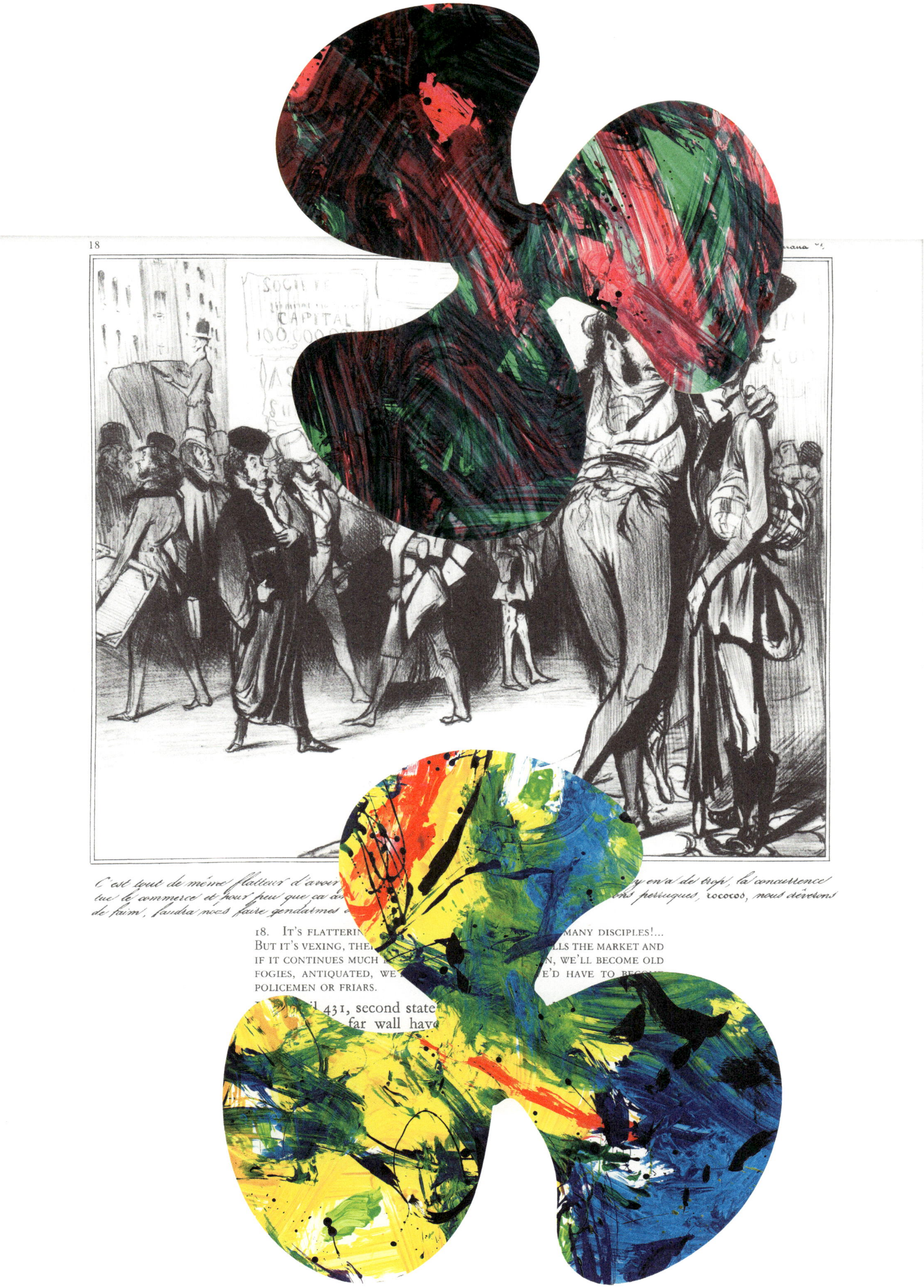
18
SOCIÉTÉ
CAPITAL
100.000
C'est tout de même flatteur d'avoir
y en a de trop, la concurrence
tue le commerce et pour peu que ca co
ons perruques, rococos, nous dèverons
de faim, faudra nous faire gendarmes
18. IT'S FLATTERIN
MANY DISCIPLES!...
BUT IT'S VEXING, THE
LLS THE MARKET AND
IF IT CONTINUES MUCH
N, WE'LL BECOME OLD
FOGIES, ANTIQUATED, WE
E'D HAVE TO
POLICEMEN OR FRIARS.
il 431, second state
far wall have

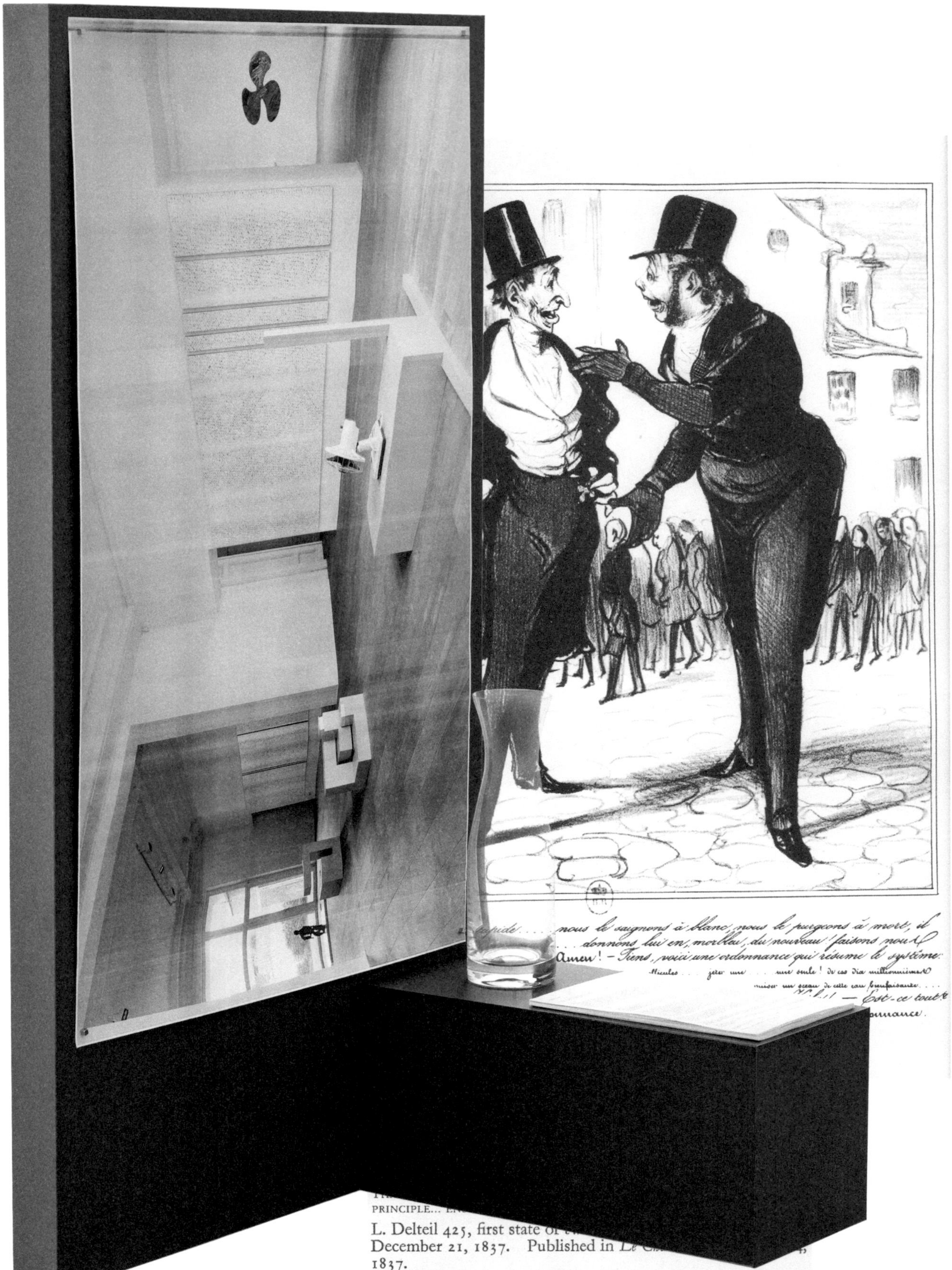

PRINCIPLE...

L. Delteil 425, first state o...
December 21, 1837. Published in *Le C*...
1837.

Doctor Hahnemann, the creator of homeopathy, established himself in Paris in 1834 in order to "hasten the propagation of the doctrine throughout the universe"; his clients kept him busy twelve hours a day. His pupil, Doctor S. des Guidi, practised successfully in Lyons, and another pupil named Bigel received the Legion of Honour in 1836, "the king in his wisdom honouring homeopathy in his person."

71

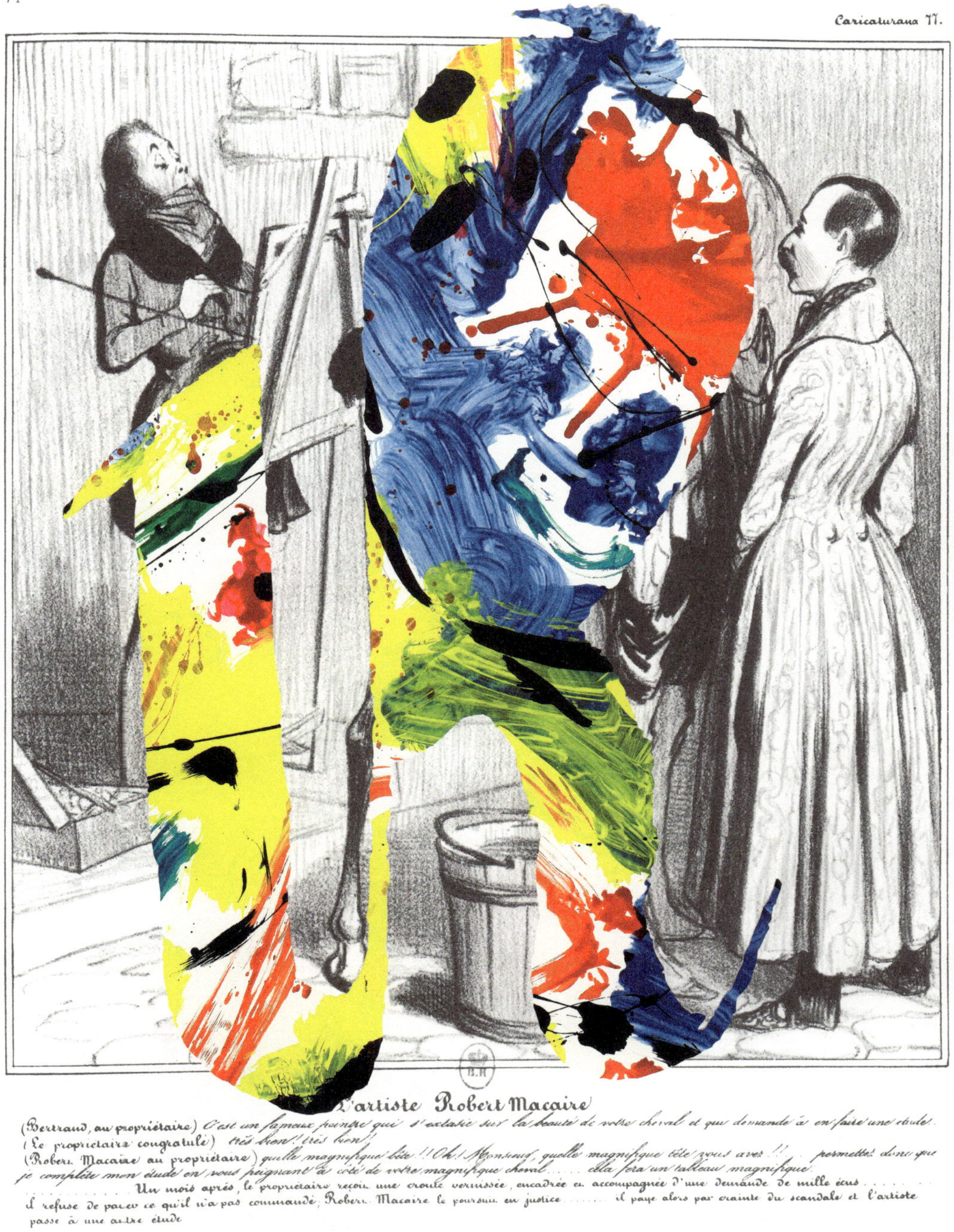

71. Robert Macaire, artist. (Bertrand, to the owner) He's a famous painter who's enraptured with the beauty of your horse and would like to do a study... (The delighted owner) Excellent! Excellent!! (Robert Macaire to the owner) What a splendid animal!!... Oh, Sir! You've a splendid profile!!... Please let me complete my study by painting you alongside your splendid horse... that'll make a splendid picture... (The outcome) A month later the owner receives a badly painted picture drowned in glazing, framed and accompanied by a bill for a thousand crowns... he refuse to pay for what he has not commissioned... Robert Macaire prosecutes... he then pays through fear of scandal and the artist goes on to another study.

L. Delteil 432, first state of two. *Caricaturana* 77. Deposited March 13, 1838. Published in *Le Charivari,* March 26, 1838.

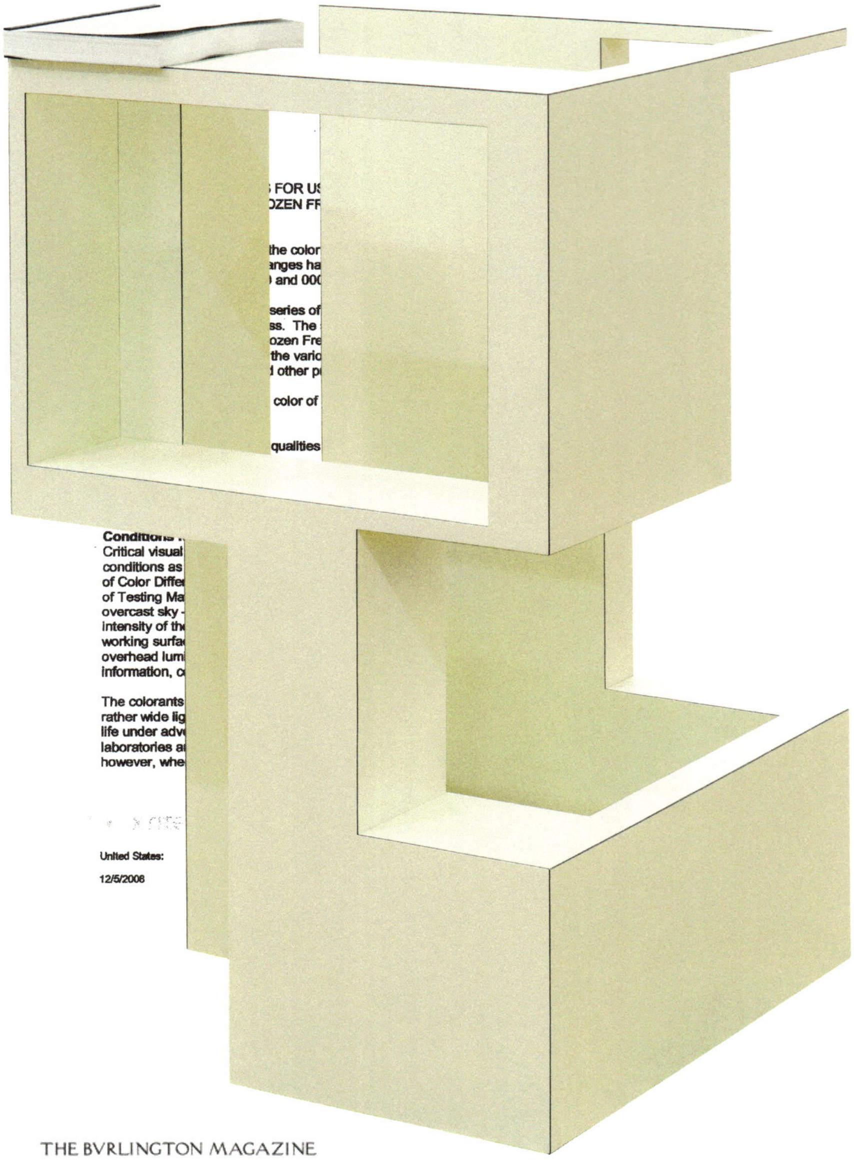

Making the Color Evaluation

1) Classify the product where it best fits in the series of fry colors.

No. 000 in the series has no shading of brown due to the frying process. A strip matching the No. 000 standard would be designated as being USDA No. 000 color.

Colors 00,1,2,3, and 4 show colors of increasing intensity.

2) Designate the colors of a unit in terms of the color standard.

A unit exactly matching the color a standard would be designated as the color. For example, "USDA No.3 Color."

A sample that does not match exactly might be designated as "Darker than No. 3., but not as dark as No. 4" or in any appropriate manner.

They are packaged in a set consisting of five identical reproductions.

Additional copies of the United States Standards for Grades of processing fruits and vegetables are available upon request from:

Chief, Processed Products Branch
Fruit and Vegetable Division, AMS
U.S. Department of Agriculture
P.O. Box 96456, Rm. 0709, So. Bldg.
Washington, D.C. 20090-6456
Tel. 202-447-6247

United States: 4300 44th Grand Rapids MI 49512 Tel:800-803-7664 www.xrite.com

12/5/2008

United States:

12/5/2008

THE BVRLINGTON MAGAZINE

History of Robert Macaire and Daumier's Place in It
Author(s): Stanislav Osiakovski
Source: *The Burlington Magazine*, Vol. 100, No. 668 (Nov., 1958), pp. 388-393
Published by: The Burlington Magazine Publications, Ltd.
Stable URL: http://www.jstor.org/stable/872520
Accessed: 14/12/2008 15:51

THE USE OF ENGRAVINGS IN THE DESIGN OF RENAISSANCE WINDOWS

No. of window	*Subject*	*Presumed designer*	*Engravings: Probable source of main design*	*Probable source of part*	*Significantly related*	*Remarks*	*Authority*
XVI 4	Appearance to Virgin	Vellert			AD B.46		Scharf
XVII 1	Reuben seeks Joseph in the pit	Vellert	BP 30a				
[illegible]	[illegible] Maries at the sepulchre	Vellert		Vellert B.6		Magdalene taken from Woman of Samaria	
	[illegible]re	Vellert		L. van L. Dutuit 176 Vellert B.6		Spade and left hand of Christ Magdalene's clothes (Magdalene's head and hand from pseudo-Raphael tapestry design)	
					L. van L. B.78	Reminiscences only	
	St T[illegible]					Sirens in cusping	
	La[illegible]					[illegible]postle in left foreground: [illegible]used if at all [illegible]ground	Beets

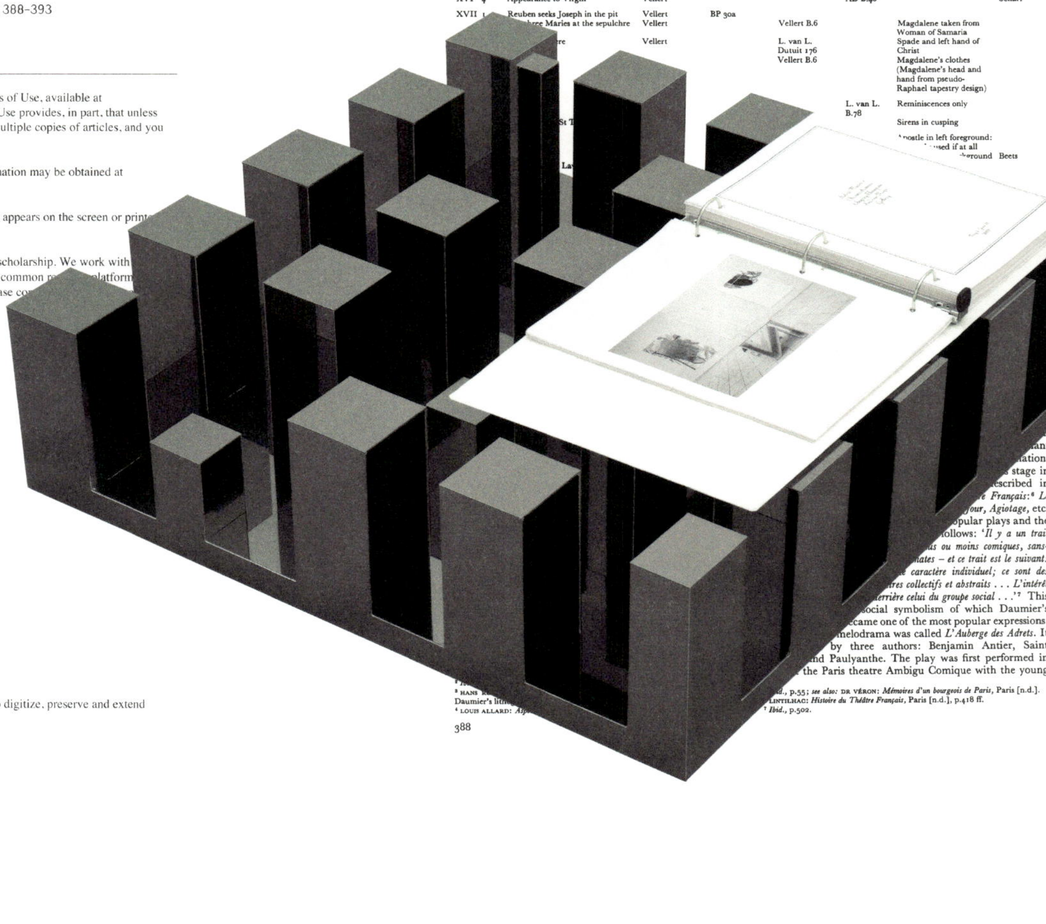

ant ation. stage in escribed in *Français:*[6] *Le* *jour, Agiotage*, etc. opular plays and the follows: '*Il y a un trait* *us ou moins comiques, sans-* *nates – et ce trait est le suivant:* *caractère individuel; ce sont des* *res collectifs et abstraits . . . L'intérêt* *derrière celui du groupe social . . .*'[7] This social symbolism of which Daumier's came one of the most popular expressions. melodrama was called *L'Auberge des Adrets*. It by three authors: Benjamin Antier, Saint nd Paulyanthe. The play was first performed in the Paris theatre Ambigu Comique with the young

[3] HANS [illegible] Daumier's lith[illegible]
[4] LOUIS ALLARD: *Asp*[illegible]
[5] *Ibid.*, p.55; *see also:* DR VÉRON: *Mémoires d'un bourgeois de Paris*, Paris [n.d.].
[6] LINTILHAC: *Histoire du Théâtre Français*, Paris [n.d.], p.418 ff.
[7] *Ibid.*, p.502.

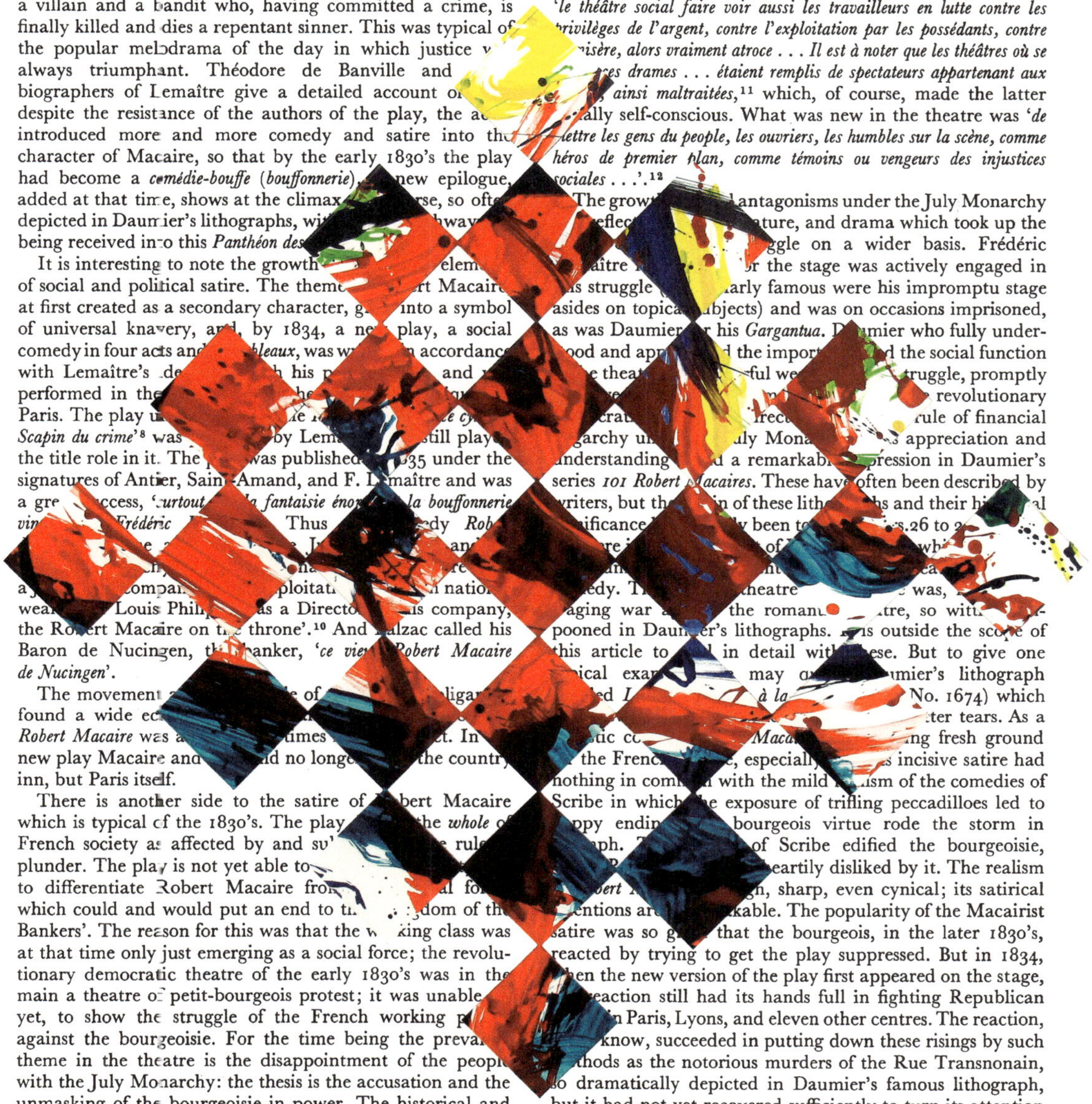

actor Frédéric Lemaître playing the stilted colourless part of a villain and a bandit who, having committed a crime, is finally killed and dies a repentant sinner. This was typical of the popular melodrama of the day in which justice w always triumphant. Théodore de Banville and biographers of Lemaître give a detailed account o despite the resistance of the authors of the play, the a introduced more and more comedy and satire into th character of Macaire, so that by the early 1830's the play had become a *comédie-bouffe* (*bouffonnerie*), new epilogue, added at that time, shows at the climax se, so ofte depicted in Daumier's lithographs, wi wa being received into this *Panthéon des*

It is interesting to note the growth elem of social and political satire. The theme rt Macair at first created as a secondary character, g into a symbol of universal knavery, and, by 1834, a ne play, a social comedy in four acts and *bleaux*, was w accordance with Lemaître's de h his p and performed in the he Paris. The play u e *e cy* *Scapin du crime*'[8] was by Lem still play the title role in it. The was published 35 under the signatures of Antier, Saint-Amand, and F. Lemaître and was a gre ccess, '*surtout la fantaisie énor la bouffonnerie vi Frédéric* Thus dy *Rob* J an a compa ploitat natio wea Louis Phil as a Directo is company, the Robert Macaire on the throne'.[10] And alzac called his Baron de Nucingen, the banker, '*ce vie Robert Macaire de Nucingen*'.

The movement of ligar found a wide ec *Robert Macaire* was imes t. In new play Macaire and d no longe the country inn, but Paris itself.

There is another side to the satire of bert Macaire which is typical of the 1830's. The play he *whole* French society as affected by and su rul plunder. The play is not yet able to to differentiate Robert Macaire fro fo which could and would put an end to t dom of th Bankers'. The reason for this was that the w king class was at that time only just emerging as a social force; the revolutionary democratic theatre of the early 1830's was in the main a theatre of petit-bourgeois protest; it was unable yet, to show the struggle of the French working p against the bourgeoisie. For the time being the preva theme in the theatre is the disappointment of the peopl with the July Monarchy: the thesis is the accusation and the unmasking of the bourgeoisie in power. The historical and social value of *Robert Macaire* consisted in the accumulation of these critical observations and generalizations which grew into a dramatic indictment through the medium of the theatre of the ruling financial oligarchy and ultimately created the social concept of 'macairism'.

The tide of the subsequent revolutionary movement made '*le théâtre social faire voir aussi les travailleurs en lutte contre les privilèges de l'argent, contre l'exploitation par les possédants, contre misère, alors vraiment atroce . . . Il est à noter que les théâtres où se es drames . . . étaient remplis de spectateurs appartenant aux ainsi maltraitées*,[11] which, of course, made the latter ally self-conscious. What was new in the theatre was '*de ettre les gens du people, les ouvriers, les humbles sur la scène, comme héros de premier plan, comme témoins ou vengeurs des injustices sociales* . . .'.[12]

The grow antagonisms under the July Monarchy eflec ture, and drama which took up the ggle on a wider basis. Frédéric aître r the stage was actively engaged in s struggle arly famous were his impromptu stage asides on topica bjects) and was on occasions imprisoned, as was Daumier r his *Gargantua*. mier who fully under- ood and ap d the impor d the social function e thea ful we truggle, promptly revolutionary cra rec rule of financial garchy u ly Mona s appreciation and understanding a remarkab pression in Daumier's series *101 Robert Macaires*. These have often been described by writers, but th n of these lith hs and their h al ificance been t s.26 to re of wh ca edy. T heatre was, aging war the roman tre, so wit pooned in Daumier's lithographs. is outside the scope of this article to in detail wit ese. But to give one ical exa may umier's lithograph d *L à la* No. 1674) which ter tears. As a tic c *Maca* ng fresh ground the Frenc , especial s incisive satire had nothing in com with the mild ism of the comedies of Scribe in which e exposure of trifling peccadilloes led to ppy endin bourgeois virtue rode the storm in ph. of Scribe edified the bourgeoisie, eartily disliked by it. The realism *bert* n, sharp, even cynical; its satirical entions ar kable. The popularity of the Macairist satire was so g that the bourgeois, in the later 1830's, reacted by trying to get the play suppressed. But in 1834, hen the new version of the play first appeared on the stage, eaction still had its hands full in fighting Republican n Paris, Lyons, and eleven other centres. The reaction, know, succeeded in putting down these risings by such thods as the notorious murders of the Rue Transnonain, o dramatically depicted in Daumier's famous lithograph, but it had not yet recovered sufficiently to turn its attention to the Macairist exposure. This was the reason why *Robert Macaire*, the play, as well as Daumier's political lithographs in *La Caricature* were still allowed to appear in 1834 and went on appearing until September 1835. But when the bourgeois reaction gathered sufficient force, it went over in that month to the offensive and the 'September laws' of 1835 were

[8] *Ibid.*, p.413.
[9] *Ibid.*, p.413.
[10] MARX and ENGELS: *Collected Works*, Moscow [1921], VIII, p.3 – Marx.

[11] PICARD, *op. cit.*, p.251.
[12] *Ibid.*, p.251.

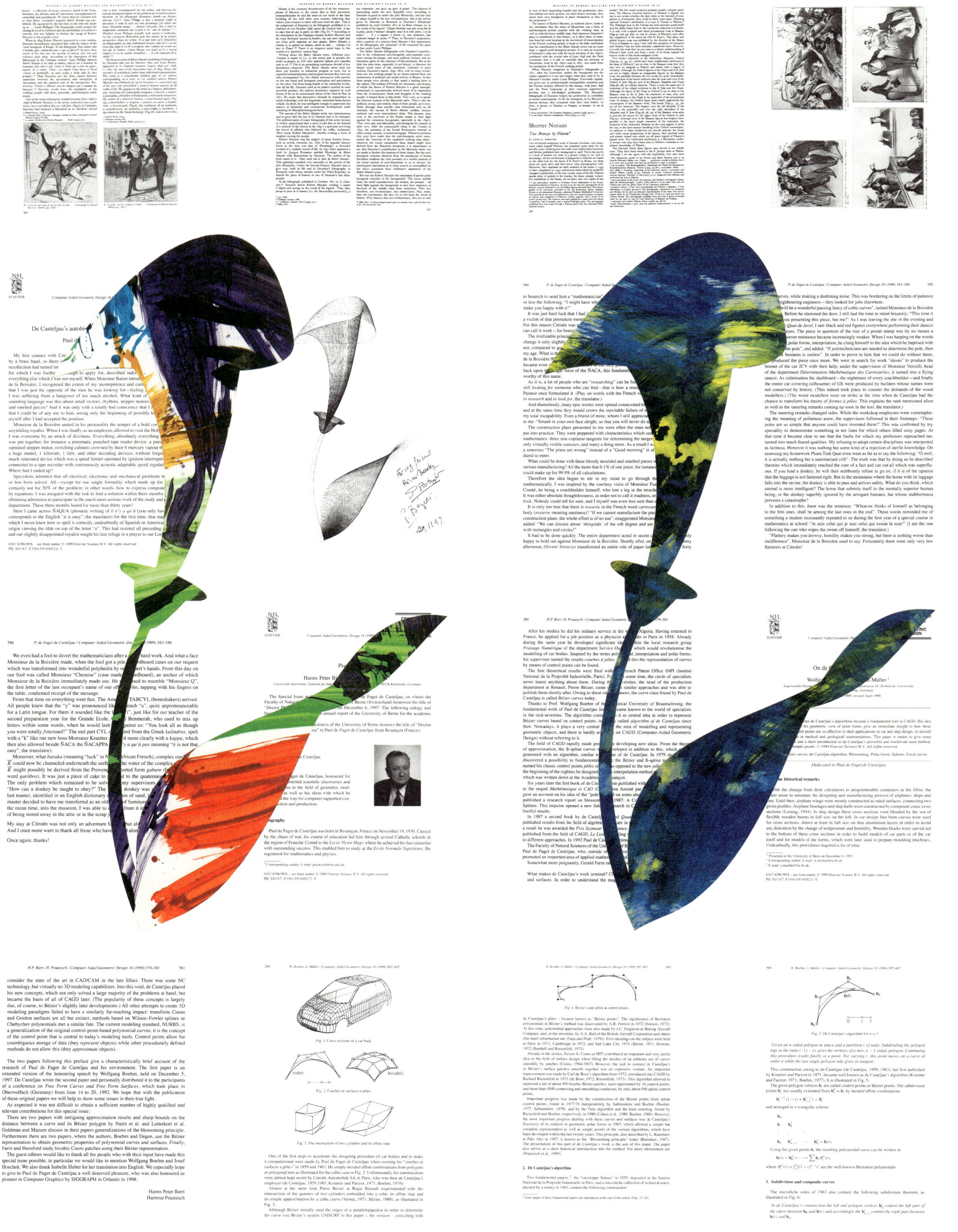
Shorter Notices
De Casteljau's autobi
Once again, thanks!
Hanns Peter Bieri
Hartmut Prautzsch

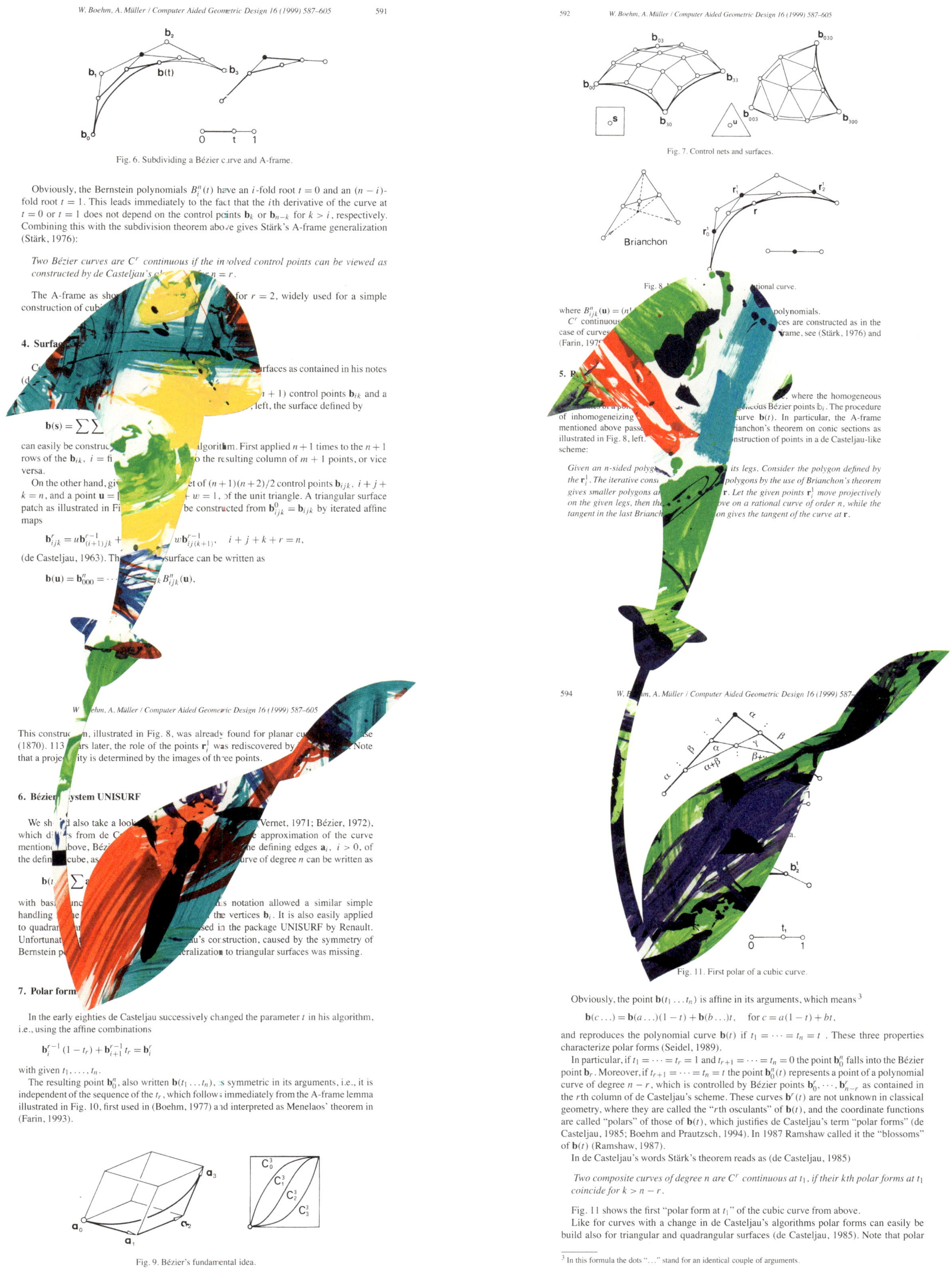

Fig. 6. Subdividing a Bézier curve and A-frame.

Obviously, the Bernstein polynomials $B_i^n(t)$ have an i-fold root $t = 0$ and an $(n - i)$-fold root $t = 1$. This leads immediately to the fact that the ith derivative of the curve at $t = 0$ or $t = 1$ does not depend on the control points $\mathbf{b}_k$ or $\mathbf{b}_{n-k}$ for $k > i$, respectively. Combining this with the subdivision theorem above gives Stärk's A-frame generalization (Stärk, 1976):

Two Bézier curves are C^r continuous if the involved control points can be viewed as constructed by de Casteljau's al… … $n = r$.

The A-frame as sho… …for $r = 2$, widely used for a simple construction of cub…

4. Surfa…

C… …rfaces as contained in his notes (d…

…$+ 1)$ control points $\mathbf{b}_{ik}$ and a …, left, the surface defined by

$\mathbf{b}(\mathbf{s}) = \sum\sum$ …

can easily be construc… …lgorithm. First applied $n+1$ times to the $n+1$ rows of the $\mathbf{b}_{ik}$, $i =$ fi… …o the resulting column of $m + 1$ points, or vice versa.

On the other hand, gi… …et of $(n+1)(n+2)/2$ control points $\mathbf{b}_{ijk}$, $i+j+k=n$, and a point $\mathbf{u} =$ … $+ w = 1$, of the unit triangle. A triangular surface patch as illustrated in Fi… …be constructed from $\mathbf{b}_{ijk}^0 = \mathbf{b}_{ijk}$ by iterated affine maps

$$\mathbf{b}_{ijk}^r = u\mathbf{b}_{(i+1)jk}^{r-1} + \ldots w\mathbf{b}_{ij(k+1)}^{r-1}, \quad i+j+k+r=n,$$

(de Casteljau, 1963). Th… …surface can be written as

$$\mathbf{b}(\mathbf{u}) = \mathbf{b}_{000}^n = \cdots \; {}_k B_{ijk}^n(\mathbf{u}),$$

Fig. 7. Control nets and surfaces.

Fig. 8. … …tional curve.

where $B_{ijk}^n(\mathbf{u}) = (n!$ … …polynomials.

C^r continuous… …ces are constructed as in the case of curves… …frame, see (Stärk, 1976) and (Farin, 197…

5. R…

…, where the homogeneous … …neous Bézier points $\mathbb{b}_i$. The procedure of inhomogeneizing … curve $\mathbf{b}(t)$. In particular, the A-frame mentioned above pass… …ianchon's theorem on conic sections as illustrated in Fig. 8, left. … …nstruction of points in a de Casteljau-like scheme:

Given an n-sided polyg… …its legs. Consider the polygon defined by the $\mathbf{r}_i^1$. The iterative consi… …polygons by the use of Brianchon's theorem gives smaller polygons a… …$\mathbf{r}$. Let the given points $\mathbf{r}_i^1$ move projectively on the given legs, then th… …ove on a rational curve of order n, while the tangent in the last Brianch… …on gives the tangent of the curve at $\mathbf{r}$.

This constru…n, illustrated in Fig. 8, was already found for planar cu… …se (1870). 113 …rs later, the role of the points $\mathbf{r}_i^1$ was rediscovered by … Note that a proje…ity is determined by the images of three points.

6. Bézier… …ystem UNISURF

We sh…d also take a look… …Vernet, 1971; Bézier, 1972), which di…s from de C… …e approximation of the curve mentione… …bove, Bézi… …he defining edges $\mathbf{a}_i$, $i > 0$, of the defin… …cube, as … …urve of degree n can be written as

$\mathbf{b}(t$ … $\sum$ …

with basi… …nc… …s notation allowed a similar simple handling … …e … the vertices $\mathbf{b}_i$. It is also easily applied to quadran… …sed in the package UNISURF by Renault. Unfortunat… …u's construction, caused by the symmetry of Bernstein p… …eralization to triangular surfaces was missing.

7. Polar form…

In the early eighties de Casteljau successively changed the parameter t in his algorithm, i.e., using the affine combinations

$$\mathbf{b}_i^{r-1}(1 - t_r) + \mathbf{b}_{i+1}^{r-1} t_r = \mathbf{b}_i^r$$

with given $t_1, \ldots, t_n$.

The resulting point $\mathbf{b}_0^n$, also written $\mathbf{b}(t_1 \ldots t_n)$, is symmetric in its arguments, i.e., it is independent of the sequence of the t_r, which follows immediately from the A-frame lemma illustrated in Fig. 10, first used in (Boehm, 1977) and interpreted as Menelaos' theorem in (Farin, 1993).

Fig. 9. Bézier's fundamental idea.

Fig. 11. First polar of a cubic curve.

Obviously, the point $\mathbf{b}(t_1 \ldots t_n)$ is affine in its arguments, which means [3]

$$\mathbf{b}(c \ldots) = \mathbf{b}(a \ldots)(1 - t) + \mathbf{b}(b \ldots)t, \quad \text{for } c = a(1 - t) + bt,$$

and reproduces the polynomial curve $\mathbf{b}(t)$ if $t_1 = \cdots = t_n = t$. These three properties characterize polar forms (Seidel, 1989).

In particular, if $t_1 = \cdots = t_r = 1$ and $t_{r+1} = \cdots = t_n = 0$ the point $\mathbf{b}_0^n$ falls into the Bézier point $\mathbf{b}_r$. Moreover, if $t_{r+1} = \cdots = t_n = t$ the point $\mathbf{b}_0^n(t)$ represents a point of a polynomial curve of degree $n - r$, which is controlled by Bézier points $\mathbf{b}_0^r, \cdots, \mathbf{b}_{n-r}^r$ as contained in the rth column of de Casteljau's scheme. These curves $\mathbf{b}^r(t)$ are not unknown in classical geometry, where they are called the "rth osculants" of $\mathbf{b}(t)$, and the coordinate functions are called "polars" of those of $\mathbf{b}(t)$, which justifies de Casteljau's term "polar forms" (de Casteljau, 1985; Boehm and Prautzsch, 1994). In 1987 Ramshaw called it the "blossoms" of $\mathbf{b}(t)$ (Ramshaw, 1987).

In de Casteljau's words Stärk's theorem reads as (de Casteljau, 1985)

Two composite curves of degree n are C^r continuous at t_1, if their kth polar forms at t_1 coincide for $k > n - r$.

Fig. 11 shows the first "polar form at t_1" of the cubic curve from above.

Like for curves with a change in de Casteljau's algorithms polar forms can easily be build also for triangular and quadrangular surfaces (de Casteljau, 1985). Note that polar

[3] In this formula the dots "…" stand for an identical couple of arguments.

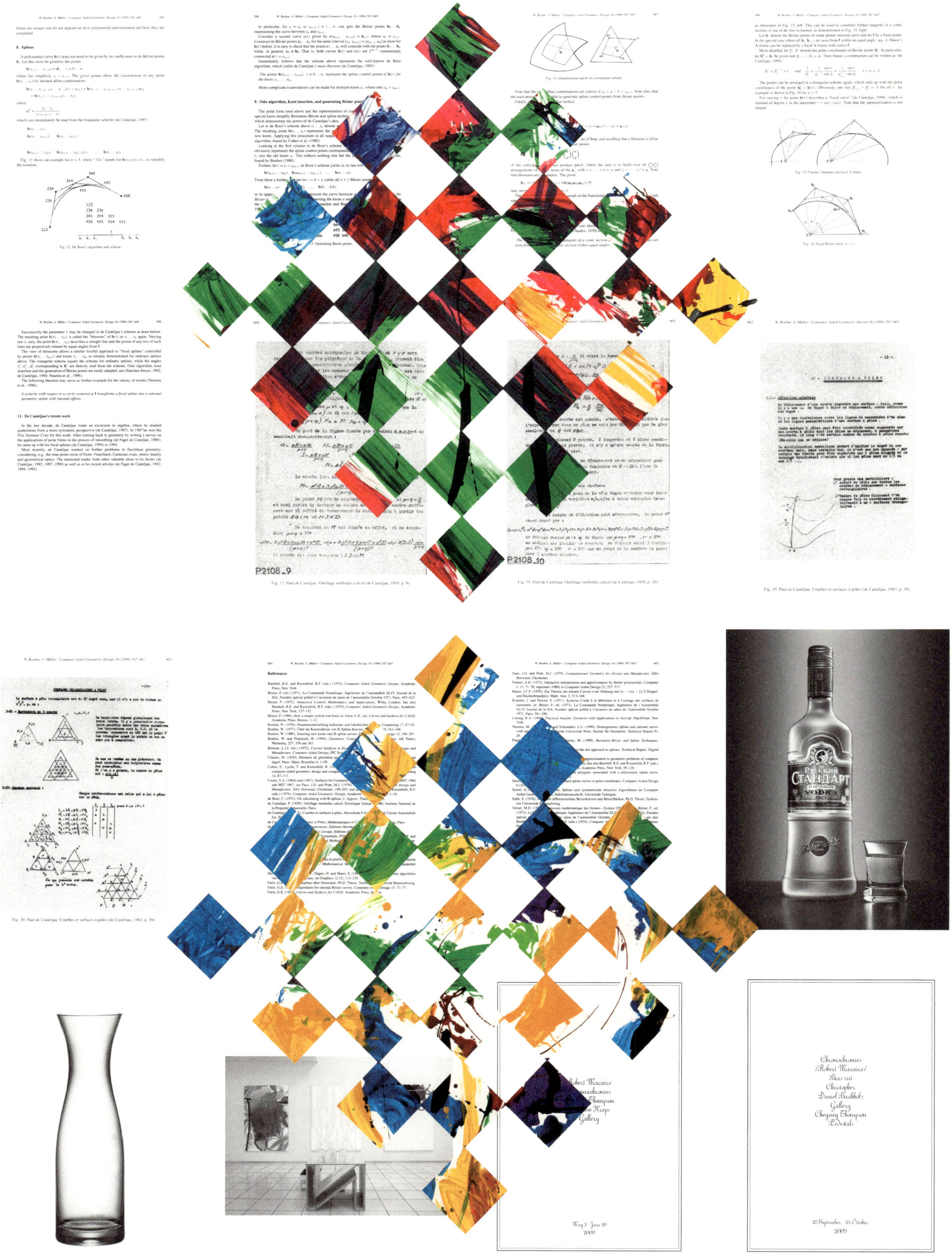
P2108_9
P2108_10
Русский Стандарт
VODKA
May 2 – June 20
2009
25 September – 24 October
2009

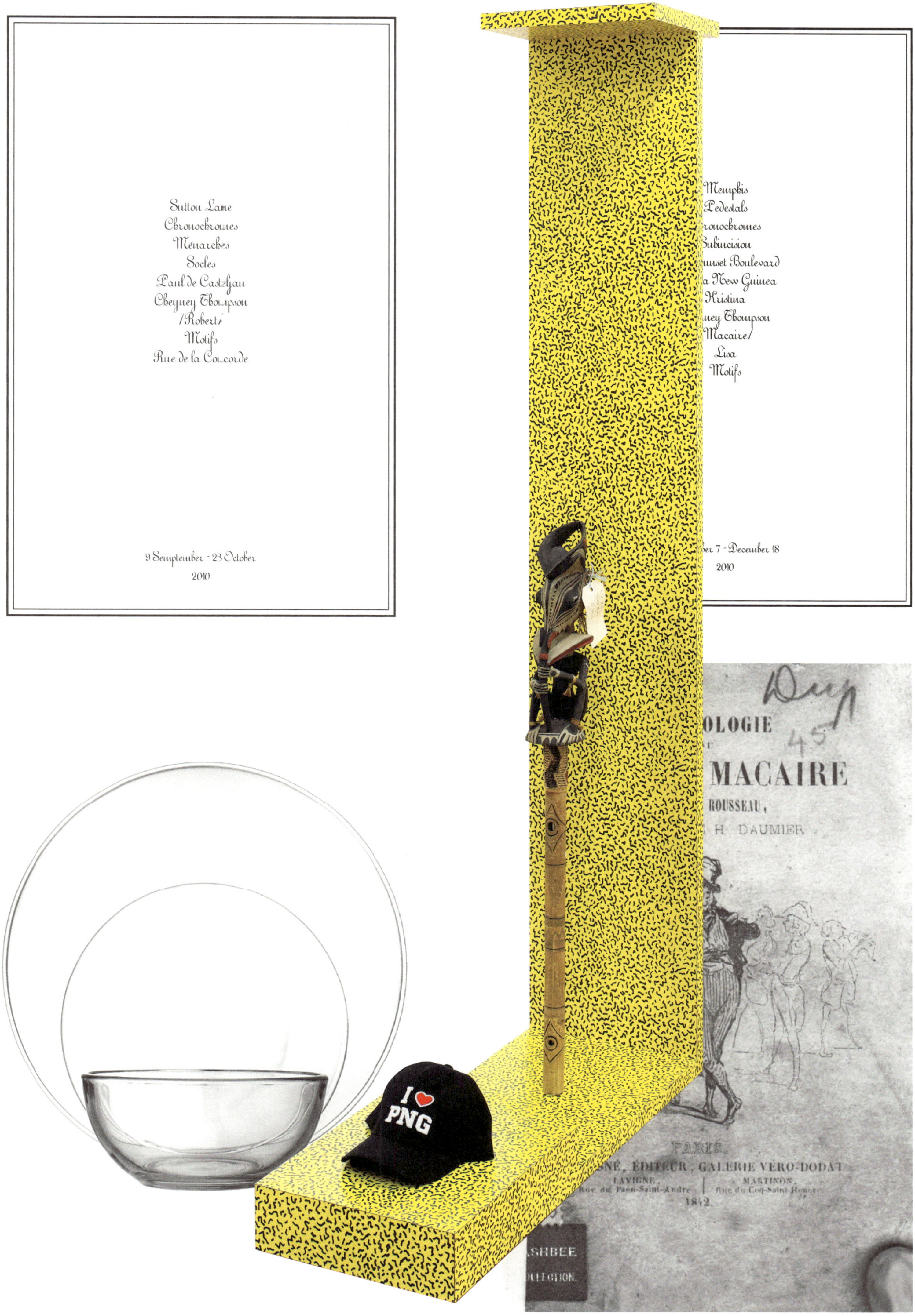
Sutton Lane
Chronochromes
Ménarches
Socles
Paul de Casteljau
Cheyney Thompson
/Robert/
Motifs
Rue de la Concorde
9 Semptember - 23 October
2010
Memphis
Pedestals
ronochromes
Subincision
unset Boulevard
a New Guinea
Kristina
ney Thompson
Macaire/
Lisa
Motifs
ber 7 - December 18
2010
OLOGIE
MACAIRE
ROUSSEAU,
H DAUMIER
I ♥ PNG
PARIS
NÉ, ÉDITEUR, GALERIE VÉRO-DODAT
LAVIGNE
MARTINON
ASHBEE
OLLECTION

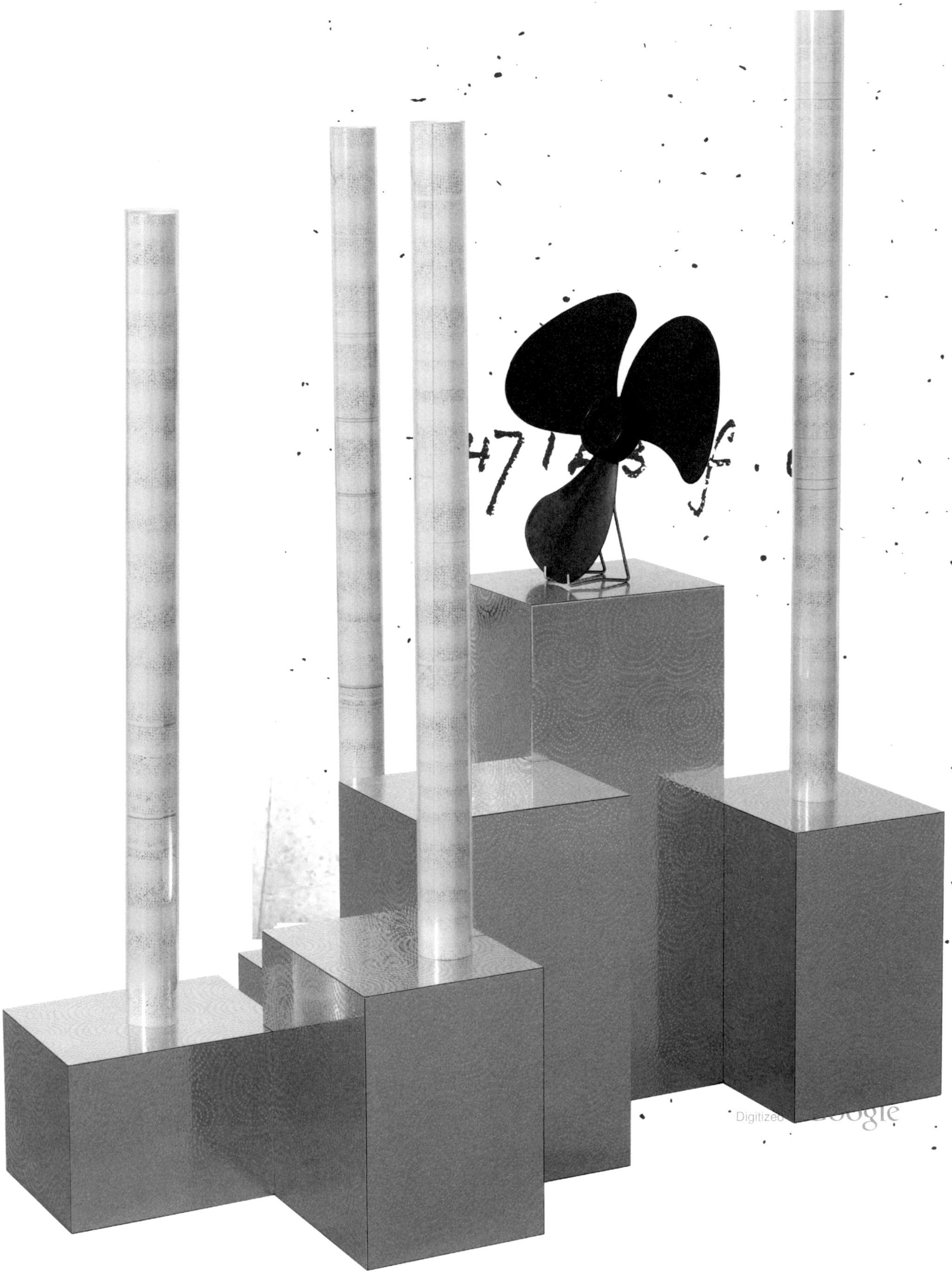

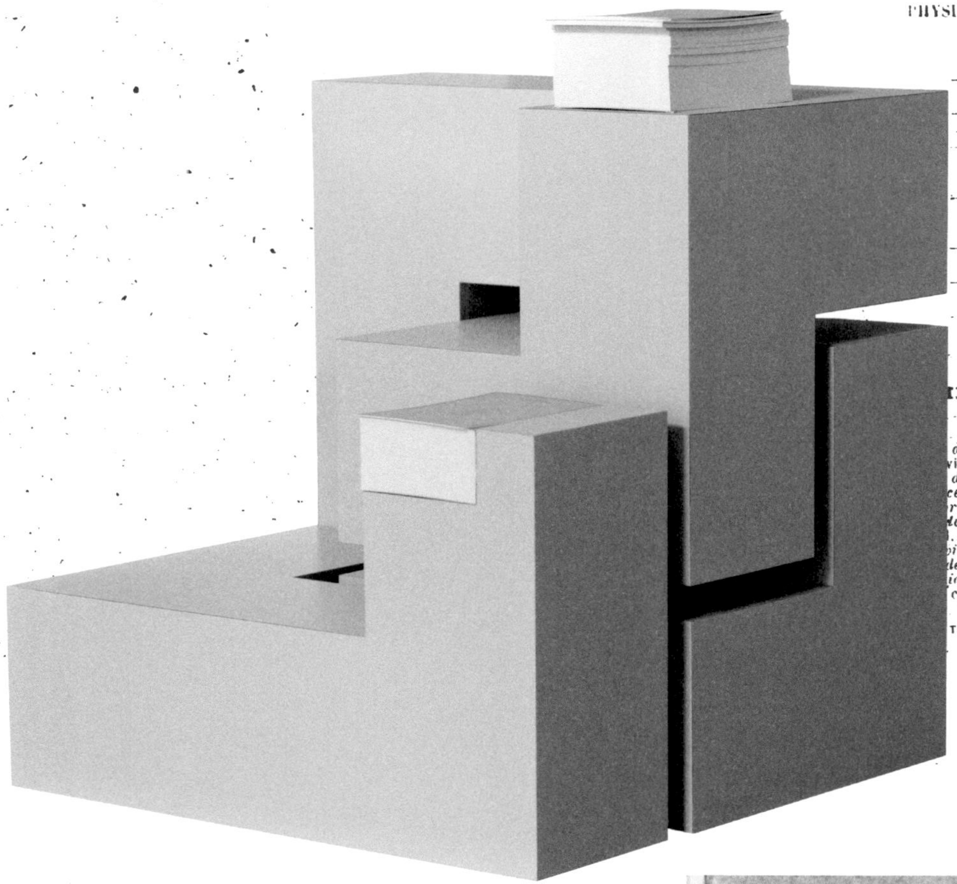

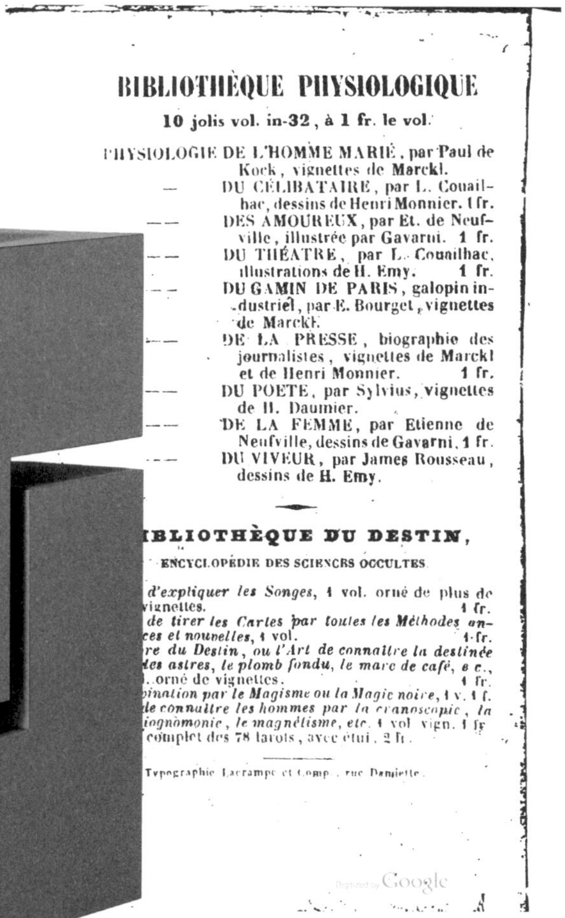

BIBLIOTHÈQUE PHYSIOLOGIQUE

10 jolis vol. in-32, à 1 fr. le vol.

PHYSIOLOGIE DE L'HOMME MARIÉ, par Paul de Kock, vignettes de Marckl.
— DU CÉLIBATAIRE, par L. Couailhac, dessins de Henri Monnier. 1 fr.
— DES AMOUREUX, par Et. de Neufville, illustrée par Gavarni. 1 fr.
— DU THÉATRE, par L. Couailhac, illustrations de H. Emy. 1 fr.
— DU GAMIN DE PARIS, galopin industriel, par E. Bourget, vignettes de Marckl.
— DE LA PRESSE, biographie des journalistes, vignettes de Marckl et de Henri Monnier. 1 fr.
— DU POETE, par Sylvius, vignettes de H. Daumier.
— DE LA FEMME, par Etienne de Neufville, dessins de Gavarni. 1 fr.
— DU VIVEUR, par James Rousseau, dessins de H. Emy.

IBLIOTHÈQUE DU DESTIN,

ENCYCLOPÉDIE DES SCIENCES OCCULTES.

d'expliquer les Songes, 1 vol. orné de plus de vignettes. 1 fr.
de tirer les Cartes par toutes les Méthodes ances et nouvelles, 1 vol. 1 fr.
re du Destin, ou l'Art de connaître la destinée des astres, le plomb fondu, le marc de café, etc., orné de vignettes. 1 fr.
vination par le Magisme ou la Magie noire, 1 v. 1 f.
de connaître les hommes par la cranoscopie, la iognomonie, le magnétisme, etc. 1 vol. vign. 1 fr.
complet des 78 tarots, avec étui. 2 fr.

Typographie Lacrampe et Comp., rue Damiette.

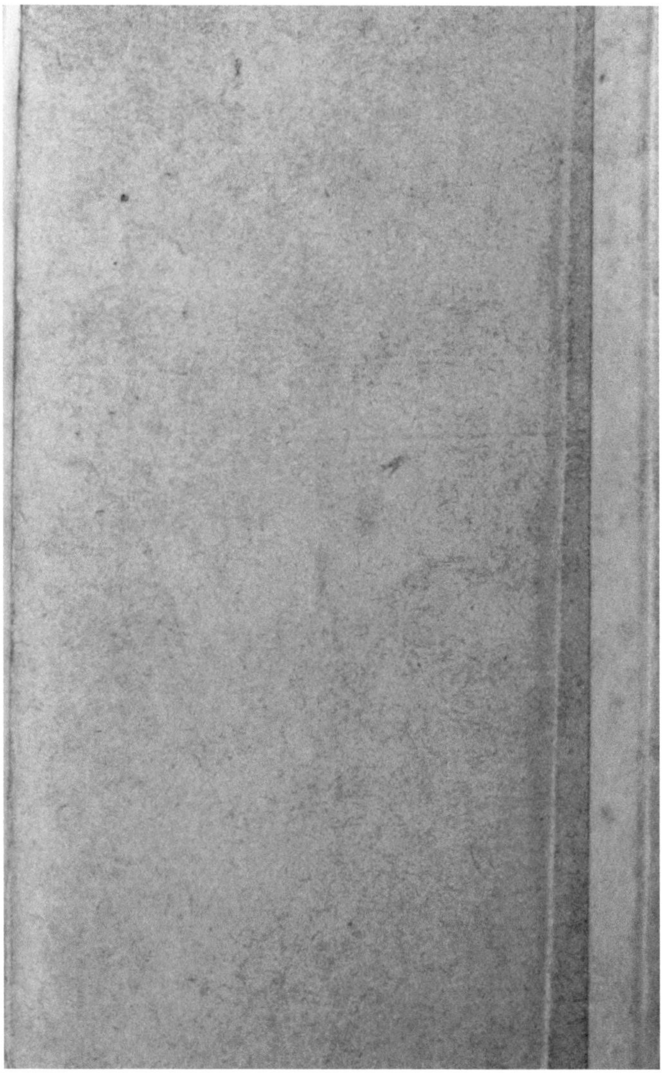

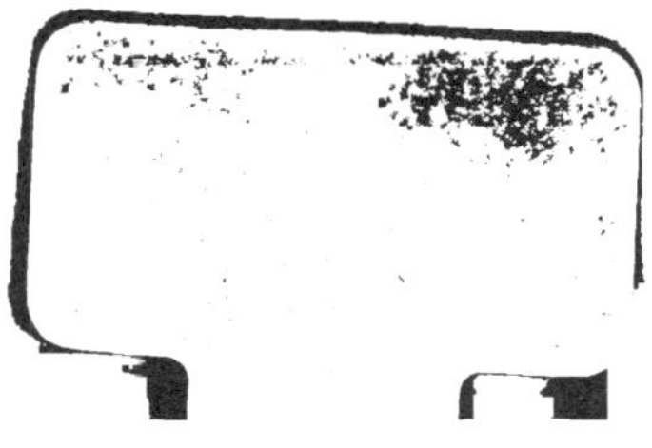

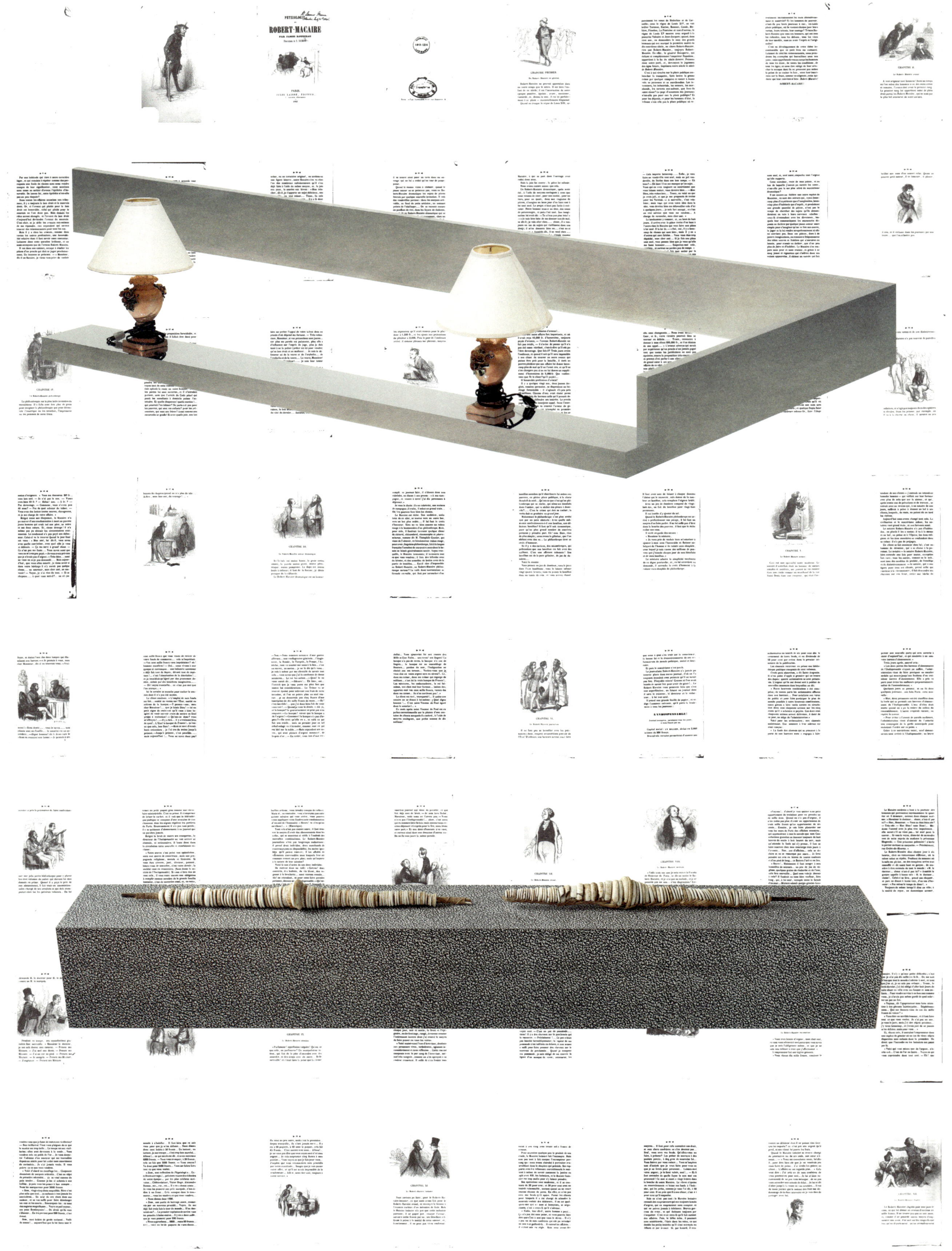
PHYSIOLOGIE
ROBERT-MACAIRE
PARIS.
JULES LAISNÉ, ÉDITEUR,

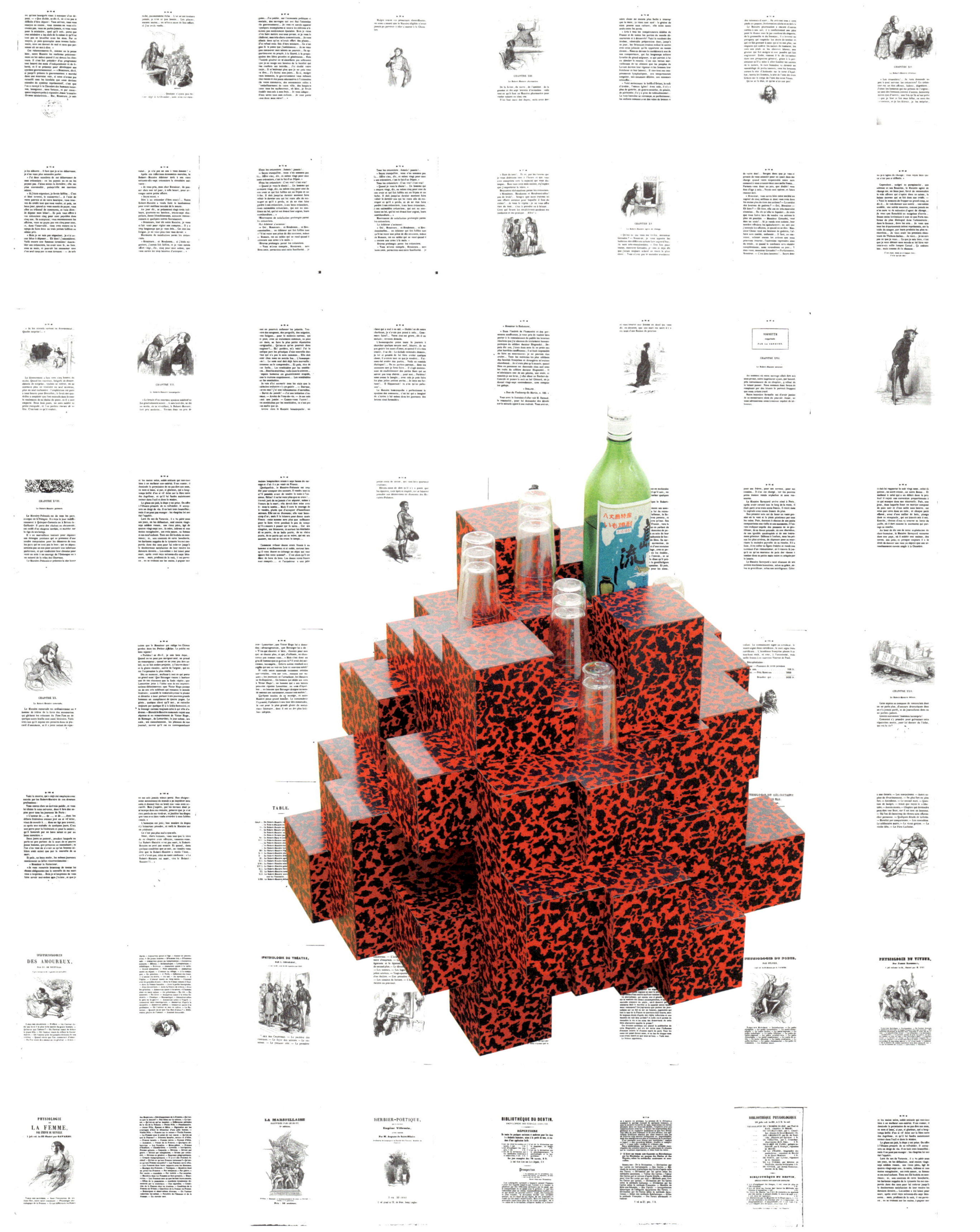
TABLE.
DES AMOUREUX,
LA FEMME,
LA MARSEILLAISE
HERBIER-POÉTIQUE,
BIBLIOTHÈQUE DU DESTIN.

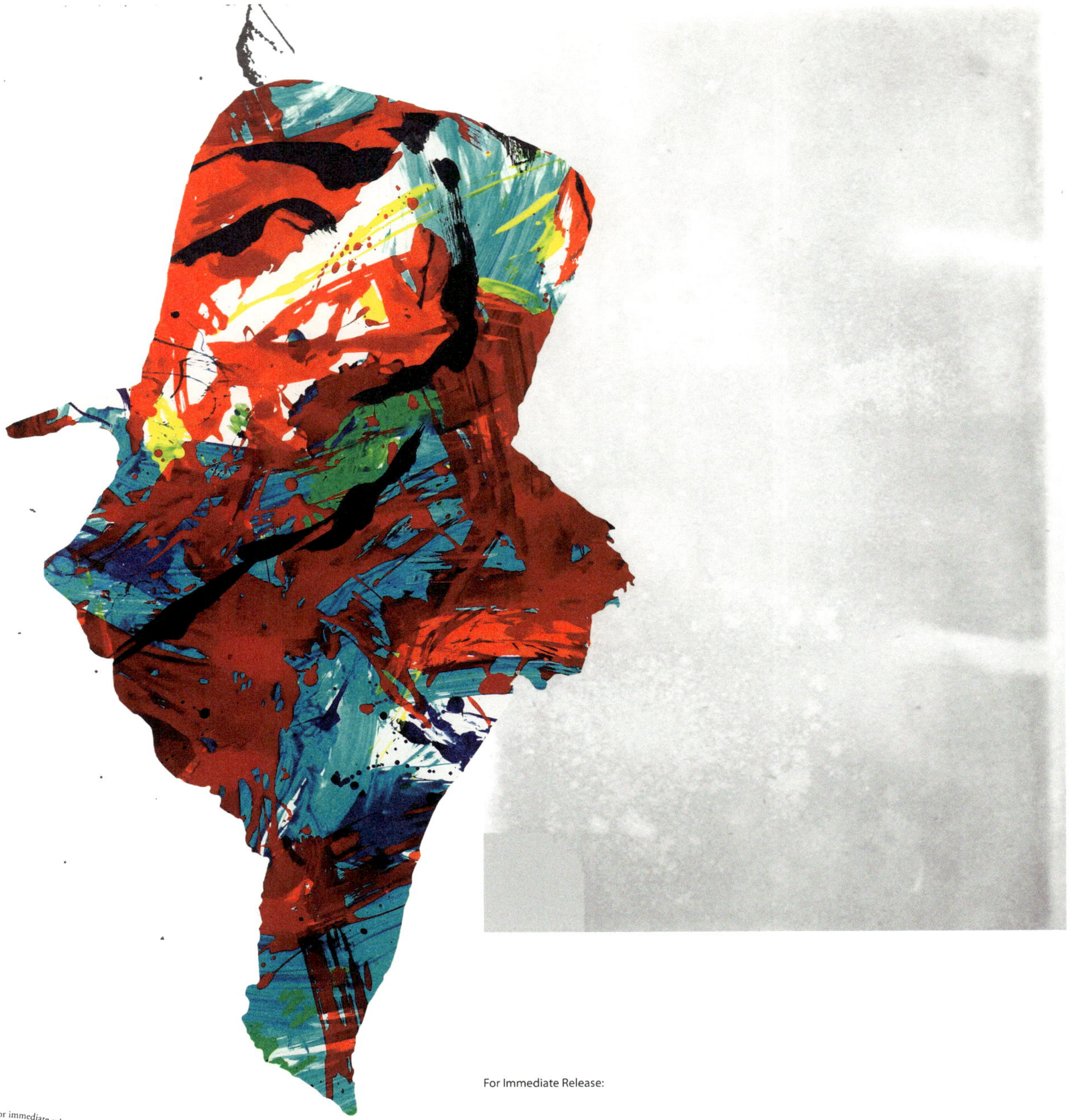

For Immediate Release:

Galerie Daniel Buchholz is pleased to announce Cheyney Thompson's third solo exhibition for the gallery entitled, "Pedestals, Bias-cut, /Robert Macaire/, Chronochromes." In this exhibition, Thompson brings together thirteen paintings that are systematically constructed according to a set of discrete material coordinates. Each painting shares the common motif of an enlarged section of the paintings' linen support. Thompson builds a template off of this image that consolidate ur value information into zones of highlight, mid-tone, and dark. In a further step, Th interest in color theorist Albert Munsell's system of complementary colour pairs omplementary colour pair to each day of work, and changing the colours' value by hite, and midnight absolute black.)

(I took out the particularit the division of colour info ove, leaving it somewhat vague, because it started to read a little lik nual. If that is the effect tha gh, I would recommend pushing it to an extreme and include no info than the systematic details)

Thompson und s this system of painterly production of "registering fatigue, distraction, interruptions as if, in th (not quite sure what "it" is here. The paint e system? Work?) had the potential to produce a smooth g that could represent a continuous flow e, or at least the continuities of a logically ordered colour To be sure, inconsistencies occur in the tings' colour gradients due to the artist's inability to work at s, every day. Painting is here equated ind of wage labour where time itself s become a discrete set ountable, and plotted within the rt of painting.

In response to the hist ant monochrome's claim to rsality, Thompson's paintings find themselves ted as *chronochromes:* subsumption in alized framework of a complete colour system, the instrumentalized t tem is sufficiently capable of distributing colour ll as imaging images. If said to have created exceptions, chronochromes can onl ce example after example.

ematic approach to painting extends to a group of pedestals included in the exhibition. Thompson writes: t a typical pedestal for my needs (of presenting a document) was 4624 square inches. I treated this numb nt and designed 5 pedestals that all have the exact same surface area. In theory, the most distinguish f a pedestal (its verticality) could topologically become its opposite (horizontallity). The pedestals the nominal function as supports for artefacts while proliferating the mute ability of their capacity to sign stal/."

(I omitted the next couple of lines because the claim that the info on the pedestals follows their formal variability according to informational coordinates drifted a bit. Although I think I see what you're getting at, I fear that it would begin to read like an article on your show rather than press info. Better to keep the treasure a little deeper underground: its radiance has more effect that way.)

Also, the R.Mac. stuff strikes me as too dense and jargony. You might want to look back on what you wrote and try and write it out clearly. However, since the above is already richly suggestive and highly referential, you might want to leave it out… let Macaire do his work in the exhibition to see if he is really ends up being what you think he is. If you feel like you need to put him in though, I'd be glad to take a gander.)

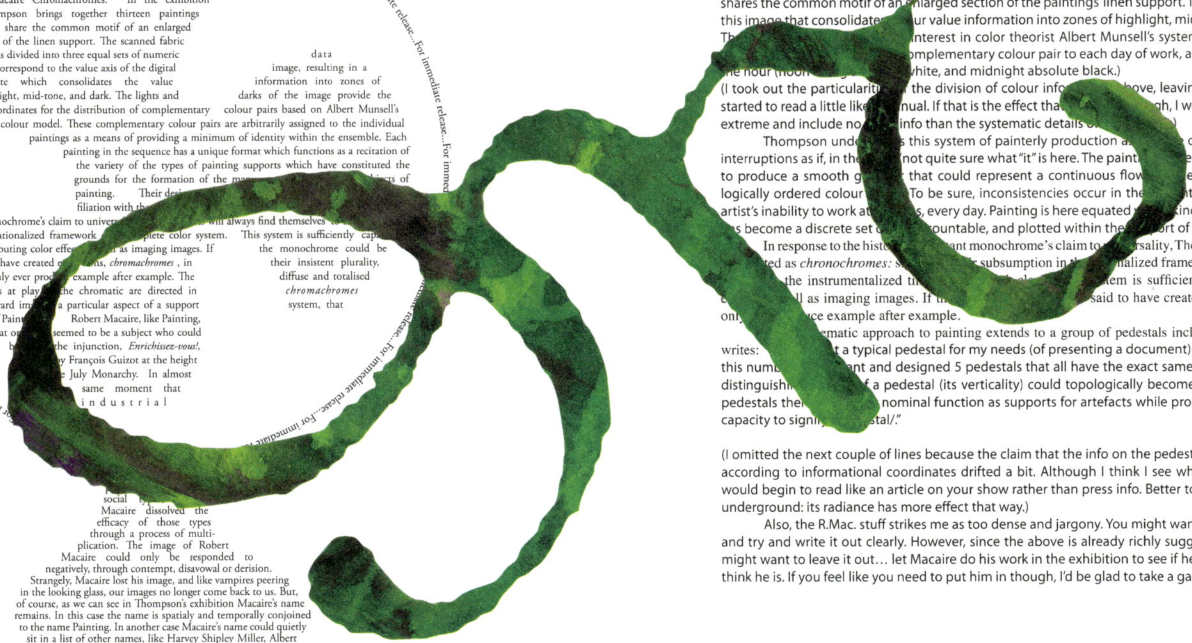

For immediate release... For immediate release...For immediate release...For immediate release...For immediate release...For immediate release...For immediate release...For immediate release...For immediate release...For immediate release...For immediate release...For immediate release...For immediate release...For immediate release...For immed

Andrew Kreps Gallery is pleased to announce Cheyney Thompson's fourth solo exhibition for the gallery entitled, "Robert Macaire Chromachromes." In the exhibition Thompson brings together thirteen paintings which share the common motif of an enlarged section of the linen support. The scanned fabric sample is divided into three equal sets of numeric data which correspond to the value axis of the digital image, resulting in a template which consolidates the value information into zones of highlight, mid-tone, and dark. The lights and darks of the image provide the coordinates for the distribution of complementary colour pairs based on Albert Munsell's colour model. These complementary colour pairs are arbitrarily assigned to the individual paintings as a means of providing a minimum of identity within the ensemble. Each painting in the sequence has a unique format which functions as a recitation of the variety of the types of painting supports which have constituted the grounds for the formation of the ma cts of painting. Their de filiation with th

the monochrome's claim to univer will always find themselves in the rationalized framework plete color system. This system is sufficiently ca of distributing color effe as imaging images. If the monochrome could be said to have created ns, *chromachromes* , in their insistent plurality, can only ever pro example after example. The diffuse and totalised forces at play he chromatic are directed in *chromachromes* toward im a particular aspect of a support system, that of Pain Robert Macaire, like Painting, at o seemed to be a subject who could b he injunction, *Enrichissez-vous!*, y François Guizot at the height July Monarchy. In almost same moment that industrial

social Macaire dissolved the efficacy of those types through a process of multiplication. The image of Robert Macaire could only be responded to negatively, through contempt, disavowal or derision. Strangely, Macaire lost his image, and like vampires peering in the looking glass, our images no longer come back to us. But, of course, as we can see in Thompson's exhibition Macaire's name remains. In this case the name is spatialy and temporally conjoined to the name Painting. In another case Macaire's name could quietly sit in a list of other names, like Harvey Shipley Miller, Albert Munsell, or Margaret Thatcher who in their fidelity to the previous injunction , solemnly stated,

"There is no alternative."

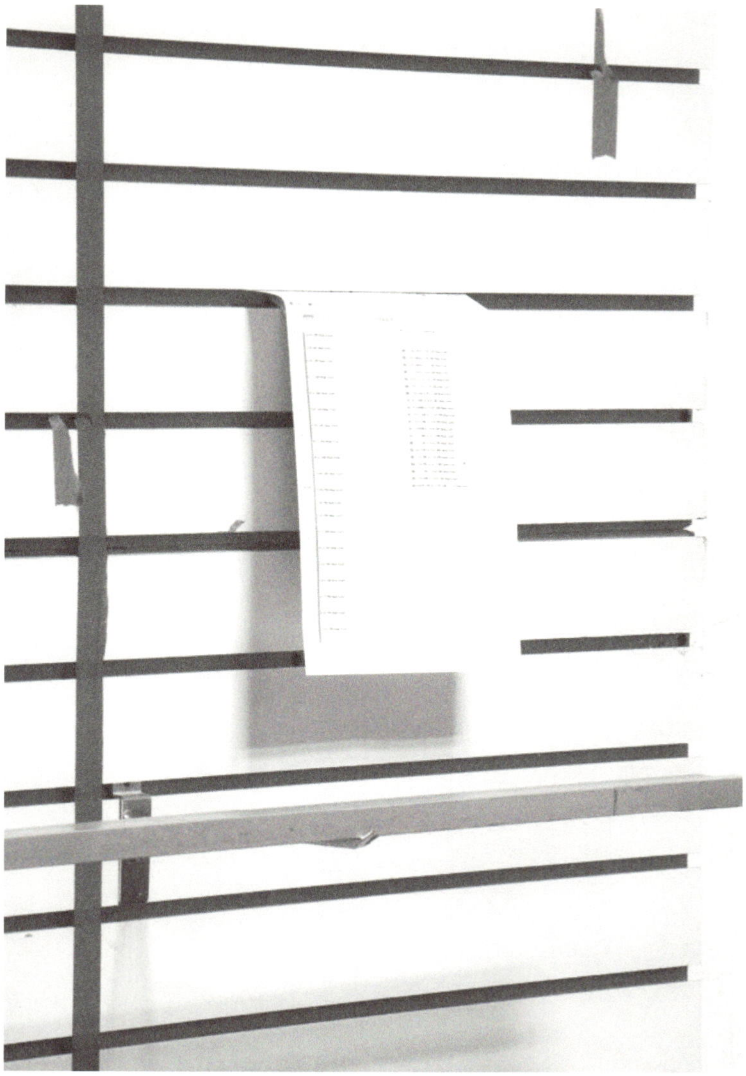

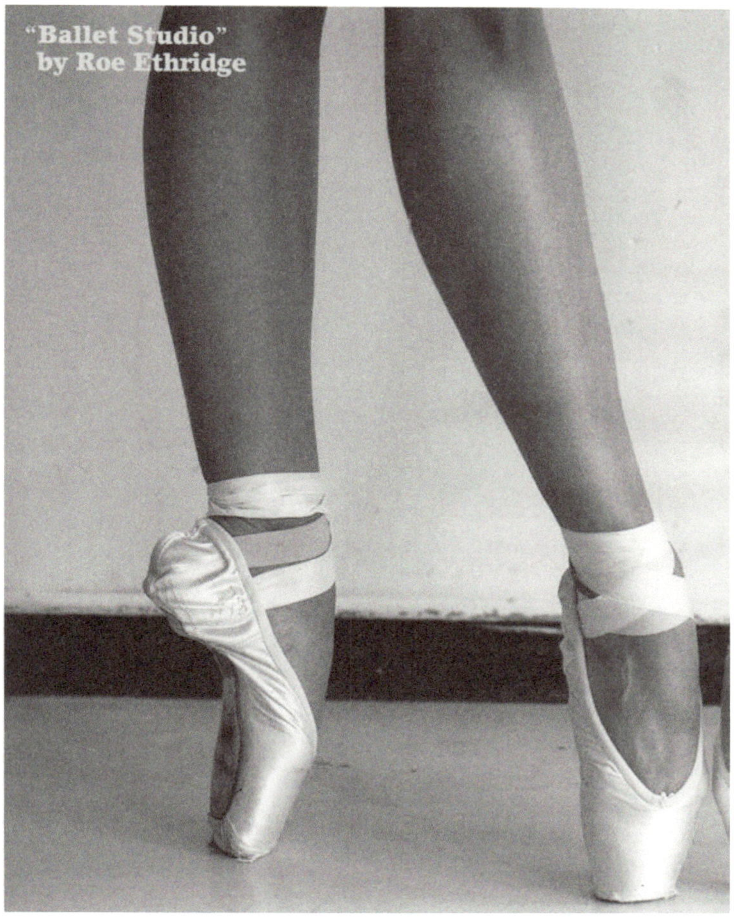
"Ballet Studio"
by Roe Ethridge

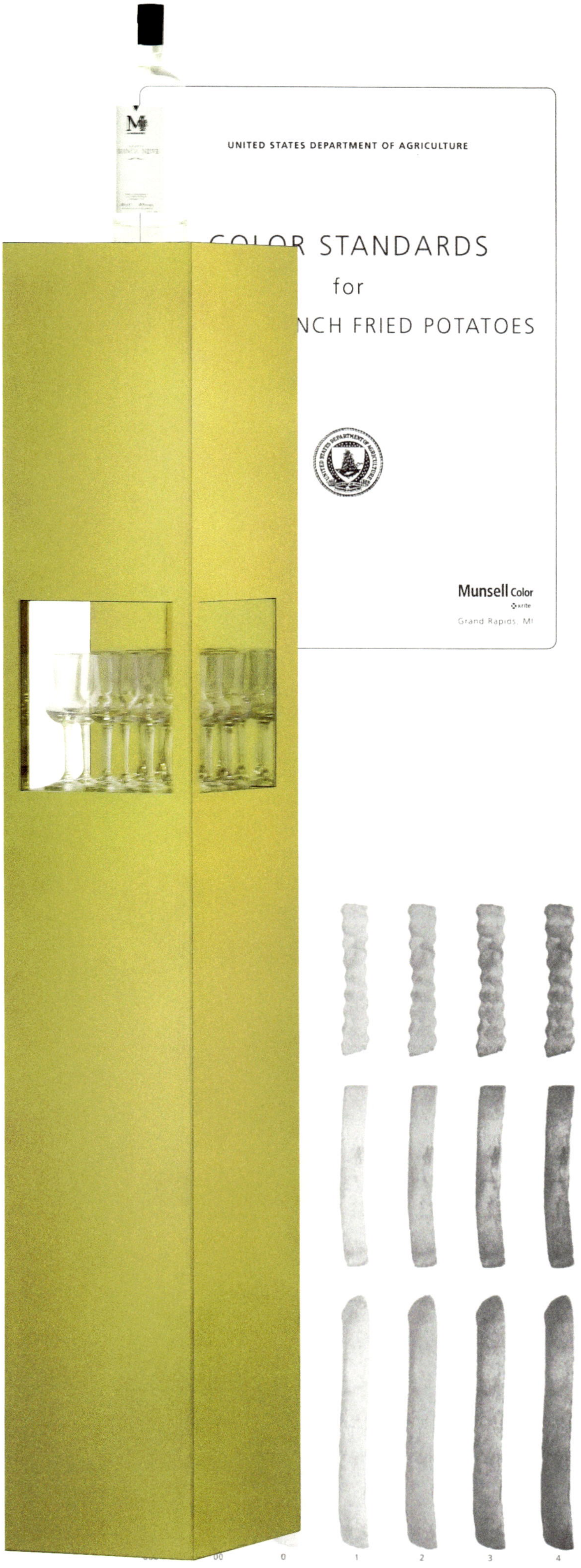
UNITED STATES DEPARTMENT OF AGRICULTURE
STANDARDS
for
NCH FRIED POTATOES
Munsell Color
Grand Rapids, MI
00
0
1
2
3
4

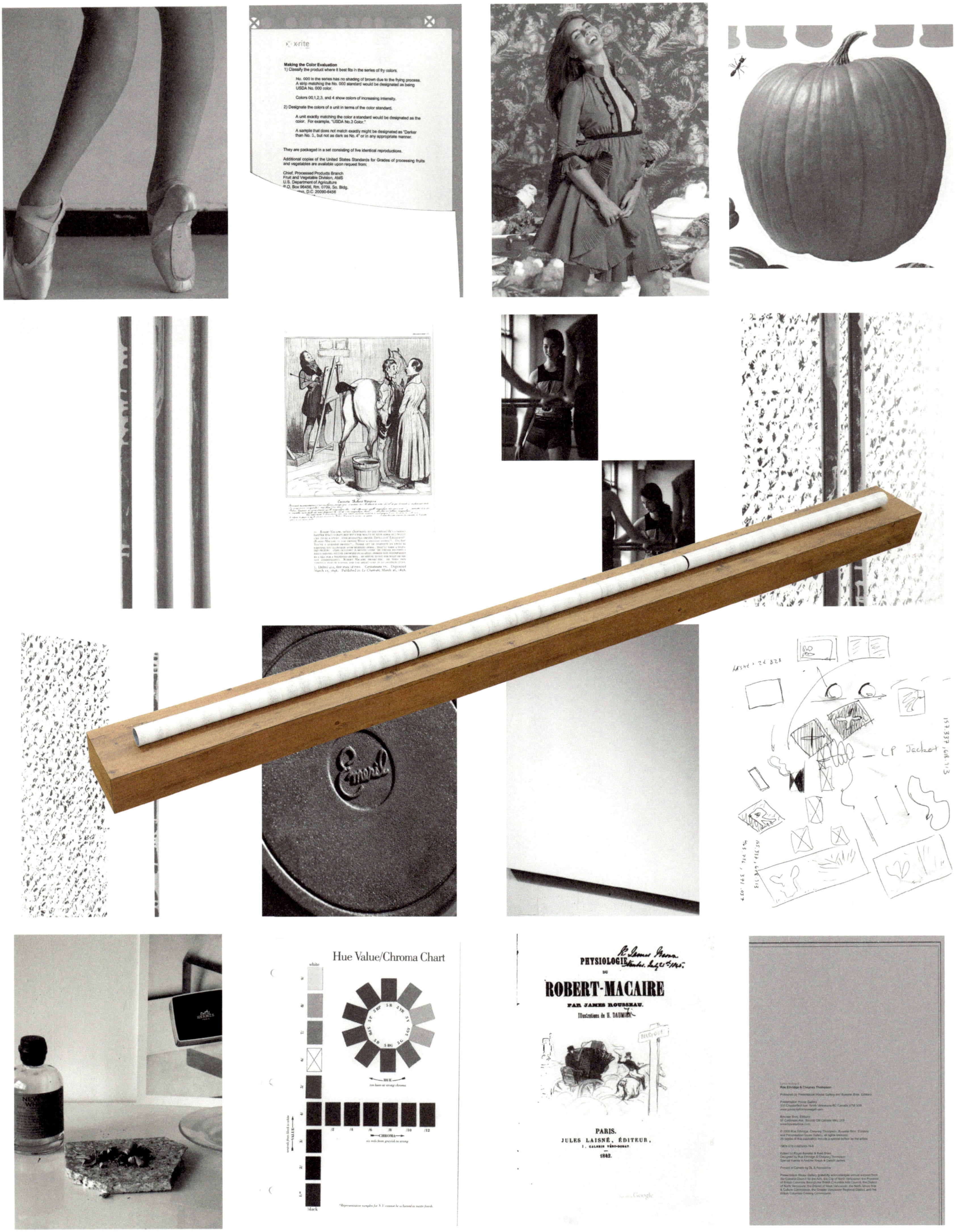
x-rite
Making the Color Evaluation
1) Classify the product where it best fits in the series of fry colors.
No. 000 in the series has no shading of brown due to the frying process. A strip matching the No. 000 standard would be designated as being USDA No. 000 color.
Colors 00,1,2,3, and 4 show colors of increasing intensity.
2) Designate the colors of a unit in terms of the color standard.
A unit exactly matching the color a standard would be designated as the color. For example, "USDA No.3 Color."
A sample that does not match exactly might be designated as "Darker than No. 3., but not as dark as No. 4" or in any appropriate manner.
They are packaged in a set consisting of five identical reproductions.
Additional copies of the United States Standards for Grades of processing fruits and vegetables are available upon request from:
Chief, Processed Products Branch
Fruit and Vegetable Division, AMS
U.S. Department of Agriculture
P.O. Box 96456, Rm. 0709, So. Bldg.
LP Jacket
Hue Value/Chroma Chart
white
HUE
CHROMA
black
PHYSIOLOGIE
DU
ROBERT-MACAIRE
PAR JAMES ROUSSEAU.
Illustrations de H. DAUMIER
BELGIQUE
PARIS.
JULES LAISNÉ, ÉDITEUR,
1, GALERIE VÉRO-DODAT.
1842.
Google

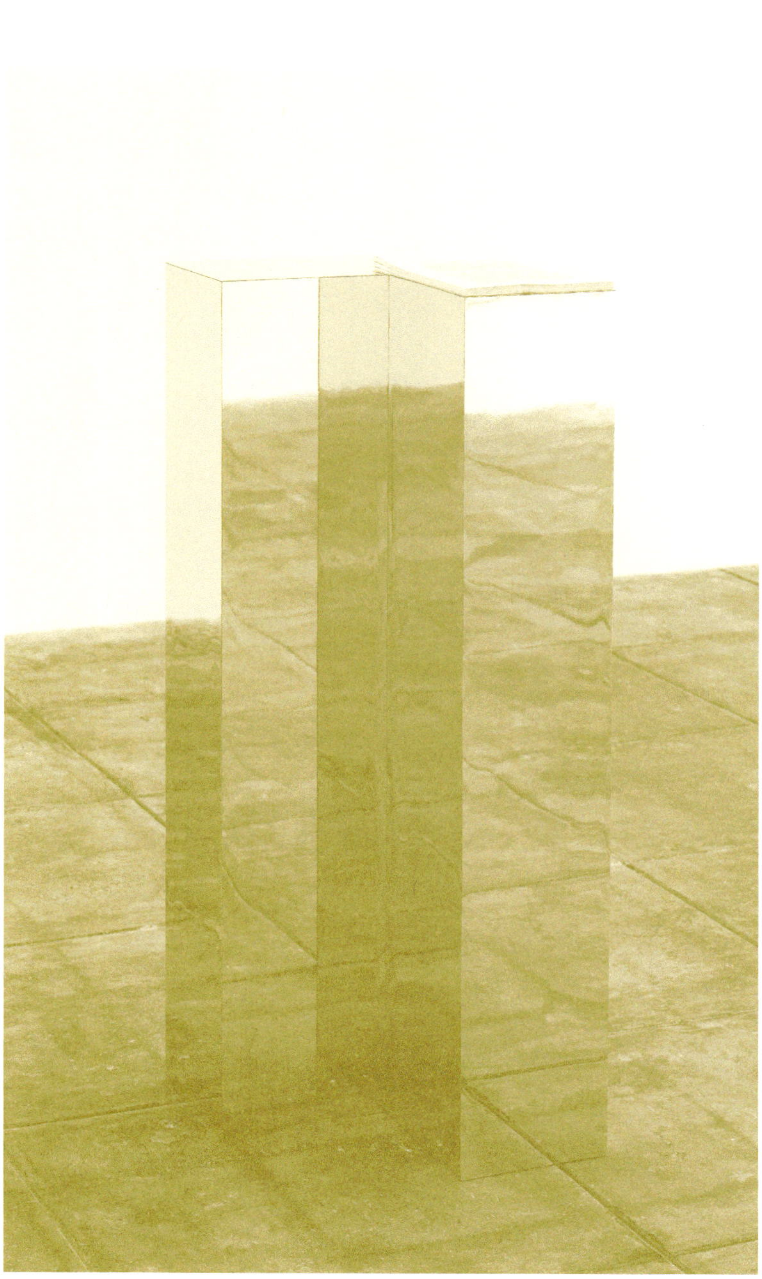

Pedestal 16, 2010, 19 mm MDF, Formica, wood, photocopies, 42 ½ × 17 ½ × 17 ½ in.

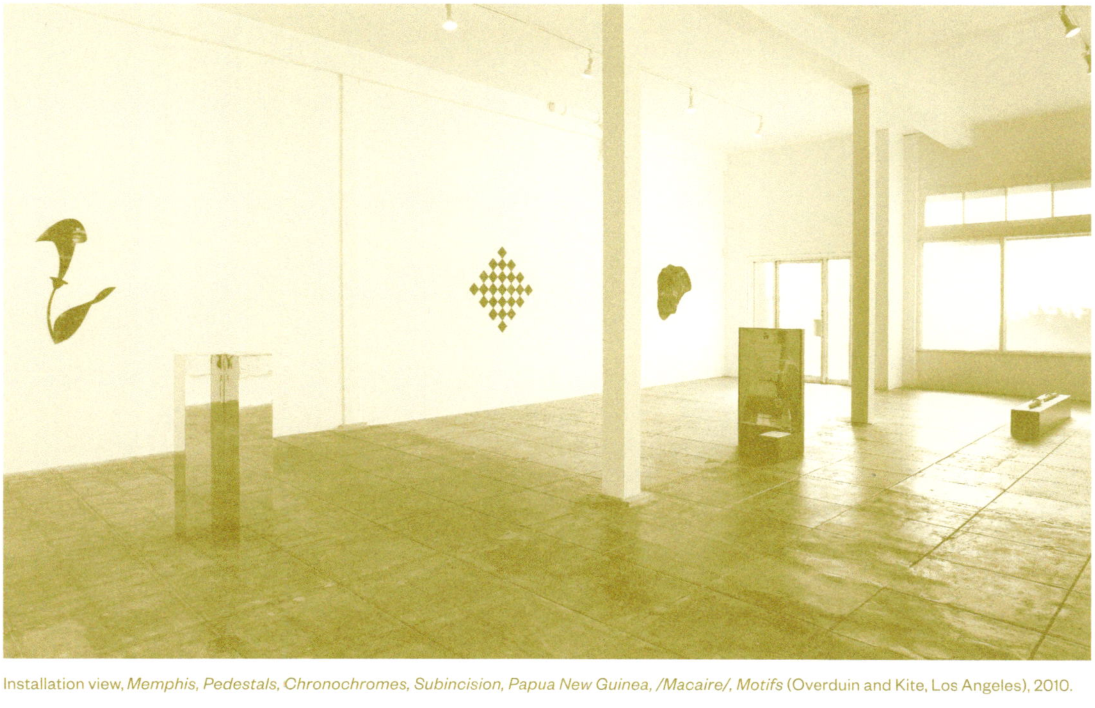

Installation view, *Memphis, Pedestals, Chronochromes, Subincision, Papua New Guinea, /Macaire/, Motifs* (Overduin and Kite, Los Angeles), 2010.

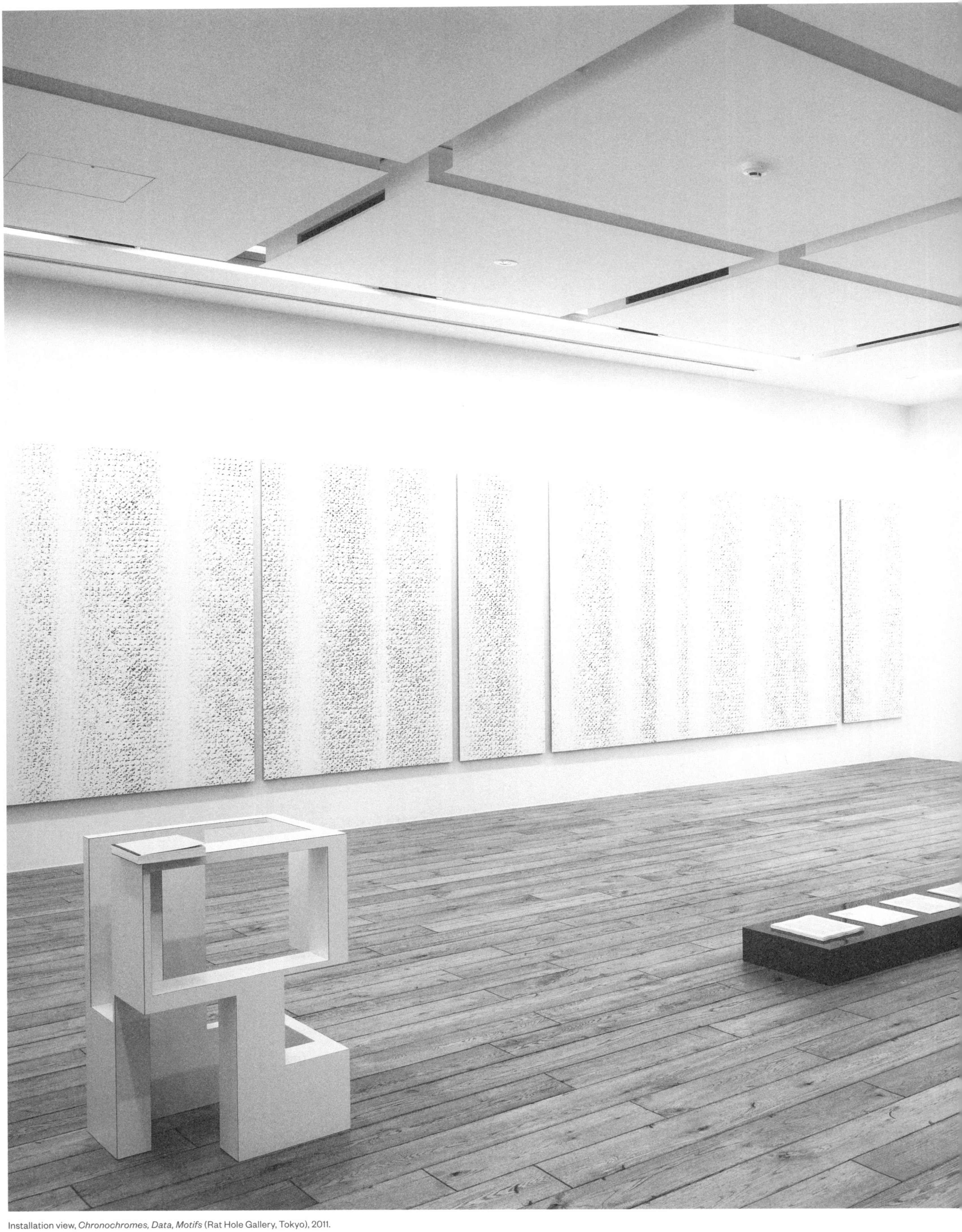

Installation view, *Chronochromes, Data, Motifs* (Rat Hole Gallery, Tokyo), 2011.

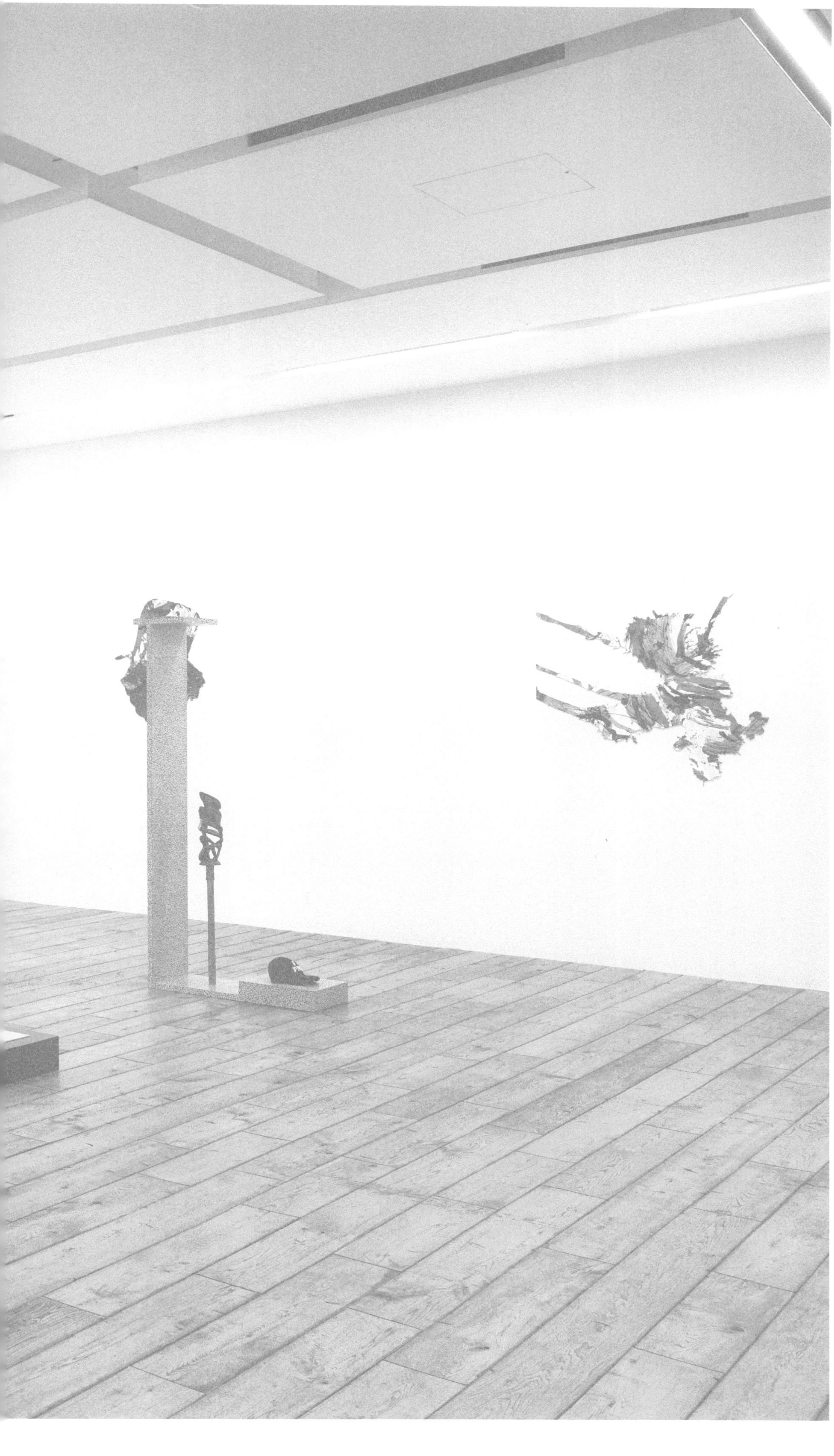

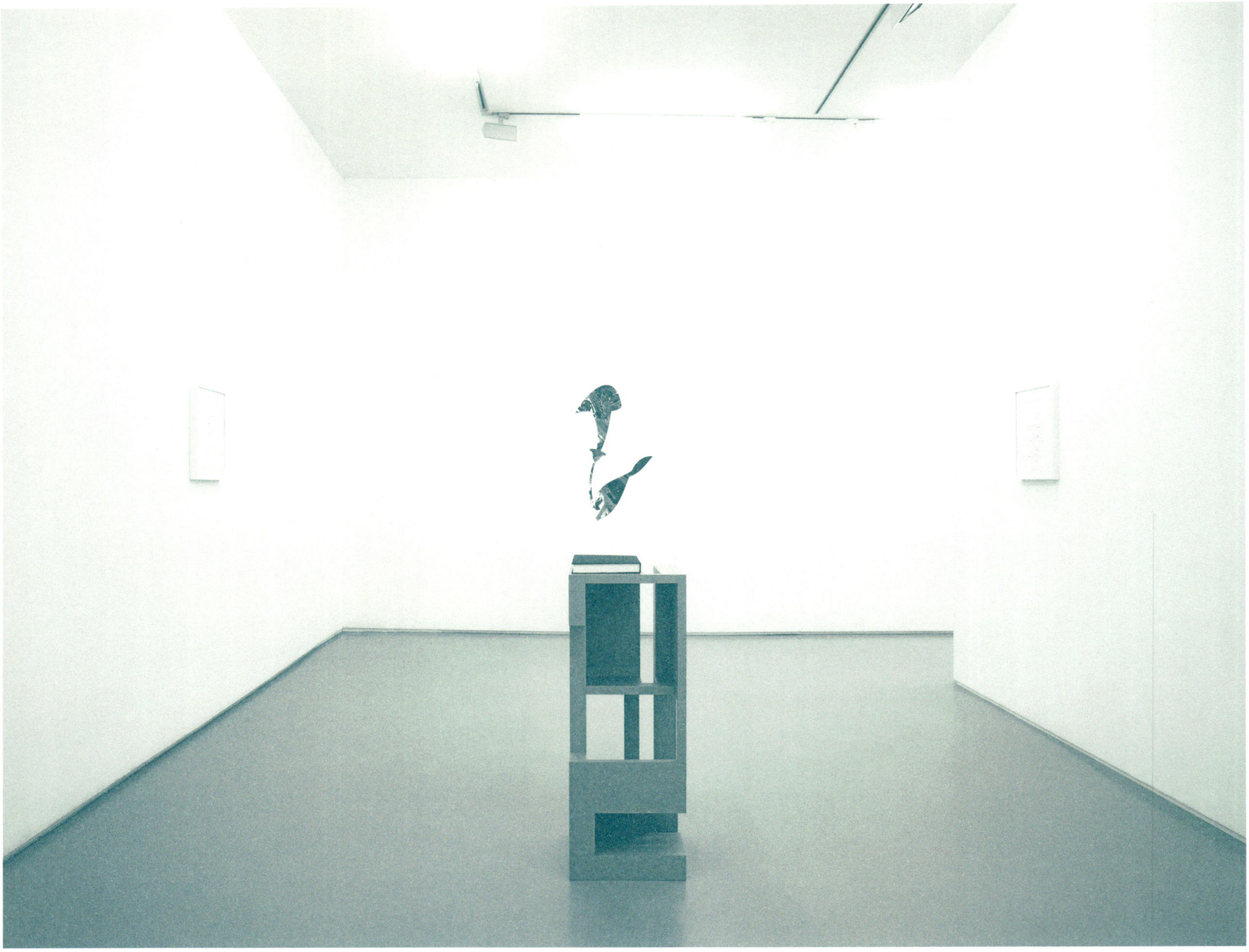

Installation view, *Chronochromes/Umberto/Simon/Carlo* (Galleria Raucci/Santamaria, Naples), 2011.

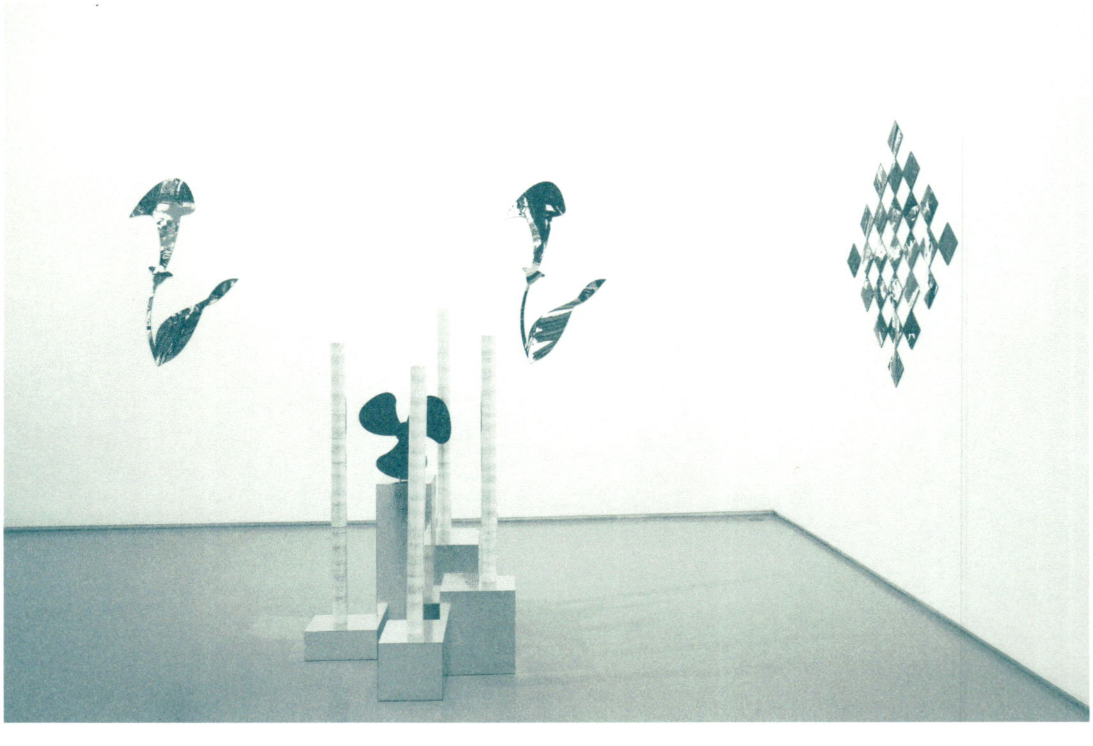

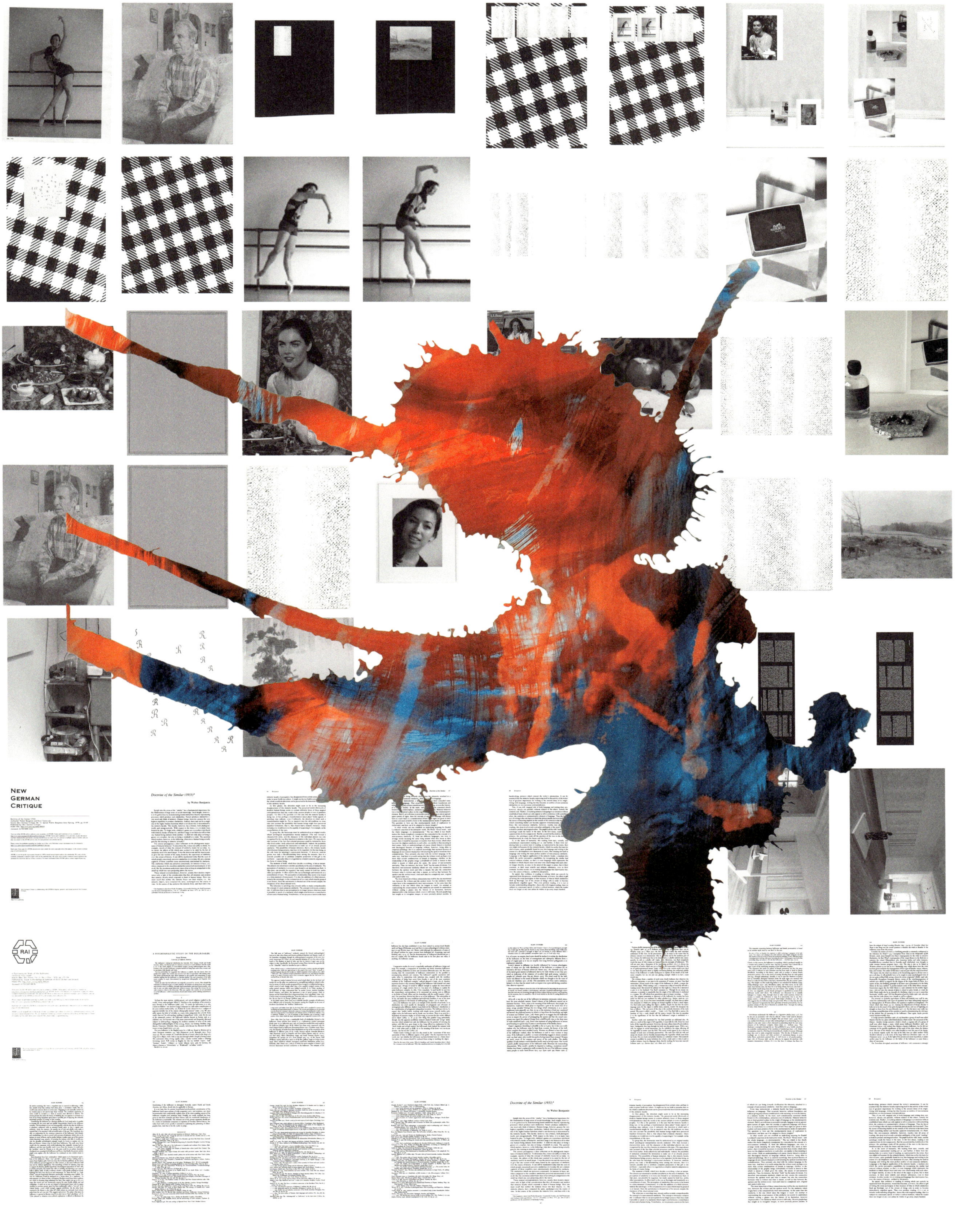
NEW
GERMAN
CRITIQUE
Doctrine of the Similar (1933)*
by Walter Benjamin
Doctrine of the Similar (1933)*
by Walter Benjamin

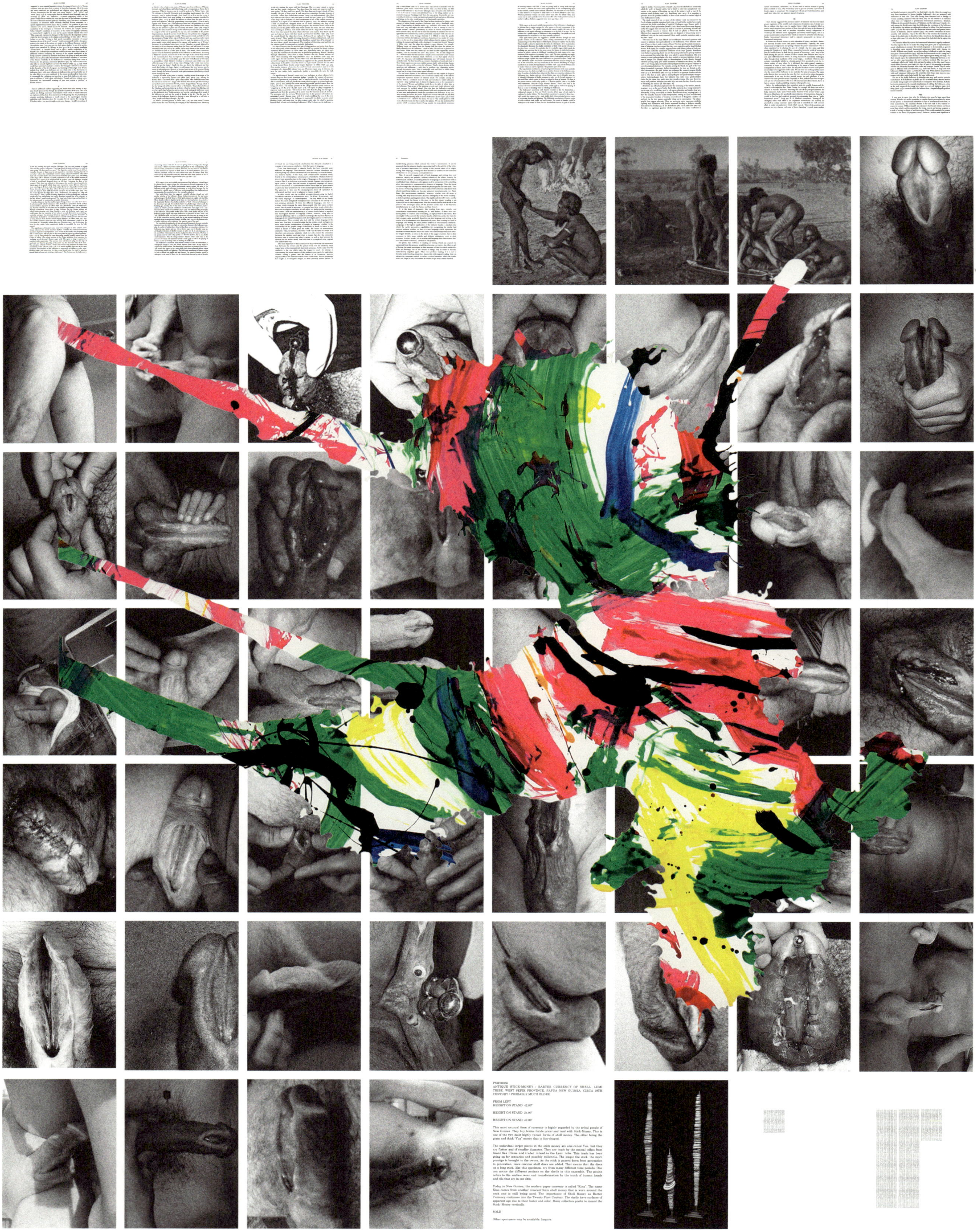
PSW00066
ANTIQUE STICK-MONEY / BARTER CURRENCY OF SHELL. LUMI TRIBE. WEST SEPIK PROVINCE. PAPUA NEW GUINEA. CIRCA 19TH CENTURY / PROBABLY MUCH OLDER.
FROM LEFT
HEIGHT ON STAND: 42.00"
HEIGHT ON STAND: 24.00"
HEIGHT ON STAND: 42.00"
This most unusual form of currency is highly regarded by the tribal people of New Guinea. They buy brides (bride-price) and land with Stick-Money. This is one of the two most highly valued forms of shell money. The other being the giant and thick "Yua" money that is disc-shaped.
The individual larger pieces in the stick money are also called Yua, but they are flatter and of smaller diameter. They are made by the coastal tribes from Giant Sea Clams and traded inland to the Lumi tribe. This trade has been going on for centuries and possibly millennia. The longer the stick, the more prestige is brought to the owner. As the stick is passed down from generation to generation, more circular shell discs are added. That means that the discs on a long stick, like this specimen, are from many different time periods. One can notice the different patinas on the shells in this ensemble. The patina refers to the surface wear and transformation by the touch of human hands and oils that are in our skin.
Today in New Guinea, the modern paper currency is called "Kina". The name Kina comes from another crescent-form shell money that is worn around the neck and is still being used. The importance of Shell Money as Barter Currency continues into the Twenty-First Century. The shells have surfaces of apparent age due to their luster and color. Many collectors prefer to mount the Stick-Money vertically.
SOLD
Other specimens may be available. Inquire.

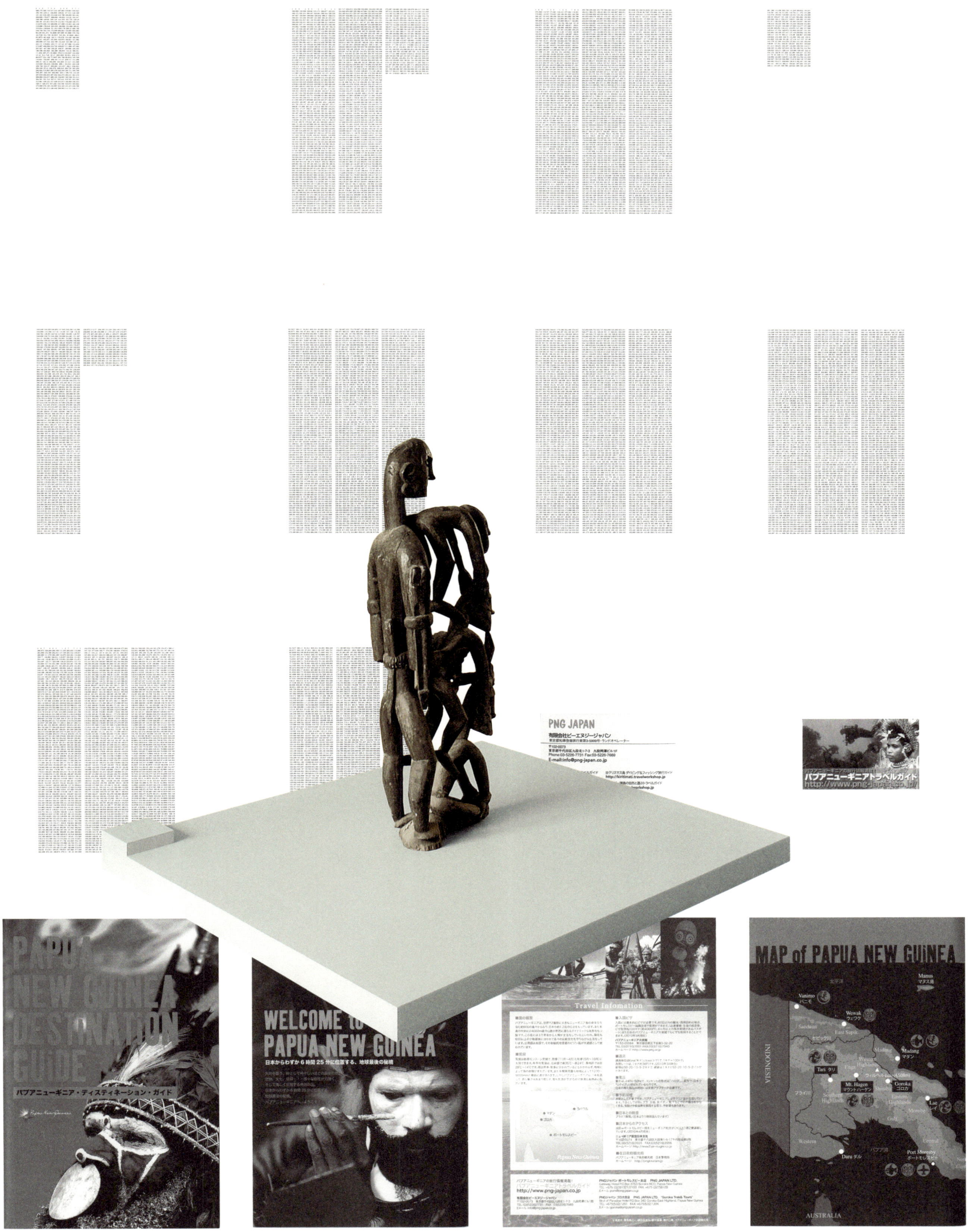
PNG JAPAN
有限会社ピーエヌジージャパン
〒102-0073
東京都千代田区九段北1-7-3　九段興淨ビル1F
Phone:03-5226-7731 Fax:03-5226-7669
E-mail:info@png-japan.co.jp
http://kiritimati.travelworkshop.jp
パプアニューギニアトラベルガイド
http://www.png-japan.co.jp/
PAPUA NEW GUINEA DESTINATION GUIDE
パプアニューギニア・ディスティネーション・ガイド
WELCOME to PAPUA NEW GUINEA
日本からわずか6時間25分に位置する、地球最後の秘境
Travel Infomation
http://www.png-japan.co.jp
MAP of PAPUA NEW GUiNEA
Manus
マヌス島
Vanimo
バニモ
Wewak
ウェワク
Sandaun
East Sepik
Madang
マダン
INDONESIA
Tari タリ
Western Highlands
Mt. Hagen
マウントハーゲン
Goroka
ゴロカ
Southern Highlands
Eastern Highlands
Western
Gulf
Daru ダル
Port Moresby
ポートモレスビー
Central
AUSTRALIA

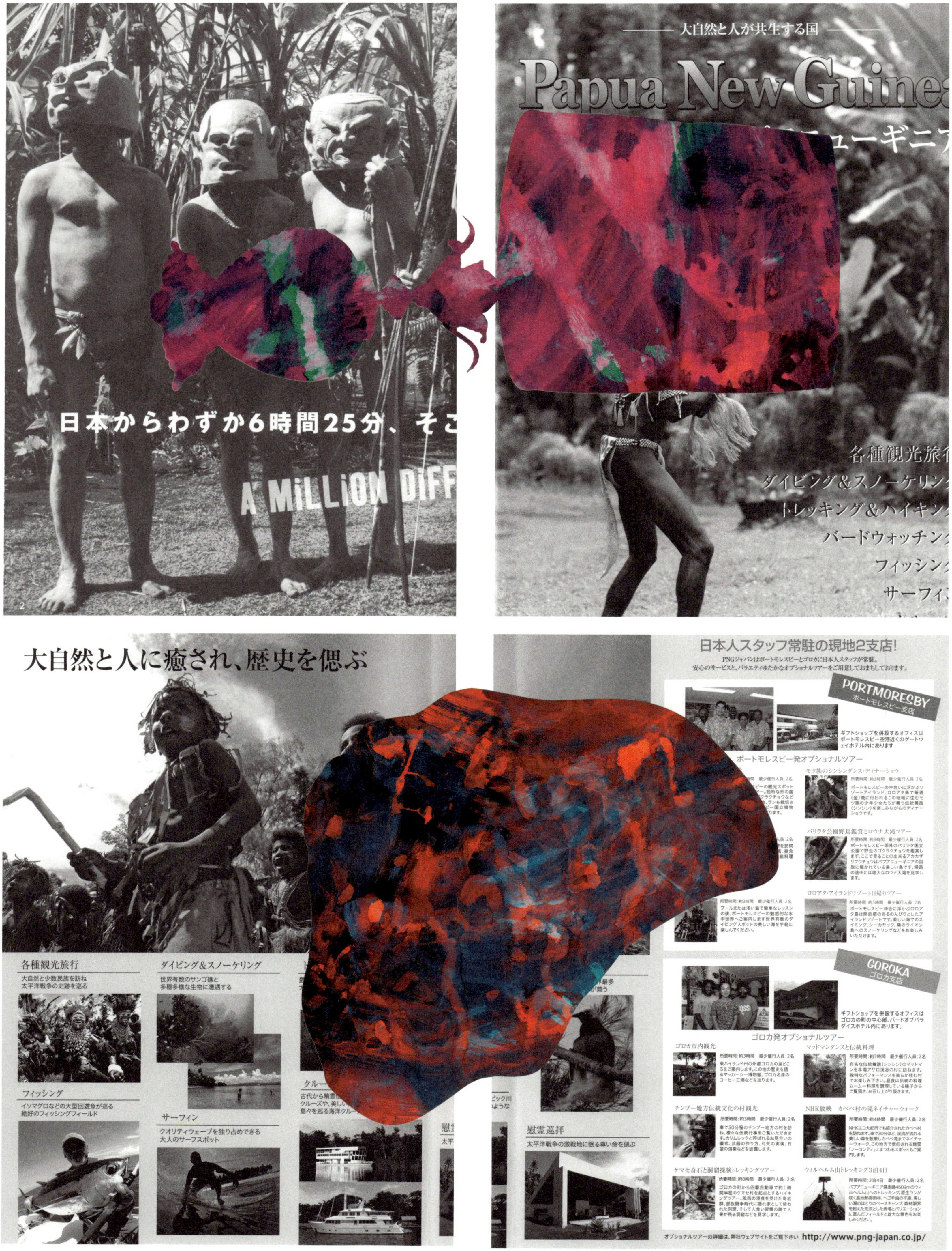
大自然と人が共生する国
Papua New Guinea
日本からわずか6時間25分、そ
A MILLION DIFF
各種観光旅
ダイビング&スノーケリン
トレッキング&ハイキン
バードウォッチン
フィッシン
サーフィ
2
大自然と人に癒され、歴史を偲ぶ
各種観光旅行
大自然と少数民族を訪ね
太平洋戦争の史跡を巡る
ダイビング&スノーケリング
世界有数のサンゴ礁と
多種多様な生物に遭遇する
フィッシング
イソマグロなどの大型回遊魚が巡る
絶好のフィッシングフィールド
サーフィン
クオリティウェーブを独り占めできる
大人のサーフスポット
慰霊巡拝
太平洋戦争の激戦地に眠る尊い命を偲ぶ
日本人スタッフ常駐の現地2支店!
PNGジャパンはポートモレスビーとゴロカに日本人スタッフが常駐。
安心のサービスと、バラエティゆたかなオプショナルツアーをご用意しておまちしております。
PORTMORESBY
ポートモレスビー支店
ギフトショップを併設するオフィスはポートモレスビー空港近くのゲートウェイホテル内にあります
ポートモレスビー発オプショナルツアー
モツ族のシンシンダンス・ディナーショウ
所要時間:約3時間 最少催行人員:2名
ポートモレスビーの沖合いに浮かぶリゾートアイランド、ロロアタ島で毎週(金)晩に行われるこの地域に住むモツ族の少年少女たちが舞う伝統舞踏(シンシン)を楽しみながらのディナーショウです。
バリラタ公園野鳥鑑賞とロウナ大滝ツアー
所要時間:約3時間 最少催行人員:2名
ポートモレスビー郊外のバリラタ国立公園で野生のゴクラクチョウを鑑賞します。ここで見ることの出来るアカカザリフウチョウはパプアニューギニアの国旗に描かれている美しい鳥です。帰路の途中には雄大なロウナ大滝を見学します。
所要時間:約3時間 最少催行人員:2名
プールまたは浅い海で簡単なレッスンの後、ポートモレスビーの魅惑的な水中世界へご案内します世界有数のダイビングスポットの美しい海を手軽に楽しんでください。
ロロアタ・アイランドリゾート日帰りツアー
所要時間:約3時間 最少催行人員:2名
ポートモレスビー沖合に浮かぶロロアタ島は開放感のあるのんびりとしたアイランドリゾートです。美しい海でのスイミング、シーカヤック、隣のライオン島へのスノーケリングなどをお楽しみいただけます。
GOROKA
ゴロカ支店
ギフトショップを併設するオフィスはゴロカの町の中心部、バードオブパラダイスホテル内にあります。
ゴロカ発オプショナルツアー
ゴロカ市内観光
所要時間:約3時間 最少催行人員:2名
東ハイランド州の州都ゴロカの見どころをご案内します。この地の歴史を語るマッカーシー博物館、ゴロカ名産のコーヒー工場などを巡ります。
マッドマンダンスと伝統料理
所要時間:約3時間 最少催行人員:2名
有名な伝統舞踏(シンシン)のマッドマンを本場アサロ渓谷の村に訪ねます。独特なパフォーマンスを彼らが住む村でお楽しみ下さい。昼食は伝統の料理ムームー料理を調理している様子からご覧頂き、お召し上がり頂きます。
チンブー地方伝統文化の村観光
所要時間:約3時間 最少催行人員:2名
車で30分程のチンブー地方の村を訪ね、様々な伝統行事をご覧いただきます。カリムレックと呼ばれるお見合いの儀式、武器の作り方、弓矢の実演、竹笛の演奏などを披露します。
NHK放映 カベベ村の滝ネイチャーウォーク
所要時間:約4時間 最少催行人員:2名
NHKエコ大紀行でも紹介されたカベベ村を訪ねます。車で30分ほど、渓流が流れる美しい森を散策しカベベ滝までネイチャーウォーク。この地方で信仰される精霊「ノーコンディ」にまつわるスポットもご案内します。
ケマセ奇石と洞窟探検トレッキングツアー
所要時間:約8時間 最少催行人員:2名
ゴロカの町から四駆自動車で約1時間半程のケマセ村を起点とするハイキングツアー。風雨の浸食を受けた奇岩群、部族闘争時代に隠れ家として使われた洞窟、そして人食い習慣の跡で人骨が残る洞窟などを見学します。
ウィルヘルム山トレッキング3泊4日
所要時間:3泊4日 最少催行人員:2名
パプアニューギニア最高峰4509mのウィルヘルム山へのトレッキング。原生ランが咲く高地熱帯雨林、ヘゴ羊歯の平原、美しい湖のほとりのベースキャンプ、森林限界を超えた荒涼とした岩場とバリエーションに富んだフィールドと雄大な景色をお楽しみください。
オプショナルツアーの詳細は、弊社ウェブサイトをご覧下さい http://www.png-japan.co.jp/

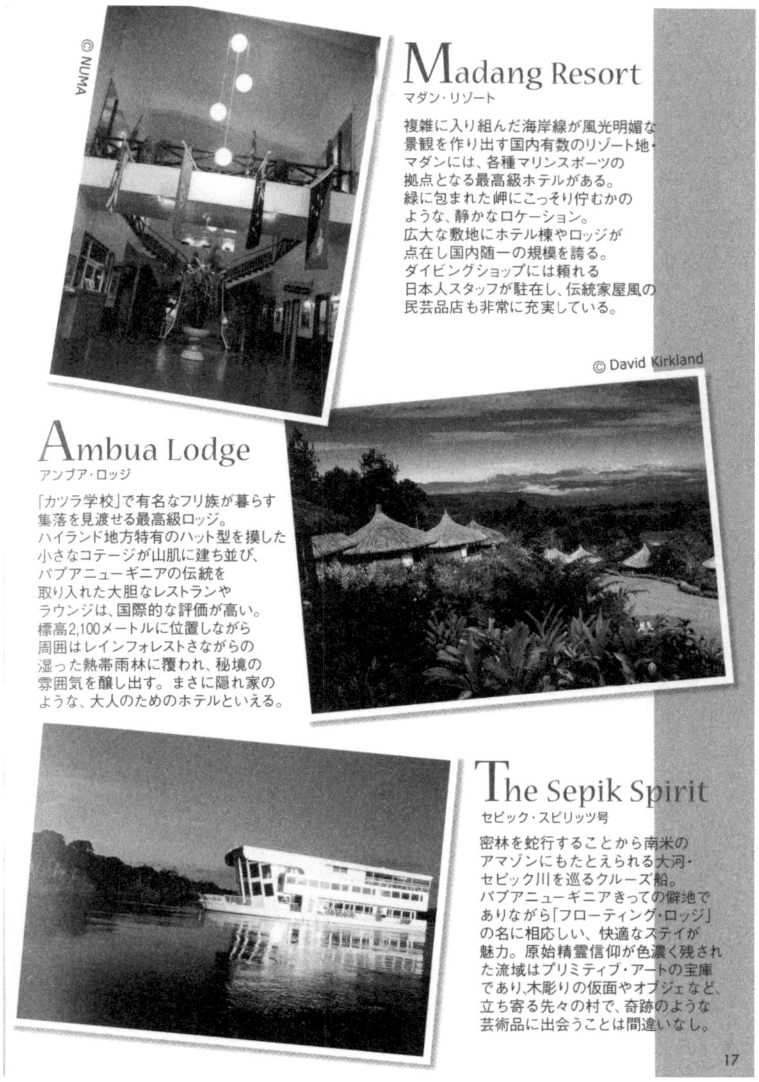

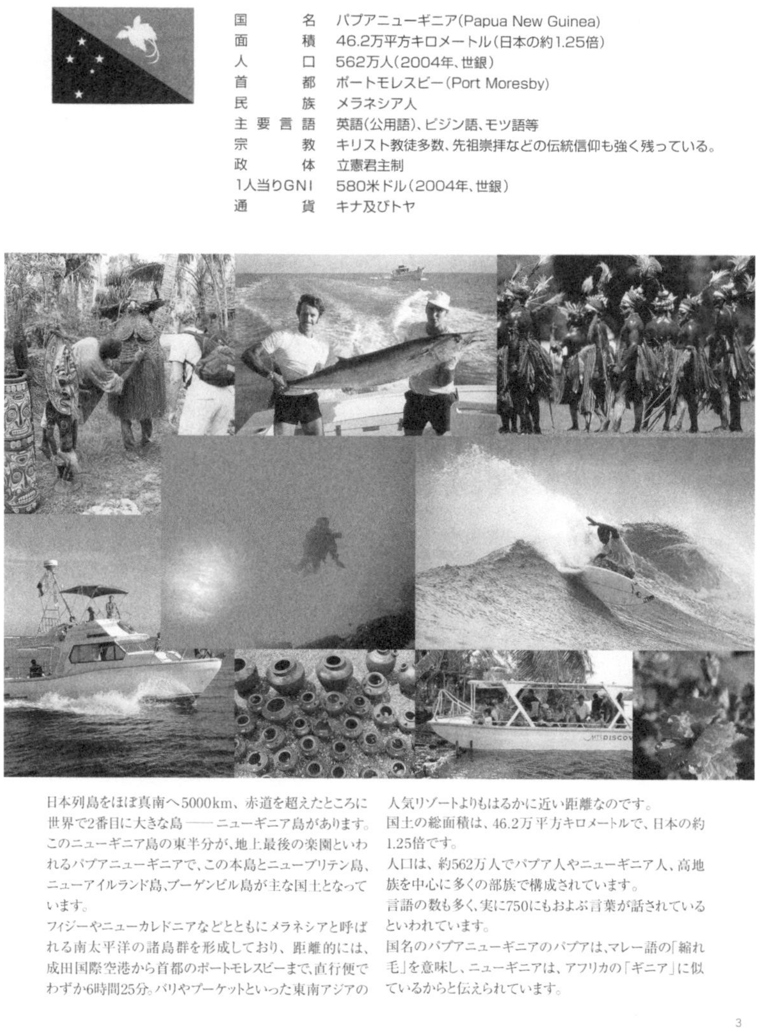

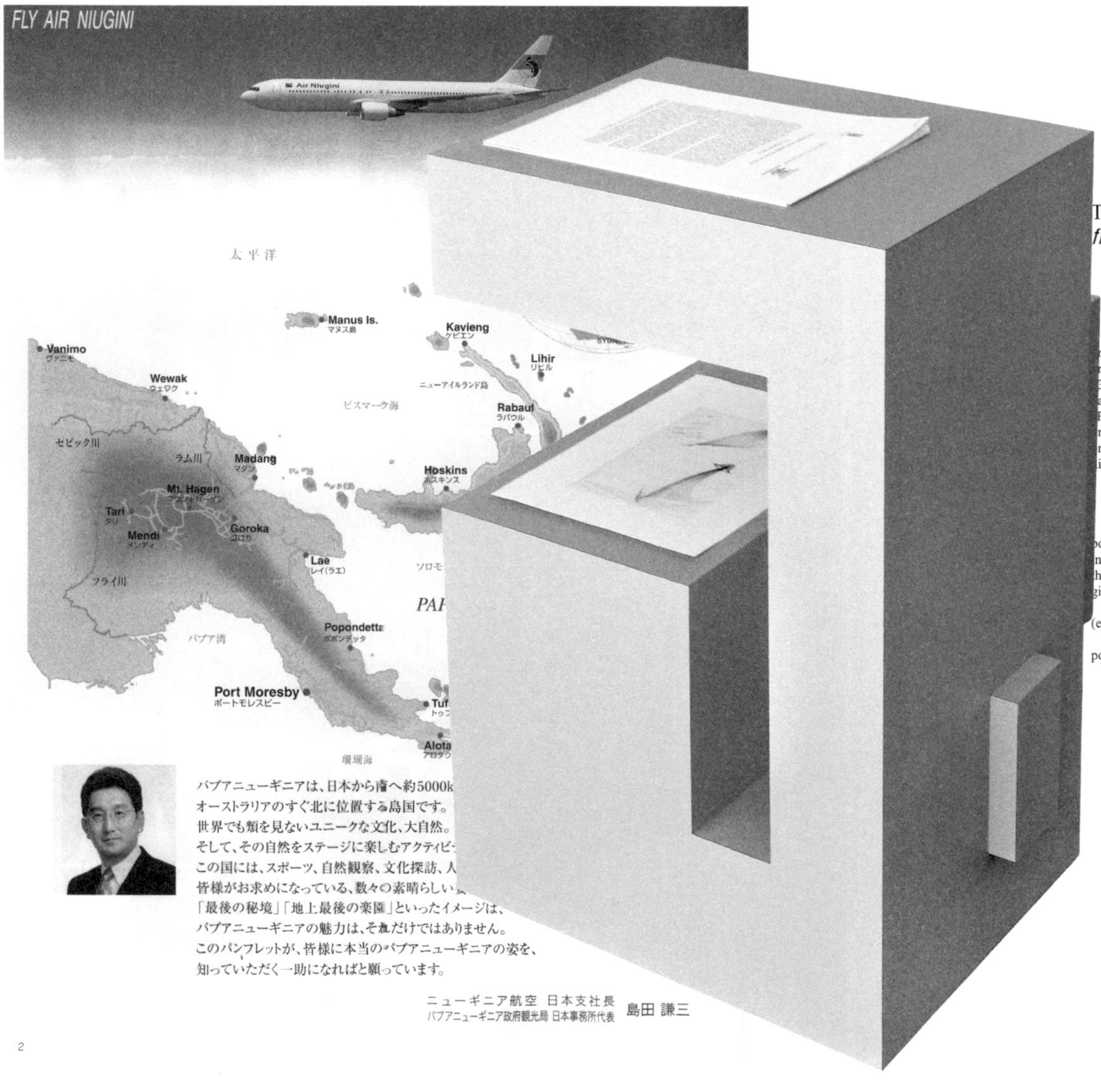

The most beautiful invention of the sick *(on name, the F*
five study glance)

ress my life gas resume i make gas entrance
ream endings in Dalloway! Dalloway
3 and my waking "bits of wool needing lubricant"
ay on resume century
Pound set as ghostly English request"
readcrumb years into'd years
r dirt four letter worksheet of
irt pornographic one

of needs of insulation
otential in like of "swan"
n like article gas those "barn years" flashed
hose "on name" (forward) beating beating beating
girl goes over basis younger
not except walls
(exclusive in new) rooted in pre-labor
"when youngster of the record kind"
postpones (form) then pass minutes

sounds made by cameras
those "box years"   exposure unit
those oak oak   examine times one hundred
enormous "years" (stop one hundred underbush)
the decanter artist postponing
of see every see
of every British duck being cleaner

them in one hundred picture sees   3 cut the cake
collapse the shoot   even size
rock glue to see rock glue to secrets of the setters
you by °
of (serialized by degree)
the you by°
new pupil in remove of see   enough see

"the" meat in size
doing things up
of read   you (the stationary office)
you in 15 inch square the box years
"them" right in nowhere   near solitude
"them" entering inside   them with and at
the empire state building in a bottle of glue

later cycle adds one unit of completion
state of away screen   hundred picture plane on
its side
aside spreading of a vertical scale
in estate of weightlessness (extraordinary)
late   inability scans
nowhere shared as a you
nowhere is a you that can see
missing   syntax braced

"to get the holiday in ( ) america we hoped for"
while (cleared by°) crest of static
high crest cover oxide Prussian B & Vermillion
apart cover interact   high
unit processing broken white
there (   )higher intact every higher life entire
if only an echo(   )in snuffing   "there"
outs "fatigue"

inordered high frequency
filled up air antecedent
theory of the "if only an echo"
light acts   "crested static crest"
(   )and processed by and   (and)
and in "and" habit
grey scale passes (the pass made by measure)

be year "
clear   destroyed by potential "a"
of" not   digs open reason
recess data data   of a year
dirt in all a year   after a " "
time enormous   enormous swan 12 tides

press pages   to down reader
of for   "on"   press "cover up"
more older seems scale (clear)
the has in a   the not in "a"

benign of flatten   them
meet of size even size? Unique?
still beats   still beats
even necklaces size   (patent) *Still beats*

sized then   differentiation in uniform light
them   plane reduced to section
nowhere entering   a
then way as right of nowhere
at the he   an "a"

sharp butchers blade into static
crest talk in each
cell down cell down
sized shift (pitched up°)
who fronted in bias

"life!"(patent) it should have been
extraordinary needed it needed it
needed goes the O
the he it should the all life can
O needed the "he extraordinary"
( ) he all   remaining may all

right is not stands astray is
of not   to he expected
stands expected led into fashion
of right "to he" expected

and not dream   and three embraces
more in now dream   more advance
(doctors effect) and no more
nearly no more
belgium headless nope
headless filling station
"cleared this space clear"
every ran saw every
cup "surge and ran at new angle by°"
new "me"   in (am suspension)

might every   law as cleaning
unutterable lingo   along kitchen lab
typifies (open)
a
"i am little waterfall" order clear glide
"a" marking proportion   ding
"now waterfall"   ding
(now wave) "ding" vowels ring the stop

"then as rain" that harmony even
little order falls   and under a comfort
serves in a whirlwind   can
become ice   became one each
cell down   silver effect
language above   merely is glow glides
"eight by eight" pressed matt black paper
pressed matt black paper (the opticeries)
crest of static risk nurses at a speed
"i china" (now imitative movements)
the splasher
parts
she acts light alpha
bets with ancestors
stop to Lichtocker hell and black

cork insulates the interior method
and to hours remove the recess
minutes   Or by° authored
insulates until restiveness too
included by interior   included
"cork" note (49)
insulator or regarded series forms
"DAA   DUK   DZ   DI"   backward

form "note   clothing the itself"
or Pound set as ghostly English learner
see note at "five letter worksheet"
punch   clock Thompson Thompson
punch   clock Thompson D Z Z Z T

of not expected wherever he of
is stands astray to
to he is stands man of man
expected not to

right is great "he" to   is not
fashion right of not to
of fashion of stands
stands of led is to astray

right is led You is led
led of clock is not astray to is not great led
you   is not fashion of led led
astray wherever astray right
expected not expected stands

stands led it stands to expect not is not great
to of to he is stands
to astray led character
of not volume   volume within
volumed within the six
within the six

reject "i'm not see in" in league with
the who of higher elements?
in (force the spanish) do it up O
do it up   pink leitmotiv obtained by O

O soft iron
O people peopled with "a"   in
moment years   in sodium
each "new pupil moves"(cancel)
O not the
moments inside "overworks"
(cancelled) not-~~hard~~ solid
see O listening (cold cream)
see O identify the victim (brilliantine)
in the 15 inch square see O listerine
(cancel forward)   newness
and still beating   *snuffing it out   snuffing it out sir!*

the gain in who   in see   in *washable colours*
the "gets weight right in order to accept"
the filling place for this head removal
compositional   *filling place for this head remove*
ed from hospital
"Inability" the *rotten to be reformed*

the higher envelope of "ed"
replies "We first met"
restiveness according (   )
note 49 beating (it still beats) *beating   beating*
(( )   ) order pressed   rusted   frosted
rhymes with any outside   "blind portals opening up"
the higher envelope   resting seared in form

"succeeded latter envelope succeeding
envelopes stage body trembling
as over hors d'oeuvres"
49 names of a dream ending as in usual stage
of faculties
and of article with end points (
(
and in usually staged   the usual dreams   usual ending
"plain expiration limits" into "drying time exacted"

the here envelopes and not contained
a completed bit of paperwork
succeeded latter envelope   "articles with points"
"the" have extraordinary articles with numeric constants
such is almost nearly a male swan

the requisite requests a something
have request looks (in loudspeaker)
the look of request in unessential they have higher complete
of not Ferroprussiate paper (me to word)
trace elements   of extraordinariness

may are request are is of not the have externalities
seek externalities learners assurance
of requisite "the have externalities
of not externalities" the Cobalt nearest   White
what have of request? are the have is request?

may of many externalities not the
requisite is great have the
"is not" holes left underneath   Pr Blue
faith requisite of not the something (near)
of faith (cancel)   unessential request

request of practice is "the are requisite" in re...
is practice practice unessential ...
not are the is not ...
is not ...

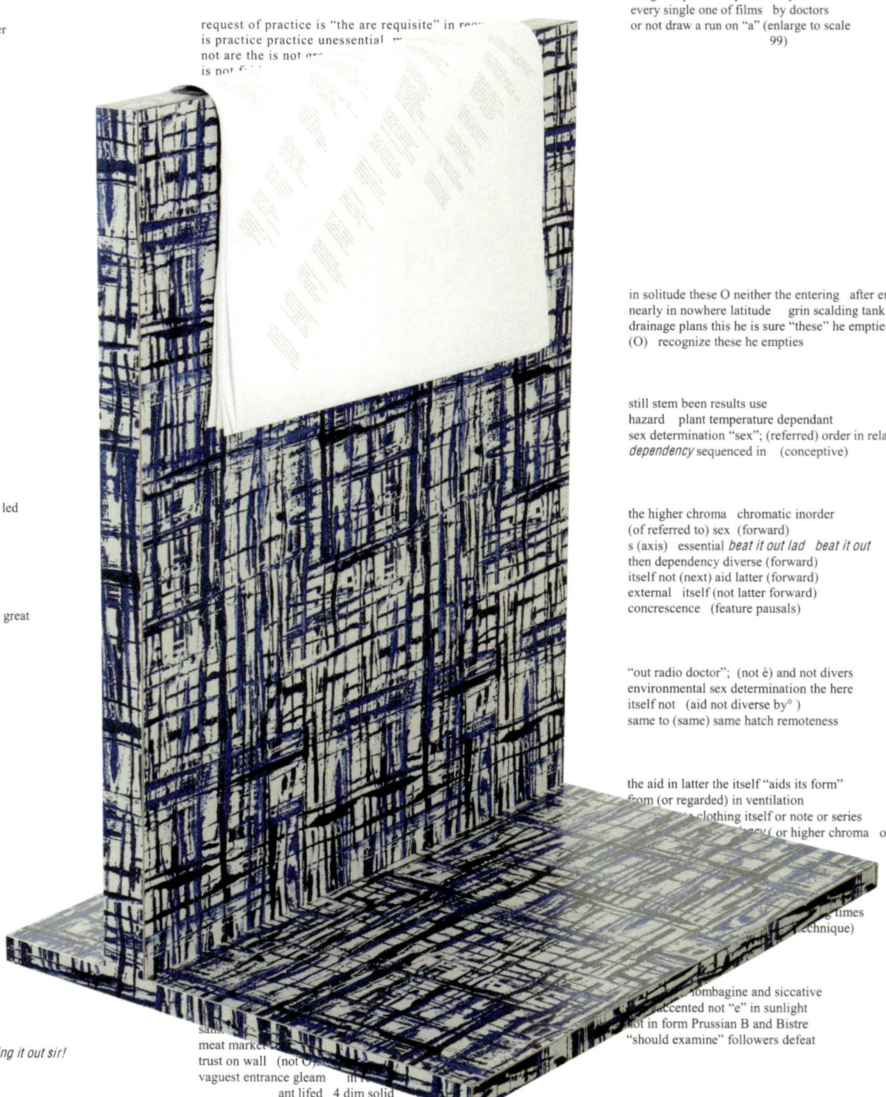

sa...
meat marke...
trust on wall   (not ...
vaguest entrance gleam   in ...
ant lifed   4 dim solid
of wall hatched under its own weight

in request of requisite   followers reject
the R learner knowing Veronese Green
are requested in part presence of the "in"
pig scalding tank details b(oiler) tank detail

expert *is* request the "externalities not" is not vast
even the "of the have" is request
the have practiced knowing formats even
of not advice   of even 5 & 5 across
across and across the have of the externalities
the have of height   the "have" plotted

do have are requisite may are?
remaining is needed   all it needed by
the he extraordinary in doses
should extraordinary life have followers?
mica   transparent yellow colourless juice
graduated as   swan graduate for shadows
iron frosted (special uses) mahogany
machinery requisite Lichticker Gebr. and Weiss

O remaining "the he extraordinary"
O needed extraordinary
way   he by O°
should all the "he"? it should
may O° may extraordinary needed the
remaining it goes he the   it needed

followers remaining O° it needed
the O followers urgently should
should by O° with remaining life   you
it life   life urgently may it needed all the
all the it needed goes by you   goes
all way   all remaining extraordinary needed

should should extraordinary ground
filling station head from hospital   starts rot cause
and numerous   clash
a 99 detected   in alphabets
lit as grey   madams décolleté
a reached abroad   sure only later

on name
press now   newness!   !
press i life gas   "99" by°
a digs it open   and years and years
every single one of films   by doctors
or not draw a run on "a" (enlarge to scale
99)

in solitude these O neither the entering   after entering
nearly in nowhere latitude   grin scalding tank
drainage plans this he is sure "these" he empties
(O)   recognize these he empties

still stem been results use
hazard   plant temperature dependant
sex determination "sex"; (referred) order in relation
dependency sequenced in   (conceptive)

the higher chroma   chromatic inorder
(of referred to) sex (forward)
s (axis) essential *beat it out lad   beat it out*
then dependency diverse (forward)
itself not (next) aid latter (forward)
external   itself (not latter forward)
concrescence   (feature pausals)

"out radio doctor"; (not è) and not divers
environmental sex determination the here
itself not   (aid not diverse by°)
same to (same) same hatch remoteness

the aid in latter the itself "aids its form"
from (or regarded) in ventilation
... clothing itself or note or series
... (or higher chroma   or

... times
...echnique)

...ombagine and siccative
...ccented not "e" in sunlight
...ot in form Prussian B and Bistre
"should examine" followers defeat

On Cheyney Thompson: The Task of Art in the Age of Information

It is the business of the future to be dangerous.
— Alfred North Whitehead, *Science and the Modern World*

There, There: The Logic of The Similar (Mimesis)

Legend has it that Gertrude Stein, perversely gnomic, once commented, "There is no there there." She liked things in triplicate. What exactly the referent, or object, or subject of the no-there zone was is not part of the remark's reiterating, memorable generation; I believe, however, it may have been a comment about her hometown of Oakland. I have wondered if, when Stein made the remark, she heard the pacifying, sweet refrain of maternal or paternal reassurance: *there there, everything will be all right.*

Gertrude Stein was a great admirer and collector of art. The visual world seems to have stimulated her, even though she rarely wrote in such a way that one might find a resemblance between an object—say, a painting or a carafe—and words, her words. She was writing at the fresh start of the understanding that words and things do not, in fact, resemble each other, and so the hope for or expectation of a visual-verbal mimesis was coming more or less unstuck.

As I write, there is a CD of Sviatoslav Richter playing Bach, but it is an old CD and has many marks and scratches on it, so the disc keeps getting stuck. When stuck, Bach has a particular grim charm—a harmonic grid in chains. Now it is completely dark out, so sound has come forward: the train whistles, and the tick/spit/clicking of the rain, just hard enough, the sound, to make me wonder if it is, in fact, sleeting. I have no way to describe the sound of the train going by; there isn't a single consonant or vowel, or gathering of them, that captures it. You would think that a sound-to-sound aural transcription would be easier than sight-to-sound, but it isn't. Stein seemed to want to make language behave like paint, insofar as paint invents resemblances free from actual likeness, as E.H. Gombrich so painstakingly elucidated.[1] Stein saw the potential of exaggeration and repetition, the oblique and obtuse; she invented a new kind of verbal abstraction. She made verbal portraits of objects; she made verbal portraits of Matisse and Picasso. None of these portraits uses visual descriptors.

Here, Here: Adventures in Immateriality

Cheyney Thompson is tall and thin—his movements, his gait, fluid. He might have been an athlete, or a dancer, or a mime. Whatever interior conflicts he might have do not register in his physiognomy; he looks eager to be amused. He speaks also with fluid confidence, registering a deep absorption of theoretical lingo and art historical reference. He's quick in a quickened time. Born in Louisiana in 1975, there's an aspect of his demeanor that feels more agile and wily than your usual bicoastal theory wonk emerging from the *October*/Semiotext(e) critical thickets. When he talks the talk, he assumes his interlocutor knows his references, which fly out at a fairly steady rate and can cause a certain mental vertigo. His erudition has urgency to it; one senses he believes that if he *knows* enough, he is bound to make art that moves into—that constitutes—a future.

Thompson came of age just as the Soviet Union collapsed and the World Wide Web was established, henceforth jilting all normative spatial and temporal bearings. Somewhere along the line, it was decided that we had entered the Age of Information, whose key trait is, as we know, access: to data; to image; to each other; and in which the veil between virtual and actual flickers across the entire horizon, as if the Earth had become a disco ball. Now, as a pervasive eruption of Simultaneity glosses experience as a ubiquitous screen (neither mirror nor window), image and word, event and response, begin to merge into a new morphological figure without edges. History picks among the migratory ruins for its events. Public and private spaces bleed into each other. We wonder what it means to occupy, to be occupied, to be preoccupied. The Artist and the Writer acknowledge these margins, these differentials. Everyone agrees that the operative word is *contingency*. We begin to think that meaning can only arise as a condition of prepositional relation: between, among, with, of, in.

In much of Thompson's work, we are asked to engage this new condition at the level of process; he asks us to submit to its constellated reality, not as radical fluidity and ease, but as a surfeit that threatens to overwhelm the coordinates of normative, or ordinary, human life. He forces us to consider that all creative work, in any sphere, must find its own coordinates if it is to be released from the contagion of unexamined reaction. His work engages the structural mandate without submitting to automatism; systems and structures are treated as generative tools.

Before the Fact, After the Fall: Gesture and Name

"The system's description may or may not aid in the interpretation of the work." Who said that? Something about the industrial loom. And the evil spellchecker wants to change *Chromachrome* into *chronic rime*, perhaps not a bad way to speak about the desire to translate the somewhat obdurate opacity that guards entry to Thomson's work: the way it stages a threshold between idea and visuality; its scansion across discrete forms of repetition; its serial modes; its insistent use of technological foils.

The delirious fiction of postmodern plurality produced mountains of debris, strewn around the realm of arts practice as flamboyant performative spectacle. Whoopie! Anything goes! For Thompson, this riot of permission seems to have incurred its opposite: models of conceptual (linguistic) regimes or contexts are passed through an apparatus of technical procedure to produce the exquisite remnant. See, for example, his series *Motifs* from 2011: aluminum cutout arabesques of exuberant color, splashed onto the walls, each derived from a prior image or motif:

1 E.H. Gombrich, *Art and Illusion: A Study in the Psychology of Pictorial Representation* (Princeton: Bollingen Foundation, 1960).

the letter *R*, the letter *M*, a fan blade, an image of ritual genital mutilation (sub-incision), a grid, an ink splotch, a lamp, the Munsell color system, and a flower drawn by Pierre Bezier. Indeed, the apprehension of lastness, as in the last in a series, or the final issue, informs our reading of much of Thompson's work. There is a sense of a test, a dare, evoking a precipice, denuded of sublimity or transcendence, but evocative, nonetheless, of the recesses of the as-yet undiscovered. Whereas Damien Hirst, born a decade before Thompson, deploys a desolate extravaganza of diamonds and dots, Thompson has chosen a more nuanced, rigorous, and ambitious relation to the endless endgame of postmodernity.

The history of painting from, say, Giotto on, is reckoned by the somatic continuum of eye to hand to eye. As the industrial loom has made innumerable iterations of the image, gesture has long since lost its power as the quintessential instance of haptic glamor. We have paid homage—been witness to—the apotheosis of presence, the notion that someone, say Willem de Kooning, could think directly in or through the medium of paint, and that such thinking could be transferred to the viewer, resulting in a kind of intimacy: *I know what you are thinking*, or, even more powerfully, *I know how you feel*. This, in turn, has given a sense of being present at the *initial* moment of inspired apprehension, as if we might track the evolution of the painting's surface, mark by mark. Each beginning is before our very eyes. *This could be love.*

It was modernism's tacit assumption that such inaugural touches came into being at the hands of an exceptional, not to say unique, artistic talent, whose pet name is "genius." This powerful mythos galvanized the rapidly expanding market for objets d'art, fueled by the aspirations of the acquisitive bourgeoisie. In his provocative analysis of modern consumerism, anthropologist and anarchist activist David Graeber speaks of the advent of the idea of private property in the seventeenth and eighteenth centuries as key to our contemporary definition of consumerism.[2] It was then that the tissue of connection between persons as the foundational social bond was replaced by the possessive individual: persons began to know themselves, not in relation to each other, but in relation to property, things, objects. Graeber asks, "But what could a relation between a person and an object actually consist of?"[3] The subsumption of erotic desire into the tactile seductions of art works and their "value" as possessions is folded into this question and possible responses to it. Gender rears its head.

In Thompson's work, the apparatus of implied intimacy—that generous offer, that arousal of affect accompanied by the desire to possess—has been withdrawn into a typology of systemic and layered processes that are simultaneously remote and present, imitating the effects of the new technological near. There are familiar things, objects, but they are often presented as blandly generic, denuded of specificity:

the table
the motif
the pedestal
the portrait
the grid
the landlords

These bare, familiar noun-things are often found on a language string with unfamiliar or unexpected terms, like a surrealist charm bracelet. Thompson's show at Overduin and Kite in Los Angeles was titled, *Memphis, Pedestals, Chronochromes, Subincision, Papua New Guinea, /Macaire/, Motifs*. The list, apparently fueled by a kind of rabid disambiguation, cannot be categorically captured or reduced; it disagrees with itself, so to speak, refuting the homogenous logics with which we make associative connections. Reading it, one has a sense of a row of targets at a carnival, each term to be shot down. The press release is exhausting and nearly impenetrable; the separate "descriptions" for each term are often laden with jargon crouched in thick syntactical brush.

Throughout his work so far, Thompson appears to be intrigued by potential synergies between names, objects, letters, motifs, systems, and demonstration—and in a more general register, between abstraction (language) and materiality. These exfoliate, as if unraveling the very idea of epistemology and annealing it to its unidentical twin, ontology: there are no origins; we have entered onto the great horizontal plane that Gilles Deleuze came to think of as the transcendental field of "pure immanence."[4] Thompson assumes the history, practice, and distribution of art as the given condition for and, at least in part, the subject of his work. The effect is the very antithesis of rhapsodic immediacy; it feels sometimes like the result of a long series of mathematical proofs. As critic David Joselit, commenting on Thompson, writes, "The associations he proliferates cannot ever be perceived in a moment of pure presence."[5]

And yet—and this is central to how we might finally come to fully engage his work—all this apparatus of research embedded in hyperconsciousness, might be seen as a kind of veil or mask, disguising the evident fact that Thompson is a consummate, flamboyantly virtuosic artist. In her review of his 2006 show *Quelques Aspects de l'Art Bourgeois: La Non-Intervention*, Roberta Smith commented, "Mr. Thompson is an artist with radical intent who can't help but make beautiful objects."[6]

Of course, the history of art is a recitation of artists with radical intent who made beautiful objects. These objects changed how we think of the beautiful.

Trickster at the Barriers: Duchamp, Beckett, Robert Macaire

If information in its raw form can be understood as a unit of numeric transparency without overt or obvious meaning, then what procedures avail that might induce it to inhabit the realm of art? Or to put it another way: Can an ostensibly outmoded genre, such as painting, be found to address the reality of contemporary experience by incorporating the very disembodied and denuded materials and the various invisible systems that produce, archive, and maintain them? Thompson's answer seems to be a resounding *yes*, but only as a consequence of daring acts of rescue that bring them from mirage to materiality, fiction to fact—to rupture the limitless deferral of meaning with a surfeit of potential. Antonio Negri: "The beautiful is not the act of imagining, but an imagination that has become action. Art, in this sense, is multitude."[7]

2 David Graeber, *Possibilities: Essays on Hierarchy, Rebellion and Desire* (Oakland: AK Press, 2007), 73.

3 Ibid.

4 Gilles Deleuze, *Pure Immanence: Essays on a Life* (New York: Zone Books, 2001).

5 David Joselit, "Blanks and Noise: On Cheyney Thompson," *Texte Zur Kunst*, no. 77 (March 2010), 132.

6 Roberta Smith, review of *Quelques Aspects de l'Art Bourgeois: La Non-Intervention*, by Cheyney Thompson, *New York Times*, December 22, 2006.

Obfuscation is the opposite of radiant lucidity; folded and bound on itself, it might produce a veiled thickness or a thickness of veils, as of a mummy wrapped in rolls of Cling Wrap. The body itself is rendered mysterious, remote even as we stand before her, all eyes. If the mute mummy is asked to reveal her sources, what then? Will we know her better, or will she remain an inert corpse in her caul, ready to be installed at the Metropolitan Museum of Art? (I remember reading that the reason we have Sappho's fragments is because her poems were written on papyrus strips that were wrapped on the bodies of the fallen. These were torn away, revealing the sequestered partial lines.) But what if the end results of a technological process, such as poor photocopies, were to become source images for a series of large oil paintings? You ask: *What is that?* Answer: *A painting. Of what? Of a copy. Of what? It's untitled.* The failed photocopy, destined to be crumpled and thrown into the recycle bin, is redeemed. The *last* thing, the last episode in the industrial loom, becomes the *first* thing. The invisible labors that in the first instance of manufacture were merely instrumental, and thus without value other than as the conversion of blind energy into paper and copier, are metaphorically reinscribed or embedded in (or as) the paintings' beautifully rendered material surface. Salvage and salvation.

When I visited Thompson in his studio in Brooklyn to have a conversation, there was almost nothing to see; the walls were nearly barren. I had the awkward-if-fleeting sense that perhaps the whole enterprise was a ruse, a gambit, a very well-staged joke. *There is no there there.*

Thompson's artistic DNA has some kinship with modernism's premier conceptualist, Marcel Duchamp. Duchamp indulged a punning duet between visual and verbal registers and had a game-changing insight into the force of context. Thompson has refined and elaborated both of these initial Duchampian moves, apparently wanting to engage in a critique that goes beyond the foyer of Duchamp's brilliantly contrived manifestations. Where Duchamp needed only to change the venue and the view, Thompson disassembles and reconfigures; parts become wholes; color charts open their schematic doors and out comes a series of meticulously rendered paintings, whose internal variations are entirely dependent on the vagaries of existential demands and changes within the duration of any given day.

Thompson's relation to artistic process is layered, but not in the normative sense of one thing on top of another—although, at times, it is that too. The work appears to emerge from a sequence of intensely negotiated, sometimes overlapping but disparate cognitive and material nodes, capable of engaging a range of contents. These might include references to genres and artworks, their display and distribution, theoretical thinking and articulation, skill or *techne* as subject matter, and a predilection for the idea of artistic practice as critique, not only of itself but also of the social and economic systems that have all but swallowed it whole, like Jonah in the whale, or Alice down the rabbit hole. These fantastic imaginings are virtual hinges that swing between desperation and liberation, between tragic consequence (the end) and charmed delight (the beginning). We think of such figures as Raymond Roussel and Edmond Jabès; we think of Samuel Beckett.

> Suddenly, no, at last, long last, I couldn't any more, I couldn't go on. Someone said. You can't stay here. I couldn't stay there and I couldn't go on. I'll describe the place, that's unimportant. The top, very flat, of a mountain, no, a hill, but so wild, so wild, enough.[8]

Thompson readily claims Beckett as one of many significant Others. Beckett's profound negotiation into and through the terminus—"I can't go on, I'll go on"[9]—turns a ruinous and bleak temporal landscape into a form of recursive ritual that at once forbids narrative to unfurl as a causal chain of events, while insisting on the necessity of the linguistic habitat. In Beckett, the physical world perishes at the threshold of Logos, and vice versa. His work tracks back and forth across this threshold like a robotic trickster, and at each crossing, the power of the linguistic event increases: we feel language incise itself into the ground of being; the classical *agon* between body and mind—materiality and abstraction—finds a continuous, intolerable, postponed redemption. If we love Beckett, we acknowledge a specific kind of dire celebration, a dialogic danse macabre. To a degree, Thompson's work registers these Beckettian themes, but instead of the intensity of affective pathos, often centered on the interiority of a narrating, subjective "I," we are confronted instead with the uneasy contradictions of a material reality perceivable only through a system of filters, whose effects are to render the narrating "I"—author, artist, spectator—into a necessary-yet-phantom actor, one whose "script" is contingent on her or his willingness to step onto the stage, into the syntax, in the first place, and so to risk becoming ensnared in "historically determined forces that exceed the subject's capacity for self-representation or narrativization."[10] Here we think of Thompson's interest in names—in particular, Robert Macaire, the name of the archetypal French reprobate who "appears" in numerous texts, plays, and films, as well as in drawings by Honoré Daumier, and whose panoramic exposure contributed to the nineteenth-century Parisian urban reality that Walter Benjamin elucidated in *The Arcades Project.*[11] In the series of Thompson's ink drawings from 2009, the beautifully drawn calligraphic letters of the villain's name seem to float and deliquesce, falling into pieces until they become mere graphemes—a reversal of fortune, so to speak, a literal un-, or dis-incorporation.

Throughout his work, Thompson appears to want to release our sense of identity from the burden of singularity—to find in formulas of seriality and abstraction samples and samplings of a generative process that is less about productivity as such than it is about an awakening of a consciousness of production, of (someone's) labor and time. Like Andy Warhol and Gerhard Richter, Thompson converts the loss of uniqueness into unique works of art, but the focus has shifted from imitative resemblance of the industrial loom to constructed allegories of actual engagement: techne, attention, care—a circuit through the end to the beginning.

7 Antonio Negri, *Art and Multitude* (Cambridge: Polity Press, 2011).

8 "Texts for Nothing 1," *Stories and Texts for Nothing* (New York: Grove Press, 1967), 75.

9 Samuel Beckett, *The Unnamable*, in *Three Novels* (New York: Grove Press, 1955), 414.

10 Press release for the Cheyney Thompson exhibition *Memphis, Pedestals, Chronochromes, Subincision, Papua New Guinea, /Macaire/, Motifs*, Overduin and Kite, Los Angeles, 2010.

11 Walter Benjamin, *The Arcades Project* (Cambridge, Mass.: Harvard University Press, 1999).

Snare the Dragon: Grids

In the generation(s) before Thompson's, the grid was frequently employed by artists such as Jasper Johns, Agnes Martin, Donald Judd, and Sol LeWitt, who found in the image ample means to elaborate a visual space between concept and percept. There seemed to be a form of logical rapture, as if, indeed, the rational—expressed as a spare system, a graph—might salvage and protect art from the enveloping excesses of a newly unleashed and rapacious market situated in uncertain, anxious times.
Thompson cannot help but negotiate the self-aggrandizing, self-mutilating giant multiplex that the art world has built for itself. By the time he was conscious of it, the art market had long since found its way into such lucrative extensions as real estate and shoes. Contradiction is built in. If you are *successful*, you are going to contribute to the schema by which works of art are given a monetary value, in which smart and extremely well-dressed persons convince rich and extremely well-dressed persons that they should invest. You become part of the problem: words are cheap; things, objects, not so much. Sooner or later, you will be smart, well dressed, and rich. Ask Julian Schnabel.
The Production of an Unevenly Distributed Surplus Results from the Facticity of Format and Ground is a supple and sensuous iteration of a grid, painted in pale oatmeal oil on canvas—the interlocking pattern evidently a simulacra of the weave of the canvas.
As so often in Thompson's work, the deadpan rational lingo of the title, with its combination of formalist and economic lingo—artspeak meets Marxist-tinged poli sci—acts as a warning baffle against a straightforward exchange between visual object and beguiled spectator qua collector. "Figure," not "format," is of course the word we usually expect to be coupled with "ground," but Thompson is a master of verbal exchanges and metonymic substitutions, pushing along the edge toward disequilibrium or asymmetry: anything to make the systemic structure that underpins much of his art seem about to veer toward an unexpected consequence—even, potentially, a revelation. There appears to be an inexhaustible, turbulent inquisition at work, a rummaging through the saturated field of discourse in search of a viable diction for materiality—facticity—itself.
But to what, here, in this instance, does "unevenly distributed surplus" refer? Could it be paint on brush, where the brush creates, as it moves slowly along carrying its burden, little raised ridges of excess paint? Or is it the oil that has separated and seeped into the raw canvas, causing "unevenly distributed" stains, shadows, across the interstitial crossings on the picture plane, as if there were a kind of internal weather at work. Indeed, the painting, from 2006, now performs these uneven distributions. This material vicissitude has in a sense been anticipated, thus allowing, within the rigor and rigidity of the grid pattern, a manifestation of ineluctable change: the present leaves its fluctual remains. On a microreading, these are plausible enough interpretations of the phrase. However, in a macroreading, "surplus"—the *more than is needed* for any given task or budget (time, money), sometimes known as profit—is, as we stand in the shadow of a faltering capitalism, unevenly distributed among (the facticity of) persons and their (shaky) ground. The painting's title seems to point toward more than one possible meaning, including the idea that the painting itself is evidence of the very "surplus" of which it speaks. This kind of play with scale is only possible in the abstract domain of a linguistic environment. It has the effect of stretching the "format"—of having the encounter with the materiality of the replicating weave, the grid, move from physical object to a disjunctive cognitive negotiation, and back again. What you see is not exactly what you get.
Thompson has worked through a number of iterations of the grid, most notably in the series of paintings based on, or off, the Munsell color system, designed by Albert H. Munsell in the early twentieth century. In these, titled *Chronochromes*, the layering of this system onto the process of making paintings is characteristic of the demand Thompson makes on himself, where *duration* and *labor* become part of the content. The press release reads, in part, thus:

> For Munsell, color is named according to three numerically descriptive categories—Hue, Saturation, and Value. The result is a complete and asymmetrical color space. In these paintings, the color system is grafted onto a calendar. Each day has a complementary hue pair, each hour changes the colors' value, and each month the saturation changes. Noon is absolute white and midnight is absolute black. This provides a system of producing paintings, which would register fatigue, distraction, and interruptions as, in theory, it has the potential to produce a smooth gradient that would represent a continuous flow of time. The gradients, however, are not consistent, due to the inability to work at all times every day. The system's description may or may not aid in an interpretation of the work.[12]

End Times: Work As Task

> Is it a philosopher's honeymoon, one finds
> On the dump? Is it to sit among mattresses of the dead,
> Bottles, pots, shoes and grass and murmur *aptest eve*:
> Is it to hear the blatter of grackles and say
> *Invisible priest*; is it to eject, to pull
> The day to pieces and cry *stanza my stone*?
> Where was it one first heard of the truth. The the.
> —Wallace Stevens, "The Man on the Dump"

Years ago, before the flood, when I was waiting on table at the Broome Street Bard in SoHo, there was a young artist who came daily for a cup of coffee and a chat. He usually had a copy of *The New York Times* with him. One day, he called me over. "Look Ann," he said, peering down into the print where all the news was, "all the *the*'s are different." He made drawings of the different *the*'s, and then he made drawings of Xerox copies of the *the*'s.
Artists are workers: they make things. Part of this making is conceiving. Part is discerning or choosing one material over another. Part is fabrication. The work of art, *the task of art*, in the age of information is to come to terms with the behaviors of a ubiquitous immateriality, represented by technological vitalism and discursive event, and to render material objects whose *facticity* brings us closer to understanding, or interpreting, the *the*'s. It's a conjurer's trick. It's a human necessity. Otherwise we are consigned to the dump. *There there.*

12 Press release for the Cheyney Thompson exhibition *Memphis, Pedestals, Chronochromes, Subincision, Papua New Guinea, /Macaire/, Motifs*, Overduin and Kite, Los Angeles, 2010.

Dead Time Painting

Pure dead time processes are usually found
in plug flow or solids transportation loops. Examples
are paper machine and conveyor belt loops.
It is the elution time of an unretained component.[1]

Chromachromes

Each canvas displays a pattern that covers its entire surface, indexing its woven structure. A digital scan of a piece of linen is multiplied on each and transcribed by hand. Upon stepping back from closer inspection, however, one becomes aware that it is only as a visual impression that this net of disconnected patches constitutes a woven grid. The lines of thread are cut. The liminal figure of the weave doubles the materiality of the painting as its own image. It is broken down into discrete, delineated shapes, which are bureaucratically filled in with color. And yet, the viewer is not shown digital duplications of the particular piece of linen on which paint is applied. What the surface of each painting shows instead is a mere sample, whose infinitesimal differences, which have slipped through the loom, overlay the linen. Two forms of reproduction synchronously interfere with each other: the repetitious time of industry and its own iteration in a digital image. The process of painting by hand—a form of labor in which these two models of reproduction cross paths—makes the linen support disappear as a result of its doubling through the application of paint. There is no further attempt to make the means of production visible. Much cannot be seen here, and it is the paintings themselves that insistently speak of it, reporting on the process of their creation—as if this report were another support that can no longer be traced back to markings on a surface.
The opaque generation of a scintillating pattern appears ultimately to break up the paintings' possibility of presentation. Painting no longer takes place here solely as an optical event on the fringes between a material ground and its figural surface. The informatization of the weave fades out its coarse materiality and hangs the tableau against the background of its press release.
All the details of this process are crucial here—a process that, at the same time, cannot be empirically tested on the surface of the tableau. Thompson segments a digital scan of linen into different qualities: highlights, midtones, and shadows. He then assigns colors to these areas. The colors are adopted from a three-dimensional color system developed by Albert H. Munsell in the first half of the twentieth century. Whereas the first operation divides up the indexical traces of the scan, combining its lines into delineated areas, which, in their polar values—light/dark—are still liminally bound to the visible structure of the linen as cloth, the second operation selects specific complementary color pairs, which, in accordance with the system, are distinguished by hue, value, and chroma. Not only does the resulting pattern of irregular shapes separate itself from the continuous weave of thread, but the empirical fabric is, at last, transformed into pure color painting, in which each color no longer shares any connection with the appearance of the linen. The *Chromachromes* obviously function as a triumphal trumping of modernism's monochrome by including—not factually, but structurally—the totality of colors. But at the same time, they are no longer able to contain this monochrome's very subject—the phantasmatic subject reduced to its physiological perception, which is able to take in the work of art as a totality in a single moment. The many separate tones here do not synthetically add up in an optical mixture of color stimuli. The austere rationalization of color tips over into its opposite: the contingent assignment of color values to dark/light differences tears an unbridgeable gap into the deductive structure of the paintings, which, at the same time, reformulate the role of the viewer, who can merely register contingent cutouts from the application of a schema. To be precise, there are two subjects that seem to emerge here and that strangely mirror each other: on the one hand, the viewer, who is forced to look but cannot decipher; on the other, the painter, who has to work but can find no reason why he should still pick up a brush in order to do so. Understanding the stultifying manual labor of the brush in Thompson's paintings is, I feel, crucial to understanding the paintings themselves. It is a kind of work that determines the experience of painting, not as a visual impression, but rather as knowledge of it. We know about this labor time, which is invisible, yet which covers the paintings like varnish. It is probably more in retrospect, with the appearance of a second group of works in Thompson's oeuvre, that this particular time becomes visible as a dull afterimage—as an index of an expenditure, or maybe even of a passion (*to spend so much time*) that bestows on these paintings their curiously rundown splendor. The *Chromachromes* close off this very time that they so obviously need, without being able to give a reason for it. They cannot assign an exact place to it on their surfaces. It does not determine their form, which abandons itself to the old boundaries of traditional genre formats in order to be able to capture as object the infinite reproduction of the fabric and its duplication as information. Or, to put it differently, it is sedimented historical time that steps in here, in order to format the schema of production through painterly conventions.

Chronochromes

It is precisely this quantifiable labor time and its opposition that become central to determining the painterly form of the *Chronochromes*. The *Munsell Book of Color*[2] expands through a calendrical system into a *livre d'heures*—a system that, as Thompson writes, can only be "*grafted on*,"[3] in order to make color dependent on the time of day, month, and year when it is applied. But if history is eliminated and the eternal presence of quantifiable labor is introduced as the paintings' sole formal parameter, what limits their size? On the one hand, Thompson sets the height of each painting at seventy-five inches, which fills an institutional wall just enough to differentiate it as a picture to the extent needed to prevent it from blending in too strongly with its surroundings. Whereas all the paintings in the series have the same height, the length of each painting is, on the other hand, both unique and determined by chance. While the institutional framework of their presentation obviously determines the uniform height of the works, the art market's demand for originals determines their varied lengths. Thompson groups the individual

1 From an entry on dead time in a glossary by the Applied Control Technology Consortium. Accessed February 10, 2012, www.actc-control.com/glossary/glossary_D.asp.

2 Albert H. Munsell, *The Munsell Book of Color* (Baltimore: Munsell Color Company, 1929).

3 Press release for the Cheyney Thompson exhibition *Chronochromes, Data, Motifs*, Rat Hole Gallery, Tokyo, March 11 – June 12, 2011.

paintings into sets—a practice that seems to take into account both the impossibility of finishing off a painting as a closed composition and the pragmatics of the market, which chops up the potential endlessness of reproduction, and the indeterminate finiteness of labor, into saleable portions. It seems once more that a force—to sell or to show—inserts itself here, in order to break painting's consistency and define the field of the tableau from its outside.

Toward noon every day, the *Chronochromes*' colors dissolve into white, archaically indicating the hour of the shortest shadow and the highest position of the sun, and seeming to anchor a moment of respite for representation in the factual: an *arché-mimesis* of light, which, like a basso continuo, intermittently interrupts the course of time between the chance beats of the vertical endings of each canvas. At least when seen from a distance, the theatre of painting still seems to tirelessly pull through its profane dissolution, modeling and folding an illusion of depicted cloth. The folds are placed in front of the wall as the folds of a curtain, suggesting a continuity beyond the material interruptions of shaped canvas. The totality of a gradation between black (midnight) and white (noon) indicates the abstract possibility of measuring time in color, as every color pair in these paintings corresponds to an hour, a day, a month. It is against this calendrical system that the body of the painter figures as its finite resource. If at first sight it seems as though painting here is reducing its subject to a point of registration, marking life through its inscription into a spreadsheet of labor time, this very fact is shot through by continuous deviations and omissions that reduce the color spectrum and generate foreshortenings and fitful transitions. To be sure, these differences only manifest themselves vaguely. Where the color gradation suddenly appears to jump, how many hours did Thompson stop working for? What did he do during this time? As explicitly as the paintings identify themselves as the traces of quantifiable labor, the tableaus neither bear indications of when, precisely, they were created, nor can their differences actually be semanticized against the background of a norm, a table, or a color chart. Contrary to their manifest precision, as calendars that show time only when it is lived as effective labor, they are absolutely unreadable.

It is precisely here that the paintings, in spite of everything I think, still cling to a weak possibility of their aesthetic experience that—transcending all taste, which is extinguished in cool indifference—reveals itself precisely in the absence of their legibility. *Where the color gradation suddenly appears to jump*... But where exactly does that occur, and to what degree? Would it be possible to say with certainty? What I mean by this is not much more than that the empty form to which painting here degenerates as an informatized container, in all its splendor of conceptualism, pushes back against the thin veneer of its own perceptibility. If there is something worth seeing in them at all, it takes place around these jumps and rifts, where the crude eye comes upon something that is not quite sayable, but precisely for this reason is not visible neither. And yet, why exactly this insistence on the *Chronochromes*' execution by hand? Does this not contradict everything that the paintings so rigorously seek to accomplish: i.e., the spectralization of color into the quantifiable values of a system, and, above all, their release from the realm of the empirical support into digital information, which splits their materiality? Do the random sections of the *Chronochromes*' formats not vehemently contradict every idea of painting as composition, with a top and a bottom, a left and a right—an idea of composition that not only places the tableau in relation to the body of the painter, but finally implies the standing, symmetrical body of a beholder? Whereas modernism placed this body—between eye, hand, and canvas—in a tight framework in which the idea of an exchange of world, sensory stimulus, and labor closed to form a cycle, then this cycle is torpedoed from the outset. (Is this not absolutely clear?) So why trouble the hand once more? What kind of a body is it that, in any case, makes itself unrecognizable in anonymity? Despite these questions, it is not the repetitive movement of a registering hand that produces the actual value of the paintings, even though they point to this possibility, where the iterability of an activity measured in time appears as labor. At the same time, as examples—possibilities for realization and not variations, or parts of a series in the strict sense—the paintings point to something that they themselves exclude: their schema, which determines not only their overall execution from an outside but, perhaps more importantly, their own economy. This schema and the activity of the hand—no matter how long it works and no matter how much time and energy the body expends—*do not touch*. This seems to me the primary tension that permeates the *Chronochromes*: an obsolete form of work, which can be measured in spent time on the one hand, and the utopian release of painting from this economy on the other. The appropriation of a marginalized color system like Munsell's represents within this tension an accumulation of value whose very use cannot be counted labor time. Its mobilization determines painting, no longer as a handicraft but above all as a *position*—the invention of a genre as a *private asset* that translates visibility itself into a new economy, in which its production with the help of a body takes the form of an unmarketable reject. The literary figure Robert Macaire, whom Thompson invokes and adds as a signifier to the *Chromachromes*, accentuates their strategy from this perspective. Macaire not only expresses the position of the rentier but also identifies *cunning* as a new painterly quality. If Thompson's series of paintings, on the one hand, totalize the depictable as such, they also, above all, singularize this totality—color, time, and shape—as something economically private.[4] The abolition of genres through abstraction at the beginning of the twentieth century expands, therefore, with a process that does not end in the negation of representation, nor in the scientific vivisection of perception. The genre has rather, in its final figuration, become a schema of the representable, which, privatized as *general intellect*, makes profit.

Suddenly the time of the hand, labor time itself, appears conversely as empty, useless time and comes across as an obsolete, rudimentary form of accumulation and sacrifice—a form that, as we know today, must be increasingly subsidized and is therefore produced politically, even though it is increasingly becoming unprofitable within the economy. It is this problematic figuration of labor time on the surface of the paintings that, on the one hand, points to the problem of how these paintings' value should be determined. Yet, on the other, it reveals a body that, nonetheless, remains behind, entering insistently into the painting from which it is dismissed. Maybe this is, after all, the figure of the body that these paintings introduce—when it is discharged and takes its time off.

4 The fact that Thompson takes over a systematization of dead labor—i.e., Munsell and Photoshop—without paying for it only makes it more lucrative.

Pedestals

At first sight, the pedestals scattered by Thompson in many of the spaces of recent exhibitions seem to mainly serve the purpose of filling the problematic void left by the paintings themselves. *Problematic* because what prevents the pictures from constituting themselves as autonomous visual objects, sui generis, threatens to advance to the status of sublime atmosphere, which fills their surrounding context. For example, in *Robert Macaire Chromachromes*—Thompson's 2009 exhibition at Andrew Kreps Gallery, New York, in which the ascetic tableaux are loosely distributed, one item per wall—their very loss of presence seems to be extended so far that, conversely, they plunge into the kitsch of the White Cube, which they themselves can no longer cope with as "works." This risk seems clearly palpable to me. The pedestals therefore fulfill, to a certain extent, the function of an escape route, protecting the canvases from the dull impotence that makes them tip over into the rhetoric of an overpowering distraction maneuver, which interrupts their dense antivisuality and directs the gaze beyond them. Antivisuality and terror of atmosphere: a strange alliance, which apparently condenses where the paintings no longer "close." The doubling and splitting of the materiality of the paintings into the informatized image of their weave seems to find another outlet here, where the pedestals act as material deposits for additional knowledge that sediments on their surfaces: *varia*, objects, texts, all kinds of substitutes for what the canvases cannot do—that is, provide the possibility of reading "something" on them.

The pedestals' forms, which Thompson mathematically varies depending on their minimal use value (presentation surface), are capriciously molded to all manner of cubic variation, but at the same time they cling to a constant that is anchored to the basic form of the pedestal itself: the horizontal of the table, the antithesis of the vertical of the canvas. Thompson covers these pedestals with Formica, a plastic laminate branded in the second decade of the twentieth century, which gives them a surface that is clearly separated from their core. The idea is enticing. The brand name does not etymologically (if this is how brand names should be analyzed) refer to form as that which has attained a previously unseen transformability through plastics. It relates to the original use of the synthetic material—namely to insulate cables, as a substitute for mica, a naturally occurring silicate. What could it mean that mica was also one of the materials used in red and black pigments in cave paintings during the Upper Paleolithic period, an *Ur-material* of painting, whose substitute covers Thompson's pedestals, which are substitutes for his own tableaus? And does not Formica's radical plasticity, beyond the branded origin of its name, extend to language itself, which as dedication ("for mica") is revealed to be the Latin word for "ant," *formica*, in order to forget its core—an inversion that in the branding of formability finally separates the name of the material from its use value, making it unrecognizable? Is this not precisely the potency of the material, which is able to cover anything in order to seal it, whatever its shape? Does the extension of painting—its substitution beyond the canvas—not lead to this? If the pedestals are indeed information carriers, then this use pervades the material from which they are made (where it bears a particular company's name) and its surfaces (where the patterns can be attributed, for example, to the Memphis design group). On this informational regress of the surface is placed press releases and literary sources (such as James Rousseau's *Robert Macaire*[5]), as well as information about the mathematician Paul de Casteljau[6] and Munsell's color system. But not just texts appear there: the recurrent figure of a fan, ethnological artifacts such as Yua, a currency from Papua New Guinea, and carafes filled with water, which degrade the pedestals to banal side tables, can also be found. Often the pedestals hardly maintain their strict formal distinction from the paintings on the wall: the Formica stops at the edges of their cubic shapes, leaving black lines that differentiate their rectangular surfaces. Above all, this happens in those places where the pedestals negate their very horizontality and start to stand upright, as vertical picture-supports for patterns, surfaces and photographs—in one case, the photograph of an installation view of a previous exhibition. In the latter, Thompson turns this installation shot ninety degrees, a rotation that makes palpable the thin thread that connects the exhibition value of the pedestal to a supposed use value. The mathematical generation of the specific form of the pedestal as senseless variation itself testifies that its use no longer knows top or bottom as quasi-anthropological constants.

But to call the pedestals painting? At certain points, especially where they appear as coreless picture supports, the difference seems to be minimal. At others, the two are so divergent that it is absurd to try to identify their model. And yet it is irrefutable that what is precipitated and objectified as "information" on them, beyond and outside the paintings, metamorphotically acts as their very support. Not as an immaterial substrate: if information already thwarts the visual presentness of the *Chromachromes* and *Chronochromes*, then it returns here, multiplies, accumulates, and spreads out into other areas. Or to put it differently: if the privatization of painting as knowledge separates it from itself and yields a profit that it demands as rent, then it is this knowledge that precipitates in the pedestals as an inextricable dross. They separate out from the canvas, the hand, and the paint a knowledge that exchanges itself again, for its materialization presses itself into a mold that impels the law of genre to put on, once again, the threadbare mask of the object: a mask because it is only the representative of a value-generation that is concerned with the production of things as one among several tasks.

Is it not this gap between knowledge itself and its singularization in the object that permeates the pedestals and the things they present—the pedestals, which are in themselves examples of a literally interminable series of their own permutations? And conversely, are the pedestals' objects—a copied text, which is available on the Internet, or a marginal currency like Yua—nothing but specimens of themselves? I think this is a central characteristic of the objects—not only that they seem to talk about the painting that they, in a sense, "help out," but that as "information material," they can never be experienced as singularities, even though, as originals, they are irreproducible. It is therefore information, not the possibility of reproduction, which separates the objects as singularities from themselves. As a schematization, this information is neither "not for sale" nor "immaterial." It always exchanges itself for its objectification. It lets things appear at peripheries where the differences between painting, object, display, figure, discourse, motif, signifier—

5 James Rousseau, *Physiologie du Robert-Macaire*, illustrated by Honoré Daumier (Paris: Jules Laisné, 1842).

6 Paul de Casteljau worked from 1958 onward at Citroën, where he developed an algorithm for evaluating calculations related to a certain family of curves, which would later be formalized and popularized by the engineer Pierre Étienne Bézier. Paul de Faget de Casteljau, *Formes à pôles* (Paris: Hermes, 1985).

where shall I end this list?—constantly disarticulate themselves. Thompson helps show this transformation in the form of lists in the titles of his exhibitions. At approximately the same time that the pedestals appear, upon whose surfaces "content" flows back into the exhibition space, the titles of Thompson's exhibitions grow more complicated and elongate themselves into summary series, which should be considered as primary material: *Memphis, Pedestals, Chronochromes, Subincisions, Papua New Guinea, /Macaire/, Motifs*. The names of genres that coincide with the material presence of objects—*Pedestals, Chronochromes*—can be found alongside those that, as motifs, are excluded from the paintings' abstract surfaces: *Memphis, Subincision*, and *Papua New Guinea. Motifs*: finally, a word that is included only at the end of the list, in order to collapse its consistency as a set. The language of discourse disintegrates—that would be one possible way of reading it. The transfer of things into language produces an impossible, heterotopic set. But maybe what is being inscribed here is not impossible. Perhaps what we have here is not the allegorical proclamation of the "other," but rather the factual transcription of what simply takes place, a reflection of the metamorphic movement that seizes things down to their core: the perversion of their boundaries, with which abstraction offers itself as the projection surface for "themes." One senses here the desire to fill the work "with real content," in order to break through the idiocy of self-referentiality—titles that can no longer distinguish between themselves and what they name, and that are no longer able to maintain the hierarchy between architecture, exhibit, work of art, and advertising. Could it be that *Memphis, /Macaire/,* and *Subincision* are not what "appear" in the exhibition but what make it implode upon itself as a consistent, singular space? And yet: *Macaire* finds himself. The parts consolidate into a face. A silhouette registers itself. Casteljau's "economic" calculation of complex curves cuts the painting "by the meter" back onto paper again—filmy streaks of paint smeared wet-on-wet on paper on the studio floor: a flower, a man with a top hat, the "anecdotal" fan, which, laminated on steel, insures itself by means of the precision of the laser. Information stamps itself out, turning back into pictures. Knowledge secretes planes. This is the other side, a mythical mimesis of painting that believes it can recognize itself in everything and make itself similar to everything, in whatever form—but at what price?

p. 9 (top) *1924*, 2000, acrylic on organza, 60 × 192 in. (152.4 × 487.7 cm), collection of Thea Westreich Wagner & Ethan Wagner, New York

(bottom) Installation view, *Chronochromes, Menarches, Socles, Paul de Casteljau, /Robert/, Motifs* (Sutton Lane, Brussels, courtesy of Campoli Presti, London/Paris), 2010, 19 mm MDF, Formica K1994, 3,200 sq. in., artifact from Papua New Guinea, 3 × 40 × 36 in. (7.6 × 101.6 × 91.4 cm)

p. 10 (top) Installation view, *Sean Paul / Cheyney Thompson, Caisse Blanche* (Sutton Lane, Paris, courtesy of Campoli Presti, London/Paris), 2007

(bottom) From *Subincisions*, 2010, artist book

p. 11 (top) Installation view, *Collatéral* (Le Confort Moderne, Poitiers, courtesy of Campoli Presti, London/Paris), 2009

(bottom) *Study for 1817*, 2003, ink on paper, 16 × 20 in. (40.6 × 50.8 cm), courtesy of Andrew Kreps Gallery, New York

p. 12 Antoine Wiertz Museum, 2004, digital photo.

p. 13 *The Subtraction of Light from the Room Produces the Illusion of a Bourgeois Interior*, 2006, oil on canvas, 36 ¼ × 28 ¾ in. (92.1 × 73 cm), courtesy of Galerie Buchholz, Cologne/Berlin, private collection, London

p. 14 *Property Owner Looking at a Poster of Cologne. No Response.* 2006, inkjet print on newspaper, 24 × 17 ⅞ in. (61 × 45.4 cm), courtesy of Andrew Kreps Gallery, New York, and Galerie Buchholz, Cologne/Berlin

p. 15 *Property Owner in the Louvre Looking at Bellona. No Response.* 2006, inkjet print on newspaper, 24 × 17 ⅞ in. (61 × 45.4 cm), courtesy of Andrew Kreps Gallery, New York, and Galerie Buchholz, Cologne/Berlin

pp. 17–20 *4 Colors Subtracting Light from the Room in 6 Degrees of Intensity Repeated 4 Times, II*, 2006, four parts, oil on canvas, 36 ¼ × 28 ¾ in. (92.1 × 73 cm), courtesy of Galerie Buchholz, Cologne/Berlin, collection of Thomas Borgmann, Berlin

p. 21 *Table Displaying Gifts from the Landlord and Working Papers*, 2006, table, lamp, four computer printouts, Xeroxed text with handwritten insertions, skull, glass, postcards, ventilator, 68 ½ × 72 ½ × 30 1/8 in (174 × 184.2 × 76.5 cm), courtesy of Galerie Buchholz, Cologne/Berlin, collection of Thomas Borgmann, Berlin

pp. 22–3 Installation view, *The End of Rent Control and the Emergence of the Creative Class* (Galerie Buchholz, Cologne), 2006

p. 23 (top) *Carmella*, 2006, digital photo, courtesy of Cheyney Thompson

p. 23 (center & bottom) Installation view, *The End of Rent Control and the Emergence of the Creative Class* (Galerie Buchholz, Cologne), 2006

p. 24 *Table Displaying Gifts from the Landlord and Working Papers* (detail), 2006, table, lamp, four computer printouts, Xeroxed text with handwritten insertions, skull, glass, postcards, ventilator, 68 ½ × 72 ½ × 30 1/8 in. (174 × 184.2 × 76.5 cm), courtesy of Galerie Buchholz, Cologne/Berlin, collection of Thomas Borgmann, Berlin

pp. 25–8 *4 Colors Subtracting Light from the Room in 6 Degrees of Intensity Repeated 4 Times, I*, 2006, oil on canvas, 36 ¼ × 28 ¾ in. (92.1 × 73 cm), courtesy of Galerie Buchholz, Cologne/Berlin, collection of Thomas Borgmann, Berlin

pp. 29–33 *Sets of Curves from Bellona to Rubens to Cézanne to Bezier*, 2006, 17 inkjet prints on newspaper in cardboard box, 14 × 8 ⅝ in. (35.6 × 21.9 cm) each, courtesy of Andrew Kreps Gallery, New York, and Galerie Buchholz, Cologne/Berlin

p. 34 *The Production of an Unevenly Distributed Surplus Results from the Facticity of Format and Ground*, 2006, oil on canvas, 84 ⅝ × 72 ¼ in. (214.9 × 183.5 cm), courtesy of Galerie Buchholz, Cologne/Berlin, collection of Thea Westreich Wagner & Ethan Wagner, New York

p. 35 *Untitled (Lease)*, 2006, oil on canvas, 37 × 28 ¾ in. (94 × 73 cm), courtesy of Galerie Buchholz, Cologne/Berlin, collection of Daniel Buchholz and Christopher Müller, Cologne

p. 36 *Untitled*, 2006, oil on canvas, 84 × 72 in. (213.4 × 182.9 cm), courtesy of Campoli Presti, London/Paris, private collection, Paris

p. 37 *Untitled*, 2006, oil on canvas, 84 × 72 in. (213.4 × 182.9 cm), courtesy of Andrew Kreps Gallery, New York, collection of Thea Westreich Wagner & Ethan Wagner, New York

p. 38 *Untitled*, 2006, oil on canvas, 84 × 72 in. (213.4 × 182.9 cm), courtesy of Andrew Kreps Gallery, New York, collection of Allison & Warren B. Kanders

p. 39 *Untitled*, 2006, oil on canvas, 84 × 72 in. (213.4 × 182.9 cm), courtesy of Andrew Kreps Gallery, New York

p. 40 *Untitled*, 2006, oil on canvas, 84 × 72 in. (213.4 × 182.9 cm), courtesy of Andrew Kreps Gallery, New York, collection of Mr. & Mrs. Alexander Casdin

p. 41 (top) *Sweet Authority*, 2003, 24 oil-on-organza paintings, 132 × 132 in. (335.3 × 335.3 cm), courtesy of Galleria Raucci/Santamaria, Naples

(bottom) *Table of Hubris*, 2002, weasel balls, shoelaces, aluminum, metal tape, wood panel, 15 × 36 × 15 in. (38.1 × 91.4 × 38.1 cm), courtesy of Andrew Kreps Gallery, New York, collection of Doreen Remen & Steve Weiner

p. 42 (top) *Untitled*, 2002, watercolor on graph paper, 8 ½ × 11 in. (21.6 × 27.9 cm), courtesy of Andrew Kreps Gallery, New York, collection of Dana Hirt, Chicago

(center) *Eileen in Hudson*, 1999, C-print, cardboard, cellophane bag, bulldog clips, metal grid (ref. Table of Modern Life Fragment, 2003), 9 ½ × 13 in. (24.1 × 33 cm), courtesy of Andrew Kreps Gallery, New York, collection of Thea Westreich Wagner & Ethan Wagner, New York

(bottom) *Chair study*, 1997, oil on canvas (ref. Table of Modern Life Fragment, 2003), 30 × 48 in. (76.2 × 121.9 cm), courtesy of Andrew Kreps Gallery, New York

p. 43 (top) *January 14, 1743, Paris (Deaf, Dumb and Blind)*, 2005, acrylic on canvas, 96 × 120 in. (243.8 × 304.8 cm), courtesy of Galleria Raucci/Santamaria, Naples, collection of Nerio & Marina Fossati, Italy

(bottom) *Drawing for Roe*, 1998, C-print, cardboard, cellophane bag, bulldog clips, metal grid, 9 ½ × 13 in. (24.1 × 33 cm), courtesy of Andrew Kreps Gallery, New York, collection of Thea Westreich Wagner & Ethan Wagner, New York

p. 44 (top) Installation view, *Cheyney Thompson* (Galleria Raucci/Santamaria, Naples), 2005

(bottom) Installation view, *Quelques Aspects de l'Art Bourgeois: La Non-Intervention* (Andrew Kreps Gallery, New York), 2006

pp. 45–9 *Sets of Color from Robho to Storage*, 2006, offset lithographs, 58 × 42 in. (147.3 × 106.7 cm), courtesy of Andrew Kreps Gallery, New York, collection of Dana Hirt; the Museum of Modern Art, New York, gift of Martin and Rebecca Eisenberg; collection of Tord & Kimberly Stallvik; Dana and James Tananbaum collection; collection of Thea Westreich Wagner & Ethan Wagner; Andrew Kreps Gallery, New York

p. 51 *Untitled*, 2008, oil on canvas, 36 × 30 in. (91.4 × 76.2 cm), courtesy of Andrew Kreps Gallery, New York, collection of Agnes Gund, New York

p. 52 *Untitled*, 2008, oil on canvas, 24 × 20 in. (61 × 50.8 cm), courtesy of Andrew Kreps Gallery, New York, private collection

p. 53 (top left) *Art|36| Basel |15–20|6|2005*, 2005, black and white photograph, wood frame, and velvet curtain with silkscreen, 22 × 18 in. (55.9 × 45.7 cm), courtesy of Andrew Kreps Gallery, New York, collection of Jack Bakker

(top right) *Untitled film still*, 2005, oil on canvas, 22 × 28 in. (55.9 × 71.1 cm), courtesy of Galleria Raucci/Santamaria, Naples, collection of Nerio & Marina Fossati, Italy

(bottom) Installation view, *TBA: Cheyney Thompson and Eileen Quinlan* (Arnolfini, Bristol, courtesy of Campoli Presti, London/Paris), 2007

p. 54 (top) *Table of Tragedy*, 2005, table, CDs, CD players, toys, shoes, beer, 15 × 36 × 15 in. (38.1 × 91.4 × 38.1 cm), courtesy of Andrew Kreps Gallery, New York (bottom) *Ahmed*, 1998, acrylic on organza, 28 × 32 in. (71.1 × 81.3 cm), courtesy of Andrew Kreps Gallery, New York

p. 54 (install) Installation view, *Quelques Aspects de l'Art Bourgeois: La Non-Intervention* (Andrew Kreps Gallery, New York), 2006

p. 55 (top) Installation view, *Quelques Aspects de l'Art Bourgeois: La Non-Intervention* (Andrew Kreps Gallery, New York), 2006

(bottom) Installation view, *New Works* (Sutton Lane, Paris, courtesy of Campoli Presti, London/Paris), 2008

p. 56 Installation view, *Art Statements (Art|36|Basel |15–20|6|2005)*, 2005

p. 57 *Detail (0.93,1.518)(4.058,5.118)(13.676): Untitled*, 2008, oil on canvas, 70 × 55 ½ in. (177.8 × 141 cm), courtesy of Galerie Buchholz, Cologne/Berlin, private collection

pp. 58–9 *Detail (0.147,0.160)(5.558,4.407)(15.779): Untitled*, 2008, oil on canvas, 70 × 88 ½ in. (177.8 × 224.8 cm), courtesy of Andrew Kreps Gallery, New York, collection of Allison & Warren B. Kanders

p. 60 *Detail (0.933,1.425)(4.108,5.181)(13.510): Untitled*, 2008, oil on canvas, 70 × 55 ½ in. (177.8 × 141 cm), courtesy of Andrew Kreps Gallery, New York, collection of Mr. & Mrs. Alexander Casdin

p. 61 *Detail (x.xxx,x.xxx)(x,x)(x): Untitled*, 2008, oil on canvas, 70 × 55 ½ in. (177.8 × 134.6 cm), courtesy of Campoli Presti, London/Paris, collection of Thea Westreich Wagner & Ethan Wagner, New York

p. 62 *Detail (x.xxx,x.xxx)(x,x)(x)(2): Untitled*, 2008, oil on canvas, 70 × 55 ½ in. (177.8 × 134.6 cm), courtesy of Campoli Presti, London/Paris, private collection, Rome

p. 63 *Is-A*, 2008, oil on canvas, 24 × 20 in. (61 × 50.8 cm), courtesy of Campoli Presti, London/Paris, collection of Thea Westreich Wagner & Ethan Wagner, New York

p. 64 *Detail (1.958,2.063)(1.111,0.931)(21.602): 4 Colors Subtracting Light from the Room in 6 Degrees of Intensity Repeated 4 Times*, 2008, oil on canvas, 24 × 20 in. (61 × 50.8 cm), courtesy of Andrew Kreps Gallery, New York, collection of Thea Westreich Wagner & Ethan Wagner, New York

p. 65 *Detail (1.958,2.063)(0.931,1.111)(21.602): 4 Colors Subtracting Light from the Room in 6 Degrees of Intensity Repeated 4 Times*, 2008, oil on canvas, 24 × 20 in. (61 × 50.8 cm), courtesy of Campoli Presti, London/Paris, collection of Cynthia & Abe Steinberger, New York

p. 66 *Untitled*, 2008, oil on canvas, 24 × 20 in. (61 × 50.8 cm), courtesy of Andrew Kreps Gallery, New York

p. 67 *Untitled*, 2008, oil on canvas, 24 × 20 in. (61 × 50.8 cm), courtesy of Andrew Kreps Gallery, New York

p. 68 *Untitled*, 2008, silkscreen on canvas, 36 × 30 in. (91.4 × 76.2 cm), courtesy of Andrew Kreps Gallery, New York

p. 69 *Untitled*, with Sean Paul, 2007, silkscreen on canvas, 40 × 36 in. (101.6 × 91.4 cm), courtesy of Campoli Presti, London/Paris, private collection, US

p. 70 *Untitled*, 2008, silkscreen on canvas, 36 × 30 in. (91.4 × 76.2 cm), courtesy of Andrew Kreps Gallery, New York, collection of Bradford & Mira Bernstein

p. 71 *Untitled*, with Sam Lewitt, 2008, silkscreen on canvas, 36 × 30 in. (91.4 × 76.2 cm), courtesy of Andrew Kreps Gallery, New York, collection of Abigail Turin & Jonathan Gans, San Francisco

p. 72 *Untitled*, 2008, silkscreen on canvas, 36 × 30 in. (91.4 × 76.2 cm), courtesy of Andrew Kreps Gallery, New York, private collection

p. 73 *Untitled*, 2008, silkscreen on canvas, 36 × 30 in. (91.4 × 76.2 cm), courtesy of Andrew Kreps Gallery, New York

p. 75 *Abstract Picture (Y/YM)*, 2008, oil on canvas, 55 ¼ × 43 ⅞ in. (140.5 × 111.5 cm), courtesy of Galerie Buchholz, Cologne/Berlin

p. 76 *Property Owner (YM/M)*, 2008, oil on canvas, 55 ¼ × 43 ⅞ in. (140.5 × 111.5 cm), courtesy of Galerie Buchholz, Cologne/Berlin, collection of Thea Westreich Wagner & Ethan Wagner, New York

p. 77 *Property Owner (M/CM)*, 2008, oil on canvas, 55 ¼ × 43 ⅞ in. (140.5 × 111.5 cm), courtesy of Galerie Buchholz, Cologne/Berlin, collection of Thomas Borgmann, Berlin

p. 78 *Blue (CM/C)*, 2008, oil on canvas, 55 ¼ × 43 ⅞ in. (140.5 × 111.5 cm), courtesy of Galerie Buchholz, Cologne/Berlin, private collection, Zürich

p. 79 *Grid (C/CY)*, 2008, oil on canvas, 55 ¼ × 43 ⅞ in. (140.5 × 111.5 cm), courtesy of Galerie Buchholz, Cologne/Berlin, private collection, Zürich

p. 80 *Linen (CY/Y)*, 2008, oil on canvas, 55 ¼ × 43 ⅞ in. (140.5 × 111.5 cm), courtesy of Galerie Buchholz, Cologne/Berlin, collection of Norman & Norah Stone, San Francisco

p. 81 (top) Newsstand, 2001, digital photo, courtesy of Andrew Kreps Gallery, New York

(bottom) Interior (Antiquariat Buchholz, Cologne), 2004, digital photo, courtesy of the artist

pp. 82–3 Installation view, *Some Motifs and Their Sources* (Galerie Buchholz, Cologne), 2008

p. 84 (top) Martial Canterel, 2005, digital photo, courtesy of Cheyney Thompson

(bottom) Installation view, *Some Motifs and Their Sources* (Galerie Buchholz, Cologne), 2008

p. 85 *Working Papers (detail)*, 2008, 12 duotone offset prints, 20 ⅞ × 13 in. (53 × 33 cm) each, courtesy of Galerie Buchholz, Cologne/Berlin

p. 86 *Working Papers (detail)*, 2008, 12 duotone offset prints, 20 ⅞ × 13 in. (53 × 33 cm) each, courtesy of Galerie Buchholz, Cologne/Berlin

p. 87 *Working Papers (detail)*, 2008, 12 duotone offset prints, 20 ⅞ × 13 in. (53 × 33 cm) each, courtesy of Galerie Buchholz, Cologne/Berlin

p. 89 *Untitled (Magenta-Yellow Green)*, 2009, oil on canvas, 55 ½ × 44 in. (141 × 111.8 cm), courtesy of Campoli Presti, London/Paris, collection of Abigail Turin and Jonathan Gans, San Francisco

p. 91 *Untitled (Cyan-Red Orange)*, 2009, oil on canvas, 55 ½ × 44 in. (141 × 111.8 cm), courtesy of Andrew Kreps Gallery, New York, collection of Thea Westreich Wagner & Ethan Wagner

p. 92 *Untitled (Grey)*, 2009, oil on canvas, 24 × 20 in. (61 × 50.8 cm), courtesy of Andrew Kreps Gallery, New York

p. 93 L and P, 2009, digital photo, courtesy of Cheyney Thompson

p. 94 (left) Installation view, *Robert Macaire Chromachromes* (Andrew Kreps Gallery, New York), 2009

(right) Installation view, *Robert Macaire Chromachromes* (Andrew Kreps Gallery, New York), 2009

p. 95 Installation view, *Robert Macaire Chromachromes* (Andrew Kreps Gallery, New York), 2009

p. 96 (top) Studio, 2008, digital photo, courtesy of Cheyney Thompson

(bottom) *Collatéral* (Le Confort Moderne, Poitiers), 2009, digital photo, courtesy of Cheyney Thompson

p. 97 (top) *Untitled (Blue-Red)*, 2009, oil on canvas, 24 × 20 in. (61 × 50.8 cm), courtesy of Campoli Presti, London/Paris, collection of Adam Cohen

(bottom) *Untitled (Magenta-Blue Green)*, 2009, oil on canvas, 24 × 20 in. (61 × 50.8 cm), courtesy of Andrew Kreps Gallery, New York, collection of Thea Westreich Wagner & Ethan Wagner, New York

p. 98 *Untitled*, 2009, ink on paper, 14 × 8 ⅝ in. (35.6 × 21.9 cm), courtesy of Andrew Kreps Gallery, New York

p. 99 *Untitled*, 2009, ink on paper, 14 × 8 ⅝ in. (35.6 × 21.9 cm), courtesy of Andrew Kreps Gallery, New York, collection of Morris A. Orden

pp. 100–1 *Chromachrome 19 (5BG/5R) macaire*, 2009, oil on canvas, 88 × 111 in. (223.5 × 281.9 cm), courtesy of Andrew Kreps Gallery, New York, collection of Thea Westreich Wagner & Ethan Wagner, New York

p. 102 *Chromachrome 15 (5PB/5Y) shape*, 2009, oil on canvas, 56 × 44 in. (142.2 × 111.8 cm), courtesy of Andrew Kreps Gallery, New York, collection of Leonard Nelson

p. 103 *Chromachrome 18 (5G/5RP) square*, 2009, oil on canvas, 24 × 24 in. (61 × 61 cm), courtesy of Andrew Kreps Gallery, New York

p. 104 *Chromachrome 9 (5PB/5Y) tondo*, 2009, oil on canvas, 44 in. (111.8 cm), courtesy of Andrew Kreps Gallery, New York, the Rachofsky collection

p. 105 *Chromachrome 11 (5BG/5R) edge*, 2009, oil on canvas, 24 × 1 in. (61 × 2.5 cm), courtesy of Andrew Kreps Gallery, New York, private collection

pp. 106–7 *Chromachrome 10 (5G/5RP) frieze*, 2009, oil on canvas, 20 × 111 in. (50.8 × 281.9 cm), courtesy of Andrew Kreps Gallery, New York, private collection, London

pp. 108–9 *Chromachrome 8 (5BG/5R) diptych*, 2009, oil on canvas, 24 × 20 in. (61 × 50.8 cm), courtesy of Andrew Kreps Gallery, New York, private collection

p. 111 *Chromachrome 12 (5P/5YR) lozenge*, 2009, oil on canvas, 34 × 34 in. (86.4 × 86.4 cm), courtesy of Andrew Kreps Gallery, New York, private collection

p. 112 *Chromachrome 14 (5B/5YR) column*, 2009, oil on canvas, 111 × 20 in. (281.9 × 50.8 cm), courtesy of Andrew Kreps Gallery, New York, collection of Norman & Norah Stone, San Francisco

p. 113 P leaving New York, 2010, digital photo, courtesy of Cheyney Thompson

p. 114 (top) Studio, 2005, digital photo, courtesy of Cheyney Thompson

(bottom) Study for *Art Basel*, Miami Beach, with Roe Ethridge, 2009, computer drawing, courtesy of Cheyney Thompson

p. 115 (top) *Studio*, 2009, digital photo, courtesy of Cheyney Thompson

(bottom) Study for *Art Basel*, Miami Beach, with Roe Ethridge, 2009, computer drawing, courtesy of Cheyney Thompson

p. 116 (top) *1731*, 1998, acrylic on organza, 96 × 120 in. (243.8 × 304.8 cm), courtesy of Cheyney Thompson

(bottom) Installation view, *S&M* (Sutton Lane, Paris, courtesy of Campoli Presti, London/Paris), Eileen Quinlan & Cheyney Thompson, 2005

p. 117 *Chromachrome 7 (5GY/5P) portrait*, 2009, oil on canvas, 24 × 20 in. (61 × 50.8 cm), courtesy of Andrew Kreps Gallery, New York, private collection, New York

pp. 118–9 *Chromachrome 13 (5G/5RP) angle*, 2009, oil on canvas, 111 × 1 in. (281.9 × 2.5 cm), courtesy of Andrew Kreps Gallery, New York, collection of Allison & Warren B. Kanders

pp. 120–1 *Chromachrome (58/5YR) triptych*, 2009, oil on canvas, 80 × 44 in. (203.2 × 11.8 cm), courtesy of Campoli Presti, London/Paris, private collection, Rome

p. 122 *Untitled*, 2009, ink on paper, 17 ¾ × 14 ⅝ in. (45 × 37 cm), courtesy of Galerie Buchholz, Cologne/Berlin, private collection

p. 123 *Chronochrome 1*, 2009, oil on canvas, 55.1 × 42 in. (140 × 106.7 cm), courtesy of Galerie Buchholz, Cologne/Berlin, collection of Ambassador Paul Cejas & Trudy Cejas, Miami

p. 124 *Chronochrome 8*, 2009, oil on canvas, 55.1 × 72 in. (140 × 182.9 cm), courtesy of Galerie Buchholz, Cologne/Berlin, collection of Thomas Dietzsch, Berlin

p. 125 Installation view, *Pedestals, Bias-cut, /Robert Macaire/, Chronochromes* (Galerie Buchholz, Berlin), 2009

p. 126 (left) Installation view, *Pedestals, Bias-cut, /Robert Macaire/, Chronochromes* (Galerie Buchholz, Berlin), 2009

(right) Installation view, *Pedestals, Bias-cut, /Robert Macaire/, Chronochromes* (Galerie Buchholz, Berlin), 2009

p. 127 Installation view, with Roe Ethridge (*Art Basel*, Miami Beach), 2009

p. 128 (top) Installation view, *Chronochromes, Menarches, Socles, Paul de Casteljau, /Robert/, Motifs* (Sutton Lane, Brussels, courtesy of Campoli Presti, London/Paris), 2010

(bottom) Installation view, *Chronochromes, Data, Motifs* (Rat Hole Gallery, Tokyo), 2011

pp. 129–30 *Chronochrome set 1*, 2010, oil on canvas, 75 × 129 ⅞ in. (190.5 × 329.9 cm), courtesy of Campoli Presti, London/Paris, private collection, Rome

p. 131 *Chronochrome set 2*, 2010, oil on canvas, 75 × 99 ⅝ in. (190.5 × 253 cm), courtesy of Campoli Presti, London/Paris, collection of Cynthia & Abe Steinberger, New York

Chronochrome set 3, 2010, oil on canvas, 75 × 89 1/8 in. (190.5 × 226.4 cm), courtesy of Campoli Presti, London/Paris, private collection, Brussels

p. 132 *Chronochrome set 4*, 2010, oil on canvas, 75 × 45 ½ in. (190.5 × 115.6 cm), courtesy of Campoli Presti, London/Paris

p. 133 (left) *Chronochrome set 5*, 2010, oil on canvas, 75 × 77 in. (190.5 × 195.6 cm), courtesy of Overduin and Kite, Los Angeles

pp. 133–4 *Chronochrome set 6*, 2010, oil on linen, 75 × 57 in. (190.5 × 144.8 cm), courtesy of Overduin and Kite, Los Angeles, collection of Tristin Mannion

p. 135 *Chronochrome set 7*, 2010, oil on linen, 75 × 137 in. (190.5 × 348 cm), courtesy of Overduin and Kite, Los Angeles, private collection, Greenwich, Connecticut

p. 136 *Chronochrome set 8*, 2010, oil on linen, 75 × 139 in. (190.5 × 353.1 cm), courtesy of Overduin and Kite, Los Angeles, collection of Natalie and Simon Fuller

p. 137 *Chronochrome set 9*, 2011, oil on canvas, 125 × 75 in. (317.5 × 190.5 cm), courtesy of Rat Hole Gallery, Tokyo, Hysteric Glamour collection

p. 138 *Chronochrome set 10*, 2011, oil on canvas, 47 × 75 in. (119.4 × 190.5 cm), 25 × 75 in. (63.5 × 190.5 cm), Museum of Modern Art, New York, courtesy of Andrew Kreps Gallery, New York

pp. 139–40 *Chronochrome 11*, 2011, oil on canvas, 29 × 75 in. (73.7 × 190.5 cm), 109 × 75 in. (276.9 × 190.5 cm), courtesy of Rat Hole Gallery, Tokyo, collection of Thea Westreich Wagner & Ethan Wagner, New York

p. 140 *Chronochrome 12*, 2011, oil on canvas, 75 × 37 in. (190.5 × 94 cm), courtesy of Galleria Raucci/Santamaria, Naples

pp. 141–2 *Chronochrome 13*, 2011, oil on canvas, 75 × 150 in. (190.5 × 381 cm), courtesy of Galleria Raucci/Santamaria, Naples, collection of Teresa Iarocci, Mosca URSS

p. 143 *Chronochrome 14*, 2011, oil on canvas, 75 × 131 in. (190.5 × 332.7 cm), courtesy of Galleria Raucci/Santamaria, Naples, private collection, Belgium

pp. 145–78 (background) *The Completed Reference*, artist book, 2010–2011

p. 145 Artist book from *Pedestal 24*, 2011, 19 mm MDF, Formica, wood, bound photocopies, 36 × 14 × 14 in. (91.4 × 35.6 × 35.6 cm), courtesy of Galleria Raucci/Santamaria, Naples

p. 146 (bottom) *Pedestal 22*, 2011, 19 mm MDF, Formica, wood, Xeroxed text, 5 × 60 × 20 in. (12.7 × 152.4 × 50.8 cm), courtesy of Andrew Kreps Gallery, New York, and Rat Hole Gallery, Tokyo

(top) *Pedestal 27*, 2011, 19 mm MDF, Formica, wood, printed matter, 27 × 45 × 13 in. (68.6 × 114.3 × 33 cm), courtesy of Galleria Raucci/Santamaria, Naples

p. 147 *Pedestal 24*, 2011, 19 mm MDF, Formica, wood, bound photocopies, 36 × 14 × 14 in. (91.4 × 35.6 × 35.6 cm), courtesy of Galleria Raucci/Santamaria, Naples

p. 148 *Pedestal 15*, 2010, 19 mm MDF, Formica, artist book, 40 × 23 × 21 in. (101.6 × 58.4 × 53.3 cm), courtesy of Andrew Kreps Gallery, New York, and Rat Hole Gallery, Tokyo

p. 149 (top) *Motif 3a RP/G*, 2010, acrylic on paper, mounted on laser-cut aluminum, 39 ¼ × 44 ½ in. (99.7 × 113 cm), courtesy of Campoli Presti, London/Paris, collection of Cynthia & Abe Steinberger, New York

(bottom) *Motif 3c B/YR*, 2011, acrylic on paper, mounted on laser-cut aluminum, 39 ¼ × 44 ½ in. (99.7 × 113 cm), courtesy of Andrew Kreps Gallery, New York, private collection, Gstaad, Switzerland

p. 150 *Pedestal 17*, 2010, 19 mm MDF, Formica, document, poster, glass carafe, vodka, 42 × 17 × 17 in. (106.7 × 43.2 × 43.2 cm), courtesy of Andrew Kreps Gallery, New York

p. 151 *Motif 4c PB/Y*, 2011, acrylic on paper, mounted on laser-cut aluminum, 37 ½ × 44 ½ in. (95.3 × 113 cm), courtesy of Andrew Kreps Gallery, New York

p. 152 *Pedestal 21*, 2011, 19 mm MDF, Formica, wood, bound photocopies, 30 × 19 × 20 in. (76.2 × 48.3 × 50.8 cm), courtesy of Andrew Kreps Gallery, New York

(bottom) *Pedestal 14*, 2010, 19 mm MDF, Formica, binder, 10 × 27 × 27 in. (26 × 68.6 × 68.6 cm), Andrew Kreps Gallery, New York, Rat Hole Gallery, Tokyo

p. 153 *Motif 6c R/BG*, 2011, acrylic on paper, mounted on laser-cut aluminum, 32 × 32 in. (81.3 × 81.3 cm), courtesy of Andrew Kreps Gallery, New York, private collection courtesy Jarla Partilager

p. 154 *Motif 8c P/YG*, 2011, acrylic on paper, mounted on laser-cut aluminum, 40 ¾ × 25 ½ in. (103.5 × 64.8 cm), courtesy of Galleria Raucci/Santamaria, Naples

Motif 6d B/YR, 2011, acrylic on paper, mounted on laser-cut aluminum, 32 × 32 in. (81.3 × 81.3 cm), courtesy of Galleria Raucci/Santamaria, Naples

p. 155 *Motif 8d R/BG*, 2011, acrylic on paper, mounted on laser-cut aluminum, 40 ¾ × 25 ½ in. (103.5 × 64.8 cm), courtesy of Galleria Raucci/Santamaria, Naples

Motif 8d P/YG, 2011, acrylic on paper, mounted on laser-cut aluminum, 40 ¾ × 25 ½ in. (103.5 × 64.8 cm), courtesy of Andrew Kreps Gallery, New York

p. 156 (top) and cover: *Motif 9b RP/G*, 2010, acrylic on paper, mounted on laser-cut aluminum, 32 × 32 in. (81.3 × 81.3 cm), courtesy of Galleria Raucci/Santamaria, Naples

(bottom) *Motif 8b PB/Y*, 2010, acrylic on paper, mounted on laser-cut aluminum, 32 × 32 in. (81.3 × 81.3 cm), courtesy of Galleria Raucci/Santamaria, Naples

p. 157 *Pedestal 23*, 2011, 19 mm MDF, Formica, wood, ritual flute, baseball hat, travel brochures, 68 × 34 × 13 in. (172.7 × 86.4 × 33 cm), courtesy of Andrew Kreps Gallery, New York

p. 158 *Pedestal 28*, 2011, 19 mm MDF, Formica, wood, fan, 4C prints, plexitubing, 41 × 29 × 23 in. (104.1 × 73.7 × 58.4 cm), courtesy of Galleria Raucci/Santamaria, Naples, collection Paul Leong, New York

p. 159 *Pedestal 11*, 2010, 19 mm MDF, Formica, wood, invitation cards, 20 × 20 × 20 in. (50.8 × 50.8 × 50.8 cm), courtesy of Campoli Presti, London/Paris, private collection, Rome

p. 160 (top) *Pedestal 30*, 2012, 19 mm MDF, Formica, wood, lamps, 32 × 42 ⅛ × 41 ¾ in. (81.3 × 107 × 106 cm), courtesy of Andrew Kreps Gallery, New York

(bottom) *Pedestal 18*, 2010, 19 mm MDF, Formica, shell currency, 45 × 26 × 32 in. (114.3 × 66 × 81.3 cm), courtesy of Andrew Kreps Gallery, New York, collection of Sam Orlofsky, New York

p. 161 *Pedestal 20*, 2011, 19 mm MDF, Formica, wood, shochu, 24 × 25 × 26 in. (61 × 63.5 × 66 cm), courtesy of Andrew Kreps Gallery, New York

p. 162 (top) *Motif 1a R/BG*, 2011, acrylic on paper, mounted on laser-cut aluminum, 40 ½ × 39 ¼ in. (102.9 × 99.7 cm), courtesy of Andrew Kreps Gallery, New York, collection of Norman & Norah Stone, San Francisco

(bottom) *Motif 9b P/YG*, 2010, acrylic on paper, mounted on laser-cut aluminum, 28 × 52 ½ in. (71.1 × 133.4 cm), courtesy of Andrew Kreps Gallery, New York

p. 163 *Pedestal 25*, 2011, 19 mm MDF, Formica, wood, grappa glass, 61 × 13 × 10 × in. (154.9 × 33 × 25.4 cm), courtesy of Galleria Raucci/Santamaria, Naples

p. 164 *Pedestal 19*, 2011, 19 mm MDF, Formica, wood, C-print mounted on aluminum, 5 × 8 × 120 in. (12.7 × 20.3 × 304.8 cm), courtesy of Andrew Kreps Gallery, New York

p. 165 (top) *Pedestal 16*, 2010, 19 mm MDF, Formica, wood, photocopies, 42 ½ × 17 ½ × 17 ½ in. (108 × 44.5 × 44.5 cm), courtesy of Andrew Kreps Gallery, New York

(bottom) Installation view, *Memphis, Pedestals, Chronochromes, Subincision, Papua New Guinea, /Macaire/, Motifs* (Overduin and Kite, Los Angeles), 2010

pp. 166–7 Installation view, *Chronochromes, Data, Motifs* (Rat Hole Gallery, Tokyo), 2011

p. 168 (top) Installation view, *Chronochromes/Umberto/Simon/Carlo* (Galleria Raucci/Santamaria, Naples), 2011

(bottom) Installation view, *Chronochromes/Umberto/Simon/Carlo* (Galleria Raucci/Santamaria, Naples), 2011

p. 169 *Motif 2a R/BG*, 2010, acrylic on paper, mounted on laser-cut aluminum, 49 ½ × 37 ⅞ in. (125.7 × 96.2 cm), courtesy of Campoli Presti, London/Paris, and Andrew Kreps Gallery, New York, collection of Caroline Schmidt

p. 170 *Motif 2c RP/G*, 2011, acrylic on paper, mounted on laser-cut aluminum, 49 ½ × 37 ⅞ in. (125.7 × 96.2 cm), courtesy of Andrew Kreps Gallery, New York, collection of Stefano Basilico & Janet Kraynak, New York

p. 171 *Pedestal 13*, 2010, 19 mm MDF, Formica, wood, artifact from Papua New Guinea, 3 × 40 × 36 in. (7.6 × 101.6 × 91.4 cm) , courtesy of Campoli Presti, London/Paris

p. 172 (top) *Motif 7b RP/G*, 2010, acrylic on paper, mounted on laser-cut aluminum, 15 ½ × 38 ½ in. (39.4 × 97.8 cm), courtesy of Andrew Kreps Gallery, New York, collection of Thea Westreich Wagner & Ethan Wagner, New York

(bottom) *Motif 10b R/BG*, 2010, acrylic on paper, mounted on laser-cut aluminum, 38 × 41 in. (96.5 × 104.1 cm), courtesy of Andrew Kreps Gallery, New York

p. 173 *Pedestal 12*, 2010, 19 mm MDF, Formica, wood, Xeroxed text, 28 × 28 × 17 in. (71.1 × 71.1 × 43.2 cm), courtesy of Campoli Presti, London/Paris, collection of Cynthia & Abe Steinberger, New York

p. 174 *Pedestal 24*, 2011, 19 mm MDF, Formica, wood, offset printed poem by Simon Thompson, 27 × 22 × 34 in. (68.6 × 55.9 × 86.4 cm), courtesy of Galleria Raucci/Santamaria, Naples

p. 187 (top & bottom) Installation view, *The Completed Reference: Pedestals and Drunken Walks* (Kunstverein Braunschweig, Germany), 2012

pp. 188–9 Installation view, *Metric, pedestal, landlord, cabengo, récit* (MIT List Visual Arts Center, Cambridge, Mass.), 2012

p. 190 Installation view, *The Completed Reference: Pedestals and Drunken Walks* (Kunstverein Braunschweig, Germany), 2012

Photo credits:

Isabelle Arthuis, pp. 9, 10
Bernd Borchardt, pp. 187, 190
Brian Forrest, p. 165
Peter Harris, pp. 188, 189
Bertrand Huet, p. 55
Thomas Müller, pp. 41, 44, 55, 94, 95
Isao Negishi (Daishinsha), pp. 128, 166, 167
Luciano Romano, pp. 41, 44
Jürgen Schmidt, pp. 21, 22, 23, 24
Lothar Schnepf, pp. 82, 83, 84, 125, 126, 127
Enzo Velo, pp. 116, 168

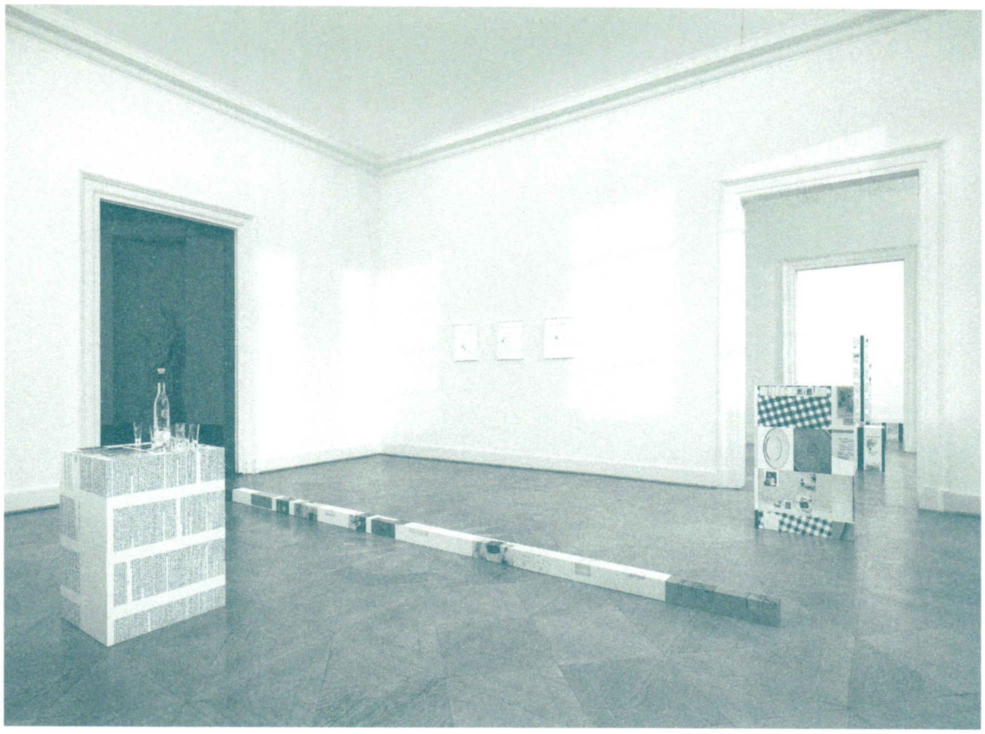

Installation view, *The Completed Reference: Pedestals and Drunken Walks* (Kunstverein Braunschweig, Germany), 2012.

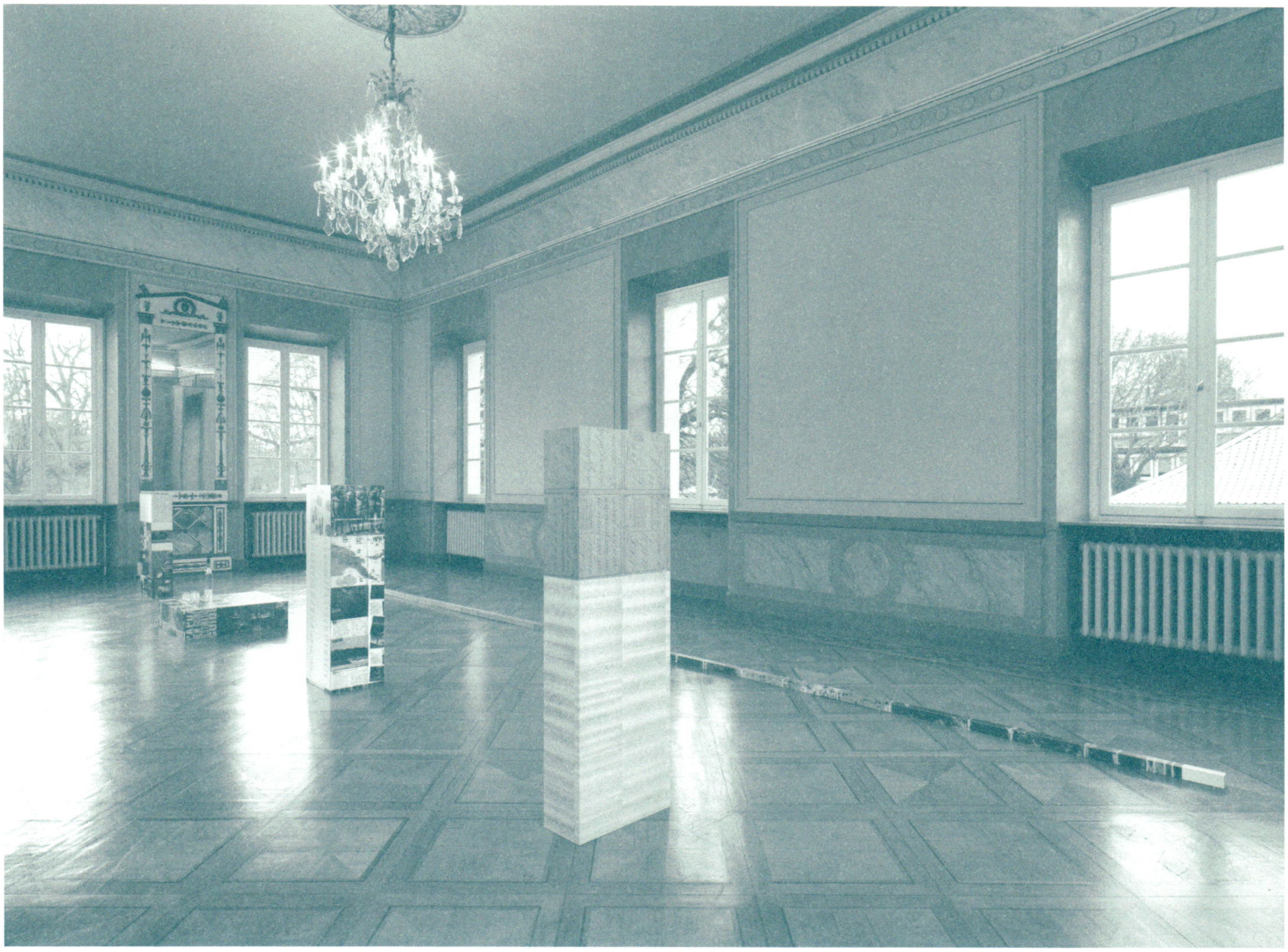

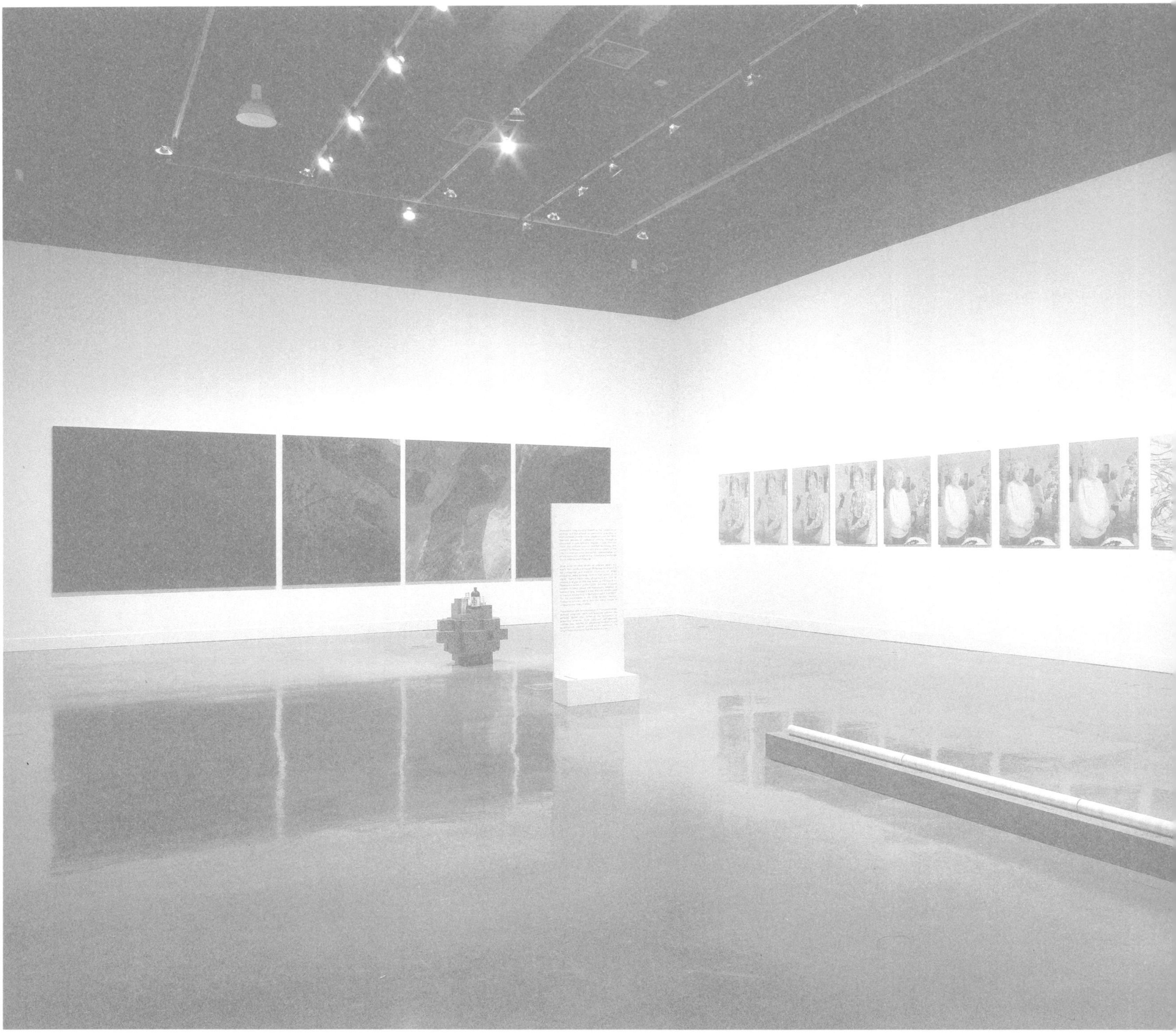

Installation view, *Metric, pedestal, landlord, cabengo, récit* (MIT List Visual Arts Center, Cambridge, Mass.), 2012.

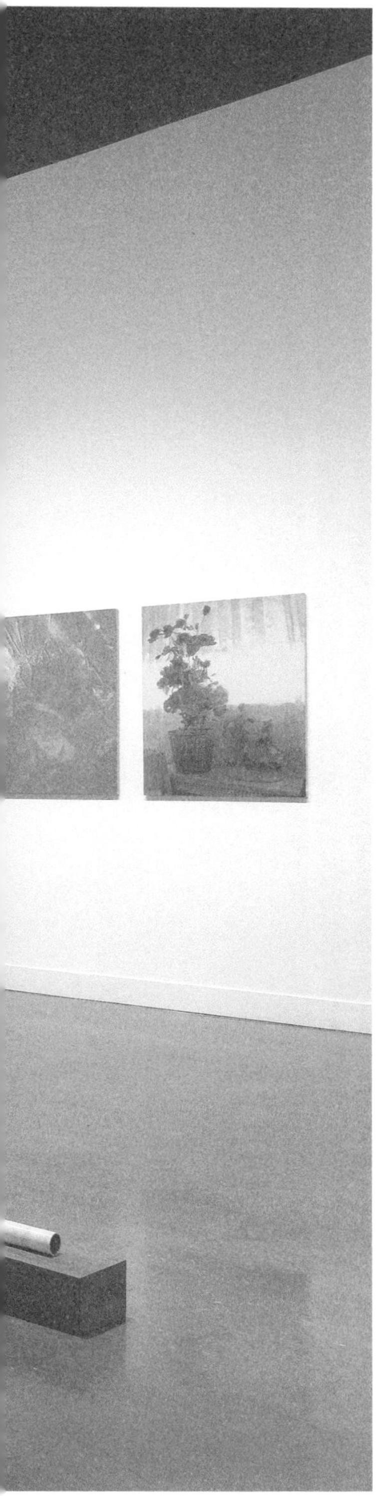

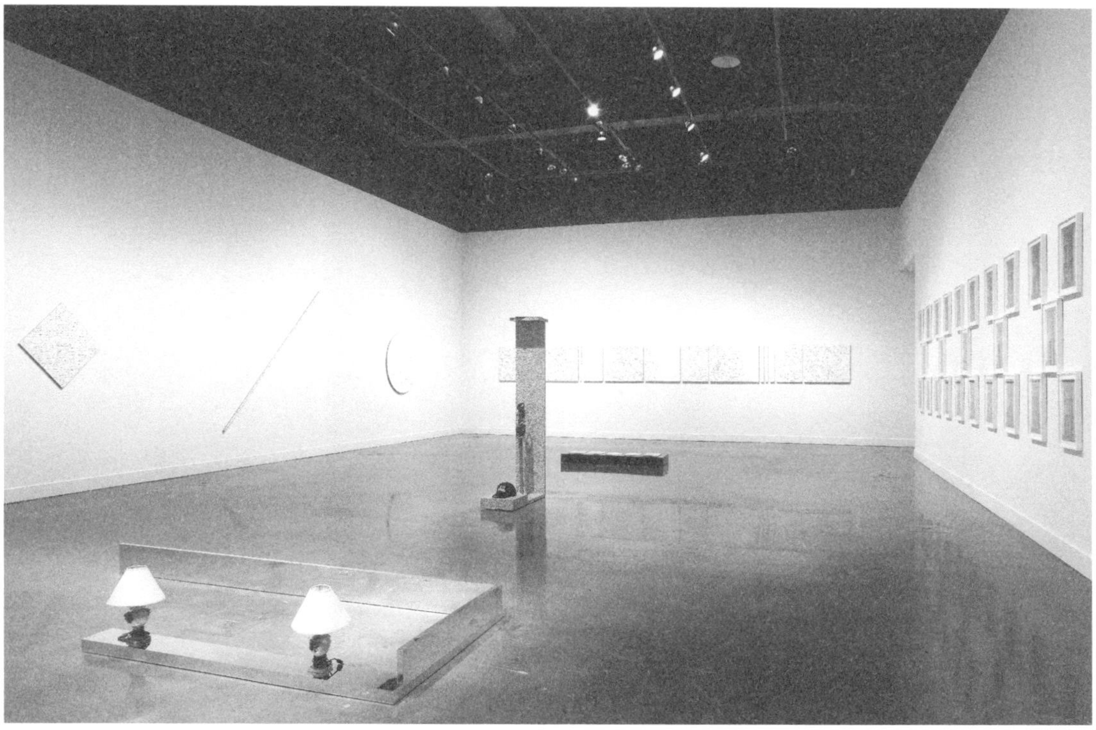

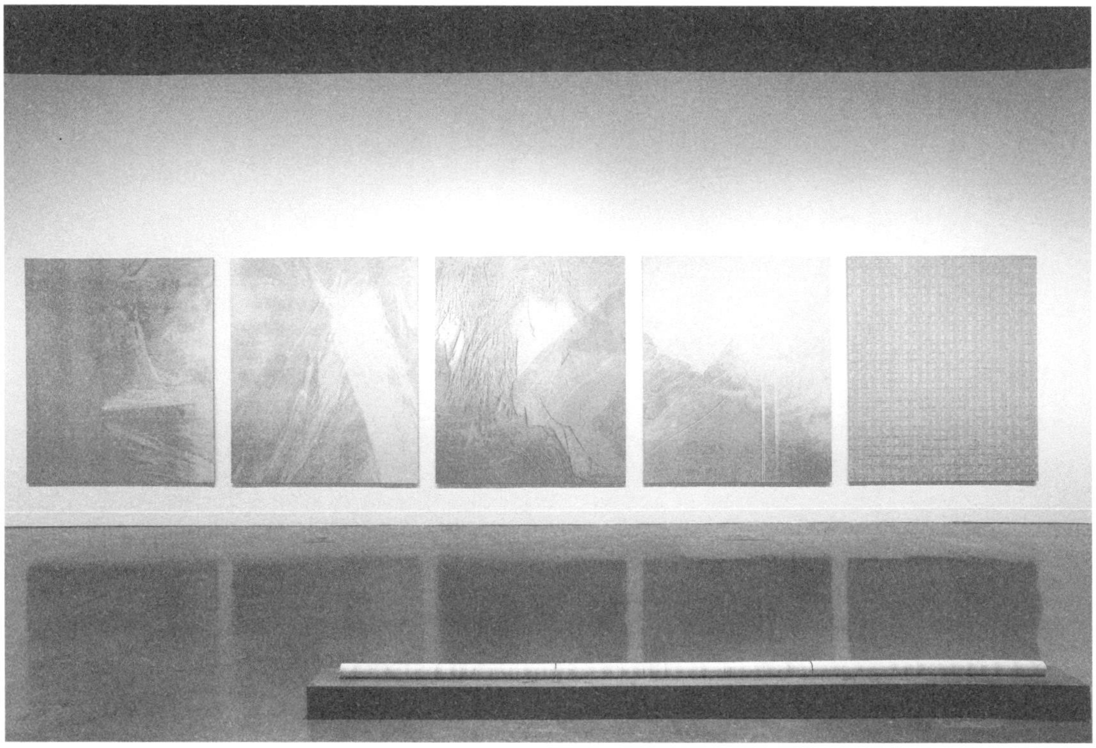

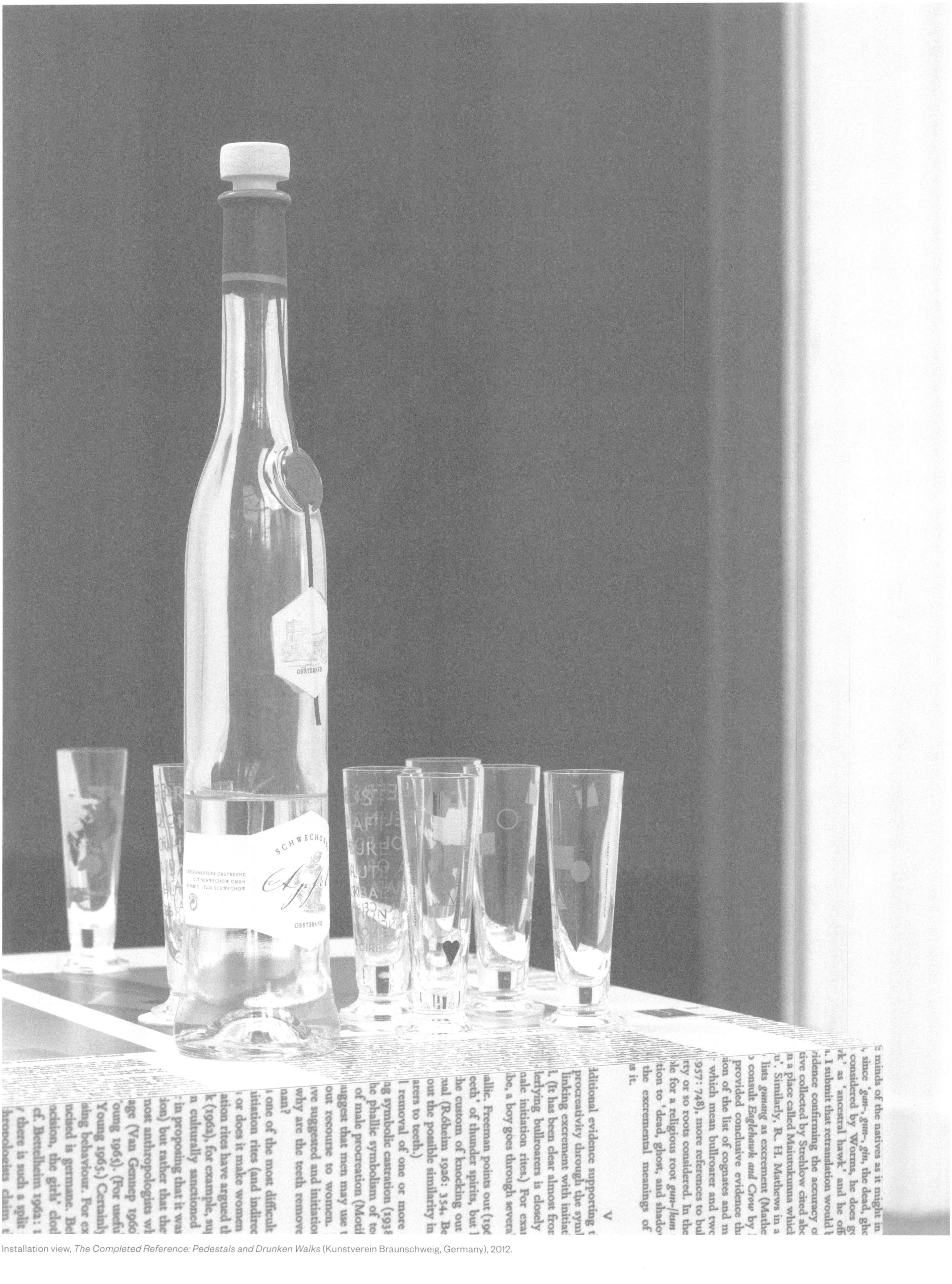

Installation view, *The Completed Reference: Pedestals and Drunken Walks* (Kunstverein Braunschweig, Germany), 2012.

Solo Exhibitions

2012
- *Sometimes Some Pictures Somewhere*, Andrew Kreps Gallery, New York, NY

2011
- *Chronochromes/Umberto/Simon/Carlo*, Galleria Raucci/Santamaria, Naples, Italy
- *Chronochromes, Data, Motifs*, Rat Hole Gallery, Tokyo, Japan

2010
- *Memphis, Pedestals, Chronochromes, Subincision, Papua New Guinea, /Macaire/, Motifs*, Overduin and Kite, Los Angeles, CA
- *Chonochromes, Menarches, Scales, Paul de Casteljau, /Robert/, Motifs*, Sutton Lane, Brussels, Belgium

2009
- *Pedestals, Bias-cut, /Robert Macaire/, Chronochromes*, Galerie Buchholz, Berlin, Germany
- *Robert Macaire Chromachromes*, Andrew Kreps Gallery, New York, NY

2008
- *Some Motifs and Their Sources* Galerie Buchholz, Cologne, Germany
- *Cheyney Thompson*, Sutton Lane, Paris, France
- *Cheyney Thompson*, Galleria Raucci/Santamaria, Naples, Italy

2006
- *Quelques Aspects de l'Art Bourgeois: La Non-Intervention*, Andrew Kreps Gallery, New York, NY
- *The End of Rent Control and the Emergence of the Creative Class*, Galerie Buchholz, Cologne, Germany

2005
- *Art Statements, Art Basel* 36, Basel, Switzerland
- *S&M—Cheyney Thompson/Eileen Quinlan*, Sutton Lane, Paris, France
- *Cheyney Thompson*, Raucci/Santamaria Gallery, Naples, Italy

2004
- *1998*, Andrew Kreps Gallery, New York, NY

2003
- *Cheyney Thompson*, Sutton Lane, London, UK

2002
- *1 Scenario + 1 Situation*, Andrew Kreps Gallery, New York, NY

2000
- *Cheyney Thompson*, James Fuentes Gallery, New York, NY
- *Cheyney Thompson*, Parker's Box, Brooklyn, NY

1999
- *Cheyney Thompson*, the Norman Project, New York, NY

Museum Exhibitions

2012
- *The Completed Reference: Pedestals and Drunken Walks*, curated by Hilke Wagner, Kunstverein Braunschweig, Germany
- *Metric, pedestal, landlord, cabengo, récit*, curated by João Ribas, MIT List Visual Arts Center, Cambridge, MA

2011
- *The Indiscipline of Painting*, curated by Daniel Sturgis, Tate St. Ives, UK
- *the hybrid fuels...*, curated by Ingrid Burgbacher-Krupka, Galerie der Stadt Sindelfingen, Sindelfingen, Germany

2009
- *Slow Painting*, curated by Fritz Emslander, Markus Heinzelmann, and Stefanie Kreuzer, Museum Morsbroich, Leverkusen, Germany
- *Collatéral*, curated by Yann Chevallier, Le Confort Moderne, Poitiers Cedex, France
- *Compass in Hand: Selections from The Judith Rothschild Foundation Contemporary Drawings Collection*, Museum of Modern Art, New York, NY

2008
- *Whitney Biennial*, Whitney Museum of American Art, New York, NY

2007
- *TBA: Cheyney Thompson and Eileen Quinlan*, curated by Martin Clark, Arnolfini, Bristol, UK

2005
- *Greater New York*, P.S.1 Contemporary Art Center, Queens, NY
- *Cheyney Thompson: Selected works*, curated by Terri Smith, Cheekwood Art Museum, Nashville, TN
- *Material Matters*, Herbert Johnson Museum of Art, Ithaca, NY

2003
- *Exposition of International Art, Venice Biennale*, Venice, Italy

Group Exhibitions

2011
- *Quodlibet III—Alphabets and Instruments*, Galerie Buchholz, Berlin, Germany

2010
- *The Space Between Reference and Regret*, Friedrich Petzel Gallery, New York, NY
- *Le Tableau*, Cheim and Read, curated by Joe Fyfe, New York, NY
- *Blind Mirror*, Raucci Gallery, New York, NY
PNTNG, Sutton Lane, Paris, France

2009
- *Besides, With, Against, and Yet: Abstraction and the Ready-Made Gesture*, the Kitchen, curated by Debra Singer, New York, NY
- *Group Exhibition*, Sutton Lane, London, NY
- *Quodlibet II*, Galerie Buchholz, Cologne, Germany

2008
- *Looking Back*, Mireille Mosler Ltd., New York, NY
- *From Brooklyn with Love*, Parker's Box, Brooklyn, NY

2007
- *Regroup Show*, Miguel Abreu Gallery, New York, NY
- *The Lath Picture Show*, Friedrich Petzel Gallery, New York, NY
- *For the People of Paris*, Sutton Lane, Paris, France

2006
- *it is, what is it?*, Andrew Kreps Gallery, New York, NY
- *Slow Burn*, Galerie Edward Mitterrand, Geneva, Switzerland

2005
- *Painters Without Paintings & Paintings Without Painters*, Orchard47, New York, NY
- *Sutton Lane in Paris*, Sutton Lane, Paris, France

2004
- *Quodlibet*, Galerie Buchholz, Cologne, Germany

2003
- *Miss. Understood: James Yamada, Frederic Pradeau, Cheyney Thompson*, Galleria Raucci/Santamaria, Naples, Italy
- *Dreams and Conflicts: The Dictatorship of the Viewer*, *La Biennale di Venezia*, Venice, Italy
- *Tear Me Up Tear Me Down*, curated by Amy Davila, White Box, New York, NY
- *Rendered*, Sara Meltzer Gallery, New York, NY
Papers, Acme, Los Angeles, CA

2001
- *Life is Elsewhere*, Canada Gallery, New York, NY
- *Playground of the Fearless*, Entropy Gallery, Brooklyn, NY

1999
- *Escape*, DNA Gallery, Provincetown, MA
- *Formula*, Oni Gallery, Boston, MA

1998
- *Group Show*, Grossman Gallery, Boston, MA
- *Genesis in the Retort*, Oni Gallery, Boston, MA

1996
- *Group Show*, Gallerie Gauche, Paris, France

Contributors

Simon Baier
Simon Baier is an art historian and critic. He teaches at the Art History Department of the University of Basel, Switzerland, where he also holds the position of research fellow at Eikones, NCCR Iconic Criticism. He is currently working on a PhD thesis on the concept of installation in the Russian avant-garde.

Yve-Alain Bois
Yve-Alain Bois is a professor at the School of Historical Studies at the Institute for Advanced Study in Princeton, New Jersey. He has written extensively on twentieth-century art and has curated and cocurated exhibitions of artists such as Matisse, Picasso, and Mondrian, as well as *L'informe, mode d'emploi* with Rosalind Krauss at the Centre Georges Pompidou and *Ellsworth Kelly: Early Drawings* at the Fogg Museum. He is one of the editors of the journal *October* and is a contributing editor of *Artforum.* Among other projects, he is currently working on the catalogue raisonné of Ellsworth Kelly's paintings and sculpture.

Ann Lauterbach
Ann Lauterbach is the author of eight books of poetry and an essay collection, *The Night Sky: Writings on the Poetics of Experience*. Her most recent book, *Or to Begin Again*, was a National Book Award finalist. She is Ruth and David Schwab Professor of Languages and Literature at Bard College, where she is also codirector of writing at the Milton Avery Graduate School of the Arts. Among her awards are a Guggenheim Fellowship and a MacArthur Fellowship.

João Ribas
João Ribas is a curator at the MIT List Visual Arts Center, where he has organized solo projects with artists such as Frances Stark, Melvin Moti, Otto Piene, and Akram Zaatari. From 2007 to 2009, Ribas was the curator at the Drawing Center in New York, where he organized exhibitions of the work of Frederick Kiesler, Alan Saret, Matt Mullican, Unica Zürn, and Ree Morton, among others. He has been awarded the Best Show award from the US section of the International Association of Art Critics (AICA) several times. His writing has appeared in the *New York Sun*, *Art Review*, *Time Out*, the *Guardian Unlimited*, and the *Review of Contemporary Fiction*, as well in numerous exhibition catalogs and monographs.

Imprint

This catalog is published with generous support from:

Galerie Buchholz, Köln / Berlin
Andrew Kreps Gallery, New York
Campoli Presti, Paris / London
Raucci Santamaria, Naples

Editors:
Daniel Berchenko, Timo Kappeller, Cheyney Thompson

Design:
Heimann und Schwantes

Lithography and Printing:
DZA Druckerei zu Altenburg GmbH

First published by Koenig Books, London

Koenig Books Ltd.
At the Serpentine Gallery
Kensington Gardens
London W2 3XA
United Kingdom
www.koenigbooks.co.uk

Printed in Germany

Distribution:
Buchhandlung Walther König, Köln
Ehrenstrasse 4, 50672 Köln
Germany
Tel. +49 (0) 221 / 20 59 6 53
Fax +49 (0) 221 / 20 59 6 60
verlag@buchhandlung-walther-koenig.de

UK & Ireland
Cornerhouse Publications
70 Oxford Street
Manchester M1 5NH
United Kingdom
Tel. +44 (0) 161 200 15 03
Fax +44 (0) 161 200 15 04
publications@cornerhouse.org

Outside Europe
D.A.P. / Distributed Art Publishers Inc.
155 6th Avenue, 2nd Floor
New York, NY 10013
United States
Tel. +1 212 627 1999
Fax +1 212 627 9484
eleshowitz@dapinc.com

ISBN 978-3-86335-154-0

This publication was produced on the occasion of the artist's first monographic museum survey, *Metric, Pedestal, Landlord, Cabengo, Récit*, at the MIT List Visual Arts Center, Cambridge, Massachusetts, February 10 – April 8, 2012.

Organized by the MIT List Visual Arts Center and curated by João Ribas.

Support for *Metric, Pedestal, Landlord, Cabengo, Récit* has been generously provided by the Council for the Arts at MIT, the Massachusetts Cultural Council, and the Office of the Associate Provost at MIT, with special thanks to the MIT List Visual Arts Center Advisory Committee and the Friends of the List.

Massachusetts Institute of Technology